Embedded Programming with Android™

About the Android Deep Dive Series

Zigurd Mednieks, Series Editor

The Android Deep Dive Series is for intermediate and expert developers who use Android Studio and Java, but do not have comprehensive knowledge of Android system-level programming or deep knowledge of Android APIs. Readers of this series want to bolster their knowledge of fundamentally important topics.

Each book in the series stands alone and provides expertise, idioms, frameworks, and engineering approaches. They provide in-depth information, correct patterns and idioms, and ways of avoiding bugs and other problems. The books also take advantage of new Android releases, and avoid deprecated parts of the APIs.

About the Series Editor

Zigurd Mednieks is a consultant to leading OEMs, enterprises, and entrepreneurial ventures creating Android-based systems and software. Previously he was chief architect at D2 Technologies, a voice-over-IP (VoIP) technology provider, and a founder of OpenMobile, an Android-compatibility technology company. At D2 he led engineering and product definition work for products that blended communication and social media in purpose-built embedded systems and on the Android platform. He is lead author of *Programming Android* and *Enterprise Android*.

Embedded Programming with Android™

Bringing Up an Android System from Scratch

Roger Ye

Addison-Wesley

New York • Boston • Indianapolis • San Francisco
Toronto • Montreal • London • Munich • Paris • Madrid
Capetown • Sydney • Tokyo • Singapore • Mexico City

Many of the designations used by manufacturers and sellers to distinguish their products are claimed as trademarks. Where those designations appear in this book, and the publisher was aware of a trademark claim, the designations have been printed with initial capital letters or in all capitals.

The author and publisher have taken care in the preparation of this book, but make no expressed or implied warranty of any kind and assume no responsibility for errors or omissions. No liability is assumed for incidental or consequential damages in connection with or arising out of the use of the information or programs contained herein.

For information about buying this title in bulk quantities, or for special sales opportunities (which may include electronic versions; custom cover designs; and content particular to your business, training goals, marketing focus, or branding interests), please contact our corporate sales department at corpsales@pearsoned.com or (800) 382-3419.

For government sales inquiries, please contact governmentsales@pearsoned.com.

For questions about sales outside the U.S., please contact international@pearsoned.com.

Visit us on the Web: informit.com/aw

Library of Congress Cataloging-in-Publication Data
Ye, Roger, author.
  Embedded programming with Android : bringing up an Android system from scratch / Roger Ye.
       pages   cm
  Includes index.
  ISBN 978-0-13-403000-5 (pbk. : alk. paper)—ISBN 0-13-403000-1 (pbk. : alk. paper)
 1. Android (Electronic resource) 2. Embedded computer systems—Programming.
3. Application software—Development. 4. Emulators (Computer programs)
5. Smartphones—Programming. I. Title.
  QA76.76.A65Y438 2016
  004.167—dc23
                                                            2015022900

Copyright © 2016 Pearson Education, Inc.

All rights reserved. Printed in the United States of America. This publication is protected by copyright, and permission must be obtained from the publisher prior to any prohibited reproduction, storage in a retrieval system, or transmission in any form or by any means, electronic, mechanical, photocopying, recording, or likewise. To obtain permission to use material from this work, please submit a written request to Pearson Education, Inc., Permissions Department, 200 Old Tappan Road, Old Tappan, New Jersey 07675, or you may fax your request to (201) 236-3290.

ARM is a trademark of ARM Ltd. Android™, Google Play™, Google and the Google logo are registered trademarks of Google Inc. CodeBench is a trademark of Mentor Graphics. Ubuntu is a trademark of Canonical. CyanogenMod® is a USPTO-registered trademark of CyanogenMod, LLC. Eclipse is a trademark of Eclipse Foundation.

ISBN-13: 978-0-13-403000-5
ISBN-10: 0-13-403000-1

Text printed in the United States on recycled paper at RR Donnelley in Crawfordsville, Indiana.
First printing, August 2015

Editor-in-Chief
Mark L. Taub

Executive Editor
Laura Lewin

Development Editor
Michael Thurston

Managing Editor
John Fuller

Project Editor
Elizabeth Ryan

Copy Editor
Jill Hobbs

Indexer
Infodex Indexing Services

Proofreader
Linda Begley

Technical Reviewers
Zigurd Mednieks
Blake Meike

Editorial Assistant
Olivia Basegio

Cover Designer
Chuti Prasertsith

Compositor
codeMantra US, LLC

*To the programmers who have great interest in embedded systems
and the latest computing devices*

Contents in Brief

Preface xv

Acknowledgments xxi

About the Author xxiii

I Bare Metal Programming 1

1. Introduction to Embedded System Programming **3**
2. Inside Android Emulator **13**
3. Setting Up the Development Environment **25**
4. Linker Script and Memory Map **39**
5. Using the C Language **63**
6. Using the C Library **93**
7. Exception Handling and Timer **125**
8. NAND Flash Support in Goldfish **183**

II U-Boot 217

9. U-Boot Porting **219**
10. Using U-Boot to Boot the Goldfish Kernel **249**

III Android System Integration 281

11. Building Your Own AOSP and CyanogenMod **283**
12. Customizing Android and Creating Your Own Android ROM **309**

IV Appendixes 339

A. Building the Source Code for This Book **341**
B. Using Repo in This Book **355**

Index 359

Contents

Preface xv

Acknowledgments xxi

About the Author xxiii

I Bare Metal Programming 1

1 Introduction to Embedded System Programming 3
What Is an Embedded System? 3
Bare Metal Programming 3
Learning Embedded System Programming 5
Software Layers in an Embedded System 7
Tools and Hardware Platform 11
The Difference between Virtual Hardware and Real Hardware 11
Summary 12

2 Inside Android Emulator 13
Overview of the Virtual Hardware 13
Configuring Android Virtual Devices 14
Hardware Interfaces 17
Serial 18
Timer 18
Summary 24

3 Setting Up the Development Environment 25
The Host and Client Environments 25
Development Environment Setup 26
Downloading and Installing Android SDK 27
Downloading and Installing the GNU Toolchain for ARM 27
Integrated Development Environment 29
Your First ARM Program 29
Building the Binary 30
Running in the Android Emulator 32
`makefile` for the Example Projects 36
Summary 38

4 Linker Script and Memory Map 39
Memory Map   39
Linker   41
- Symbol Resolution   42
- Relocation   46
- Section Merging   49
- Section Placement   50

Linker Script   51
- Linker Script Example   53

Initializing Data in RAM   56
- Specifying Load Address   58
- Copying `.data` to RAM   58

Summary   61

5 Using the C Language 63
C Startup in a Bare Metal Environment   63
- Stack   65
- Global Variables   68
- Read-Only Data   68
- Startup Code   68

Calling Convention   78
- Calling C Functions from Assembly Language Code   79
- Calling Assembly Language Functions from C Code   81

Goldfish Serial Port Support   81
- Check Data Buffer   87
- Data Input and Output   88
- Unit Test of Serial Functions   90

Summary   92

6 Using the C Library 93
C Library Variants   93
- C Library Variants in an Operating System   93
- C Library Variants in Bare Metal Environment   94

Newlib C Library   96
Common Startup Code Sequence   97
CS3 Linker Scripts   97
Customized CS3 Startup Code for the Goldfish Platform   103

Contents   xi

System Call Implementations   104
Running and Debugging the Library   112
Using Newlib with QEMU ARM Semihosting   116
    Semihosting Support in Newlib C   117
    Semihosting Example Code   118
Summary   122

7 Exception Handling and Timer   125

Goldfish Interrupt Controller   125
The Simplest Interrupt Handler   128
    Interrupt Support Functions   129
    Implementation of the Simplest Interrupt Handler   132
Nested Interrupt Handler   140
    Implementation of the Nested Interrupt Handler   142
    Testing Nested Interrupts and Discovering the Processor Mode Switch   155
Testing System Calls/Software Interrupts   163
Timer   164
    Goldfish-Specific Timer Functions   172
    U-Boot API   172
Real-Time Clock   172
    Unit Test of Timer and RTC   174
Summary   181

8 NAND Flash Support in Goldfish   183

Android File System   183
NAND Flash Properties   185
NAND Flash Programming Interface in the Goldfish Platform   187
Memory Technology Device Support   188
MTD API   189
    U-Boot API to Support NAND Flash   205
    Goldfish NAND Flash Driver Functions   205
NAND Flash Programming Interface Test Program   206
    NAND Flash Information from the Linux Kernel   206
    NAND Flash Test Program   210
Summary   216

II U-Boot 217

9 U-Boot Porting 219
Introducing U-Boot 219
Downloading and Compiling U-Boot 220
Debugging U-Boot with GDB 224
Porting U-Boot to the Goldfish Platform 227
- Creating a New Board 228
- Processor-Specific Changes 229
- Board-Specific Changes 229
- Device Driver Changes 239

Summary 246

10 Using U-Boot to Boot the Goldfish Kernel 249
Building the Goldfish Kernel 249
Prebuilt Toolchain and Kernel Source Code 250
Running and Debugging the Kernel in the Emulator 252
Booting Android from NOR Flash 254
- Creating the RAMDISK Image 256
- Creating the Flash Image 258
- Booting Up the Flash Image 258
- Source-Level Debugging of the Flash Image 266

Booting Android from NAND Flash 270
- Preparing system.img 270
- Booting from NAND Flash 271

Summary 280

III Android System Integration 281

11 Building Your Own AOSP and CyanogenMod 283
Introducing AOSP and CyanogenMod 283
Setting Up an Android Virtual Device 284
AOSP Android Emulator Build 288
- AOSP Build Environment 288
- Downloading the AOSP Source 289
- Building AOSP Android Emulator Images 290
- Testing AOSP Images 292

CyanogenMod Android Emulator Build 297

Downloading the CyanogenMod Source 297
Building CyanogenMod Android Emulator Images 298
Testing CyanogenMod Images 302
Summary 307

12 Customizing Android and Creating Your Own Android ROM 309

Supporting New Hardware in AOSP 309
    Building the Kernel with AOSP 317
    Building U-Boot with AOSP 322
    Booting Android with U-Boot from NAND Flash 323
Supporting New Hardware in CyanogenMod 332
    Building the Kernel with CyanogenMod 334
    Building U-Boot and Booting Up CyanogenMod 337
Summary 338

IV Appendixes 339

A Building the Source Code for This Book 341

Setting Up the Build Environment 341
Setting Up a Virtual Machine 344
Organization of Source Code 344
Source Code for Part I 345
    Building and Testing from the Command Line 345
    Building and Testing in Eclipse 346
Source Code for Part II 350
Source Code for Part III 352
    Building AOSP 352
    Building CyanogenMod 353

B Using Repo in This Book 355

Resources for Repo 355
Syncing a New Source Tree In Minutes 355
Downloading Git Repositories Using Local Manifest 356

Index 359

Preface

Computing is becoming more and more pervasive. Computing devices are evolving from traditional desktop computers to tablets and mobile devices. With the newer platforms, embedded computing is playing a more important role than the traditional mainframe- and desktop-based computing. Embedded system programming looks very different in various usage scenarios. In some cases, it consists of application programming using the assembly and C languages on top of the hardware directly. In other cases, it takes place on top of a real-time operating system (RTOS). In the most complicated case, it can be a desktop-based system using a modern operating system such as Linux or Windows.

Due to the many different usage scenarios and hardware architectures that are possible, it is very difficult to teach embedded programming in a standard way in a school or university. There are simply too many hardware platforms based on a multitude of very different architectures. The processors or microprocessors can be as simple as 8-bit models or as complicated as 32-bit or even 64-bit devices. In most cases, students learn about embedded programming on a dedicated hardware reference board and use the compiler and debugger from a particular company. Obviously, this kind of development environment is unique and difficult to duplicate. To overcome these challenges, this book uses virtualization technology and open source tools to provide a development environment that any programmer can easily obtain from the Internet.

Who Should Read This Book

If you want to learn embedded system programming, especially embedded system programming on Android, this is the book for you. For starters, you may want to get some hands-on experience while you read a book. This book includes plenty of examples for you to try out. The good thing is that you don't need to worry about having a hardware platform or development tools. All examples in this text are built using open source tools that you can download from the Internet, and all of them can be tested on the Android emulator. The source code is hosted in GitHub. Appendix A describes the build environment setup and explains how to work with the source code in GitHub.

> **Note**
>
> Git is a version control tool used by many open source projects. If you are new to it, you can search for "git" or "GitHub" on the Internet to find tutorials on its use. A free book on GitHub, *Pro Git* by Scott Chacon, can also be downloaded from the following address:
>
> http://git-scm.com/book/en/v2
>
> GitHub is a free git repository on the Internet that can be used to host open source projects. You can find the git repositories in this book at the following address:
>
> https://github.com/shugaoye/

If you have just started your career as an embedded system software engineer, your first project may be porting U-Boot to a new hardware platform. This book gives you the detailed steps on how to port U-Boot to the Android emulator.

If you are an experienced software developer, you may know that it is quite difficult to debug a complex device driver in your project. In this book, we explore a way to separate the debugging of the hardware interface from the device driver development. We explain how to debug serial ports, interrupt controllers, timers, the real-time clock, and NAND flash in a bare metal environment. We then explain how to integrate these examples with U-Boot drivers. The same method can also be used for Linux or Windows driver development.

To take full advantage of this book, you should be familiar with the C language, basic operating system concepts, and ARM assembly language. Ideally, readers will be graduates in computer science or experienced software developers who want to explore low-level programming knowledge. For professionals who work on Android system development, this is also a good reference book.

How This Book Is Organized

In this book, we discuss the full spectrum of embedded system programming—from the fundamental bare metal programming to the bootloader to the boot-up of an Android system. The focus is on instilling general programming knowledge as well as developing compiler and debugging skills. The objective is to provide basic knowledge about embedded system programming as a good foundation, thereby providing a path to the more advanced areas of embedded system programming.

The book is organized in a very process-oriented way. You can decide how to read this book based on your individual circumstance—that is, in which order to read chapters and explore subtopics. An explanation of how each part of the book relates to the others will help you make this decision.

The book consists of three parts. Part I focuses on so-called bare metal programming, which includes the fundamentals of low-level programming and Android system programming. Chapters 1 through 4 provide essential knowledge related to bare metal programming, including how to run programs on the hardware directly using assembly language code. In Chapter 5, the focus moves to the C programming language. The rest of Part I explores the minimum set of hardware interfaces necessary to boot a Linux kernel using U-Boot. In Chapters 5 to 8, we focus on the hardware interface programming of serial ports, interrupt controllers, the real-time clock, and NAND flash controllers in the bare metal programming environment.

Part II begins with Chapter 9, which covers how to port U-Boot to the goldfish platform. Using U-Boot, we can boot the Linux kernel and Android system, as explained in Chapter 10. The work completed in Chapters 5 through 8 can contribute to the U-Boot porting by isolating the hardware complexity from the driver framework in U-Boot. The same technique can be used in the Linux driver development as well. In Part II, we also use the file system images from the Android SDK to boot the Android system. To support two different boot processes (NOR and NAND flash), we must customize the file system from the Android SDK. Because this work takes place at the binary level, we are restricted to performing customization at the file level; that is, we cannot change the content of any files. Strategies to customize the file system are covered in Part III.

In Part III, we move from the bootloader to the kernel to the file system. We use a virtual device to demonstrate how to build a customized ROM for an Android device. We explore ways to support a new device and to integrate the bootloader and Linux kernel in the Android source code tree. In Chapter 11, we delve into the environment setup process and the standard build process for the Android emulator. In Chapter 12, we create a customized ROM for the virtual device including the integration of U-Boot and the Linux kernel. At the end of this chapter, readers will have a complete picture just like the Android system developers do at the mobile device manufacturing level.

A detailed introduction to each of the book's chapters follows. Part I, "Bare Metal Programming" consists of Chapters 1 to 8 focusing on so-called bare metal programming:

- Chapter 1, "Introduction to Embedded System Programming," gives a general introduction to embedded system programming. It also explains the scope of this book.
- Chapter 2, "Inside Android Emulator," introduces the Android emulator and gives a brief introduction to the hardware interfaces used throughout the book.
- Chapter 3, "Setting Up the Development Environment," details the development environment and tools used in our project. It also provides the first example, which gives us a chance to test our environment.
- Chapter 4, "Linker Script and Memory Map," covers the basics of developing an assembly program. We use two examples to analyze how a program is assembled and linked. After we have a binary image, we analyze how it is loaded into the Android emulator and then started.
- Chapter 5, "Using the C Language," introduces the C startup code and explains how we move from assembly language to a C language environment. We also begin to explore the goldfish hardware interfaces of the goldfish platform. Likewise, we explore the serial port of the goldfish platform.
- Chapter 6, "Using the C Library," presents details on how to integrate a C runtime library into a bare metal programming environment. We introduce different flavors of C runtime libraries and use Newlib as an example to illustrate how to integrate a C runtime library.
- Chapter 7, "Exception Handling and Timer," explores the interrupt controllers, timer, and real-time clock (RTC) of the goldfish platform. We work through various examples that demonstrate ways to handle these hardware interfaces. All example code developed in the chapter can subsequently be used for U-Boot porting in Chapter 9.
- Chapter 8, "NAND Flash Support in Goldfish," explores the NAND flash interface of the goldfish platform. This is also an important part of U-Boot porting. In Chapter 10, we explore how to boot the Android system from NAND flash.

Part 2, "U-Boot" consists of Chapters 9 and 10, which introduce the processes of U-Boot porting and debugging. After we have a working U-Boot image, we can use it to boot our own goldfish kernel and the Android image.

- Chapter 9, "U-Boot Porting," gives the details on U-Boot porting.
- Chapter 10, "Using U-Boot to Boot the Goldfish Kernel," discusses how to build a goldfish Linux kernel on our own. This kernel image is then used to demonstrate the various scenarios to boot the goldfish Linux kernel using U-Boot. Both the NOR flash and NAND flash boot-up processes are discussed.

Part 3, "Android System Integration" considers how to integrate U-Boot and the Linux kernel into the Android Open Source Project (AOSP) and CyanogenMod source trees.

- Chapter 11, "Building Your Own AOSP and CyanogenMod," gives the details on Android emulator builds in AOSP and CyanogenMod.
- Chapter 12, "Customizing Android and Creating Your Own Android ROM," teaches you how to create your own Android ROM on a virtual Android device. This Android ROM can be brought up by U-Boot, which we created in Chapter 9.

Example Code

Throughout this book, many examples are available to test the content in each chapter. It is recommended that you input and run the example code while you read this book. Doing so will give you good hands-on experiences and provide you with valuable insight so that you will better understand the topics covered in each chapter.

For Chapters 3 through 8, the directory structure organizes the code by chapter. Some folders are common to all of the examples, such as those containing include and driver files. All other folders are chapter specific, such as c03, c04, and c05; these folders contain the example code in that chapter.

The common makefile is `makedefs.arm`, which is found in the top-level directory. Individual makefiles are also provided for each example. Following is a template of the makefile for example code. The `PROJECTNAME` is defined as the filename of an example code. This makefile template is used for the individual projects in Chapters 3 through 8.

```
#
# The base directory relative to this folder
#
ROOT=../..
PROJECTNAME=

#
# Include the common make definitions.
#
include ${ROOT}/makedefs.arm
```

```
#
# The default rule, which causes the ${PROJECTNAME} example to be built.
#
all: ${COMPILER}
all: ${COMPILER}/${PROJECTNAME}.axf

#
# The rule to debug the target using Android emulator.
#
debug:
        @ddd --debugger arm-none-eabi-gdb ${COMPILER}/${PROJECTNAME}.axf &
        @emulator -verbose -show-kernel -netfast -avd hd2 -shell -qemu -monitor telnet::6666,server -s -S -kernel ${COMPILER}/${PROJECTNAME}.axf

#
# The rule to clean out all the build products.
#
clean:
        @rm -rf ${COMPILER} ${wildcard *~}

#
# The rule to create the target directory.
#
${COMPILER}:
        @mkdir -p ${COMPILER}

#
# Rules for building the ${PROJECTNAME} example.
#
${COMPILER}/${PROJECTNAME}.axf: ${COMPILER}/${PROJECTNAME}.o
${COMPILER}/${PROJECTNAME}.axf: ${PROJECTNAME}.ld
SCATTERgcc_${PROJECTNAME}=${PROJECTNAME}.ld
ENTRY_${PROJECTNAME}=ResetISR

#
# Include the automatically generated dependency files.
#
ifneq (${MAKECMDGOALS},clean)
-include ${wildcard ${COMPILER}/*.d} __dummy__
endif
```

The rest of source code in this book can be found on GitHub at *https://github.com/shugaoye/*. Please refer to Appendix A for the details.

Conventions Used in This Book

The following typographical conventions are used in this book:

- *Italic* indicates URLs.
- `<!-- Bold in angle brackets -->` is used to signify comments in the code or console output.
- `Constant-width type` is used for program listings, as well as within paragraphs to refer to program elements such as variable and function names, databases, data types, environment variables, statements, and keywords.
- **`Constant-width bold type`** shows commands or other text that should be typed in by the user.
- `Constant-width italic type` shows text that should be replaced with the user-supplied values or with the values determined by the context.

> **Note**
> A Note signifies a tip, suggestion, or general note.

Acknowledgments

I am grateful to Laura Lewin and Bernard Goodwin, both executive editors at Pearson Technology Group, who gave me the opportunity to publish this book with Addison-Wesley. I would like to thank the team from Addison-Wesley. Michael Thurston was the developmental editor; he reviewed all the chapters and gave me valuable suggestions on the content presentation. Olivia Basegio and Michelle Housley helped me to coordinate with the team at Addison-Wesley. Project editor Elizabeth Ryan ensured that this project adhered to schedule. I would also like to thank the copy editor, Jill Hobbs, who did a great job improving the readability of this book.

This book could not have been published without technical review. I would like to thank all of the reviewers for identifying errors and for providing valuable feedback about the content. Thanks are especially due to the Android experts, Zigurd Mednieks and G. Blake Meike. They are co-authors of Android-related books, including *Enterprise Android* and *Programming Android*.

I also want to thank all of my friends and colleagues at Motorola and Emerson. We had a wonderful time working on many great products that contributed to the technology boom that has occurred in the past 10 years. Together, we witnessed the introduction of the high-tech products that have changed our lives today.

Last but not least, I would like to thank my dearest wife and my lovely daughter, who gave me lots of support and encouragement along the way while I worked on this book.

About the Author

Roger Ye is an embedded system programmer who has great interest in embedded systems and the latest technologies related to them. He has worked for Motorola, Emerson, and Intel as an engineering manager. At Motorola and Emerson, he was involved in embedded system projects for mobile devices and telecommunications infrastructures. He is now an engineering manager at Intel Security, leading a team that develops Android applications.

Roger now lives in China with his wife Bo Quan and his daughter Yuxin Ye. You can find more information about him at GitHub: *https://github.com/shugaoye/*.

Bare Metal Programming

1. Introduction to Embedded System Programming
2. Inside Android Emulator
3. Setting Up the Development Environment
4. Linker Script and Memory Map
5. Using the C Language
6. Using the C Library
7. Exception Handling and Timer
8. NAND Flash Support in Goldfish

1
Introduction to Embedded System Programming

In primary school, when I read my first textbook, I believed that it definitely told the truth of the world. Now, many years later, when I look back, I understand that each book tells the truth of the world from the author's perspective.

The same idea applies to the world of embedded system programming. Many books about this subject have been published, and each author inevitably shares his or her own experiences with this approach from his or her own point of view. Likewise, in this book, I share my own knowledge about embedded system programming from my past working experiences. In this chapter, I introduce embedded system programming from that perspective.

What Is an Embedded System?

An embedded system is a computing device or component that provides a dedicated functionality to the end user. It could be part of a larger system, or it could be a stand-alone device. Many appliances and other devices in our world could be called embedded systems. Some of these items we use directly every day, such as DVD players, scanners, printers, switches, and routers. Others are hidden inside larger systems, such as base stations, satellites, elevator controls, car engine controls, hospital equipment controls, and imaging systems.

Embedded systems may also be either a single simple device or a complex system. They include both low-cost devices and complicated, high-cost systems. Such devices and components can use any hardware architecture that meets the design goal.

Clearly, it is very difficult to provide a complete picture of such a broad topic. In this book, we will explore the world of embedded systems through a typical example and look at the general development of embedded system programming.

Bare Metal Programming

Bare metal programming means you write your code directly on top of the hardware; that is, there are no other software layers beneath your program. This practice is very common when programming a microcontroller (MCU).

Many books focus on embedded programming, but few of them discuss bare metal programming in detail. However, if you do a search on the Internet about bare metal programming, you'll find many articles and discussions of this topic. The reason books don't typically cover bare metal programming is because such programming relies heavily on the hardware. Consequently, it is difficult to make a book on this topic generic enough that all readers can benefit from it. When we talk about bare metal programming, we have to refer to a specific hardware reference board. Of course, not all readers will have that board in hand. In this book, a virtualization environment is used to resolve this hardware dependency issue. Specifically, the Android emulator is used as a hardware reference board.

There are many reasons why someone might want to do bare metal programming, but hardware limitations in the simplest systems could be one of the major motivations. In the simplest embedded system, a microcontroller may be used. The hardware resources in such a system may be very limited, such that it cannot afford to run its own operating system. A small program running directly on the hardware is the only choice in this situation.

We can also sometimes do bare metal programming in advanced or complicated systems. In a complicated system populated with microprocessors, there may be an operating system in the end-user environment. However, for chip-level hardware verification in a research lab, for example, it may be too difficult to verify the initial chip using the entire software stack with an operating system. The most straightforward way to do this is to create a simple environment directly on top of the hardware so that the chip designer and verification team can focus on the hardware verification itself. If you have ever worked on a hardware reference board development team, you know that the initial code for many hardware modules is provided by the verification team or the hardware designer. They provide code snippets running directly on hardware, rather than relying on an operating system. In fact, the device driver developer for an operating system may develop the hardware driver based on the testing code while using the hardware specification as a reference.

Bare metal programming is mostly done in C and assembly language, because both can be used with no—or at least minimal—runtime library support. That means we can load our program anywhere we choose in memory. We can run our program by implementing the reset vector, so that the hardware first fetches an instruction. Subsequently, we can add a C runtime library to do simple, yet useful things like providing error messages with the `printf` function.

To make it possible for you to follow along as we go from "bare metal" upward in this book, we'll use assembly language, C, and virtualized hardware that you can download and run on your computer—namely, the Android "goldfish" emulator. We'll write our own programs from the first line of the code. Initially, that program will be in assembly language, but we'll try to move to the C language as soon as we can. Along the way, we'll explore the hardware interfaces and create experimental code directly on the virtual hardware. We'll reuse this exploratory code later during U-Boot porting.

> **Note**
> The virtual hardware board known as "goldfish" is the virtual hardware defined in the Android emulator. It is discussed in detail in Chapter 2.

As we finish building the system, we'll try to integrate the existing technology as much as possible so that we can reduce the time needed to build the final system. We'll integrate code from the C runtime library, reuse code for hardware peripherals, and build the boot-loader (U-Boot), goldfish kernel, and file system step by step. By the end of this book, you should have a clear idea of how an embedded system is built and what the development environment looks like.

As it progresses through these steps, this book emphasizes hands-on practices. In addition, you may have to do some exploration on your own to find details relating to ARM architecture, assembly or C programming, and the Android system. Following are some helpful resources:

- *ARM System Developer's Guide*, by Andrew N. Sloss, Dominic Symes, and Chris Wright
- ARM Architecture Reference Manual ARMv7-A and ARMv7-R edition
- RealView Platform Baseboard for ARM1176JZF-S
- *Embedded Android*, by Karim Yaghmour
- *Building Embedded Linux Systems*, by Karim Yaghmour, Jon Masters, Gilad Ben-Yossef, and Philippe Gerum
- *Programming Embedded System in C and C++*, by Michael Barr

The terms *bare metal programming* and *embedded system programming* are both used in this book. Bare metal programming is a kind of very straightforward programming that takes place on top of the hardware. There are not many resource management activities involved in this practice; those needed refer to hardware-related resources such as the CPU, memory, interrupts, and storage. By comparison, embedded system programming is a broader term, referring to any kind of programming on top of the hardware—including both bare metal programming and programming for a real-time operating system (RTOS). In reality, there is not always a clear-cut distinction between bare-metal programming and RTOS programming, so use of the broader label for this activity may be warranted in some cases.

As a program becomes increasingly more complicated, you tend to be moving from bare metal programming toward RTOS programming. Simple resource management such as interrupt handling and memory management can exist in bare metal programming. When you start to use the C library and make function calls to `malloc()`, for example, you are starting to manage memory allocation. When you add multiple tasks in the infinite loop to handle different functions, you are starting to deal with scheduling. When you make your bare metal programming as complicated as a bootloader, you are on your way to enabling an embedded operating system.

Learning Embedded System Programming

To learn embedded system programming, you need a basic knowledge of electronics, digital electronics, microcontrollers, and both assembly language and C.

With this essential knowledge, the first step is to start a real project and learn the basic development process. From this real project, you can get hands-on experience with the development environment setup, build, and debug phases as they relate to the hardware board. While working on the project, you will inevitably encounter all kinds of challenges. As you resolve them one by one, you will improve your analytical skills and make connections among all your existing hardware and software knowledge. This is a tough and painful cycle to navigate, and one that it is difficult to teach in a classroom.

To reduce the learning curve, it is helpful to practice in a virtualization environment first. In a virtualization environment, you have more freedom to play with the hardware compared to what you can do on the real hardware board. In addition, you usually have better means to debug and analyze the target in a pure software environment. For example, you can do source-level debugging much more easily on the virtualized hardware board in either QEMU or the Android emulator. In such an environment, you can easily transfer the debugging process from one layer to the other—something that is very difficult to do in a real hardware board. We will take advantage of this ability in Chapter 9, when we do source-level debugging to analyze the boot up process from U-Boot to the Linux kernel.

After you gain enough experience by working through the projects in this book, you will be ready to start a project with a real hardware board. You will find there are a lot of similarities in terms of programming between the real hardware and the virtualized hardware—but you will also notice some differences between the two. In a real-world project, you may find that the hardware problems are mixed together with software issues. In particular, it is extremely difficult to work on the boot-up process of the first version of a hardware board. Both hardware and software engineers have to work together to overcome the challenges in the initial startup phase. You also have to use many more debugging and analysis tools in the real hardware environment, many of which are unique to a particular hardware platform. When you move to other projects, you'll have to learn to use new tools as well. However, the more tools you have used, the more confidence you will have in your ability to learn to use new ones. Ideally, you should try to isolate the issues or challenges you encounter in programming so that you have to deal with only one or two of them at a time. In this way, you can simplify complex issues before you try to attack them.

After you complete a few projects successfully, you may start to work on more challenging tasks in the embedded system development domain. Gaining operating system knowledge, especially with RTOS, may become something you want to explore. You may start to work on more complicated hardware interfaces as well, such as USB or Ethernet. These layered software stacks start from a hardware layer. For example, you may have to become familiar with the Ethernet protocol, the IP protocol, the TCP protocol, and continuing up to application-level protocols to work on some network interface-related embedded projects. To deal with all these challenges, you can consult many books about operating systems and dedicated hardware interfaces that are available for reference, besides exploiting what you learn from working with these directly.

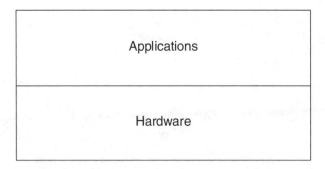

Figure 1.1 A simple embedded system architecture

Even though the scope and nature of the various embedded system programming projects can be highly diverse, the basic knowledge used to conquer each project is quite similar. This book is designed to help you work on your first project with the guidance on essential knowledge and examples.

Software Layers in an Embedded System

The type of application determines the software architecture of an embedded system. The software architecture of an embedded system can be as simple as the microcontroller-based application shown in Figure 1.1. This kind of application might be found in a device like a thermometer or an electronic oven.

There is only one single software layer in this kind of system, which is the application itself. The application controls the hardware directly. It usually initializes the hardware first and runs in an infinite loop to perform a dedicated function. For an example, a thermometer application may initialize the sensor first and then run in an infinite loop to read the temperature repeatedly.

A more complicated embedded system may include all the layers found in a general-purpose computer, as shown in Figure 1.2. Such a system usually includes a processor that can support a full operating system. The system starts from the bootloader, which initializes the hardware peripherals and loads the operating system. Once the operating system is ready, a few applications run on top of the operating system to perform multiple functions. Typical examples include a mobile phone, a GPS navigator, and a base station. Note that the layers in the actual software stack in a system depend on the specific application; that is, the layers in Figure 1.2 are highly generalized. For an example, a system can be designed with firmware or without firmware. The firmware can be a bootloader, BIOS, or codec for a DSP. A bootloader usually disappears after the system is up. In some special cases, firmware may stay in memory and provide some runtime services after the system is running. For an example, the latest UEFI-based BIOS includes UEFI runtime services—a set of services provided by the BIOS instead of operating system. Any operating system running on a hardware with UEFI BIOS can utilize UEFI runtime services.

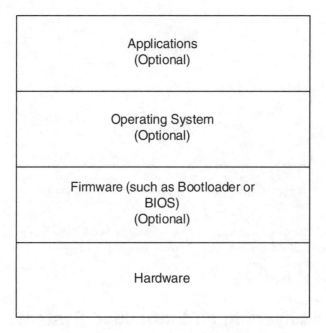

Figure 1.2 An embedded system with full software stacks

Vendors usually provide different microprocessor models to meet the demands of different embedded applications. We can use the popular ARM processors as an example to see how we might use different processor series to meet different requirements. To handle the dynamic demands from various applications, the ARM architecture has evolved into a set of product series. Currently, four series of ARM processors are available based on the targeted applications:

- CORTEX-A: High-performance processors for open operating systems
- CORTEX-R: Exceptional performance processors for real-time applications
- CORTEX-M: Cost-sensitive solutions for deterministic microcontroller applications
- SecurCore: Processors for high-security applications
- FPGA Cores: Processors for FPGA

SecurCore and FPGA Cores usually can be designed as a specific hardware component and are used as part of a bigger system. The software inside this kind of processor is usually firmware, which relies on the programming languages used by hardware designers instead of those used by software programmers, such as Verilog or HDL.

The CORTEX-M series includes microcontrollers. The system architecture in this case resembles that depicted in Figure 1.1. The software applications usually run on top of the hardware directly and perform the dedicated functions. This kind of application software is also called firmware, because it is burned inside a read-only memory (ROM) in the device. Firmware does not change after the application is shipped to the market.

The system architecture of CORTEX-R or CORTEX-A is similar to that depicted in Figure 1.2. The difference between these two lies in the kind of operating system that can be supported. CORTEX-R is more suitable for real-time operating systems, whereas CORTEX-A can support full operating systems. Due to hardware limitations, the CORTEX-R series cannot support a full operating system, while CORTEX-A can run a real-time operating system without any problem. The key difference between a real-time operating system and a full operating system is that the number of tasks and the memory usage are predetermined before the system starts up in a RTOS. This makes the scheduler in a RTOS much simpler than the one in a full operating system.

> **Note**
> The ARM processor that the Android emulator emulates is ARM926EJ-S, which is the entry-point processor capable of supporting a full operating system.

In the first part of this book, we discuss the programming languages and the hardware interfaces of the typical hardware peripherals used in embedded system development. The system architecture is similar to that shown in Figure 1.3. In Chapter 5, we discuss the serial port supported in goldfish. In Chapter 7, we cover interrupt handling, timers, and RTC. In Chapter 8, we look at NAND flash programming in the goldfish platform.

The second part of the book begins with Chapter 9, where we port U-Boot to the goldfish platform. All the hardware peripherals that we support in the first part of the book can be supported in U-Boot. The system diagram relevant to this case is shown in Figure 1.4.

In Chapter 10, we build the goldfish Linux kernel and demonstrate how to boot Android using U-Boot and the goldfish kernel to have a complete system. The original

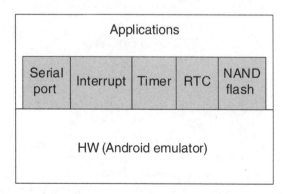

Figure 1.3 System diagram for the first part of the book

10 Chapter 1 Introduction to Embedded System Programming

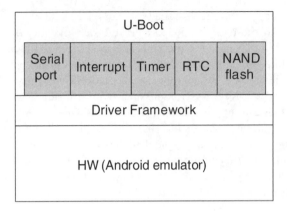

Figure 1.4 System diagram in Chapter 9

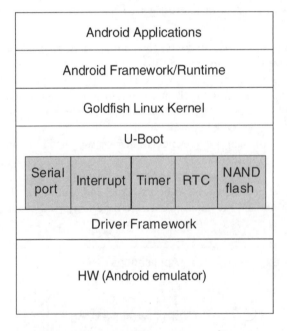

Figure 1.5 The Android system in this book

Android file system from Android SDK is used to demonstrate the final system. This system diagram is shown in Figure 1.5.

In the third part of the book, we continue to use the system diagram depicted in Figure 1.5. The difference is that we build everything from scratch, including the Android file system (e.g., Android framework, runtime, and system applications).

Tools and Hardware Platform

The GNU toolchain is increasingly being used for embedded software development. Thanks to the many contributions made by the programming community, the GNU toolchain can support most of the hardware architecture. It has become the most popular choice for embedded system programmers.

With the maturity of virtualization technology, it is possible to practice embedded programming using virtual hardware instead of a real hardware reference board. From an educational point of view, teaching or learning embedded programming using the GNU toolchain on top of a virtual hardware can be very valuable. With this approach, both time and space limitations can be dramatically reduced. With many virtualization technologies, QEMU is definitely the best choice for practicing embedded system programming. It can support multiple hardware architectures and instruction sets. It has built-in implementation that can support many hardware reference boards from TI, Freescale, Intel, and other vendors.

QEMU could have been used in this book to simulate the hardware reference board. However, QEMU is a general emulator that can emulate many hardware boards, and the maturity levels of those hardware boards may be quite different. Considering the maturity level of various boards supported by QEMU, the Android emulator is a better choice for this purpose. The Android emulator is based on QEMU. Google customized a few things based on a specific version of QEMU and included those functions in the Android SDK. The major changes include virtual hardware (goldfish) support and the addition of a layer that supports Android Virtual Device Manager. The Android emulator offers very helpful display support, keyboard, and power management simulation capabilities. As mentioned earlier, it is built for a special virtual hardware platform called goldfish, which was developed by Google and runs on top of QEMU. Although there is not a formal hardware specification for the Google goldfish platform, we can explore its details by investigating the goldfish kernel code to find the necessary hardware information.

By comparison, QEMU is much more suitable for the development of various virtualization technologies. It is more advanced and is changed rapidly by its user/developer community. Meanwhile, the Android emulator is suitable as the basis for developing Android applications or for learning programming as in this book. In both cases, the reliability of the emulator itself is the major consideration.

The Difference between Virtual Hardware and Real Hardware

Even though it is very convenient to use a hardware emulator to learn embedded programming, you must remain aware of the differences between the real hardware platform and the virtual environment. The good news with emulators is that you do not need to worry about damaging the hardware if you make mistakes. You can also do source code-level debugging without any difficulties. It can be very challenging to perform source code-level debugging in the initial hardware startup on a real hardware platform. Special tools like the JTAG debugger and flashing tool must be used for the initial debugging effort. Another thing to consider is that the virtual environment can never be completely identical to the real hardware. Some functionality may be missing in QEMU for a particular hardware board, or certain features may differ in the virtual and real versions. For an example, QEMU supports the ARM Versatile Express board and most of the functionalities of the Versatile Express board work on QEMU. However, there are still some differences between the virtualized platform and the real hardware. In Chapter 9, when we port U-Boot to the goldfish platform, we will refer to the Versatile Express code base; at that time, we will more fully explore the differences between Versatile Express QEMU and the real Versatile Express board.

Luckily, using the Android emulator, we do not have to worry about the differences between the virtual hardware and the real hardware. The goldfish platform is a pure virtual hardware platform from Google. The hardware specification is whatever Google has defined in the Android emulator source code.

Summary

This chapter provided an overview of embedded system programming in general and bare metal programming in particular. We discussed the system architectures of different kinds of embedded system applications and mapped the different system architectures to the different chapters in this book. Finally, we briefly considered the development tools and hardware platform that will be used in this book.

2
Inside Android Emulator

In this chapter, we look at the Android emulator from a hardware perspective. The Android emulator was developed by Google to allow Android application developers to test Android applications without relying on real hardware. This emulator is built on top of the open source virtual machine QEMU. QEMU is a project that is under active development by the open source community. It can support multiple hardware architectures, including ARM, x86, and MIPS, among others. The Android emulator supports three hardware architectures: ARM, x86, and MIPS. Given that most of the mobile devices currently available in the market are designed for ARM architecture, in this book we chose to use an ARM-based instance of the Android emulator.

Overview of the Virtual Hardware

Before we dive into programming, let's take a look at the virtual hardware that we will use throughout the book. Because there is not a hardware specification for what we usually have for a real hardware platform, we must study the goldfish kernel source code to figure out the details. Luckily, both the Android emulator and the goldfish Linux kernel are open source projects, so we can readily obtain the source code and play with them. Figure 2.1 shows the user interface of the Android emulator.

The Android emulator and goldfish kernel source code can be found at the following locations:

- Android emulator: *https://android.googlesource.com/platform/external/qemu/*
- Goldfish kernel: *https://android.googlesource.com/kernel/goldfish.git*

As mentioned earlier, the Android emulator can support multiple processor architectures, such as ARM, x86, and MIPS. In this book, we look at the ARM architecture. The Android emulator supports many hardware features likely to be found on mobile devices, including the following:

- An ARMv5 CPU and the corresponding memory-management unit (MMU)
- A 16-bit LCD display
- One or more keyboards (a qwerty-based keyboard and associated phone buttons)

14   Chapter 2   Inside Android Emulator

Figure 2.1   Android emulator

- A sound chip with output and input capabilities
- Flash memory partitions (emulated through disk image files on the development machine)
- A GSM modem, including a simulated SIM card
- A camera, using a webcam connected to your development computer
- Sensors like an accelerometer, using data from a USB-connected Android device

Figure 2.2 shows a block diagram of the Android emulator hardware. For a different hardware architecture, such as x86 or MIPS, all hardware peripherals are the same except the CPU.

Configuring Android Virtual Devices

To use the emulator, we must first create one or more Android Virtual Device (AVD) configurations. In each configuration, we specify an Android platform to run in the emulator and the set of hardware options and emulator skin we want to use. Then, when we launch the emulator, we specify the AVD configuration that we want to load.

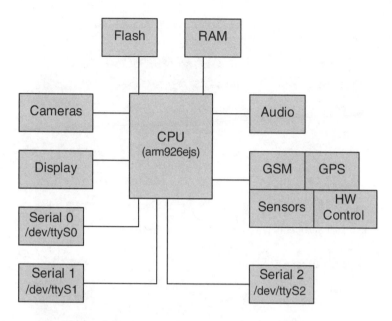

Figure 2.2 Goldfish platform hardware block diagram

> **Note**
>
> The Android platform discussed here includes the target version of Android and CPU architecture. In Figure 2.3, we create an AVD for Android 4.0.3 and an ARM processor. To create an AVD for a particular Android version, you must download the SDK platform and system images for that version using Android SDK Manager. If you are using Linux, you can start Android SDK Manager from the command line:
>
> `$ android sdk`
>
> Each Android Virtual Device can be considered a specific virtual hardware device with a particular software and hardware configuration. The hardware configuration specifies the processor architecture, such as x86 or ARM, as well as peripherals such as memory, screen size, or a camera. The software configuration specifies the Android version with or without Google services. In Parts I and II (Chapters 1–10) of this book, we use the configuration defined in Figure 2.3. In Part III, we use a more recent Android version to discuss the integration of U-Boot and the Linux kernel with Android source code.

Each AVD functions as an independent device, with its own private storage for user data, SD card, and so on. When we launch the emulator with an AVD configuration, it automatically loads the user data and SD card data from the AVD directory. By default, the emulator stores the user data, SD card data, and cache in the AVD directory.

To create and manage AVDs, we can use the AVD Manager user interface (UI) or the Android tool that is included in the SDK, as shown in Figure 2.3.

Chapter 2 Inside Android Emulator

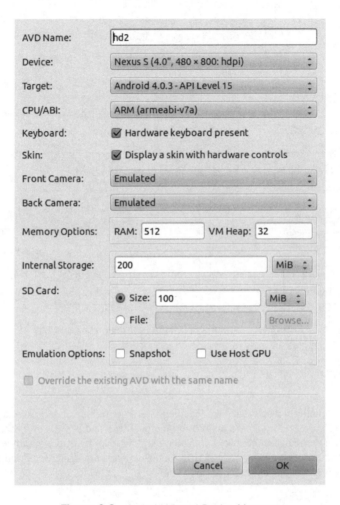

Figure 2.3 Android Virtual Device Manager

After we download and install the Android SDK, we can start AVD Manager from the command line using the following command. The command android can be found in the `${SDK ROOT}/tools` folder.

$ android avd

In Figure 2.3, we created a configuration with the AVD name hd2. This configuration includes 512MB RAM, a 4-inch WVGA screen, 200MB internal flash memory, and 100MB SD card storage.

After an emulator instance is created, this instance can be launched using the following command:

```
emulator -avd <avd_name> [<options>]
```

Hardware Interfaces

Given that our topic here is embedded system programming, we are more interested in the hardware programming interface of the Android emulator. Let's discuss a few hardware interfaces that we'll use throughout this book. Most of goldfish-specific hardware interfaces are defined in the Linux kernel source code, found at `arch/arm/mach-goldfish/include/mach/hardware.h`. Memory-mapped input/output (I/O) is used by goldfish hardware peripherals; this type of I/O uses the same address space to address both memory and I/O devices. The memory and registers of the I/O devices are mapped to the processor address space. In the goldfish platform, all hardware interfaces share a common base address: 0xff000000. For the virtual address, the base address is 0xfe000000.

> **Note**
>
> You need only the kernel source for the analysis in Parts I and II of this book. We will discuss the Android source code tree in Part III. There are two versions of goldfish kernel that we will use in this book. You can check out branch android-goldfish-2.6.29 for Parts I and II for reference. In Part III, we will use version android-goldfish-3.4, as we will compile the Android 4.4.x source tree. Refer to Appendix B for details on the source code used in this book.

Looking at the startup log of the goldfish kernel (shown later in this chapter), we get a quick overview of the hardware interfaces that support the Android emulator. Table 2.1 summarizes the goldfish hardware programming interfaces.

Table 2.1 Hardware Registers and Interrupts

Hardware	C Language Definition	Base Address Offset	Interrupt
Serial 1	GOLDFISH_TTY_BASE	(0x2000)	4
Timer	GOLDFISH_TIMER_BASE	(0x3000)	3
Audio	GOLDFISH_AUDIO_BASE	(0x4000)	15
Memlog	GOLDFISH_MEMLOG_BASE	(0x6000)	
RTC	GOLDFISH_RTC_BASE	(0x10000)	10
Serial 2	GOLDFISH_TTY1_BASE	(0x11000)	11
Serial 3	GOLDFISH_TTY2_BASE	(0x12000)	12
Ethernet	GOLDFISH_smc91x_BASE	(0x13000)	13
Frame Buffer	GOLDFISH_FB_BASE	(0x14000)	14
Event	GOLDFISH_EVENTS_BASE	(0x16000)	18
NAND Flash	GOLDFISH_NAND_BASE	(0x17000)	
Pipe	GOLDFISH_PIPE_BASE	(0x18000)	19
Switch 0	GOLDFISH_SWITCH0_BASE	(0X19000)	20
Switch 1	GOLDFISH_SWITCH1_BASE	(0x1a000)	21

Table 2.2 Serial Hardware

Serial Hardware	Base Address	Interrupt
Serial 1	0xff002000	4
Serial 2	0xff011000	11
Serial 3	0xff012000	12

The following sections provide a quick look at the serial and timer interfaces as examples. Throughout this book, we introduce the hardware interfaces that we port to U-Boot and bare metal environment. In Chapter 5, we discuss serial hardware. Interrupt controllers are discussed in Chapter 7. In Chapter 8, we discuss the NAND flash hardware.

Serial

The goldfish platform includes three serial ports. Table 2.2 shows the base addresses of these ports.

There are five 32-bit registers, listed next, which can be used to handle the data communication of serial ports. The definitions of these registers can be found in the goldfish kernel source in the file drivers/char/goldfish_tty.c.

- **PUT_CHAR** at offset 0x0 is a write-only register. Writing a value to it puts a character onto the console.
- **BYTES_READY** at offset 0x4 returns the number of characters waiting to be read from the console. This register is read-only.
- **CMD** at offset 0x8 is a write-only register. Writing a command performs one of four actions:
    - CMD_INT_DISABLE (0) disables the console interrupt.
    - CMD_INT_ENABLE (1) enables the console interrupt.
    - CMD_WRITE_BUFFER (2) copies DATA_LEN bytes from virtual address DATA_PTR to the console.
    - CMD_READ_BUFFER (3) copies DATA_LEN bytes from the console to virtual address DATA_PTR. The number of bytes should not exceed that specified by BYTES_READY.
- **DATA_PTR** at offset 0x10 is a write-only register. The value in this register is the virtual address used in the read and write buffer commands.
- **DATA_LEN** at offset 0x14 is a write-only register. The value in this register is the number of bytes to copy with the read or write buffer commands.

Timer

The offset for the timer controller is found at 0x3000. There are six 32-bit registers, listed next, defined in arch/arm/mach-goldfish/include/mach/timer.h. Time is represented by a flowing 64-bit counter.

- **TIME_LOW** at offset 0x0 returns the lowest 32-bit from the 64-bit counter. It also latches the high 32 bits into TIME_HIGH. You must read TIME_LOW before reading TIME_HIGH to get consistent values. TIME_LOW is a read-only register.
- **TIME_HIGH** at offset 0x4 is a read-only register storing the top 32 bits of the 64-bit counter. It should be read only after reading the TIME_LOW value.
- **ALARM_LOW** at offset 0x8 is a write-only register storing the lowest 32 bits of the next alarm value. To get consistent results, the ALARM_HIGH value should be stored first when setting an alarm. When the counter value matches the alarm value, an interrupt is triggered.
- **ALARM_HIGH** at offset 0xc is a write-only register storing the top 32 bits of the next alarm value. Writing to this register does not update the internal 64-bit alarm register. Updating is done on writes to ALARM_LOW.
- **CLEAR_INTERRUPT** at offset 0x10 is a write-only register. When written to, it will clear an interrupt previously posted by the alarm.
- **CLEAR_ALARM** at offset 0x14 is a write-only register. It is used to clear a timer interrupt.

Example 2.1 shows the goldfish kernel (shipped with Android SDK) startup log. We will refer to it when we debug the boot-up process later.

Example 2.1 Goldfish Kernel Startup Log

```
Uncompressing
Linux ..............................................................
........................ done, booting the kernel.
goldfish_fb_get_pixel_format:167: display surface,pixel format:
  bits/pixel:   16
  bytes/pixel:  2
  depth:        16
  red:          bits=5 mask=0xf800 shift=11 max=0x1f
  green:        bits=6 mask=0x7e0 shift=5 max=0x3f
  blue:         bits=5 mask=0x1f shift=0 max=0x1f
  alpha:        bits=0 mask=0x0 shift=0 max=0x0
Initializing cgroup subsys cpu
Linux version 2.6.29-gea477bb (kroot@kennyroot.mtv.corp.google.com) (gcc version
4.6.x-google 20120106 (prerelease) (GCC) ) #1 Wed Sep 26 11:04:45 PDT 2012
```

We can see that the kernel version is 2.6.29 in Example 2.1. This version is built with Android 4.0.3 SDK.

```
CPU: ARMv7 Processor [410fc080] revision 0 (ARMv7), cr=10c5387f
CPU: VIPT nonaliasing data cache, VIPT nonaliasing instruction cache
```

Chapter 2 Inside Android Emulator

```
Machine: Goldfish
Memory policy: ECC disabled, Data cache writeback
Built 1 zonelists in Zone order, mobility grouping on.  Total pages: 130048
Kernel command line: qemu.gles=1 qemu=1 console=ttyS0 android.qemud=ttyS1
androidboot.console=ttyS2 android.checkjni=1 ndns=1
Unknown boot option 'qemu.gles=1': ignoring
Unknown boot option 'android.qemud=ttyS1': ignoring
Unknown boot option 'androidboot.console=ttyS2': ignoring
Unknown boot option 'android.checkjni=1': ignoring
PID hash table entries: 2048 (order: 11, 8192 bytes)
Console: colour dummy device 80x30
Dentry cache hash table entries: 65536 (order: 6, 262144 bytes)
Inode-cache hash table entries: 32768 (order: 5, 131072 bytes)
Memory: 512MB = 512MB total
Memory: 515584KB available (2900K code, 707K data, 124K init)
```

The memory size is initialized to 512MB, which is the size we defined in Figure 2.3.

```
Calibrating delay loop... 235.11 BogoMIPS (lpj=1175552)
Mount-cache hash table entries: 512
Initializing cgroup subsys debug
Initializing cgroup subsys cpuacct
Initializing cgroup subsys freezer
CPU: Testing write buffer coherency: ok
net_namespace: 936 bytes
NET: Registered protocol family 16
bio: create slab <bio-0> at 0
NET: Registered protocol family 2
IP route cache hash table entries: 16384 (order: 4, 65536 bytes)
TCP established hash table entries: 65536 (order: 7, 524288 bytes)
TCP bind hash table entries: 65536 (order: 6, 262144 bytes)
TCP: Hash tables configured (established 65536 bind 65536)
TCP reno registered
NET: Registered protocol family 1
checking if image is initramfs... it is
Freeing initrd memory: 176K
```

Following is a list of hardware interfaces initialized by the kernel, along with the corresponding device name, base address, and interrupt number. For an example, serial port 1 is initialized with device name `goldfish_tty`, base address 0xff002000, and interrupt number 4.

goldfish_new_pdev goldfish_interrupt_controller at ff000000 irq -1

goldfish_new_pdev goldfish_device_bus at ff001000 irq 1

goldfish_new_pdev goldfish_timer at ff003000 irq 3

goldfish_new_pdev goldfish_rtc at ff010000 irq 10

goldfish_new_pdev goldfish_tty at ff002000 irq 4

goldfish_new_pdev goldfish_tty at ff011000 irq 11

goldfish_new_pdev goldfish_tty at ff012000 irq 12

goldfish_new_pdev smc91x at ff013000 irq 13

goldfish_new_pdev goldfish_fb at ff014000 irq 14

goldfish_new_pdev goldfish_audio at ff004000 irq 15

goldfish_new_pdev goldfish_mmc at ff005000 irq 16

goldfish_new_pdev goldfish_memlog at ff006000 irq -1

goldfish_new_pdev goldfish-battery at ff015000 irq 17

goldfish_new_pdev goldfish_events at ff016000 irq 18

goldfish_new_pdev goldfish_nand at ff017000 irq -1

goldfish_new_pdev qemu_pipe at ff018000 irq 19

goldfish_new_pdev goldfish-switch at ff01a000 irq 20

goldfish_new_pdev goldfish-switch at ff01b000 irq 21

goldfish_pdev_worker registered goldfish_interrupt_controller

goldfish_pdev_worker registered goldfish_device_bus

goldfish_pdev_worker registered goldfish_timer

goldfish_pdev_worker registered goldfish_rtc

goldfish_pdev_worker registered goldfish_tty

goldfish_pdev_worker registered goldfish_tty

goldfish_pdev_worker registered goldfish_tty

goldfish_pdev_worker registered smc91x

goldfish_pdev_worker registered goldfish_fb

goldfish_pdev_worker registered goldfish_audio

goldfish_pdev_worker registered goldfish_mmc

goldfish_pdev_worker registered goldfish_memlog

```
goldfish_pdev_worker registered goldfish-battery
goldfish_pdev_worker registered goldfish_events
goldfish_pdev_worker registered goldfish_nand
goldfish_pdev_worker registered qemu_pipe
goldfish_pdev_worker registered goldfish-switch
goldfish_pdev_worker registered goldfish-switch
ashmem: initialized
Installing knfsd (copyright (C) 1996 okir@monad.swb.de).
yaffs Sep 26 2012 11:04:43 Installing.
msgmni has been set to 1007
alg: No test for stdrng (krng)
io scheduler noop registered
io scheduler anticipatory registered (default)
io scheduler deadline registered
io scheduler cfq registered
allocating frame buffer 480 * 800, got ffa00000
console [ttyS0] enabled
loop: module loaded
nbd: registered device at major 43
goldfish_audio_probe
tun: Universal TUN/TAP device driver, 1.6
tun: (C) 1999-2004 Max Krasnyansky <maxk@qualcomm.com>
smc91x.c: v1.1, sep 22 2004 by Nicolas Pitre <nico@cam.org>
eth0 (smc91x): not using net_device_ops yet
eth0: SMC91C11xFD (rev 1) at e080c000 IRQ 13 [nowait]
eth0: Ethernet addr: 52:54:00:12:34:56
```

Next, NAND flash is initialized with the NAND flash size, page size, spare area size, and erase block size. There are three NAND flash devices found, which are mounted as system, data, and cache.

```
goldfish nand dev0: size c5e0000, page 2048, extra 64, erase 131072
goldfish nand dev1: size c200000, page 2048, extra 64, erase 131072
goldfish nand dev2: size 4000000, page 2048, extra 64, erase 131072
mice: PS/2 mouse device common for all mice
*** events probe ***
events_probe() addr=0xe0814000 irq=18
events_probe() keymap=qwerty2
```

```
input: qwerty2 as /devices/virtual/input/input0
goldfish_rtc goldfish_rtc: rtc core: registered goldfish_rtc as rtc0
device-mapper: uevent: version 1.0.3
device-mapper: ioctl: 4.14.0-ioctl (2008-04-23) initialised: dm-devel@redhat.com
logger: created 64K log 'log_main'
logger: created 256K log 'log_events'
logger: created 64K log 'log_radio'
Netfilter messages via NETLINK v0.30.
nf_conntrack version 0.5.0 (8192 buckets, 32768 max)
CONFIG_NF_CT_ACCT is deprecated and will be removed soon. Please use
nf_conntrack.acct=1 kernel paramater, acct=1 nf_conntrack module option or
sysctl net.netfilter.nf_conntrack_acct=1 to enable it.
ctnetlink v0.93: registering with nfnetlink.
NF_TPROXY: Transparent proxy support initialized, version 4.1.0
NF_TPROXY: Copyright (c) 2006-2007 BalaBit IT Ltd.
xt_time: kernel timezone is -0000
ip_tables: (C) 2000-2006 Netfilter Core Team
arp_tables: (C) 2002 David S. Miller
TCP cubic registered
NET: Registered protocol family 10
ip6_tables: (C) 2000-2006 Netfilter Core Team
IPv6 over IPv4 tunneling driver
NET: Registered protocol family 17
NET: Registered protocol family 15
RPC: Registered udp transport module.
RPC: Registered tcp transport module.
802.1Q VLAN Support v1.8 Ben Greear <greearb@candelatech.com>
All bugs added by David S. Miller <davem@redhat.com>
VFP support v0.3: implementor 41 architecture 3 part 30 variant c rev 0
goldfish_rtc goldfish_rtc: setting system clock to 2013-05-20 13:29:09 UTC (1369056549)
Freeing init memory: 124K
mmc0: new SD card at address e118
mmcblk0: mmc0:e118 SU02G 100 MiB
 mmcblk0:
init: cannot open '/initlogo.rle'
```

Chapter 2 Inside Android Emulator

NAND flash partitions are mounted as block devices in the following section of the log.

```
yaffs: dev is 32505856 name is "mtdblock0"
yaffs: passed flags ""
yaffs: Attempting MTD mount on 31.0, "mtdblock0"
yaffs_read_super: isCheckpointed 0
save exit: isCheckpointed 1
yaffs: dev is 32505857 name is "mtdblock1"
yaffs: passed flags ""
yaffs: Attempting MTD mount on 31.1, "mtdblock1"
yaffs_read_super: isCheckpointed 0
yaffs: dev is 32505858 name is "mtdblock2"
yaffs: passed flags ""
yaffs: Attempting MTD mount on 31.2, "mtdblock2"
yaffs_read_super: isCheckpointed 0
init: cannot find '/system/etc/install-recovery.sh', disabling 'flash_recovery'
init: untracked pid 47 exited
eth0: link up
```

Summary

In this chapter, we looked inside the Android emulator. We discussed how to use Android Virtual Device Manager to configure an instance of the Android emulator. We then took a close look at two common hardware interfaces—the serial interface and the timer interface. Understanding the hardware is the first step in any embedded system programming process.

3

Setting Up the Development Environment

Now that we have an overview of the virtual hardware platform, in this chapter we set up the development environment that we will use first. After that, we create a small test program to verify the development environment.

The Host and Client Environments

In embedded system development, we usually have a host environment and a client environment (or device). The host environment is what we use to develop software and build the system. The client environment is what we use to test our software. In our case, we use a Linux environment as our host and the Android emulator as our emulated device for the testing. Most ARM development toolchains support Linux, Windows, and Mac OS X. We use Ubuntu 12.04LTS as the host development environment in this book.

First, we need to install the GNU toolchain for ARM development and the Android SDK in the host. The Android emulator is part of the Android SDK. It includes a special version of QEMU, a machine emulator capable of emulating various devices including ARM-based machines. We can write ARM assembly language or C programs, compile those programs using the GNU toolchain, and execute and test them in the Android emulator.

The Android emulator, like QEMU, can support the gdb interface. This is a good way to monitor the program running in the Android emulator. We can connect to the emulator through gdb and then perform debugging in a step-by-step manner. To have a better user interface, ddd can be used together with gdb. The setup procedures and scripts should be able to be ported to other Linux distributions quite easily.

The two lists that follow define the client and host environments. We can think of the client configuration as the hardware specification of a device. The host configuration, in contrast, is the specification of your work environment. Before you can start your project work, you would give these specifications to your IT staff so that they can obtain (purchase) hardware and software according to your specifications.

In the next section, we discuss the development environment that you have to set up yourself as a developer.

Following is the configuration of the client environment:

- Android emulator (AVD defined in Figure 2.3)
- Processor: ARM (armeabi-v7a)
- Display: 4.0", 480x800:hdpi
- Memory: 512MB RAM
- Flash: 200MB NAND flash
- 100MB SD card
- Front and back cameras
- Qwerty-based keyboard and phone buttons
- GSM modem
- Accelerometer

Following is the configuration of the host environment:

- Ubuntu 12.04LTS
- Sourcery CodeBench Lite Edition
- Android SDK
- ddd

Development Environment Setup

To set up the development environment, we must first download the toolchain for ARM and the Android SDK. Both Android and embedded system development are fast-moving, dynamic technologies, so we have to select particular versions of the ARM toolchain and the Android SDK as the base for this book. Otherwise, we will be trying to shoot a moving target—which makes it very difficult to follow the explanations and discussions.

The version of the ARM toolchain used in this book is CodeBench Lite arm-2013.11. The version of the Android SDK used in this book is the ADT bundle released at 20140702. Neither version is currently available directly from the Mentor Graphics or Google website. However, we still can get them using direct links; we'll see how to download them later in this chapter.

With the latest version of CodeBench Lite, Mentor Graphics has removed it from its website for both the ARM and x86 architectures. You can get a trial version after you register on the company's website.

Google has also removed support for the ADT bundle that uses Eclipse as an integrated development environment (IDE) from its website. You can download an SDK-only package or a version integrated with Android Studio.

To make it easier to download and install the ARM toolchain or Android SDK, you can download an installation script and run it in your Ubuntu environment. Here is the link to that script: *https://github.com/shugaoye/build/blob/master/bin/install.sh*.

You can also follow the instructions in the next two subsections to download and install both the ARM toolchain and the Android SDK by yourself.

Downloading and Installing Android SDK

Android SDK can be downloaded from *http://developer.android.com*. This software development kit is distributed in a few different formats—we will use the Android Developer Tools (ADT) bundle. This package includes the Android SDK and Eclipse ADT plugins. As mentioned earlier, you can find a stand-alone version of Android SDK or Android Studio with the link given in the previous section, but not the ADT bundle. Instead, we must use a direct link to download this bundle.

To download the ADT bundle used in this book, choose one of the following links based on your Ubuntu environment:

- x86_64 version of the ADT bundle: *https://dl.google.com/android/adt/adt-bundle-linux-x86_64-20140702.zip*
- x86 version of the ADT bundle: *https://dl.google.com/android/adt/adt-bundle-linux-x86-20140702.zip*

The ADT bundle provides everything you need to start developing applications, including a version of the Eclipse IDE with built-in ADT to streamline your Android application development.

After downloading the package, unpack the ZIP file (named `adt-bundle-<os_platform>.zip`) and save it to an appropriate location, such as a `Development` directory in your home directory. Eclipse can be found in the `adt-bundle-<os_platform>/eclipse/` folder. The Android SDK can be found in the `adt-bundle-<os_platform>/sdk/` folder.

To build the Android source code in Part III of this book, you should set up an x86_64 Ubuntu environment. In this environment, you can download and install the package using the following commands:

```
$ cd $HOME

$ wget -O ~/Downloads/adt-bundle-linux-x86_64-20140702.zip
https://dl.google.com/android/adt/adt-bundle-linux-x86_64-20140702.zip

$ unzip ~/Downloads/adt-bundle-linux-x86_64-20140702.zip
```

Downloading and Installing the GNU Toolchain for ARM

Many prebuilt ARM toolchains are available for free to developers. They usually provide toolchains in various formats to build different targets. For example, the Linaro organization supports Linux-based devices running on ARM processors (*http://www.linaro.org/*). Linaro provides separate toolchains for ARM EABI, GNU/Linux, and 64-bit GNU/Linux, among others. Google also provides its own toolchain to build the Android kernel or Android Open Source Project (AOSP); you can get a build environment and prebuilt toolchain from Google at *http://source.android.com/index.html*.

In this book, we will use the ARM toolchain from Mentor Graphics. This company offers a product family called Sourcery CodeBench for embedded software development. Included in this family is a free product called Sourcery CodeBench Lite. The GNU toolchain for ARM can be downloaded from Mentor Graphics at the following link: *http://www.mentor.com/embedded-software/sourcery-tools/sourcery-codebench/editions/lite-edition/*.

A few different toolchain formats for ARM are available on Mentor Graphics' website. We need these two:

- **Toolchain for ARM EABI/ELF:** Intended for real-time operating systems or "bare metal" systems where no operating system is present. This toolchain should not be used to build Linux kernels or applications.

- **Toolchain for GNU/Linux:** Intended for systems running "full" Linux—that is, Linux on CPUs with an MMU. This kind of toolchain can be used to build both the Linux kernel and applications.

The reason why organizations provide toolchains in different formats for a processor architecture, such as ARM, is because the target environment is different in each case. For example, we cannot use the toolchain for GNU/Linux in a bare metal environment. The C library in the GNU/Linux toolchain is Glib C; this large C runtime library is suitable for a full operating system and desktop environment, but not for an embedded system. The toolchain for ARM EABI/ELF, in contrast, is usually compiled with a much smaller C library, such as NEWLIB (we will discuss this library later); it can be used in a bare metal environment. In Part I of this book, we use the toolchain for ARM EABI/ELF to compile all examples. In Parts II and III, we use both the ARM EABI/ELF and GNU/Linux toolchains.

As mentioned earlier, the official download page for CodeBench Lite for ARM and x86 has been removed by Mentor Graphics and replaced with a page for downloading the CodeBench trial version. However, direct download links for the previous version are still available. We can download both packages using the following commands:

```
$ wget -O ~/Downloades/arm-2013.11-24-arm-none-eabi-i686-pc-linux-gnu.tar.bz2
https://sourcery.mentor.com/public/gnu_toolchain/arm-none-eabi/arm-2013.11-24-
arm-none-eabi-i686-pc-linux-gnu.tar.bz2

$ wget -O ~/Downloads/arm-2013.11-33-arm-none-linux-gnueabi-i686-pc-linux-gnu.
tar.bz2 http://sourcery.mentor.com/public/gnu_toolchain/arm-none-linux-gnueabi/
arm-2013.11-33-arm-none-linux-gnueabi-i686-pc-linux-gnu.tar.bz2
```

After downloading these packages, we can see the compressed files in the download folder. We can then extract those files into our home directory.

```
$ ls
arm-2013.11-24-arm-none-eabi-i686-pc-linux-gnu.tar.bz2
arm-2013.11-33-arm-none-linux-gnueabi-i686-pc-linux-gnu.tar.bz2
```

```
$ tar xvfj ~/Downloads/arm-2013.11-24-arm-none-eabi-i686-pc-linux-gnu.tar.bz2
$ tar xvfj ~/Downloads/arm-2013.11-33-arm-none-linux-gnueabi-i686-pc-linux-gnu.tar.bz2
```

After installing or decompressing the toolchain, you need to add it to your PATH environment variable so that you can run the compilation tools without specifying the full path.

```
$ export PATH=$HOME/{your installation folder}/bin:$PATH
```

To make this change permanent in your environment, you might want to add it to the startup script .bashrc. I created a script file that you can download and use in .bashrc; it's found at the following link: *https://github.com/shugaoye/build/blob/master/bin/setup.sh*.

To have a better user interface for gdb, we can install ddd on Ubuntu:

```
$ sudo apt-get install ddd
```

Integrated Development Environment

We use Eclipse as the IDE or editor in this book, because we are working on low-level programming. Eclipse is a development environment that can handle multiple programming languages. You can use it as a development environment for Android applications as well as for system-level development using C or assembly language. All examples in this book can be built and edited both from the command line and in Eclipse. Appendix A explains how to import a project into Eclipse.

Your First ARM Program

After we have set up the environment, we're ready to create a simple ARM program to verify our development environment is working correctly. The typical first program in many programming language books is to print "Hello World!" on the standard output. However, it is difficult to do this in just a few lines of assembly language. We can create a similar program when we move to the C language later. Before we start to test the first program, we check out source code from the open source repository GitHub. Appendix A provides more details about the source code in this book. Right now, we can use the following commands to get the source code into our home directory:

```
$ mkdir book
$ cd book
$ git clone https://github.com/shugaoye/bo.git
$ ls -F
c03/   c05/   c07/   drivers/   makedefs       README.md
c04/   c06/   c08/   include/   makedefs.arm
```

The example code for Chapters 3 to 8 is located in folders c03 to c08. The folders include and drivers contain common files.

Example 3.1 Adding Two Numbers (c03/c03e1/c03e1.S)

```
...
ResetISR:                  @ The starting address after power-up
        mov   r0, #5       @ Load register r0 with the value 5
        mov   r1, #4       @ Load register r1 with the value 4
        add   r2, r1, r0   @ Add r0 and r1 and store in r2
ResetISR_STOP:
b ResetISR_STOP            @ Infinite loop to stop execution
...
```

The source code for the first example can be found in the folder `c03/c03e1`. In the first assembly program, we add two numbers together using registers.

The assembly program source file consists of a sequence of statements, one per line. Each statement has the following format:

```
label:     instruction          @ comment
```

As this is the first assembly language program we'll create in this book, let's recap the essential assembly language elements we will use here:

- A *label* is a convenient way to refer to the location of the instruction in memory. It can be used wherever an address can appear—for example, as an operand of a branch instruction. The label name can consist of letters, numbers, underscores (_), and dollar signs ($).
- A comment starts with the symbol @; the characters that appear after this symbol are ignored.
- An instruction could be an ARM instruction or an assembler directive. Assembler directives are commands to the assembler. Assembler directives always start with a period (.).

Example 3.1 shows a very simple ARM assembly program that adds two numbers.

After powering up the board, the processor will start from the reset address in memory. The example program is loaded at the reset address after powering up the board so that we can run it. Such a bare metal application is started from the reset of system.

Building the Binary

To build the project, you can invoke the `make` command in the folder `c03/c03e1`:

```
$ make DEBUG=1 VERBOSE=1
```

```
arm-none-eabi-gcc -marm -mno-thumb-interwork -mabi=aapcs-linux -march=armv5te
-fno-common -ffixed-r8 -msoft-float -fno-builtin -ffreestanding -MD -g -D DEBUG
-Dgcc -o gcc/c03e1.o -c c03e1.S
```

```
arm-none-eabi-ld -T c03e1.ld --entry ResetISR -o gcc/c03e1.axf gcc/c03e1.o /opt/
arm-2012.03/bin/../lib/gcc/arm-none-eabi/4.6.3/../../../../arm-none-eabi/lib/
libm.a /opt/arm-2012.03/bin/../lib/gcc/arm-none-eabi/4.6.3/../../../../arm-none-
eabi/lib/libc.a /opt/arm-2012.03/bin/../lib/gcc/arm-none-eabi/4.6.3/libgcc.a
```

From this output of `makefile`, you can see that `arm-none-eabi-gcc` is invoked to assemble the source file into the object file `c03e1.o`. The object file is then linked to the executable file `c03e1.axf` using `arm-none-eabi-ld`. In the command line, we supply two parameters. The macro `DEBUG=1` turns on the debug build so that the executable includes debug information and can be debugged using gdb. With the macro `VERBOSE=1`, the debug information from assembler and linker is displayed during the build process.

To assemble the file manually, we can also directly invoke the GNU toolchain's assembler `as`, as shown in the following command:

```
$ arm-none-eabi-as -g -march=armv5te -o gcc/c03e1.o -c c03e1.S
```

The `-o` option specifies the output filename.

> **Note**
> Cross-compilation toolchains are always prefixed with the target architecture for which they are built, to avoid name conflicts with the host toolchain. For the sake of readability, we will refer to tools without the prefix in this book. For example, we will refer to `as` instead of `arm-none-eabi-as` for the assembler.

To generate the executable file manually, we can invoke the GNU toolchain's linker `ld`, as shown in the following command:

```
$ arm-none-eabi-ld -T c03e1.ld --entry ResetISR --gc-sections -o gcc/c03e1.axf gcc/c03e1.o
```

This command does the same thing as the one in `makefile`. We don't need to specify all of the library files right now, because we won't use any C library functions just yet. Use of C library functions is explained in Chapter 6.

Once again, the `-o` option specifies the output filename. The option `-Tc03e1.ld` specifies the link script filename (link script files are covered in Chapter 4).

Before we test the executable, we can look into it using the tool `nm`. To view the address assignment for various labels, run the `nm` command as shown here:

```
$ arm-none-eabi-nm gcc/c03e1.axf
00010000 T ResetISR
0001000c t ResetISR_STOP
00030000 T _bss
00030000 T _data
00030000 T _ebss
00030000 T _edata
00010010 T _etext
00010000 T _text
```

Note the address assignment for the labels `ResetISR` and `ResetISR_STOP`. The address assigned for `ResetISR` is 0x00010000—an address at the memory location of 64KB. The label `ResetISR_STOP` appears after three instructions. Each instruction is 4 bytes in size; hence `ResetISR_STOP` is assigned at the address `ResetISR+12` (0x0001000C). Labels with addresses larger than 0x00030000 are intended for data in RAM; we will discuss them again in Chapter 4, when we talk about link scripts.

The output file created by the command `ld` is in a format called ELF (executable and linkable format). Various file formats are available for storing executable code. The ELF format works well when you use it in an operating system environment. Because we plan to run the program on hardware directly (bare metal environment), we will have to convert it to a simpler file format called binary format.

A file in binary format contains consecutive bytes from a specific memory address. No other additional information is stored in the file. This format is convenient for flash programming tools, because all that has to be done when programming is to copy each byte in the file, to a consecutive address starting from a specified base address in memory.

The GNU toolchain's `objcopy` command can be used to convert between different object file formats. A common usage of the command is given here:

objcopy -O <output-format> <in-file> <out-file>

To convert `c03e1.axf` to binary format, use the following command:

$ arm-none-eabi-objcopy -O binary gcc/c03e1.axf gcc/c03e1.bin

Running in the Android Emulator

When the ARM processor is reset, it starts executing from flash memory (or ROM) and invokes the reset vector. On the Android emulator, we assume the flash memory is located starting at address 0x0. The instructions present at the beginning of the flash memory will be executed.

In the Android emulator, a file has to be specified that will be treated as flash memory. Both the ELF format and the BIN format can be used in the Android emulator. The Android emulator behaves a little differently while loading these two different formats. That is, when loading an ELF format, the Android emulator starts from the loading address that is defined in the link script. In our case, this address is 0x00010000 (at the address 64KB). In contrast, when loading a BIN format, a small bootloader is executed. After that, the emulator jumps to the address 0x00010000 (64KB). This is why we choose 0x00010000 as the loading address in the link script.

> **Note**
> We will discuss the small bootloader in QEMU again in Chapter 10. There, we'll get a clearer understanding of how a binary image is managed by QEMU and by the Android emulator.

The binary file c03e1.axf generated from the preceding step can be used for testing. After reset, the processor will start executing from the loading address in this case, and the instructions from the program will be executed. The command to invoke the emulator follows:

```
$ emulator -verbose -show-kernel -netfast -avd hd2 -shell -qemu -s -S -kernel gcc/c03e1.axf
...
emulator: Initializing hardware OpenGLES emulation support
QEMU waiting for connection on: telnet:localhost:6666,server
```

Let's look at various command-line options for this command:

- `-verbose`: Turns on the debug information about the emulator.
- `-show-kernel`: Turns on the debug information about the kernel, which can be a bare metal program, bootloader, or Linux kernel.
- `-avd hd2`: Specifies the AVD name that we created in Chapter 2.
- `-shell`: Specifies that a debug console should be created on the current console. This option will prove useful later, when we discuss goldfish kernel boot.

All options after `-qemu` are passed to the built-in QEMU inside the emulator:

- `-kernel`: Specifies that the c03e1.axf file represents the flash memory.
- `-s`: Specifies that QEMU opens a gdbserver on TCP port 1234.
- `-S`: Specifies that the CPU will be held until a command is invoked in the QEMU monitor or gdb.

After the emulator starts, the user interface will appear as shown in Figure 3.1.

For a better view of what is happening in CPU, we can start ddd using the following commands:

```
$ ddd --debugger arm-none-eabi-gdb gcc/c03e1.axf
```

In the gdb command-line window, use the `target` command to connect to the QEMU gdbserver:

```
Copyright © 1999-2001 Universität Passau, Germany.
Copyright © 2001 Universität des Saarlandes, Germany.
Copyright © 2001-2004 Free Software Foundation, Inc.
(gdb) target remote localhost:1234
0x00010000 in ?? ()
```

Select Machine Code Windows in the View menu, and you will see that the current instructions are being executed, as shown in Figure 3.2.

34 Chapter 3 Setting Up the Development Environment

Figure 3.1 Android emulator user interface

To view the contents of the registers, from the DDD menu we can select Status > Registers.... A register status window like that shown in Figure 3.3 appears. Before the program's execution begins, the contents of the registers can be found as in Figure 3.3. Note that all registers have a value of zero except for register pc. The value of register pc is where the program will start.

Running in the Android Emulator   35

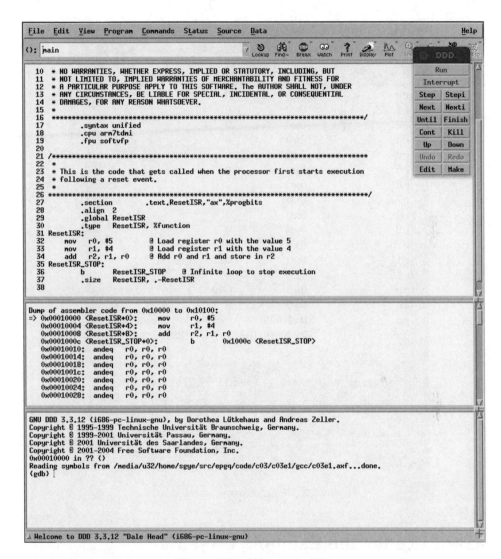

Figure 3.2 ddd user interface

We can execute the instruction step by step from the DDD window while we continually check each register's status in the registers status window. The system executes the instructions and, after their completion, keeps looping infinitely. Figure 3.4 shows the contents of the registers after the CPU goes into infinite loop. Notice the value in register r2—this register contains the result of the addition and should match the expected value of 9. We can also see the two addends stored in registers r0 and r1.

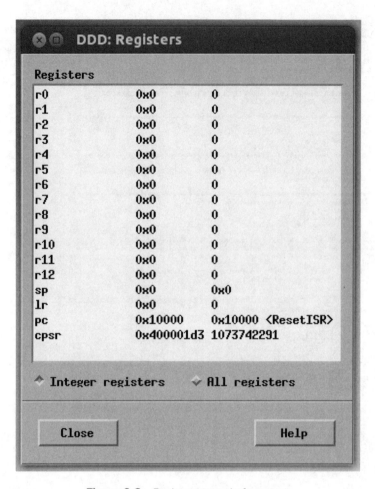

Figure 3.3 Register status before start

`makefile` for the Example Projects

To simplify the build and debug process, a standard `makefile` template will be used for all example projects in this book. This `makefile` template supports the following build targets:

- `all`: This is the default build target, which is used when you don't specify any arguments.
- `clean`: This target cleans up the project to remove all generated files, such as `.o` and `.axf` files.

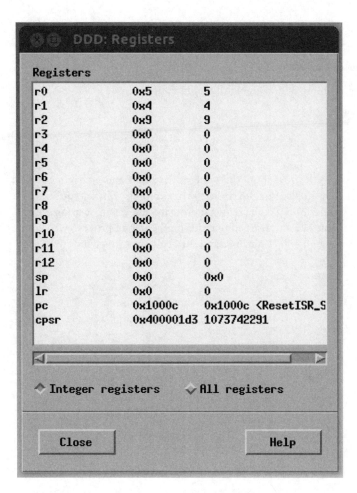

Figure 3.4 Register status after the execution

- debug: This target launches the gdb in the ddd user interface first and then starts the Android emulator.

There are various options in the makefile template as well, which can be applied when a build target is made. The most common options are DEBUG and VERBOSE:

- DEBUG: When set to DEBUG=1, a debug build will be produced. We must use the debug build feature with gdb.
- VERBOSE: When set to VERBOSE=1, the actual build command will be displayed on the console. This helps to debug the makefile itself.

Following is an example of building a debug version with the build process information displayed on the console:

```
$ make DEBUG=1 VERBOSE=1
```

Here's an example of debugging the build target:

```
$ make debug
```

Summary

In this chapter, we learned about the setup of development environments and tools. We also created a simple program to start programming. Thanks to this simple example, we now know how to build a bare metal program and debug it using gdb/ddd in the Android emulator. We also learned that during the debug process, we can monitor the system status through gdb commands and the registers status window.

4
Linker Script and Memory Map

In Chapter 3, we set up the development environment and developed a simple assembly language program to verify the environment. In this chapter, we continue to explore assembly language programming. We study how the executable image is organized and how it loads into memory before running. To understand this process, we first consider memory mapping. We next study basic concepts such as symbol resolution, relocation, and section merging. With these basic concepts as the foundation, we then discuss linker scripts using an example.

Memory Map

In an embedded system, we usually have memory in the form of RAM and ROM. The flash memory or ROM is usually a kind of read-only memory. It is a useful secondary form of storage, like a hard disk, but it is not convenient to store variables in flash memory. Instead, these variables should be stored in RAM, so that they can be easily modified. It is possible to store read-only data in ROM, but the read speed in ROM is much slower than in RAM. Thus, for performance reasons, we usually avoid this approach. The common practice is to load code and data from ROM to RAM first, and then to execute the program in RAM. Even though we don't really have NOR flash support in the Android emulator, we can use RAM to emulate it. We emulate NOR flash using RAM in Chapter 10 in section on booting Android from NOR flash memory.

> **Note**
> Flash memory is an electronic, nonvolatile computer storage medium that can be electrically erased and reprogrammed. Reading from NOR flash is similar to reading from random-access memory (RAM). In turn, NOR flash memory can be used as execute in place (XIP) memory. In other words, programs stored in NOR flash can be executed directly from that location without needing to be copied into RAM first. This option is very useful in certain use cases, although we usually copy code and data from NOR flash to RAM to execute for performance reasons. NAND flash works much like block devices, such as hard disks. The data and programs in NAND flash must be copied into RAM first before they can be accessed.

Chapter 4 Linker Script and Memory Map

To have better control over both our program and memory, we need to understand how the entire memory space is built. In a real hardware board, there may be multiple RAM and ROM resources. For example, the application processor may have RAM to run the operating system and applications. The graphic processor may have its own RAM to deal with graphics display. The processors may have regions that overlap with each other, or the graphic processor's registers may be mapped into the application processor's memory range. The map that describes the usage of the entire memory space is called a memory map. The memory map of the goldfish board is shown in Figure 4.1.

The memory map in Figure 4.1 includes only the memory regions that we use in this book. There may be other things that should be put in this memory map to have a complete picture. At the lower address starting from 0x00000000, there is a block of 64KB memory for interrupt vectors or system reserves. We load our program starting at address 0x00010000, which is at the 64KB boundary of memory.

Bare metal programming needs minimal memory resources. In the programming examples found in Chapters 5 to 8, we need less than 128KB of space to store our

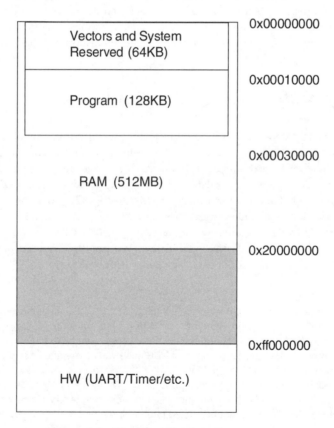

Figure 4.1 Virtual goldfish board memory map

programs. This 128KB memory can be represented as 0x20000 in hexadecimal. The addresses 0x00030000 to 0x20000000 are RAM space for data. We created a device hd2 with 512MB RAM in Chapter 2, so the entire RAM space was 512MB in that case. The 512MB memory ends at address 0x20000000. In the higher address space, we have goldfish-specific hardware interfaces, which have a base address starting from 0xff000000.

We load programs at 0x00010000 because the Android emulator is based on QEMU. QEMU can load a Linux kernel and RAMDISK using the -kernel and -initrd options. These options load two binary files into the emulated memory: the kernel binary at address 0x00010000 (64KB) and the RAMDISK binary at address 0x00800000 (8MB). Then QEMU prepares the kernel arguments and jumps at 0x00010000 (64KB) to execute the kernel. QEMU recognizes multiple binary formats. In our example code, we build the executable in both ELF (.axf) and BIN (.bin) format; QEMU supports both of them.

To place the program into the appropriate memory regions, we must understand how the assembler and the linker assemble the program into a file image and how the file image is loaded into different memory regions. We explore those topics next.

Linker

In Chapter 3, it took us two steps to generate the ELF-format executable. We generated the object file first using the assembler as. We then used the linker ld to link the object file into an executable in ELF format. We will look more closely at the linking step in this section.

Linking is the process of combining various pieces of code and data to form a single executable that can be loaded into memory. Linking can be done at compilation time, at load time (by loaders), or at runtime (by application programs). When we write a multi-file program, each file is assembled individually into object files; the linker then combines these object files to form the final executable.

In Figure 4.2, we have three assembly source files (a.S, b.S, and c.S). After we assemble them into object files, we use the linker to create the final executable, abc.axf.

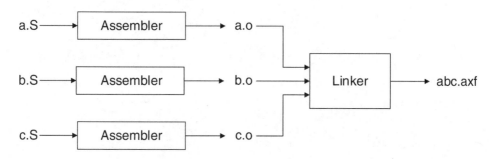

Figure 4.2 Role of the linker

While combining the object files together, the linker performs symbol resolution and relocation. Let's look into these operations in detail.

> **Note**
>
> The book *Linkers and Loaders* by John R. Levine is an excellent reference for this chapter. In this book, you can find more information about symbol resolution, section merging, various file formats, and more. The executable output from the linker usually includes the following sections:
>
> - **bss segment:** Contains uninitialized global variables.
> - **Data segment:** Contains global variables that are initialized.
> - **Text segment:** Contains code and constant data. This segment can be located in read-only memory or RAM.

Symbol Resolution

In a single-file program, while producing the object file, the assembler replaces all references to labels with their corresponding addresses. In contrast, in a multi-file program, if any references to labels are defined in another file, the assembler marks these references as "unresolved." When these object files are subsequently passed to the linker, the linker determines the values for these references from the other object files, and patches the code with the correct values.

To demonstrate the symbol resolution performed by the linker, let's use an example that sums an array of integers. The two files will be assembled and their symbol tables will be examined to show the presence of the unresolved references.

Main Program of Example c04e1

The file `sum-sub.S` contains the `sum` subroutine, and the file `c04e1.S` invokes the subroutine with the required arguments. The sources of the files are shown in Example 4.1.

Example 4.1 c04e1.S: Summing an Array of Integers (code\c04\c04e1)

```
    .syntax unified
    .cpu arm7tdmi
    .fpu softvfp

    .section .data
data1:
    .word   0

    .section .text.ResetISR
    .align
    .global ResetISR
    .type ResetISR, %function
```

```
ResetISR:
    b start                 @ Skip over the data
arr:
    .byte 2, 4, 8, 16, 32   @ Read-only array of bytes
eoa:                        @ Address of end of array + 1
    .align
start:
    ldr    r0, =arr         @ r0 = &arr
    ldr    r1, =eoa         @ r1 = &eoa
    bl     sum              @ Invoke the sum subroutine
    ldr    r0, =data1       @ r0 = &data1
    str    r3, [r0]         @ result in r3 and store it to data1
ResetISR_STOP:
    b ResetISR_STOP         @ Infinite loop to stop execution
    .size ResetISR, .-ResetISR
```

The code in Example 4.1 calls a subroutine (sum) to sum an array of data. Before it does so, it prepares the start address of an array in register r0 (arr) and the end address of an array in register r1 (eoa). After it returns from sum, the return value is stored in register r3 at memory location data1.

This code also uses the assembler directives .byte, .word, and .align. These assembler directives are described next.

> **Note**
>
> Refer to *ARM System Developer's Guide* by Andrew N. Sloss, Dominic Symes, and Chris Wright for more information on the ARM assembly language. Only the directives used in the chapter are introduced here.

.byte Directive

The byte-sized arguments of .byte are assembled into consecutive bytes in memory. Similar directives are .2byte and .4byte, for storing 16-bit values and 32-bit values, respectively. The general syntax follows:

.byte   exp1 (8bit), exp2 (8bit), ...
.2byte   exp1 (16bit), exp2 (16bit), ...
.4byte   exp1 (32 bit), exp2 (32 bit), ...

The .word directive has the same effect as .4byte.

Chapter 4 Linker Script and Memory Map

The arguments to the `.byte` directives could be simple integer literals, represented as binary (prefixed by 0b or 0B), octal (prefixed by 0), decimal or hexadecimal (prefixed by 0x or 0X). The integers could also be represented as character constants (character surrounded by single quotes), in which case the ASCII value of the character will be used. Finally, the arguments could be C expressions constructed out of literals and other symbols. Examples are shown here:

```
pattern:   .byte 0b01010101, 0b00110011, 0b00001111
npattern:  .byte npattern - pattern
halpha:    .byte 'A', 'B', 'C', 'D', 'E', 'F'
dummy:     .4byte 0xDEADBEEF
nalpha:    .byte 'Z' - 'A' + 1
```

`.align` Directive

ARM requires that the instructions be present in 32-bit aligned memory locations. The address of the first byte, which encompasses the 4 bytes in an instruction, should be a multiple of 4. To adhere to this practice, the `.align` directive can be used to insert padding bytes until the next byte address will be a multiple of 4.

Subroutine of Example c04e1

Example 4.2 shows the source code of the subroutine `sum`. It takes two input parameters in register r0 (the start address of the array) and register r1 (the end address of the array). The result is stored in register r3 (the sum of the array) at the memory location `data2`.

Example 4.2 sum-sub.S: Subroutine Definition (code\c04\c04e1)

```
    .syntax unified
    .cpu arm7tdmi
    .fpu softvfp

    .section .data
data2:
    .word 0

    .section .text.sum
    .align
    .global sum

sum:
    mov    r3, #0          @ r3 = 0
```

```
loop:
    ldrb    r2, [r0], #1        @ r2 = *r0++         ; Get array element
    add     r3, r2, r3          @ r3 += r2           ; Calculate sum
    cmp     r0, r1              @ if (r0 != r1)      ; Check if hit end-of-array
    bne     loop                @ goto loop          ; Loop
    ldr     r0, =data2          @ r0 = &data2
    str     r3, [r0]            @ result in r3 and store it to data2
    mov     pc, lr              @ pc = lr            ; Return when done
```

In the subroutine, the .global directive is used to declare sum as a function that can be invoked from other files. In the C language, all variables declared outside functions are visible to other files, until explicitly identified as static. In assembly, all labels are static, which means they are local (to the file), until the code explicitly states that they should be visible to other files, indicated via the .global directive.

The files are assembled, and the symbol tables can be dumped using the nm command:

```
$ arm-none-eabi-as -g -o gcc/c04e1.o c04e1.S
$ arm-none-eabi-as -g -o gcc/sum-sub.o sum-sub.S
$ arm-none-eabi-nm -n gcc/c04e1.o
         U sum
00000000 T ResetISR
00000000 d data1
00000004 t arr
00000009 t eoa
0000000c t start
00000020 t ResetISR_STOP

$ arm-none-eabi-nm -n gcc/sum-sub.o
00000000 d data2
00000000 T sum
00000004 t loop
```

For now, let's focus on the letter in the second column, which specifies the symbol type. The character 't' indicates that the symbol is defined in the text section. The character 'u' indicates that the symbol is undefined. An uppercase letter indicates that the symbol is .global.

It is evident that the symbol `sum` is defined in `sum-sub.o` and is not resolved yet in `c04e1.o`. When the linker is invoked, the symbol references will be resolved, and the executable will be produced.

We can see that the label `eoa` is not aligned in the 4-bytes boundary. If we remove the `.align` directive, we will get the following error message:

```
$ arm-none-eabi-as -g  -o gcc/c04e1.o c04e1.S
```

c04e1.S: Assembler messages:

c04e1.S: Error: unaligned opcodes detected in executable segment

Relocation

Relocation is the process of changing addresses already assigned to labels. This will also involve patching up all label references to reflect the newly assigned address. Primarily, relocation is performed for merging and placing sections. To understand the process of relocation, an understanding of the concept of sections is essential.

Code and data have different runtime requirements. For example, code can be placed in read-only memory, whereas data might require read-write memory. It would be convenient for code and data to not be interleaved. For this purpose, programs are divided into sections. Most programs have at least two sections: `.text` for code and `.data` for data. The assembler directives `.text` and `.data` are used to switch back and forth between the two sections.

It helps to imagine each section as a bucket. When the assembler hits a section directive, it puts the code/data following the directive in the selected bucket. Thus the code/data that belong to a particular section appear in contiguous locations.

Let's use `ld` to create the result in ELF format for further analysis:

```
$ arm-none-eabi-ld -T c04e1.ld --entry ResetISR --gc-sections -o gcc/c04e1.axf
gcc/c04e1.o gcc/sum-sub.o
```

Once we have the ELF-format executable file `c04e1.axf`, we can see how the assembler rearranges data into sections by examining Figure 4.3.

In the output of `c04e1.o` and `sub-sum.o` from the `nm` command, notice that the start address is 0x0 in both object files. After the linking is complete, the function `sum` starts at 0x10030 in the `.text` section, as shown in Figure 4.3.

Also notice how the assembly source code maps to the object file, which is dumped using the `objdump` command. We can compare the output from this command with Figure 4.3.

We can use `objdump` to dump the address arrangement of the `.text` section with option -d:

```
$ arm-none-eabi-objdump -d gcc/c04e1.axf
```

```
gcc/c04e1.axf:      file format elf32-littlearm


Disassembly of section .text:

00010000 <ResetISR>:
   10000:       ea000001        b       1000c <start>
```

```
00010004 <arr>:
   10004:       10080402        .word   0x10080402
   10008:       20              .byte   0x20

00010009 <eoa>:
   10009:       00              .byte   0x00
        ...

0001000c <start>:
   1000c:       e59f0010        ldr     r0, [pc, #16]   ; 10024 <ResetISR_STOP+0x4>
   10010:       e59f1010        ldr     r1, [pc, #16]   ; 10028 <ResetISR_STOP+0x8>
   10014:       eb000005        bl      10030 <sum>
   10018:       e59f000c        ldr     r0, [pc, #12]   ; 1002c <ResetISR_STOP+0xc>
   1001c:       e5803000        str     r3, [r0]

00010020 <ResetISR_STOP>:
   10020:       eafffffe        b       10020 <ResetISR_STOP>
   10024:       00010004        .word   0x00010004
   10028:       00010009        .word   0x00010009
   1002c:       00030000        .word   0x00030000

00010030 <sum>:
   10030:       e3a03000        mov     r3, #0

00010034 <loop>:
   10034:       e4d02001        ldrb    r2, [r0], #1
   10038:       e0823003        add     r3, r2, r3
   1003c:       e1500001        cmp     r0, r1
   10040:       1afffffb        bne     10034 <loop>
   10044:       e59f0004        ldr     r0, [pc, #4]    ; 10050 <loop+0x1c>
   10048:       e5803000        str     r3, [r0]
   1004c:       e1a0f00e        mov     pc, lr
   10050:       00030004        .word   0x00030004
```

With option -s, we can use objdump to dump the address arrangement of the .data section:

$ arm-none-eabi-objdump -s gcc/c04e1.axf

gcc/c04e1.axf: file format elf32-littlearm

48   Chapter 4 Linker Script and Memory Map

```
Contents of section .text:
 10000 010000ea 02040810 20000000 10009fe5  ........ .......
 10010 10109fe5 050000eb 0c009fe5 003080e5  .............0..
 10020 fefffffea 04000100 09000100 00000300  ................
 10030 0030a0e3 0120d0e4 033082e0 010050e1  .0... ...0....P.
 10040 fbffff1a 04009fe5 003080e5 0ef0a0e1  .........0......
 10050 04000300                              ....
Contents of section .data:
 30000 00000000 00000000                     ........
Contents of section .ARM.attributes:
 ........
```

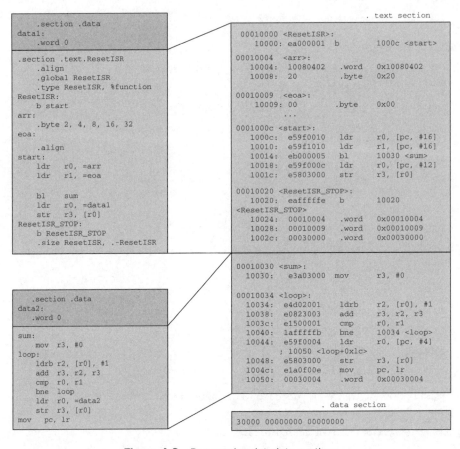

Figure 4.3 Rearranging data into sections

As shown in Figure 4.3, the code section starts from 0x10000 to 0x0002FFFF. The .data section starts at 0x00030000—the starting address for data1 and data2, which are used to store the result in memory.

Now that we have an understanding of sections, let's look into the primary reasons for which relocation is performed.

Section Merging

When dealing with multi-file programs, the sections with the same name (for example, .text) might appear in each file. The linker is responsible for merging the sections from the input files into the corresponding sections of the output file. By default, the sections with the same name from each file are placed contiguously, and the label references are patched to reflect the new address.

The effects of section merging can be seen by looking at the symbol table of the object files and the corresponding executable file. The output of the example program that sums an array of numbers can be used to illustrate section merging. The symbol table of its object files c04e1.o and sum-sub.o and the symbol table of its executable file c04e1.axf are shown here:

```
$ arm-none-eabi-nm -n gcc/c04e1.o
         U sum
00000000 T ResetISR
00000000 d data1
00000004 t arr
00000009 t eoa
0000000c t start
00000020 t ResetISR_STOP
$ arm-none-eabi-nm -n gcc/sum-sub.o
00000000 d data2
00000000 T sum
00000004 t loop
$ arm-none-eabi-nm -n gcc/c04e1.axf
00010000 T ResetISR
00010000 T _text
00010004 t arr
00010009 t eoa
0001000c t start
00010020 t ResetISR_STOP
00010030 T sum
```

```
00010034 t loop
00010054 T _etext
00030000 D _data
00030000 d data1
00030004 d data2
00030008 D _bss
00030008 D _ebss
00030008 D _edata
```

> **Note**
>
> The symbol `loop` has the address 0x4 in `sum-sub.o` and the address 0x10034 in `c04e1.axf`, because the `.text` section of `sum-sub.o` is placed immediately after the `.text` section of `c04e1.o`. The symbols `data1` and `data2` have the address 0x0 in both `c04e1.o` and `sum-sub.o`. After linking, `data1` is assigned at address 0x00030000 and `data2` is assigned at address 0x00030004; both of these addresses are found in the RAM area.

Section Placement

When a program is assembled, each section is assumed to start from address 0. In turn, labels are assigned values relative to the start of the section. When the final executable is created, the section is placed at an address X. In addition, all references to the labels defined within the section are incremented by X, so that they point to the new location. These kinds of object modules are usually called relocatable code. A relocatable program might run at the address that is assigned by linker. This is important, because linkage can happen at runtime instead of during compilation. For example, all shared libraries are linked at runtime instead of build time.

To allow the linker to correct all address references to the proper execution values, the code must follow certain guidelines. For example, it cannot jump to an absolute memory address to produce a relocatable object file. A detailed discussion of how to write relocatable code is beyond the scope of this book; please refer to the documentation for your compiler for the details. When writing such code for the ARM architecture, you can refer to *RealView Compilation Tools Developer Guide* from ARM.

The placement of each section at a particular location in memory and the patching of all references to the labels in the section are handled by the linker. The effects of section placement can be seen by looking at the symbol table of the object file and the corresponding executable file.

Example 3.1 can be used to illustrate section placement. We first assemble the file `c03e1.s`. From the output, we can see that the address for labels is assigned starting from 0 within a section.

```
$ arm-none-eabi-as -g -o gcc/c03e1.o c03e1.S
arm-none-eabi-nm -n gcc/c03e1.o
00000000 T ResetISR
0000000c t ResetISR_STOP
```

To make things clearer, we can place the .text section at address 0x100 at the link stage, as follows:

```
$ arm-none-eabi-ld -Ttext=0x100 --entry ResetISR -o gcc/c03e1.axf gcc/c03e1.o
$ arm-none-eabi-nm -n gcc/c03e1.axf
00000100 T ResetISR
0000010c t ResetISR_STOP
00008110 A __bss_end__
00008110 A __bss_start
00008110 A __bss_start__
00008110 T __data_start
00008110 A __end__
00008110 A _bss_end__
00008110 A _edata
00008110 A _end
00080000 N _stack
```

When the executable is created, the linker is instructed to place the text section at address 0x100 with the option -Ttext=0x100. The addresses for labels in the .text section are reassigned starting from 0x100, and all label references are patched to reflect the new locations.

Let's look at the symbol type from nm output. As we mentioned earlier, uppercase means the symbol is global, whereas lowercase means the symbol is local. The symbol type 'T' or 't' indicates the symbol is in the text section. The symbol type 'A' indicates the symbol's value is absolute and will not be changed by further linking. The symbol type 'N' means the symbol is a debugging symbol.

Linker Script

As mentioned in the previous section, section merging and placement are handled by the linker. The programmer can control how the sections are merged, and at which locations they are placed in memory, through a linker script file.

The linker script is used to control the behavior of the linker. This script is written in the linker's command language. Its main purpose is to describe how the sections in the input files should be mapped into the output file, and to control the memory layout of the output file.

The linker always uses a linker script. If you do not supply one yourself, the linker will use a default script that is compiled into the linker executable. You can use the `--verbose` command-line option to display the default linker script. Certain command-line options, such as `-r` or `-N`, will affect the default linker script as well.

You may supply your own linker script by using the `-T` command-line option. When you do so, your linker script will replace the default linker script.

For the details on using linker scripts, you can refer to the user's manual for the GNU linker, which can be found online or in the installation folder of Sourcery CodeBench Lite.

A very simple linker script file is shown in Example 4.3.

Example 4.3 Basic Linker Script

```
SECTIONS {
        . = 0x00010000;
        .text : {
                abc.o (.text);
                def.o (.text);
        }
}
```

Let's see what we can find in this simple linker script:

- The `SECTIONS` command is the most important linker command; it specifies how the sections are to be merged and at which locations they are to be placed.
- Within the block following the `SECTIONS` command, the period (.) represents the location counter. The location is always initialized to 0x0 at the beginning. It can be modified by assigning a new value to it. Setting the value to 0x0 at the beginning is superfluous.
- The third line specifies that the `.text` sections from the input files `abc.o` and `def.o` should go into the `.text` section of the output file.

The linker script can be further simplified and generalized by using the wildcard character * instead of individually specifying the filenames, as shown in Example 4.4.

Example 4.4 Wildcard in Linker Scripts

```
SECTIONS {
        . = 0x00010000;
        .text : { * (.text); }
}
```

If the program contains both `.text` and `.data` sections, the `.data` section merging and location details can be specified as shown in Example 4.5.

Example 4.5 Multiple Sections in Linker Scripts

```
SECTIONS {
        . = 0x00010000;
        .text : { * (.text); }
        . = 0x00030000;
        .data : { * (.data); }
}
```

Here, the `.text` section is located at `0x10000` and the `.data` section is located at 0x30000. Note that, if the location counter is not assigned a different value, the `.text` and `.data` sections will be located at adjacent memory locations.

Linker Script Example

To demonstrate the use of linker scripts, we'll use the assembly code in Example 4.6 and the linker script in Example 4.7 to explore how they work. Example 4.6 is a slightly modified version of the "sum of arrays" program found in Example 4.1. The linker script shown in Example 4.7 controls the placement of the program's `.text`, `.rodata`, and `.data` sections.

Example 4.6 c04e2.S: Code of the Modified Summing a Data Array Program (code\c04\c04e2)

```
    .syntax unified
    .cpu arm7tdmi
.fpu softvfp

    .section  .data
data1:
    .word 0

    .section .rodata
arr:
    .byte 2, 4, 8, 16, 32      @ Read-only array of bytes
eoa:

    .section .text.ResetISR
    .align
    .global ResetISR
    .type ResetISR, %function
```

```
ResetISR:
    ldr    r0, =arr            @ r0 = &arr
    ldr    r1, =eoa            @ r1 = &eoa

    bl     sum                 @ Invoke the sum subroutine
    ldr    r0, =data1          @ r0 = &data1
    str    r3, [r0]            @ Result in r3 and store it to data1
ResetISR_STOP:
    b ResetISR_STOP            @ Infinite loop to stop execution
    .size ResetISR, .-ResetISR
```

Example 4.7 c04e2.ld: Linker Script of Summing a Data Array Program (code\c04\c04e2)

```
MEMORY
{
    FLASH (rx)  : ORIGIN = 0x00010000, LENGTH = 128K
    SRAM  (rwx) : ORIGIN = 0x00030000, LENGTH = 512M}

SECTIONS
{
    .text :
    {
        _text = .;
        KEEP(*(.isr_vector))
        *(.text*)
        *(.rodata*)
        _etext = .;
    } > FLASH

    .data : AT(ADDR(.text) + SIZEOF(.text))
    {
        _data = .;
        *(vtable)
        *(.data*)
        _edata = .;
    } > SRAM

    .bss :
```

```
    {
        _bss = .;
        *(.bss*)
        *(COMMON)
        _ebss = .;
    } > SRAM
}
```

The only change here is that the array now appears in the .rodata section. Also note that the branch instruction to skip over the data is no longer required, because the linker script will place the .text and .rodata sections in the appropriate locations. As a result, statements can be placed in the program, in any convenient way, and the linker script will take care of storing the sections correctly in memory.

When the program is linked, the linker script is passed as a parameter to the linker, as shown in the following commands:

$ arm-none-eabi-as -o gcc/c04e2.o c04e2.S

$ arm-none-eabi-as -o gcc/sum-sub.o sum-sub.S

$ arm-none-eabi-ld -T c04e2.ld -o gcc/c04e2.axf gcc/c04e2.o gcc/sum-sub.o

The option -T c04e2.ld specifies that the file c04e2.ld is to be used as the linker script. As usual, we can dump the symbol table to gain insight into how the sections are placed in memory:

$ arm-none-eabi-nm -n gcc/c04e2.axf

00010000 T ResetISR

00010000 T _text

00010014 t ResetISR_STOP

00010024 T sum

00010028 t loop

00010048 t arr

0001004d T _etext

0001004d t eoa

00030000 D _data

00030000 d data1

00030004 d data2

00030008 D _bss

00030008 D _ebss

00030008 D _edata

From this symbol table, it is obvious that the .text section is placed starting from address 0x10000 and the .rodata section is placed starting after the .text section. The label `ResetISR` appears at the start of the `.text` section, and the label `arr` appears at the start of the `.rodata` section. The placement information can be seen in Example 4.7.

Initializing Data in RAM

Now that we know how to write linker scripts, we can place data in either RAM or ROM using sections. If it is read-only data, we can place it in ROM, just as we did in Example 4.6 and Example 4.7. In those examples, we placed the read-only data array `arr` into the `.rodata` section and the `.rodata` section into ROM. We placed the variables `data1` and `data2` in RAM, because we need to use them to store the result. But what should we do if some variables have initial values and we need to change those values later? This problem isn't handled through the high-level programming, because the program loader should have done everything before the high-level program is ready to execute. In embedded system programming, not all RAM data is initialized when the power is turned on. As a consequence, we have to do something special to initialize the variables in RAM, if there are initial values assigned to them.

In the following examples, we examine how the data in RAM can be initialized with values from ROM.

Example 3.1 showed the addition of two numbers in which registers were used to store the two numbers and the result. In Example 4.8 and Example 4.9, we will change this program to use RAM to store the number and the result. The code is modified to load two variables from RAM, add them, and store the result in a variable in RAM. The two variables and the space for result are placed in the `.data` section.

Example 4.8 c04e3.S: Adding Data in RAM (code/c04/c04e3)

```
        .data
val1:   .4byte 10       @ First number
val2:   .4byte 30       @ Second number
result: .space 4        @ space for the result

        .section    .text.ResetISR,"ax",%progbits
        .align
        .global ResetISR
        .type   ResetISR, %function
ResetISR:
    /* Add and store result. */
    ldr     r0, =val1       @ r0 = &val1
    ldr     r1, =val2       @ r1 = &val2

    ldr     r2, [r0]        @ r2 = *r0
    ldr     r3, [r1]        @ r3 = *r1
```

```
        add     r4, r2, r3      @ r4 = r2 + r3

        ldr     r0, =result     @ r0 = &result

        str     r4, [r0]        @ *r0 = r4
ResetISR_STOP:
        b       ResetISR_STOP   @ Infinite loop to stop execution
```

When the program is linked, the linker script is similar to the one in Example 4.7. The dump of the symbol table of c04e3.axf is shown here:

$ arm-none-eabi-nm -n gcc/c04e3.axf

00010000 T ResetISR

00010000 T _text

0001001c t ResetISR_STOP

0001002c T _etext

00030000 D _data

00030000 d val1

00030004 d val2

00030008 d result

0003000c D _bss

0003000c D _ebss

0003000c D _edata

The variables val1, val2, and result are loaded in RAM at 0x00030000, 0x00030004, and 0x00030008, respectively. However, RAM is volatile memory, so it is not possible to directly make the data consist of the initial values available in RAM on power-up.

Even though we don't really have flash memory in locations 0x00010000 to 0x00030000, we can still treat this range as flash memory from a programming perspective.

All code and data should be stored in flash memory before power-up. On power-up, a startup code is supposed to copy the data from flash memory to RAM, and then proceed with the execution of the program. This process will help assign initial values to the variables in RAM. In the C language, we can have both initialized variables and un-initialized variables. This is how the initialized variable is initialized in an embedded system, when the system is started. Thus the program's .data section has two addresses: a load address in flash memory (ROM) and a runtime address in RAM.

> **Note**
>
> In ld parlance, the load address is called LMA (load memory address), and the runtime address is called VMA (virtual memory address.).

In Example 4.8, there is no initialization code. We add the following two modifications in Example 4.8 to make the program work correctly:

- The linker script must be modified to specify both the load address and the runtime address for the .data section.
- A small piece of code should copy the .data section from flash memory (load address) to RAM (runtime address).

Specifying Load Address

Let's revisit the linker script in Example 4.7 for a moment. If the load address is not explicitly specified, it defaults to the runtime address. If data is to be placed in RAM during execution, however, the load address should correspond to flash memory and the runtime address should correspond to RAM.

A load address different from the runtime address can be specified using the AT keyword:

`.data : **AT**(ADDR(.text) + SIZEOF(.text))`

The AT keyword specifies the load address of the .data section. An address or symbol (whose value is a valid address) could be passed as an argument to AT. In Example 4.7, the load address of .data is specified as the location after all the code in flash memory has executed, which is equal to _etext.

> **Note**
>
> Symbols can be created on the fly within the SECTIONS command by assigning values to them. In the linker script in Example 4.7, _etext is assigned the value of the location counter at that position; it contains the address of the next free location in flash memory at the end of the code. This value will be used later to specify where the .data section is to be placed in flash memory. Note that _etext itself will not be allocated any memory—it is just an entry in the symbol table.

Copying .data to RAM

To copy the data from flash memory to RAM, the following information is required:

- Address of the data in flash memory (_etext), which is the same as the end of the code
- Address of the data in RAM (_data)
- Size of the .data section (_edata to _data)

With this information, the data can be copied from flash memory to RAM using the code in Example 4.9, which is a modified version of the previous examples.

Example 4.9 c04e4.S: Adding Data in RAM with copy (code/c04/c04e4)

```
        .data
val1:   .4byte 10       @ First number
val2:   .4byte 30       @ Second number
result: .space 4        @ 1 byte space for result
```

```
        .section     .text.ResetISR,"ax",%progbits
        .align       2
        .global      ResetISR
        .type        ResetISR, %function
ResetISR:
        ldr     r0, =_etext
        ldr     r1, =_data
        ldr     r2, =_edata
        subs    r2, r2, r1
copy:
        ldrb    r4, [r0], #1
        strb    r4, [r1], #1
        subs    r2, r2, #1
        bne     copy

        /* Add and store result. */
        ldr     r0, =val1       @ r0 = &val1
        ldr     r1, =val2       @ r1 = &val2

        ldr     r2, [r0]        @ r2 = *r0
        ldr     r3, [r1]        @ r3 = *r1
        add     r4, r2, r3      @ r4 = r2 + r3

        ldr     r0, =result     @ r0 = &result
        str     r4, [r0]        @ *r0 = r4
ResetISR_STOP:
        b ResetISR_STOP         @ Infinite loop to stop execution
```

The program is assembled and linked using the linker script c04e4.ld, which is the same as in Example 4.7. As usual, we can build the example using the make command:

$ make DEBUG=1
```
  AS    c04e4.S
  LD    gcc/c04e4.axf
```
$ make debug

Using a makefile target of debug, this program can be executed and tested in the Android emulator. We can trace and observe the execution using gdb.

60 Chapter 4 Linker Script and Memory Map

> **Note**
>
> In a real system with SDRAM, the memory should not be accessed immediately. That is, the memory controller must be initialized before performing a memory access. Our code works because our simulated memory does not require the memory controller to be initialized.
>
> If you want to investigate memory initialization code, you can refer to a particular board's initialization code in U-Boot. In U-Boot, you can find board initialization code in the folder `board/[vendor]/[board model]`. For example, you can find the memory initialization code for Freescale P1010 in file `board/freescale/p1010rdb/ddr.c`.

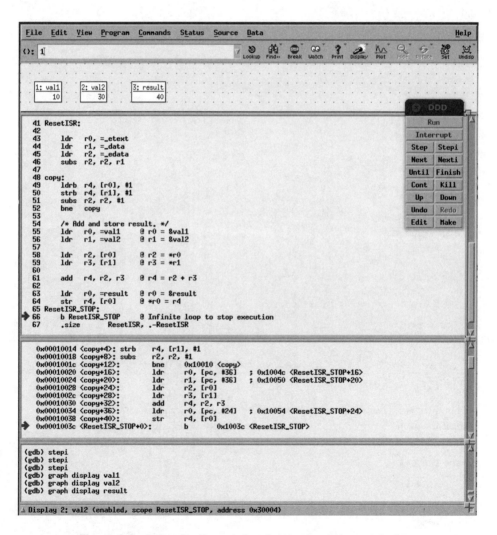

Figure 4.4 Debugging the code in gdb using the ddd user interface

After the program begins executing, we can monitor the variables `val1`, `val2`, and `result` in ddd, as shown in Figure 4.4. In the figure, notice that variables `val1` and `val2` are initialized after the code copies their values from the load addresses in flash memory.

Summary

After we set up the development environment, we can start to develop applications in a bare metal environment. In this chapter, we explored the first few steps necessary to begin this development. We learned how a program is assembled by the assembler and linked by the linker. We also learned how a program is loaded into the system memory after it is assembled and linked to a file. Finally, we saw that the system memory should be initialized after power-up, so that the program can start properly.

With this knowledge, we are ready to move on to C language programming.

5

Using the C Language

When we learned how to do bare metal programming in the last chapter, we created a bare metal application using assembly language. Once that step is complete, we want to move to the C language programming environment as soon as possible. With C, we are able to work more efficiently and can capitalize on better portability of our code. In this chapter, we explore how to switch from working with assembly language programs to the C language environment. The C language environment is prepared by a piece of assembly code called C startup code. After discovering how this code works, we consider how to call a C function from assembly language versus how to call an assembly function from the C language.

C Startup in a Bare Metal Environment

It is not possible to directly execute C code when the processor comes out of a device reset. Unlike programs written in assembly language, C programs need some basic prerequisites to be satisfied before they will run. This section describes those prerequisites and explains how to meet them.

Before transferring control to C code, the following steps have to be set up correctly:

- Prepare the stack for code written in the C language.
- Initialize global variables to be used by C. This includes both initialized data and uninitialized data.
  - The initialized data should be stored in the `.data` section.
  - The uninitialized data should be stored in the `.bss` section.
- The read-only data can be stored in ROM after the code section. We store this data in the `.rodata` section.

Let's use the serial port support in goldfish platform to demonstrate C language programming. We will enhance this example step by step throughout this chapter. This example will also be reused when we work on the U-Boot in Chapter 9. By the end of this section, we will be able to perform the necessary setup, transfer control to the C code, and execute it.

This example can be found in the folder c05/c05e1 and includes the following files:

- startup.S: The startup code that performs the necessary setup before control is transferred to the C code.
- c05e1.c: The C code that includes the main() function.
- Makefile: The makefile to build this project.
- c05e1.ld: The linker script for the project.

Let's look at the main() function, which is shown in Example 5.1.

Example 5.1 C Code Called in Assembly Language (code/c05/c05e1/c05e1.c)

```c
#define NULL 0

const int UART_IO_BASE = 0xff002000;

char *uart_name = "goldfish UART 1";

/* remove this, when port to u-boot */
struct serial_device {
    /* enough bytes to match alignment of following func pointer */
    char    name[16];

    int     (*start)(void);
    int     (*stop)(void);
    void    (*setbrg)(void);
    int     (*getc)(void);
    int     (*tstc)(void);
    void    (*putc)(const char c);
    void    (*puts)(const char *s);
    struct serial_device    *next;
};

struct serial_device goldfish_drv;

int strlen(const char * s)
{
    const char *sc;

    for (sc = s; *sc != '\0'; ++sc)
    /* nothing */;
```

```c
        return sc - s;
}

int main(int argc, char *argv[])
{
    int i = 0, len = 0;

    if(argc > 0) {
        for (i = 0; i < argc; i++) {
            len = strlen(argv[i]);
        }
    }

    len = strlen(uart_name);

    return len;
}
```

In this example code, pay attention to the following variables:

- `UART_IO_BASE` is a `const` integer variable and should be placed in the `.rodata` section.
- `char *uart_name` is initialized data and should be placed in the `.data` section.
- `struct serial_device goldfish_drv` is uninitialized data and should be placed in the `.bss` section.

To call the `main()` function in Example 5.1 from assembly code, we must first prepare the stack.

Stack

C uses the stack for storing local (auto) variables, passing function arguments, and storing return addresses, among other things. It is essential that the stack be set up correctly before control is transferred to C code.

Stacks are highly flexible in the ARM architecture, as the implementation is completely left to the software. To make sure that code generated by different compilers is interoperable, ARM has created the ARM Architecture Procedure Call Standard (AAPCS). The register that is used as the stack pointer and the direction in which the stack grows are both dictated by the AAPCS. For example, according to the AAPCS, register r13 should be used as the stack pointer and the stack should be full descending.

Chapter 5 Using the C Language

> **Note**
>
> **Type of Stack**
>
> The stack may be accessed in four different ways: empty descending (ED), empty ascending (EA), full descending (FD), or full ascending (FA). The direction differs in terms of how the stack pointer is changed and how the item on the stack is referred to. The diagrams here present two options.
>
>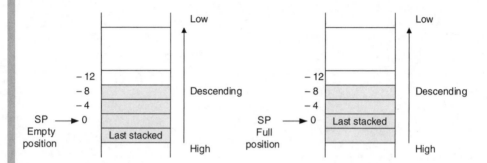
>
> **Empty Descending**
> The push operation puts values onto the stack in descending order. The stack pointer sp points to the next empty location. The pop operation increases sp and copies an item from the stack.
>
> **Full Descending**
> The push operation puts values onto the stack in descending order. The stack pointer sp points to the last item. The pop operation copies an item from the stack and increments sp.

In the ARM architecture, there are seven processor modes in total: six privileged modes (abort, fast interrupt request, interrupt request, supervisor, system, and undefined) and one nonprivileged mode (user). When the processor enters different modes, the registers that are used may be slightly different. These registers, which are called banked registers, are shown in Figure 5.1.

All banked stack pointers have to be initialized as shown in the following code. In this code, we fill in the stack space with a special pattern STACK_FILL first. Next, we switch to the specific processor mode to fill in the banked register r13 (sp) with the address of the stack pointer. To switch to the specific processor mode, we set the current program status register CSPR with the processor mode and interrupt status.

```
init_stack:
    /* Initialize the stack pointer and fill the .stack section */
    LDR     r1,=__stack_start__
    LDR     r2,=__stack_end__
    LDR     r3,=STACK_FILL
```

C Startup in a Bare Metal Environment

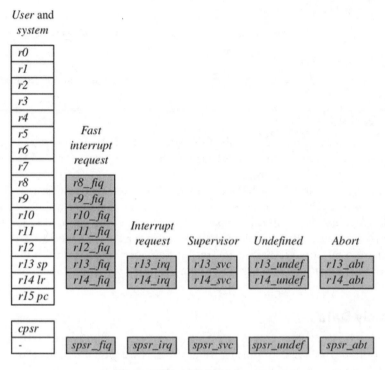

Figure 5.1 ARM register set

```
1:
        CMP     r1,r2
        STMLTIA r1!,{r3}
        BLT     1b

/* Initialize stack pointers for all ARM modes */

        MSR     CPSR_c,#(IRQ_MODE | I_BIT | F_BIT)
        LDR     sp,=__irq_stack_top__           /* set the IRQ stack pointer */

        MSR     CPSR_c,#(FIQ_MODE | I_BIT | F_BIT)
        LDR     sp,=__fiq_stack_top__           /* set the FIQ stack pointer */

        MSR     CPSR_c,#(SVC_MODE | I_BIT | F_BIT)
        LDR     sp,=__svc_stack_top__           /* set the SVC stack pointer */

        MSR     CPSR_c,#(ABT_MODE | I_BIT | F_BIT)
        LDR     sp,=__abt_stack_top__           /* set the ABT stack pointer */
```

```
            MSR     CPSR_c,#(UND_MODE | I_BIT | F_BIT)
            LDR     sp,=__und_stack_top__           /* set the UND stack pointer */

            MSR     CPSR_c,#(SYS_MODE | I_BIT | F_BIT)
            LDR     sp,=__c_stack_top__             /* set the C stack pointer */
```

Global Variables

When C code is compiled, the compiler places the initialized global variables in the .data section. The .data section must be copied from flash memory to RAM during startup.

All uninitialized global variables are initialized to zero during the startup. This step needs to be performed in the C startup code (discussed later in this chapter). When C programs are compiled, a separate section called .bss is used to hold the uninitialized variables. Because all of these variables have the same value (zero), they do not have to be stored in flash memory. Before transferring control to C code, however, the memory locations corresponding to these variables have to be initialized to zero.

Read-Only Data

GCC places global variables marked as const in a separate section, called .rodata. The .rodata section is also used for storing string constants. Because the contents of .rodata section will not be modified, it can be placed in flash memory.

Startup Code

Now that we know the prerequisites, we can create the linker script and the startup code. In the linker script, we need to specify the placements of the following sections:

- .isr_vector
- .text
- .rodata
- .data
- .bss
- .stack

Figure 5.2 shows the locations of the various sections. The .rodata section is placed immediately after the .text section in flash memory. The load address of the .data section in RAM is placed after the .rodata section as well as in flash memory. The C startup code copies the data section from its load address to its runtime address (refer to the .data section in Figure 5.2). The .bss section is placed immediately after the .data section in RAM. Symbols to locate the start of .bss and the end of .bss are also created in the linker script. The stack and banked stacks are placed after the .bss section. The

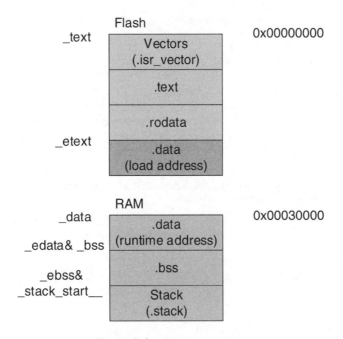

Figure 5.2 Section placements

memory-mapped hardware registers are allocated in RAM as well, such as the hardware registers for UART or the timer (starting at address 0xff000000).

Before we look at the linker script in Example 5.2, let's revisit some of the concepts underlying linker scripts. Sections are started with a period (.), such as .data and .text. All other items are symbols that are used to define the value of an address or a general value. When we define symbols, the prevailing convention is to use an underscore (_) prefix for the symbols representing the value of an address, such as _text or _data. We can use all uppercase letters to identify constants, such as C_STACK_SIZE or IRQ_STACK_SIZE. As mentioned in Chapter 4, a period (.) represents the location counter. For example, using _edata=., we can assign the current address to a symbol.

The linker script in Example 5.2 matches the section placements in Figure 5.2. The .text section is started from the address 0x10000. The label _text is the start address of the .text section, and the label _etext is the end address of the .text section. The load address of .data section is placed after the .rodata section, which is started from _etext. The start label and the end label of the .data section are _data and _edata, respectively. These items give the runtime address of the .data section. The .bss section is placed after the .data section. The start and the end of the .bss section are _bss and _ebss, respectively. The stack is placed after the .bss section. The stack pointers (__irq_stack_top__, __fiq_stack_top__, __svc_stack_top__, __abt_stack_top__, __und_stack_top__, and __c_stack_top__) for each processor mode are defined inside the stack section.

Example 5.2 Linker Script for C Code (code/c05/c05e1.ld)

```
OUTPUT_ARCH(arm)
ENTRY(_start)

MEMORY
{
    FLASH (rx) : ORIGIN = 0x00010000, LENGTH = 128K
    RAM (rwx)  : ORIGIN = 0x00030000, LENGTH = 512M}

/* The sizes of the stacks used by the application. NOTE: You can adjust them
according to your requirements. */
C_STACK_SIZE   = 512;
IRQ_STACK_SIZE = 256;
FIQ_STACK_SIZE = 256;
SVC_STACK_SIZE = 256;
ABT_STACK_SIZE = 256;
UND_STACK_SIZE = 256;

/* The size of the heap used by the application. NOTE: You can adjust it
according to your requirements. */
HEAP_SIZE = 0;

SECTIONS
{
  . = 0x10000;
  _text = .;                           /* This is the start of .text section. */
  .text : {
    KEEP(*(.isr_vector))
    _start = .;
    *(.start)
    *(.text)
    *(.text.*)
    *(.rodata)
    *(.rodata.*)
    . = ALIGN(4);
  } > FLASH
```

C Startup in a Bare Metal Environment

```
    _etext = .;             /* This is the end of .text section and the load address
                               of .data section. */

.data   : AT(ADDR(.text) + SIZEOF(.text)){
        _data = .;          /* This is the start of .data section in RAM and the
                               runtime address of .data section. */
        *(.data)
} > RAM

. = ALIGN(4);
.bss : {
        _edata = .;                     /* This is the end of .data section. */
        data_size = _edata - _data;
        __bss_start = .;
        _bss = .;                       /* This is the start of .bss section. */
        *(.bss)
} > RAM

/* The stack pointers defined here below are used in Example 5.3. */
.stack (NOLOAD)      : {
        _ebss = .;                      /* This is the end of .bss section. */
        bss_size = _ebss - _bss;
        __stack_start__ = . ;           /* This is the start of stack. */

        . += IRQ_STACK_SIZE;
        . = ALIGN (4);
        __irq_stack_top__ = . ;

        . += FIQ_STACK_SIZE;
        . = ALIGN (4);
        __fiq_stack_top__ = . ;

        . += SVC_STACK_SIZE;
        . = ALIGN (4);
        __svc_stack_top__ = . ;

        . += ABT_STACK_SIZE;
```

```
            . = ALIGN (4);
            __abt_stack_top__ = . ;

            . += UND_STACK_SIZE;
            . = ALIGN (4);
            __und_stack_top__ = . ;

            . += C_STACK_SIZE;
            . = ALIGN (4);
            __c_stack_top__ = . ;

            *(.stack)
            __stack_end__ = .;                    /* **This is the end of stack.** */
    } > RAM
}
```

Once we understand the linker script, we are ready to investigate the C startup code in Example 5.3. This startup code includes the following parts:

- Code to copy the .data from flash memory to RAM: The start of the load address of the .data section is at label _etext. The size of the .data section is _edata − _data. The .data section is initialized from the load address in flash memory.
- Code to zero out the .bss section: The size of the .bss section is _ebss − _bss. The startup code fills all of locations in this range with values of zero.
- Code to set up the stack pointer: After the .bss section is initialized to zero, the code initializes the stack space with the pattern STACK_FILL and sets up the stack pointers for all processor modes.
- Branch to main(): After everything is ready, the entry point of the C function can be called.

Example 5.3 C Startup Assembly Code (code/c05/c05e1/startup.S)

```
/* Standard definitions of mode bits and interrupt (I & F) flags in PSRs */

    .equ    I_BIT,      0x80    /* when I bit is set, IRQ is disabled */
    .equ    F_BIT,      0x40    /* when F bit is set, FIQ is disabled */

    .equ    USR_MODE,   0x10
    .equ    FIQ_MODE,   0x11
```

```
    .equ    IRQ_MODE,       0x12
    .equ    SVC_MODE,       0x13
    .equ    ABT_MODE,       0x17
    .equ    UND_MODE,       0x1B
    .equ    SYS_MODE,       0x1F

/* Constant to prefill the stack */
    .equ    STACK_FILL,     0xAAAAAAAA

    .arch armv5te
    .fpu softvfp

    .global    version
    .section   .rodata
    .align     2
.LC0:
    .ascii     "Copyright (c) 2013, Roger Ye. All rights reserved.\012"
    .ascii     "\000"

    .data
    .align     2
    .type      version, %object
    .size      version, 4
/* **We use this variable to store the pointer to the version information string.** */
version:
    .word      .LC0

/***************************************************************************
 *
 * This code is called when the processor first starts execution
 * following a reset event.
 *
 ***************************************************************************/
    .section   .text.ResetISR,"ax",%progbits
    .align     2
    .global    ResetISR
    .type      ResetISR, %function
```

Chapter 5 Using the C Language

```
ResetISR:
    /* Copy data from load address to runtime address in RAM. The load address is
at _etext and the runtime address is at _data. */
    ldr     r0, =_etext
    ldr     r1, =_data
    ldr     r2, =_edata
    sub     r2, r2, r1

    @@ Handle data_size == 0
    cmp     r2, #0
    beq     init_bss
copy:
    ldrb    r4, [r0], #1
    strb    r4, [r1], #1
    subs    r2, r2, #1
    bne     copy

    /* This code zeroes out the .bss section. The .bss start address is _bss and
the end address is _ebss. */
init_bss:
    @@ Initialize .bss
    ldr     r0, =_bss
    ldr     r1, =_ebss
    sub     r2, r1, r0

    @@ Handle bss_size == 0
    cmp     r2, #0
    beq     init_stack


    mov     r4, #0
zero:
    strb    r4, [r0], #1
    subs    r2, r2, #1
    bne     zero

init_stack:
    /* Fill the .stack section with the pattern STACK_FILL. */
    LDR     r1,=__stack_start__
    LDR     r2,=__stack_end__
```

```
        LDR     r3,=STACK_FILL
1:
        CMP     r1,r2
        STMLTIA r1!,{r3}
        BLT     1b

        /* Initialize stack pointers for all ARM modes. */
        MSR     CPSR_c,#(IRQ_MODE | I_BIT | F_BIT)
        LDR     sp,=__irq_stack_top__           /* set the IRQ stack pointer */

        MSR     CPSR_c,#(FIQ_MODE | I_BIT | F_BIT)
        LDR     sp,=__fiq_stack_top__           /* set the FIQ stack pointer */

        MSR     CPSR_c,#(SVC_MODE | I_BIT | F_BIT)
        LDR     sp,=__svc_stack_top__           /* set the SVC stack pointer */

        MSR     CPSR_c,#(ABT_MODE | I_BIT | F_BIT)
        LDR     sp,=__abt_stack_top__           /* set the ABT stack pointer */

        MSR     CPSR_c,#(UND_MODE | I_BIT | F_BIT)
        LDR     sp,=__und_stack_top__           /* set the UND stack pointer */

        MSR     CPSR_c,#(SYS_MODE | I_BIT | F_BIT)
        LDR     sp,=__c_stack_top__             /* set the C stack pointer */

        /* Call main() in C code. */
call_main:
        mov     r0, #1                          /* set argc = 1 */
        ldr     r1, =version                    /* set argv[1] = version */
        bl      main                            /* call main() function. */

ResetISR_STOP:
        b       ResetISR_STOP   @ Infinite loop to stop execution
        .size   ResetISR, .-ResetISR
```

To build a debug version, we have to include the option DEBUG=1 on the command line. Without this option, you won't be able to do source-level debugging. We can execute the make command with the debug option as follows:

```
$ make DEBUG=1 VERBOSE=1
```

Chapter 5 Using the C Language

```
arm-none-eabi-gcc -marm -mno-thumb-interwork -mabi=aapcs-linux -march=armv5te
-fno-common -ffixed-r8 -msoft-float -fno-builtin -ffreestanding -Os -fstack-usage
-fdata-sections -MD -Wall -Wstrict-prototypes -Wno-format-nonliteral -c -g -D
DEBUG -Dgcc -o gcc/c05e1.o c05e1.c

arm-none-eabi-gcc -marm -mno-thumb-interwork -mabi=aapcs-linux -march=armv5te
-fno-common -ffixed-r8 -msoft-float -fno-builtin -ffreestanding -MD -g -D DEBUG
-Dgcc -o gcc/startup.o -c startup.S

arm-none-eabi-ld -T c05e1.ld --entry ResetISR -o gcc/c05e1.axf gcc/c05e1.o
gcc/startup.o /media/u32/home/sgye/arm-2012.03/bin/../lib/gcc/arm-none-
eabi/4.6.3/../../../../arm-none-eabi/lib/libm.a /media/u32/home/sgye/arm-
2012.03/bin/../lib/gcc/arm-none-eabi/4.6.3/../../../../arm-none-eabi/lib/
libc.a /media/u32/home/sgye/arm-2012.03/bin/../lib/gcc/arm-none-eabi/4.6.3/
libgcc.a

arm-none-eabi-objcopy -O binary gcc/c05e1.axf gcc/c05e1.bin
```

Since this is a simple project, we can also build the project with gcc directly:

$ arm-none-eabi-gcc -nostdlib -o gcc/c05e1.axf -T c05e1.ld c05e1.c startup.S

The -nostdlib option is used to specify that the standard C library should not be linked in. We will discuss the standard C library further in Chapter 6.

A dump of the symbol table provides a better picture of how things have been placed in memory:

$ arm-none-eabi-nm -n gcc/c05e1.axf

```
00000000 A HEAP_SIZE

00000010 a USR_MODE

00000011 a FIQ_MODE

00000012 a IRQ_MODE

00000013 a SVC_MODE

00000017 a ABT_MODE

0000001b a UND_MODE

0000001f a SYS_MODE

00000040 a F_BIT

00000080 a I_BIT

00000100 A ABT_STACK_SIZE

00000100 A FIQ_STACK_SIZE

00000100 A IRQ_STACK_SIZE

00000100 A SVC_STACK_SIZE

00000100 A UND_STACK_SIZE

00000200 A C_STACK_SIZE

00010000 T _start
```

```
00010000 A _text
00010000 T strlen
00010020 T main
0001005c T ResetISR
00010074 t copy
00010084 t init_bss
0001009c t zero
000100a8 t init_stack
000100f0 t call_main
000100fc t ResetISR_STOP
00010170 T UART_IO_BASE
00010184 A _etext
00030000 D _data
00030000 D version
00030004 D uart_name
00030008 D __bss_start
00030008 D _bss
00030008 D _edata
00030008 B goldfish_drv
00030010 D data_size
00030038 B __stack_start__
00030038 B _ebss
00030068 B bss_size
00030138 B __irq_stack_top__
00030238 B __fiq_stack_top__
00030338 B __svc_stack_top__
00030438 B __abt_stack_top__
00030538 B __und_stack_top__
00030738 B __c_stack_top__
00030738 B __stack_end__
aaaaaaaa a STACK_FILL
```

Notice that the const integer variable UART_IO_BASE is placed in flash memory (the .rodata section). The initialized data uart_name is placed in the .data section. The uninitialized data goldfish_drv is placed in the .bss section. Refer to the memory map in Figure 4.1 to see an illustration of the memory range of flash memory and RAM.

Table 5.1 APCS Register Use Convention

Register	APCS Name	APCS Role
r0	a1	Argument 1/integer result/scratch register
r1	a2	Argument 2/scratch register
r2	a3	Argument 3/scratch register
r3	a4	Argument 4/scratch register
r4	v1	Register variable 1
r5	v2	Register variable 2
r6	v3	Register variable 3
r7	v4	Register variable 4
r8	v5	Register variable 5
r9	sb/v6	Static base/register variable 6
r10	sl/v7	Static limit/register variable 7
r11	fp	Frame pointer
r12	ip	Scratch register/specialist use by linker
r13	sp	Lower end of current stack frame
r14	lr	Link address/scratch register
r15	pc	Program counter

Calling Convention

We can transfer control from assembly language to C by calling the main() function. At this point, we can build a UART test program on top of our code. Using this UART test program, we can understand the hardware for goldfish, enabling us to easily port U-Boot to the goldfish platform in Chapter 9. Before we explore this topic in more depth, let's spend some time looking at the calling convention for ARM. If we fully understand this calling convention, we are more likely to handle the function calls between assembly language and C language properly. The discussion here is based on the example code in this chapter. If you would prefer a more advanced discussion of the calling convention, the manual *Procedure Call Standard for the ARM Architecture* (APCS) is a good reference; this free book can be downloaded from the ARM website.

Table 5.1 shows the register usage in APCS.

Before the caller makes a function call to the callee—that is, before a function (callee) is called—registers should be filled or saved according to the convention outlined in Table 5.1. Registers r0–r3 are used to pass arguments into a function. They can be used inside the function for any purpose. Register r0 is typically used to get the value provided when the function returns. The function (callee) fills in register r0 before returning to the caller. The caller should expect the contents of registers r0–r3 to be trashed (i.e., overwritten) when a function call returns.

After control is transferred into the callee, r4–r8 are registers that any called function is required to save. Therefore they must have unchanged values when control returns to the calling routine (e.g., the main program). If the called function needs these registers for extra workspace, then it must save them.

Next, we discuss how to call a C function from assembly language code. We then consider how to call an assembly language function from C code.

Calling C Functions from Assembly Language Code

We use the startup code in Example 5.3 to analyze how to call a C function from assembly language. The first C function that we call in this way is `main()` in `startup.S`. To demonstrate how to pass arguments, we pass the version information stored in flash memory to `main()` as an argument. The prototype of the `main()` function is

`int main (int argc, char *argv[])`

The arguments `argc` and `argv` are typically used as command-line arguments. The first argument, `argc`, indicates the number of command-line variables available in `argv`. The second argument, `argv`, is an array containing a string. In this example code, we need to pass only one character string from the startup code to `main()`, so we have the following code in `startup.S`:

```
...
mov     r0, #1
ldr     r1, =version
bl      main
```

Register r0 is the first argument, which is `argc` in `main()`; we assign value 1 to it. The variable `argv` is a string array that is equivalent to a pointer in the C language. We pass the address of the version information to register r1 as the second argument. Refer to the following code snippet:

```
        .global    version
        .section   .rodata
        .align     2
.LC0:
        .ascii     "Copyright (c) 2013, Roger Ye. All rights reserved.\012"
        .ascii     "\000"

        .data
        .align     2
        .type      version, %object
        .size      version, 4
version:
        .word      .LC0
```

80 Chapter 5 Using the C Language

The version information (.LC0) is stored in the .rodata section, which is located in flash memory. The label of version comprises initialized data in the .data section; it is initialized with a value of .LC0.

As mentioned in Chapter 3, several make targets are available in Makefile. We can use the target debug to execute the binary file c05e1.axf in the Android emulator and then use the following command to check the status of this operation:

$ make debug

The debug target of Makefile is equivalent to the following two commands:

$ emulator -verbose -show-kernel -netfast -avd hd2 -shell -qemu -s -S -kernel gcc/c05e1.axf

$ ddd --debugger arm-none-eabi-gdb gcc/c05e1.axf

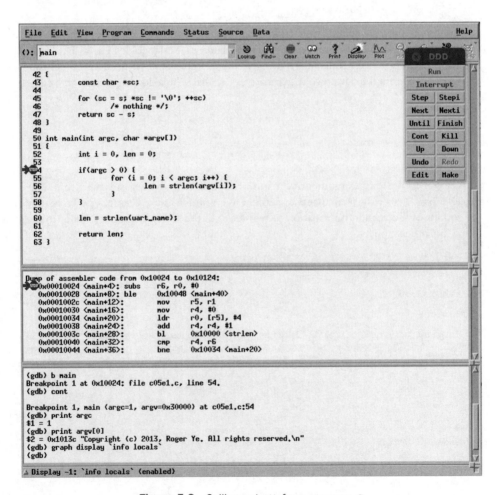

Figure 5.3 Calling main() from startup.S

At the bottom of Figure 5.3, notice the command-line prompt for gdb. We can execute gdb commands from the (gdb) command prompt.

After we set a breakpoint at `main()`, we can print out `argc` and `argv[0]` from the (gdb) prompt. In Figure 5.3, notice the address of `argv[0]`(0x1013c), which is located in flash memory. The return value from `main()` is the length of the string `uart_name`. We can check the value of register r0 after `main()` returns in the startup file `startup.S`.

Calling Assembly Language Functions from C Code

To call an assembly language function from C, the assembly code must be defined in an assembly subroutine. This subroutine has to be defined as global using the `.global` directive. The assembly language function must handle arguments and return values according to APCS. An example of calling an assembly function from C language can be found later in this chapter, in Example 5.4 (`getbaseaddr`).

Goldfish Serial Port Support

As mentioned earlier, we will be exploring goldfish hardware from this chapter onward. Now that we can write programs using the C language, it is a good time for us to add hardware support in our code. Serial ports are a good starting point for us. Once we know how to handle serial ports, we can start to print debug messages on the console. This is a very useful method when debugging the system.

In this section we will extend c05e1 to support goldfish serial port functionalities. Using this example, we will explore the serial port functionalities and see how to call assembly functions from C language programs. The example code in this section can be found in the folder `c05/c05e2` and includes the following files:

- `serial_goldfish.c`: The C code to implement serial port functions
- `goldfish_uart.S`: The assembly code to implement serial port–specific functions
- `startup.S`: The startup code that performs the necessary setup before control is transferred to C code
- `c05e2.c`: The C code to implement the test driver and the `main()` function
- `Makefile`: The makefile to build this project
- `c05e2.ld`: The linker script of the project

> **Note**
>
> From this example onward, the project files in the example code can be divided into common files and project-specific files. Common files can be reused in multiple projects; they are found in the folder named `drivers`. In c05e2, `serial_goldfish.c` and `goldfish_uart.S` are common files. Project-specific files are located in the project folder. In the example c05e2, project-specific files can be found in the folder `c05/c05e2`.

For the startup code, `startup.S` is the same as in Example 5.3. After control is transferred from assembly language to C language, a few unit test cases for the serial port are implemented in the function `main()`. In `serial_goldfish.c`, we implement most of the functions related to serial port operations. A set of functions defined in U-Boot are implemented in this example, which we will then reuse in the U-Boot porting later in this book. A U-Boot data structure for serial device is used in this example as follows:

```
struct serial_device {
    /* This is a data structure that we need to support in U-Boot serial driver. */
    char        name[16];
    int         (*start)(void);
    int         (*stop)(void);
    void        (*setbrg)(void);
    int         (*getc)(void);
    int         (*tstc)(void);
    void        (*putc)(const char c);
    void        (*puts)(const char *s);
    struct serial_device    *next;
};
```

To implement the list of functions in `struct serial_device`, we need to initialize the base address of the registers first. We will implement this in assembly language so that we can handle both physical and virtual addresses. The function prototype in C language follows:

```
void *getbaseaddr(void);
```

This function does not take any parameters. The base address is returned as a void pointer. Example 5.4 shows the implementation in assembly language.

Example 5.4 UART Functions in Assembly Language (drivers/goldfish_uart.S)

```
...
#ifndef ENTRY
#define ENTRY(name) \
    .globl name; \
    ALIGN; \
    name:
#endif

#ifndef WEAK
#define WEAK(name)  \
    .weak name;     \
    name:
#endif
```

```
#ifndef END
#define END(name)    \
   .size name, .-name
#endif

/* If symbol 'name' is treated as a subroutine (gets called, and returns)
 * then use ENDPROC to mark 'name' as STT_FUNC for the benefit of
 * static analysis tools such as the stack depth analyzer.
 */
#ifndef ENDPROC
#define ENDPROC(name)  \
   END(name)
#endif

...
   .text
#define GOLDFISH_TTY_PUT_CHAR_PHYS (IO_START + GOLDFISH_TTY2_BASE)
#define GOLDFISH_TTY_PUT_CHAR_BASE (IO_BASE + GOLDFISH_TTY2_BASE)

   .macro    addruart,rx
     /* See if the MMU is enabled and select appropriate base address */
     mrc    p15, 0, \rx, c1, c0
     tst    \rx, #1
     ldreq  \rx, =GOLDFISH_TTY_PUT_CHAR_PHYS
     ldrne  \rx, =GOLDFISH_TTY_PUT_CHAR_BASE
   .endm
ENTRY(getbaseaddr)
   addruart r0
   mov  pc, lr
ENDPROC(getbaseaddr)
...
```

An assembly macro function addruart is called in getbaseaddr. In addruart, it gets the MMU state through the mrc instruction. If MMU is enabled, it loads the virtual address. Otherwise, it loads the physical address. Refer to Chapter 2 for the hardware specifications of the goldfish serial port. The return value consisting of the base address is stored in register r0.

In Example 5.5, the static function `goldfish_init()` is responsible for initializing the data structure for the serial device. In this case, it initializes a global variable `gtty` by calling `getbaseaddr()`. In the goldfish platform, serial ports 0 and 1 are used by the Android emulator itself. When we start the emulator with the command-line option `-shell`, serial port 2 can be used as standard input/output. This is why we initialize serial port 2 (`GOLDFISH_TTY2_BASE`) in the code example. We also implement a function `default_serial_console()` that returns the data structure `serial_device`.

Example 5.5 goldfish_init/default_serial_console (drivers/serial_goldfish.c)

```
...
void *getbaseaddr(void);
static struct goldfish_tty gtty = {0, 0};

static int goldfish_init(void)
{
    void *base = 0;

    base = gtty.base;
    if(!base) {
        /* Initialize base address as UART2 */
        gtty.base = getbaseaddr();
    }
    debug ("goldfish_init(), gtty.base=%x\n", gtty.base);

    return 0;
}
...
static struct serial_device goldfish_drv = {
    .name     = "goldfish_serial",
    .start    = goldfish_init,
    .stop     = goldfish_disable_tty,
    .setbrg   = goldfish_setbrg,
    .putc     = goldfish_putc,
    .puts     = default_serial_puts,
    .getc     = goldfish_getc,
    .tstc     = goldfish_tstc,
};
```

```
struct serial_device *default_serial_console(void)
{
    return &goldfish_drv;
}

void goldfish_initialize(void)
{
    debug("goldfish_initialize()\n");
    // serial_register(&goldfish_drv);
}

#ifdef __BARE_METAL__
void default_serial_puts(const char *s)
{
    struct serial_device *dev = &goldfish_drv;
        while (*s)
            dev->putc(*s++);
}
#endif
...
```

The hardware registers used in the serial port functions are defined in a header file hardware.h as shown in Example 5.6. This file is created based on two Linux kernel files from the goldfish Linux kernel: include/asm-arm/arch-goldfish/irqs.h and arch/arm/mach-goldfish/include/mach/hardware.h. In hardware.h, both the interrupt number and the base address of hardware registers are defined.

Example 5.6 Hardware Interface Definitions in the Goldfish Platform (include/hardware.h)

```
#ifndef __ASM_ARCH_HARDWARE_H
#define __ASM_ARCH_HARDWARE_H

/* include/asm-arm/arch-goldfish/irqs.h */
/* #define _ARCH-GOLDFISH_IRQS_H */
#define IRQ_PDEV_BUS    (1)
#define IRQ_TIMER       (3)
#define IRQ_TTY0        (4)
#define IRQ_RTC         (10)
```

```c
#define IRQ_TTY1         (11)
#define IRQ_TTY2         (12)
#define IRQ_smc91x       (13)
#define IRQ_FB           (14)
#define IRQ_AUDIO        (15)
#define IRQ_EVENTS       (16)
#define IRQ_PIPE         (17)
#define IRQ_SWITCH0      (18)
#define IRQ_SWITCH1      (19)
#define IRQ_RANDOM       (20)

#define LAST_IRQ RANDOM_IRQ
#define NR_IRQS (LAST_IRQ + 1)

/*
 * Where in virtual memory the I/O devices (timers, system controllers,
 * and so on)
 */
#define IO_BASE        0xfe000000               // VA of I/O
#define IO_SIZE        0x00800000               // How much?
#define IO_START       0xff000000               // PA of I/O

#define GOLDFISH_INTERRUPT_BASE          (0x0)
#define GOLDFISH_INTERRUPT_STATUS        (0x00)    // Number of pending interrupts
#define GOLDFISH_INTERRUPT_NUMBER        (0x04)
#define GOLDFISH_INTERRUPT_DISABLE_ALL   (0x08)
#define GOLDFISH_INTERRUPT_DISABLE       (0x0c)
#define GOLDFISH_INTERRUPT_ENABLE        (0x10)

#define GOLDFISH_PDEV_BUS_BASE     (0x1000)
#define GOLDFISH_PDEV_BUS_END      (0x100)

#define GOLDFISH_TTY_BASE          (0x2000)
#define GOLDFISH_TIMER_BASE        (0x3000)
#define GOLDFISH_AUDIO_BASE        (0x4000)
#define GOLDFISH_MEMLOG_BASE       (0x6000)
#define GOLDFISH_RTC_BASE          (0x10000)
#define GOLDFISH_TTY1_BASE         (0x11000)
#define GOLDFISH_TTY2_BASE         (0x12000)
```

```
#define GOLDFISH_smc91x_BASE    (0x13000)
#define GOLDFISH_FB_BASE        (0x14000)
#define GOLDFISH_EVENTS_BASE    (0x15000)
#define GOLDFISH_NAND_BASE      (0x16000)
#define GOLDFISH_PIPE_BASE      (0x17000)
#define GOLDFISH_SWITCH0_BASE   (0X19000)
#define GOLDFISH_SWITCH1_BASE   (0x1a000)

/* Macro to get at I/O space when running virtually */
#define IO_ADDRESS(x)  ((x) + IO_START)
```

After we initialize the base address for the serial device, we can implement functions to perform such actions as sending data, receiving data, and checking data in the buffer.

Check Data Buffer

Before we try to retrieve data from a serial port, we usually check the available data first. As shown in Example 5.7, the function goldfish_tstc is implemented for this purpose.

Example 5.7 Check Data Buffer: goldfish_tstc() (drivers/serial_goldfish.c)

```
static int goldfish_tstc(void)
{
    int count = 0;
    void *base = 0;

    base = gtty.base;
    if(!base) {
        goldfish_init();
        base = gtty.base;
    }

    if(base) {
        count = *((int *)(base + GOLDFISH_TTY_BYTES_READY));
        if(count) {
            debug ("goldfish_tstc(), gtty.base=%x, base=%x, count=%d\n", gtty.base, base, count);
        }
    }

    return count;
}
```

In the function `goldfish_tstc`, the number of bytes of available data can be checked by reading the value of the register GOLDFISH_TTY_BYTES_READY.

Data Input and Output

Once we find there is data in the serial port, we can use two functions to retrieve data from the data buffer. We can get a data stream using the function `goldfish_gets()`, or we can get a single character using `goldfish_getc()`. To send a character to a serial port, we can use `goldfish_putc()`. The implementation of these functions is shown in Example 5.8.

Example 5.8 Data Input and Output: goldfish_getc(), goldfish_gets(), and goldfish_putc() (drivers/serial_goldfish.c)

```
static void goldfish_gets(char *s, int len)
{
    void *base = 0;

    base = gtty.base;
    if(!base) {
        goldfish_init();
        base = gtty.base;
    }

    *((uint32_t *)(base + GOLDFISH_TTY_DATA_PTR)) = (uint32_t)s;
    *((uint32_t *)(base + GOLDFISH_TTY_DATA_LEN)) = len;
    *((uint32_t *)(base + GOLDFISH_TTY_CMD)) = GOLDFISH_TTY_CMD_READ_BUFFER;
}

static void goldfish_putc(const char c)
{
    void *base = 0;
    base = gtty.base;
    if(!base) {
        goldfish_init();
        base = gtty.base;
    }

    if(c) {
        *((uint32_t *)(base + GOLDFISH_TTY_PUT_CHAR)) = (uint32_t)c;
```

```
    }
}
static int goldfish_getc(void)
{
    char buf[128];
    uint32_t count;
    unsigned int data = 0;
    void *base = 0;
    base = gtty.base;
    if(!base) {
    goldfish_init();
    base = gtty.base;
    }
    debug ("goldfish_getc(), gtty.base=%x, base=%x\n", gtty.base, base);
    if(base) {
        count = *((int *)(base + GOLDFISH_TTY_BYTES_READY));
        if(count == 0) {
        return -1;
        }
        goldfish_gets(buf, 1);
        data = buf[0];
    }
    return (int) data;
}
```

To retrieve data, the goldfish platform uses three registers to handle the data buffer. In the function `goldfish_gets()`, the first parameter s is written to register GOLDFISH_TTY_DATA_PTR and the length of data buffer s is written to register GOLDFISH_TTY_DATA_LEN. After that, the command GOLDFISH_TTY_CMD_READ_BUFFER is sent to GOLDFISH_TTY_CMD. This command instructs the serial device to copy data from the UART buffer to the data buffer. The function `goldfish_getc()` actually calls `goldfish_gets()` to get a single character. Unlike for the input data, the goldfish platform uses a dedicated register GOLDFISH_TTY_PUT_CHAR to send a character to the serial port. This is exactly what we can see in the output function `goldfish_putc()`. The data stream output function `default_serial_puts()` actually calls `goldfish_putc()` to do its work.

Unit Test of Serial Functions

After we have the serial device implementation, we can test these U-Boot driver functions in the emulator. Five test cases are implemented in the `main()` function, as shown in Example 5.9.

Example 5.9 Serial Device Unit Test (c05/c05e2/c05e2.c)

```
#include <serial_goldfish.h>

/* We will run the unit test of serial driver in main() */
int main(int argc, char *argv[])
{
    struct serial_device *drv;
    int c;

    /* Unit test 1: default_serial_console*/
    drv = default_serial_console();

    /* Unit test 2: goldfish_init */
    drv->start();

    /* Unit test 3: default_serial_puts & goldfish_putc */
    if(argc == 1) {
        drv->puts(argv[0]);
    }

    /* Unit test 4: goldfish_tstc */
    while (1) {
        if(drv->tstc()) {
        /* Unit test 5: goldfish_getc */
            c = drv->getc();
            drv->putc(c);
            if(c == 'q') break;
        }
    }
    return 1;
}
```

Now that we have everything ready, we can build the project from the project folder as follows:

```
$ make DEBUG=1
    CC      c05e2.c
    AS      startup.S
    CC      ../../drivers/serial_goldfish.c
    AS      ../../drivers/goldfish_uart.S
    LD      gcc/c05e2.axf
```

As we have done in previous chapters, we can start the debug session using the command `make debug`. The emulator will be started with the option `-shell`. With this option, serial port 2 will be connected to the current console.

Figure 5.4 shows the console log. As you can see in this figure, the copyright information is printed out through `drv->puts(argv[0])`. The console can be used as a standard input and output device. When the user presses the key "q", the program will quit. When the program exits from `main()`, it returns to the startup code. In the startup code, the program goes into an infinite loop after `main()`.

```
emulator: nand_add_dev: cache,size=0x4200000,file=/home/sye1/.android/avd/hd2.av
d/cache.img
emulator: Initializing hardware OpenGLES emulation support
emulator: ERROR: Could not load OpenGLES emulation library: libOpenglRender.so:
cannot open shared object file: No such file or directory
emulator: WARNING: Could not initialize OpenglES emulation, using software rende
rer.
QEMU waiting for connection on: telnet::6666,server
emulator: Kernel parameters: qemu.gles=0 qemu=1 console=ttyS0 android.qemud=ttyS
1 androidboot.console=ttyS2 android.checkjni=1 ndns=1
goldfish_tty_add id=0 base=ff002000 80 0
goldfish_tty_add id=1 base=ff011000 80 0
goldfish_tty_add id=2 base=ff012000 80 0
emulator: Trace file name is not set

emulator: autoconfig: -scale 1
emulator: Could not open file: (null)/system/build.prop: No such file or directo
ry
emulator: control console listening on port 5554, ADB on port 5555
emulator: can't connect to ADB server: Connection refused
emulator: ping program: /media/u32/home/sgye/src/Android/android-emulator-201309
28/qemu/objs/ddms
Copyright (c) 2013, Roger Ye. All rights reserved.
abcdefgh
```

Figure 5.4 Debug console of the serial device

Summary

To use the C language when programming, we have to meet several prerequisites. The most important one discussed in this chapter is the calling convention, known as ARM Procedure Call Standard (APCS). It defines the rules or protocols followed by assembly and C language programs. With this protocol, we can call C functions from assembly language programs, and we can call assembly language functions from C code.

We also started to explore the goldfish hardware, and will continue to do so in the rest of this book. In this chapter, we implemented the goldfish serial driver. To make it reusable later in U-Boot porting, we implemented this serial driver with a data structure, `serial_device`. We tested this serial driver in the Android emulator and found that it gives us the ability to print a debug log on the console. This will prove very helpful when debugging other hardware interfaces in the following chapters.

Using the C Library

In the previous chapter, we learned how to use C language in the bare metal programming environment. However, a few things are still missing from our knowledge base. One of the fundamental topics we haven't covered yet is use of the standard C library functions, such as `printf`, `scanf`, `malloc`, and so on. Usually, the C library has dependencies on operating system (OS) services. The operating system provides these services through system calls. Because there is not an operating system in a bare metal environment, we have to implement these system calls ourselves. That is the major topic discussed in this chapter.

C Library Variants

When a C library is used in a bare metal environment, it usually comes with several variants, simply because there is no operating system available. The standard C library, in contrast, is usually built on top of an operating system environment, such as UNIX or Windows. It relies on the operating system environment to provide functionalities such as file I/O, memory management, and timers.

C Library Variants in an Operating System

In a bare metal environment, none of those services is available. Instead, variants—whose differences reflect the functionality of the specific C library—are used. In the standard operating system environment, we have variants of C libraries that differ in terms of their formats, such as static linked or shared libraries. However, the functionality is the same in all variants, other than the different linkage methods. As shown in Table 6.1, Microsoft C Run-Time libraries include six format libraries based on different build options.

Table 6.1 Microsoft C Run-Time Libraries (CRT)

C Run-Time Library	Associated DLL	Characteristics	Option	Preprocessor Directives
`libcmt.lib`	None, static link	Multithreaded, static link.	`/MT`	`_MT`
`msvcrt.lib`	`msvcr110.dll`	Multithreaded, dynamic link (import library for `MSVCR110.DLL`). Be aware that if you use the Standard C++ Library, your program will need `MSVCP110.DLL` to run.	`/MD`	`_MT, _DLL`
`libcmtd.lib`	None, static link	Multithreaded, static link (debug).	`/MTd`	`_DEBUG, _MT`
`msvcrtd.lib`	`msvcr110d.dll`	Multithreaded, dynamic link (import library for `MSVCR110D.DLL`) (debug).	`/MDd`	`_DEBUG, _MT, _DLL`
`msvcmrt.lib`	None, static link	C Runtime static library. Used for mixed managed/native code.	`/clr` `/clr:oldSyntax`	
`msvcurt.lib`	None, static link	C Runtime static library compiled as 100% pure MSIL code. All code complies with the ECMA URT specification for MSIL.	`/clr:pure`	

C Library Variants in Bare Metal Environment

For the C library in a bare metal environment, we will focus on how the system call stubs are implemented, as illustrated in Figure 6.1. The system call stubs should provide some services that would otherwise be provided by operating system. However, we don't really have an operating system, so we are not able to provide full operating system services. Thus, the C library in a bare metal environment is usually not able to provide all C library functions per the standard.

The variants of the C library for a bare metal environment may have different names, such as hosting/semihosting or none/nohost/semihost, but other than semihost/semihosting functionality, the variants may not implement everything per the C language standard. These library variants provide most of the C library functions according to the C language standard, except for the functions relating to strings, memory handling, and

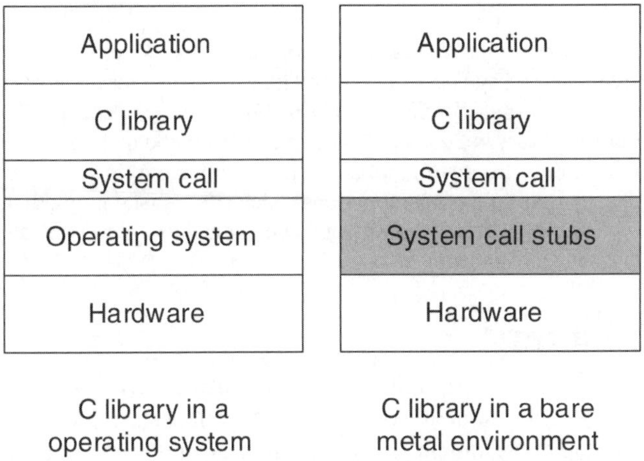

Figure 6.1 C library and system call

file-based I/O handling. The developer for an embedded system must be fully aware of the capability of the system and the C library that is built on the top of the system. The most popular C library variants in embedded system are Newlib, uclibc, and Bionic. They implement the standard C library based on their own systems with minor differences.

To provide better debugging capabilities, a special implementation of the system call stubs is provided in an embedded system called the semihosting or semihost C library. Semihosting or semihost is a mechanism that enables code running on an embedded system to communicate and use the input/output facilities on a host computer that is running a debugger. The host environment being discussed here is the environment introduced in Chapter 3—that is, the environment that we use to do development work, such as coding, compilation, and debugging. The semihost/semihosting library variant provides implementations of most of the standard C library functions, including file I/O. The file I/O will be directed through the debugger and will be performed on the host system. For example, printf/scanf will use the debugger console window and fread/fwrite will operate on files on the host system. This emulated I/O can be used only in a debugging environment. The semihosting variant is typically used together with a kind of debugging environment during development. For product release, however, the semihosting variant should not be used. We will explore this process in the second example (c06e2) in this chapter.

Many C library implementations are available for embedded programming. The choice of which to use depends heavily on the selection of the toolchain. The commercial toolchain known as RealView Development Suite (from ARM) has its own C library implementation. This variant is similar to those offered by other silicon vendors such as TI, NXP, and Freescale. For open source toolchains, Newlib is the most popular choice for the C library. As we are using Sourcery CodeBench Lite in this book, we will use Newlib's offering as an example when we discuss C library support in a bare metal programming environment.

> **Note**
>
> For the same source code of a C library, variants can be built for different target platforms. For example, Newlib C in Sourcery CodeBench Lite can be built for the ARM platform in the toolchain `arm-none-eabi` or for the MIPS platform in the toolchain `mips-sde-elf`. Similarly, the GNU C library in Sourcery CodeBench Lite can be built for the ARM platform in the toolchain `arm-none-linux-gnueabi` or for the MIPS platform in the toolchain `mips-linux-gnu`. Please refer to the Sourcery CodeBench Lite website for more details about various builds of Newlib C (*http://www.mentor.com/embedded-software/sourcery-tools/sourcery-codebench/editions/lite-edition/*).

Newlib C Library

In Chapter 5, we learned how to build a program starting from the hardware reset in an assembly language environment. We also created simple startup code that initializes the programming environment for the C language and transfers control from the assembly language to the C language. In a real product, the startup code is somewhat more complicated than what we have seen in our examples. However, the basic concept underlying the code is the same. In this chapter, we will use the commercial implementation of startup code (CS3) from Mentor Graphics' Sourcery CodeBench Lite rather than trying to build complicated startup code on our own. In this way, we can focus on the essentials of building an embedded system instead of implementing everything by ourselves.

In this chapter, we will create two code examples. We will use them to illustrate how we can use C libraries in an embedded system development environment. In the first code example (c06e1), we will implement the necessary stubs in Newlib so that we can run the example code using Newlib on the goldfish platform. In the second code example (c06e2), we will test the semihosting environment supported by QEMU so that we can see how semihosting can help in the embedded system development environment.

In the first code example, the following files are created based on the example code in Chapter 5. These files are divided into two groups: common files and project-specific files. Common files are generic files that will be reused throughout the book; project-specific files are used for only this example.

Common files:

- `startup_cs3.S`: The startup code that performs the necessary setup before the control is transferred to the C code. It is based on the Sourcery CodeBench CS3 startup code.
- `syscalls_cs3.c`: The implementation of the system service stubs.
- `serial_goldfish.c`: The C code to implement serial functions. It is the same as in Chapter 5.
- `goldfish_uart.S`: The assembly code for implementing serial port–specific functions. It is the same as in Chapter 5.

Project-specific files:

- c06e1.c: The code for the test driver implementing main() function.
- Makefile: The makefile for building this project.
- c06e1.ld: The linker script for the project.

Common Startup Code Sequence

In Chapter 3, we introduced the ARM Toolchain Sourcery CodeBench. We use the free edition Sourcery CodeBench Lite in this book. CS3 is the low-level board support library provided as part of Sourcery CodeBench. It provides a consistent set of conventions for processor and board-level initialization, language runtime setup, and interrupt and trap handler definition.

Sourcery CodeBench supports a number of built-in reference platforms. For each supported system, CS3 provides a set of linker scripts describing the system's memory map. A board support library provides generic reset, startup, and interrupt handlers. All of these scripts and libraries follow a standard set of conventions across a range of processors and boards.

CS3 Linker Scripts

CS3 may provide multiple linker scripts for different configurations using the same board. For example, on some boards, CS3 may support running the program from either RAM or ROM (flash memory). In CS3 terminology, each of these different configurations is referred to as a profile.

Because goldfish is not supported by Sourcery CodeBench directly, we have to create a new link script file for goldfish to work with the CS3 startup sequence, as shown in Example 6.1. The link script for the general profile (arm-none-eabi/lib/generic.ld) is used as the basis to be modified for the goldfish platform.

Example 6.1 Linker Script (code/c06/c06e1/c06e1.ld)

```
OUTPUT_FORMAT ("elf32-littlearm", "elf32-bigarm", "elf32-littlearm")
ENTRY(__cs3_reset)
SEARCH_DIR(.)
GROUP(-lgcc -lc -lcs3 -lcs3hosted -lcs3arm)
MEMORY
{
    flash (rx) : ORIGIN = 0x00010000, LENGTH = 128K /* Defined ROM size and the start address */
    ram (rwx)  : ORIGIN = 0x00030000, LENGTH = 512M /* Defined RAM size and the start address */
}
```

Chapter 6 Using the C Library

```
/* These force the linker to search for particular symbols from
 * the start of the link process and thus ensure the user's
 * overrides are picked up
 */
EXTERN(__cs3_reset __cs3_reset_generic)
EXTERN(__cs3_start_asm __cs3_start_asm_sim)
/* Bring in the interrupt routines and vector */
INCLUDE arm-names.inc
EXTERN(__cs3_interrupt_vector_arm)
EXTERN(__cs3_start_c main __cs3_stack __cs3_heap_end)
/* Force exit to be picked up in a hosted or OS environment
EXTERN(exit atexit) */
/* Provide fall-back values */
PROVIDE(__cs3_heap_start = _end);
PROVIDE(__cs3_heap_end = __cs3_region_start_ram + __cs3_region_size_ram);
PROVIDE(__cs3_region_num = (__cs3_regions_end - __cs3_regions) / 20);
/* Ensure that Newlib runs the finalizers
__libc_fini = _fini; */
PROVIDE(__cs3_stack = __cs3_region_start_ram + __cs3_region_size_ram);
SECTIONS
{
  .text :
  {
    CREATE_OBJECT_SYMBOLS
    __cs3_region_start_flash = .;          /* We put .text section in flash */
    _ftext = .;
    *(.cs3.region-head.flash)
   ASSERT (. == __cs3_region_start_flash, ".cs3.region-head.flash not permitted");
    __cs3_interrupt_vector = __cs3_interrupt_vector_arm;
    *(.cs3.interrupt_vector)
    /* Make sure we pulled in an interrupt vector  */
    ASSERT (. != __cs3_interrupt_vector_arm, "No interrupt vector");
    PROVIDE(__cs3_reset = __cs3_reset_generic);
    *(.cs3.reset)
    __cs3_start_asm_sim = DEFINED(__cs3_start_asm) ? __cs3_start_asm : __cs3_start_asm_sim;
```

```
    *(.text.cs3.init)
    *(.text .text.* .gnu.linkonce.t.*)
    *(.plt)
    *(.gnu.warning)
    *(.glue_7t) *(.glue_7) *(.vfp11_veneer)
    *(.ARM.extab* .gnu.linkonce.armextab.*)
    *(.gcc_except_table)
} >flash
.eh_frame_hdr : ALIGN (4)
{
    KEEP (*(.eh_frame_hdr))
    *(.eh_frame_entry .eh_frame_entry.*)
} >flash
.eh_frame : ALIGN (4)
{
    KEEP (*(.eh_frame)) *(.eh_frame.*)
} >flash
/* .ARM.exidx is sorted, so it has to go in its own output section   */
PROVIDE_HIDDEN (__exidx_start = .);
.ARM.exidx :
{
    *(.ARM.exidx* .gnu.linkonce.armexidx.*)
} >flash
PROVIDE_HIDDEN (__exidx_end = .);
.rodata : ALIGN (4)
{
    *(.rodata .rodata.* .gnu.linkonce.r.*)

    . = ALIGN(4);
    KEEP(*(.init))

    . = ALIGN(4);
    __preinit_array_start = .;
    KEEP (*(.preinit_array))
    __preinit_array_end = .;

    . = ALIGN(4);
```

```
        __init_array_start = .;
        KEEP (*(SORT(.init_array.*)))
        KEEP (*(.init_array))
        __init_array_end = .;

        . = ALIGN(4);
        KEEP(*(.fini))

        . = ALIGN(4);
        __fini_array_start = .;
        KEEP (*(.fini_array))
        KEEP (*(SORT(.fini_array.*)))
        __fini_array_end = .;

        . = ALIGN(0x4);
        KEEP (*crtbegin.o(.ctors))
        KEEP (*(EXCLUDE_FILE (*crtend.o) .ctors))
        KEEP (*(SORT(.ctors.*)))
        KEEP (*crtend.o(.ctors))

        . = ALIGN(0x4);
        KEEP (*crtbegin.o(.dtors))
        KEEP (*(EXCLUDE_FILE (*crtend.o) .dtors))
        KEEP (*(SORT(.dtors.*)))
        KEEP (*crtend.o(.dtors))

        . = ALIGN(4);
        __cs3_regions = .;
        LONG (0)
        LONG (__cs3_region_init_ram)
        LONG (__cs3_region_start_ram)
        LONG (__cs3_region_init_size_ram)
        LONG (__cs3_region_zero_size_ram)
        __cs3_regions_end = .;
        . = ALIGN (8);
        _etext = .;
    } >flash
```

```
  ASSERT (!(__cs3_region_init_ram & 7), "__cs3_region_init_ram not aligned")
  ASSERT (!(__cs3_region_start_ram & 7), "__cs3_region_start_ram not aligned")
  ASSERT (!(__cs3_region_init_size_ram & 7), "__cs3_region_init_size_ram not aligned")
  ASSERT (!(__cs3_region_zero_size_ram & 7), "__cs3_region_zero_size_ram not aligned")
  .data : ALIGN (8)
  {
      __cs3_region_start_ram = .;   /* This is the runtime address of .data section */
      __cs3_data_load = LOADADDR (.data);
      __cs3_region_init_ram = _etext;  /* This is the load address of .data section */
KEEP(*(.jcr))
      *(.got.plt) *(.got)
      *(.shdata)
      *(.data .data.* .gnu.linkonce.d.*)
      . = ALIGN (8);
      *(.ram)
      . = ALIGN (8);
      _edata = .;
  } >ram AT>flash
  .bss : ALIGN (8)
  {
      *(.shbss)
      *(.bss .bss.* .gnu.linkonce.b.*)
      *(COMMON)
      . = ALIGN (8);
      *(.ram.b .bss.ram)
      . = ALIGN (8);
      _end = .;
      __end = .;
  } >ram
  /* __cs3_region_init_ram = __cs3_region_start_ram; */
  __cs3_region_init_size_ram = _edata - __cs3_region_start_ram;
```

```
            __cs3_region_zero_size_ram = _end - _edata;
            /* Default to 1MB of heap */
            __cs3_region_size_ram = ALIGN (1024) - __cs3_region_start_ram + 1M;

            .stab 0 (NOLOAD) : { *(.stab) }
            .stabstr 0 (NOLOAD) : { *(.stabstr) }
            /* DWARF debug sections.
             * Symbols in the DWARF debugging sections are relative to
             * the beginning of the section, so we begin them at 0
             */
            /* DWARF 1 */
            .debug          0 : { *(.debug) }
            .line           0 : { *(.line) }
            /* GNU DWARF 1 extensions */
            .debug_srcinfo  0 : { *(.debug_srcinfo) }
            .debug_sfnames  0 : { *(.debug_sfnames) }
            /* DWARF 1.1 and DWARF 2 */
            .debug_aranges  0 : { *(.debug_aranges) }
            .debug_pubnames 0 : { *(.debug_pubnames) }
            /* DWARF 2 */
            .debug_info     0 : { *(.debug_info .gnu.linkonce.wi.*) }
            .debug_abbrev   0 : { *(.debug_abbrev) }
            .debug_line     0 : { *(.debug_line) }
            .debug_frame    0 : { *(.debug_frame) }
            .debug_str      0 : { *(.debug_str) }
            .debug_loc      0 : { *(.debug_loc) }
            .debug_macinfo  0 : { *(.debug_macinfo) }
            /* DWARF 2.1 */
            .debug_ranges   0 : { *(.debug_ranges) }
            /* SGI/MIPS DWARF 2 extensions */
            .debug_weaknames 0 : { *(.debug_weaknames) }
            .debug_funcnames 0 : { *(.debug_funcnames) }
            .debug_typenames 0 : { *(.debug_typenames) }
            .debug_varnames  0 : { *(.debug_varnames) }

            .note.gnu.arm.ident 0 : { KEEP (*(.note.gnu.arm.ident)) }
```

```
  .ARM.attributes 0 : { KEEP (*(.ARM.attributes)) }
  /DISCARD/ : { *(.note.GNU-stack) }
}
```

All of the changes are highlighted in bold. As the link script in Example 6.1 shows, very few changes were made on top of the original link script. We updated the memory space for both RAM and ROM for the goldfish platform. The original link script is used to load the program into RAM for execution. We want to place the code in ROM and the data in RAM in our code example. __cs3_region_init_ram is set to _etext in ROM instead of the original __cs3_region_start_ram in RAM. Pay attention to the C structure __cs3_regions; it is defined in the CodeBench Lite header file arm-none-eabi/include/cs3.h.

```
struct __cs3_region
{
  unsigned long flags;       /* Flags for this region.  None defined yet.  */
  __cs3_byte_align8 *init;   /* Initial contents of this region.  */
  __cs3_byte_align8 *data;   /* Start address of region.  */
  size_t init_size;          /* Size of initial data.  */
  size_t zero_size;          /* Additional size to be zeroed.  */
};
extern const struct __cs3_region __cs3_regions[];
```

The fields init and data should be initialized to __cs3_region_init_ram (load address) and __cs3_region_start_ram, respectively. __cs3_region_init_ram points to the initialized data that needs to be copied to RAM at __cs3_region_start_ram (runtime address) during the CS3 initialization. The field init_size is the size of initialized data section. The field zero_size is the size of the .bss section, which needs to be set to zero during the CS3 initialization.

Customized CS3 Startup Code for the Goldfish Platform

Since we are using the CS3 startup code to build our example, our own startup code is much simpler compared to the startup code used in Chapter 5.

CS3 divides the startup sequence into three phases:

1. The hard reset phase (__cs3_reset) includes actions such as initializing the memory controller and setting up the memory map.
2. The assembly initialization phase (__cs3_start_asm) prepares the stack to run C code, and jumps to the C initialization function.

Example 6.2 Startup Code (code/c06/c06e1/startup_cs3.S)

```
    .text
    .code 32

    .global __cs3_reset

__cs3_reset:
    /* Add peripherals and memory initialization here */
    LDR r0, =__cs3_start_asm
    MOV lr,pc        /* set the return address */
    BX  r0

__cs3_start_asm:
    /* Set up stack and call C initialization */
    LDR sp, =__cs3_stack
    LDR r0, =__cs3_start_c
    MOV lr,pc        /* set the return address */
    BX  r0
    .end
```

3. The C initialization phase (__cs3_start_c) is responsible for initializing the data areas, running constructors for statically allocated objects, and calling main.

The hard reset and assembly initialization phases are necessarily written in assembly language. When the system resets, there may not yet be any stack available to hold the compiler temporary files, or perhaps no RAM may be accessible that can hold the stack. These phases do the minimum work necessary to prepare the environment for running simple C code. To meet the minimum requirements before we make a call to __cs3_start_c, we provide our own implementation of __cs3_reset and __cs3_start_asm in Example 6.2. In this example, notice that we actually did nothing in the hard reset and assembly initialization phases, because we are running in an emulator. All of the necessary setup for these two phases has been done by the host system. This is one of the major differences between the virtual hardware and the physical hardware.

In the startup code, we set the stack pointer to the symbol __cs3_stack, which is the stack pointer defined in the linker script. Next, we jump to __cs3_start_c to begin the C initialization phase. If we debug the code, we'll find that the control will go to our main() function eventually.

System Call Implementations

The real work to make the Newlib C library operate on the goldfish platform comes in implementing the required system calls. In the Newlib user manual for the C library, there is a list of system call stubs that we have to implement to use Newlib in our environment. If you use the C library on a system that complies with the POSIX.1 standard (also known as IEEE 1003.1), most of these functions are supplied by your operating system.

In the embedded system, you will at least need to provide do-nothing stubs (or functions with minimal functionality) to allow your programs to link with the subroutines in libc.a. These minimal-functionality functions should fail gracefully when OS services are not available. There are a total of 18 functions implemented in Example 6.3. Except for _init, _read, _write, and _sbrk, the functions are just minimal implementations that return an indicator of success or failure to the caller. In the system calls _init, _read, and _write, we implement console input/output using the serial port implementation we developed in Chapter 5. In the system call _sbrk, we implement basic memory management logic so that we can support malloc in using the heap.

Example 6.3 Standard System Call Implementation (drivers/syscalls_cs3.c)

```
#include <sys/stat.h>
#include <sys/unistd.h>
#include <serial_goldfish.h>

#include <errno.h>
#undef errno
extern int errno;

/*
 environ
 A pointer to a list of environment variables and their values.
 For a minimal environment, this empty list is adequate:
 */
char *__env[1] = { 0 };
char **environ = __env;

/*
 * init
 * Initialize serial data structure.
 */
void _init(void) {
    struct serial_device *drv;

    drv = default_serial_console();   /* Get the data structure serial_device. */
    drv->start();         /* Call goldfish_init to initialize the base address. */
```

```
        return;
}

/*
 * write
 * Write a character to a file. 'libc' subroutines will use this system routine
 * for output to all files, including stdout.
 * Returns -1 on error or number of bytes sent.
 */
int _write(int file, char *ptr, int len) {
    int n;
    struct serial_device *drv;

    drv = default_serial_console();    /* Get the data structure serial_device. */

switch (file) {
/* We use serial port for both standard out and error. They can be directed to
different I/O devices. */
    case STDOUT_FILENO: /* stdout */
        for (n = 0; n < len; n++) {
            drv->putc(*ptr++); /* Call goldfish serial function to send a character to serial port. */
        }
        break;
    case STDERR_FILENO: /* stderr */
        for (n = 0; n < len; n++) {
            drv->putc(*ptr++); /* Call goldfish serial function to send a character to serial port. */
        }
        break;
    default:
        errno = EBADF;
        return -1;
    }
    return len;
}

/*
 * read
```

System Call Implementations

```
 * Read a character to a file. 'libc' subroutines will use this system routine
for input from all files, including stdin.
 * Returns -1 on error or blocks until the number of characters have been read.
 */
int _read(int file, char *ptr, int len) {
    int n, len1;
    int num = -1;
    char c;
    struct serial_device *drv;

    drv = default_serial_console();    /* Get the data structure serial_device. */
    len1 = drv->tstc();
    /* We implement a blocking read here. */
    while (len1 <= 0) {
        len1 = drv->tstc();                      /* Check the pending input. */
    }

    if(len1) {
        if(len1 > len) {
            /* len is the buffer size. We cannot read more than buffer size. */
            len1 = len;
        }

        num = 0;

        switch (file) {
            case STDIN_FILENO:
                for (n = 0; n < len1; n++) {
                    c = drv->getc();             /* Read input from serial port. */
                    *ptr++ = c;
                    num++;
                }
                break;
            default:
                errno = EBADF;
                return -1;
        }
    }
    return num;
}
```

Chapter 6 Using the C Library

```c
/*
 * sbrk
 * Increase program data space.
 * Malloc and related functions depend on this.
 */
#define STACK_BUFFER 65536 /* Reserved stack space in bytes. */
static char *heap_end = 0;

void * _sbrk(int incr) {
    /* Both __cs3_heap_start and __cs3_heap_end are defined by the linker. Refer to
linker script in Example 6.1. */
    extern char __cs3_heap_start;
    extern char __cs3_heap_end;
    char *prev_heap_end;

    if (heap_end == 0) {
        heap_end = &__cs3_heap_start;
    }
    prev_heap_end = heap_end;
    if (heap_end + STACK_BUFFER + incr > &__cs3_heap_end) {
        /* Heap and stack collision */
        errno = ENOMEM;
        _write(STDERR_FILENO, "Error in _sbrk!\n", 16);
        return (void *)0;
    }
    heap_end += incr;

    return (void *) prev_heap_end;
}

/*
 * Exit a program without cleanup.
 *
 */
void _exit(int status) {
    _write(1, "exit", 4);
    while (1) {
        ;
    }
}
```

```
/*
 * open
 * Open a file. A minimal implementation without file system:
 * */
int _open (const char *name, int flags, int mode)
{
errno = ENOSYS;
return -1; /* Always fails. */
}

int _close(int file) {
    return -1;
}
/*
 * execve
 * Transfer control to a new process. Minimal implementation (for a system without processes):
 */
int _execve(char *name, char **argv, char **env) {
    errno = ENOMEM;
    return -1;
}

/*
 * fork
 * Create a new process. Minimal implementation (for a system without processes):
 */
int _fork(void) {
    errno = EAGAIN;
    return -1;
}

/*
 * fstat
 * Status of an open file. For consistency with other minimal implementations in these examples,
 * all files are regarded as character special devices.
```

```
 * The sys/stat.h header file required is distributed in the 'include'
subdirectory for this C library.
 */
int _fstat(int file, struct stat *st) {
    st->st_mode = S_IFCHR;
    return 0;
}

/*
 * getpid
 * Process-ID; this is sometimes used to generate strings unlikely to conflict
with other processes.
 * Minimal implementation, for a system without processes:
 */
int _getpid(void) {
    return 1;
}

/*
 * isatty
 * Query whether output stream is a terminal. For consistency with the other
minimal implementations:
 */
int _isatty(int file) {
    switch (file){
    case STDOUT_FILENO:
    case STDERR_FILENO:
    case STDIN_FILENO:
        return 1;
    default:
        //errno = ENOTTY;
        errno = EBADF;
        return 0;
    }
}

/*
 * kill
 * Send a signal. Minimal implementation:
```

```c
 */
int _kill(int pid, int sig) {
    errno = EINVAL;
    return (-1);
}

/*
 * link
 * Establish a new name for an existing file. Minimal implementation:
 */
int _link(char *old, char *new) {
    errno = EMLINK;
    return -1;
}

/*
 * lseek
 * Set position in a file. Minimal implementation:
 */
int _lseek(int file, int ptr, int dir) {
    return 0;
}

/*
 * stat
 * Status of a file (by name). Minimal implementation:
 */
int _stat(const char *filepath, struct stat *st) {
    st->st_mode = S_IFCHR;
    return 0;
}

/*
 * unlink
 * Remove a file's directory entry. Minimal implementation:
 */
int _unlink(char *name) {
    errno = ENOENT;
    return -1;
```

```
}
/*
 * wait
 * Wait for a child process. Minimal implementation:
 */
int _wait(int *status) {
    errno = ECHILD;
    return -1;
}
```

We implemented _init, _read, _write, and _sbrk in Example 6.3. For all other stubs, we just simply provide a return value.

- _init is part of the runtime startup sequence instead of the system call. We add codes in it to initialize the data structure for serial ports. The serial initialization function (drv->start()) is called here rather than in main() as in Example 5.9.
- _read is a system call to read data from a file. We implement a blocking read using drv->tstc() and drv->getc(). We call drv->tstc() to check the available data in the serial buffer first. If there is no data, we continue polling the serial buffer and wait for input data. Once input data are available in the serial buffer, we read the number of bytes of data and make sure that the total number is smaller than the temporary data buffer size, which is supplied by the calling function.
- _write is a system call that writes data to a file. In our implementation, we support serial input/output only, and _write uses the serial driver function drv->putc() to send data to serial port.
- _sbrk is a basic memory management system call used in UNIX and UNIX-like operating systems to control the amount of memory allocated to the data segment of the process. In the embedded system, the C library uses it to manage the heap. Since malloc() depends on this memory system, we have to implement it. A static character pointer variable heap_end is used to remember the end of the used data memory in heap. When _sbrk is called for the first time, heap_end is initialized to the beginning of the heap at __cs3_heap_start. Later, when _sbrk is called again, it increases heap_end per the request. We must make sure that, after it is increased, the used heap size will not exceed the end of the heap (__cs3_heap_end) once the amount of memory kept for the stack is deducted (STACK_BUFFER_SIZE). Both __cs3_heap_start and __cs3_heap_end are defined in the linker script (Example 6.1).

Running and Debugging the Library

After we have implemented all of the necessary elements for Newlib, we are ready to test it. The unit test code is shown in Example 6.4.

Example 6.4 Unit Test Code (c06/c06e1/c06e1.c)

```c
#include <stdio.h>
#include <stdlib.h>
#include <sys/unistd.h>

/* We will run the unit test of serial driver in main() */
int main(int argc, char *argv[])
{
    int c = 0, i = 0;
    char *buffer = 0;

    /* Unit test 1: write() */
    write(STDERR_FILENO, "Hello, World!\n1", 15);

    while (1) {
        /* Unit test 2: malloc() */
        buffer = malloc(128 + i*16);

        /* Unit test 3: printf() */
        printf(". buffer=%x\n", (unsigned int)buffer);

        /* Unit test 4: getchar(), this is a blocking read */
        c = getchar();

        /* Unit test 5: putchar() */
        putchar(c);

        /* Unit test 6: free() */
        if(c != 's') {
            free(buffer);
        }

        if(c == 'q') {
            printf("\nExit from main()...\n");
            break;
        }
        i++;
    }

    return 1;
}
```

In Example 6.4, we implement a similar test scenario as Example 5.9. In Example 5.9, we got our input from a serial port and printed it to the serial port. We processed the character q in a special way; that is, if we encountered this character, we ended the program. Example 6.4, however, looks more like standard C code instead of platform-specific code, especially compared to Example 5.9. In this example, all of the serial port–specific codes have been moved to the system calls inside Newlib. The six test cases in this code test the C library functions `write`, `malloc`, `printf`, `getchar`, `putchar`, and `free`. To test `malloc` and `free`, we handle the special character s separately, skipping the function call `free` after a `malloc` call so that we can observe the memory is not freed in the heap.

To build the project, we invoke make in the project folder:

```
$ make DEBUG=1
  CC    c06e1.c
  AS    ../../drivers/startup_cs3.S
  CC    ../../drivers/serial_goldfish.c
  AS    ../../drivers/goldfish_uart.S
  CC    ../../drivers/syscalls_cs3.c
  LD    gcc/c06e1.axf
```

As usual, we run the following command to start the program for testing:

```
$ make debug
ddd --debugger arm-none-eabi-gdb gcc/c06e1.axf &
emulator -verbose -show-kernel -netfast -avd hd2 -shell -qemu -s -S -kernel gcc/c06e1.axf
...
emulator: Initializing hardware OpenGLES emulation support

emulator: ERROR: Could not load OpenGLES emulation library: libOpenglRender.so: cannot open shared object file: No such file or directory

emulator: WARNING: Could not initialize OpenglES emulation, using software renderer.

emulator: Kernel parameters: qemu.gles=0 qemu=1 console=ttyS0 android.qemud=ttyS1 androidboot.console=ttyS2 android.checkjni=1 ndns=1

goldfish_tty_add id=0 base=ff002000 80 0

goldfish_tty_add id=1 base=ff011000 80 0

goldfish_tty_add id=2 base=ff012000 80 0

emulator: Trace file name is not set
...
emulator: autoconfig: -scale 1

emulator: Could not open file: (null)/system/build.prop: No such file or directory
```

```
emulator: control console listening on port 5554, ADB on port 5555
```

```
emulator: can't connect to ADB server: Connection refused
```

```
emulator: ping program: /media/u32/home/sgye/src/Android/android-
emulator-20130928/qemu/objs/ddms
```

```
goldfish_init(), gtty.base=ff012000
```

We can view the debugging process in the console output in Figure 6.2 and in the ddd debug screen in Figure 6.3.

From the console output, we can see that `make debug` actually launches ddd and the emulator. With the option `-s`, the gdb server is set to listen to the TCP port 1234. After we connect to the target in ddd, we can set a breakpoint in `main` and start to debug the test code.

Notice that the system call `write` produces the output "Hello, World!" in the serial console. The C library functions `printf`, `getchar`, and `putchar` can be verified during this series of interactions with the serial console. The serial console is waiting for input after "Hello, World!" to be printed. When we press a key on the keyboard, a debug message is printed to show the memory address return from `malloc`. The first address returned from `malloc` is 0x30d60. After that, it always returns the address 0x311f0 in lines 2 and, because we called the `free` function before we called `malloc` in the next loop. When we input a special character s to skip the `free` function, the return address increases to 0x31298. This occurs because the previously allocated memory is not released.

```
goldfish_add_device: goldfish-switch, base ff01b000 1000, irq 21 1
emulator: autoconfig: -scale 1
emulator: Could not open file: (null)/system/build.prop: No such file or directo
ry
emulator: control console listening on port 5554, ADB on port 5555
emulator: sent '0012host:emulator:5555' to ADB server
emulator: ping program: /media/u32/home/sgye/src/Android/android-emulator-201309
28/qemu/objs/ddms
Warning: XmStringGetNextComponent: unknown type 170285352

Warning: XmStringGetNextComponent: unknown type 170208520

goldfish_init(), gtty.base=ff012000
Hello, World!
1. buffer=30d60
2. buffer=311f0
3. buffer=311f0
s. buffer=31298
4. buffer=31298
5. buffer=31298
s. buffer=31370
6. buffer=31370
7. buffer=31370
```

Figure 6.2 Debug console output of the test code

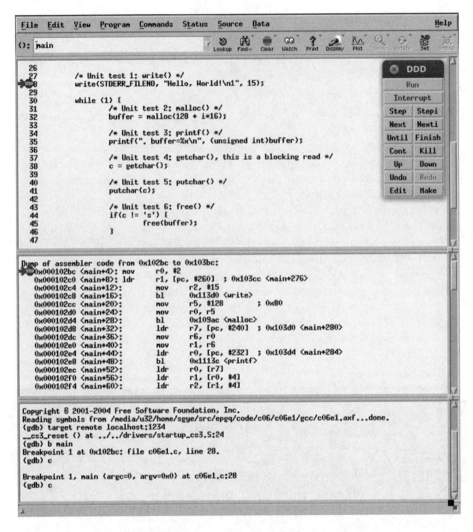

Figure 6.3 The ddd session of the test code

Using Newlib with QEMU ARM Semihosting

Now let's look at the semihosting version of the C library in the embedded system environment. Luckily, the virtual machine used by the Android emulator is QEMU, which supports semihosting. We can modify the previous test code a little to test the semihosting version of Newlib. Even though QEMU supports semihosting nicely, it is not a major function needed by the Android emulator. In fact, the semihosting support in the Android emulator is very buggy. It may be broken from version to version. To test this functionality smoothly, I uploaded a stable version of the Android emulator in SourceForge; we will use this version of the Android emulator to test the code in this section.

Semihosting Support in Newlib C

Semihosting enables codes running on an ARM target to communicate and use the input/output facilities on a host computer that is running a debugger. In our environment, we can use the gdbserver inside QEMU to support semihosting.

Examples of these facilities include keyboard input, screen output, and disk I/O. For example, we can use this mechanism to enable functions in the C library, such as `printf()` and `scanf()`, to use the screen and keyboard of the host instead of the screen and keyboard on the target system. This is useful because development hardware often does not have exactly the same input and output facilities as the final system. Semihosting enables the host computer to provide these facilities.

Semihosting is implemented by a set of defined software instructions. For example, SVCs generate exceptions from program control. The application invokes the appropriate semihosting call and then the debug agent handles the exception. The debug agent provides the required communication with the host.

The same semihosting interface is used across all of the debug agents provided by ARM. When we are debugging applications on the development platform, the semihosted operations follow the workflow shown in Figure 6.4.

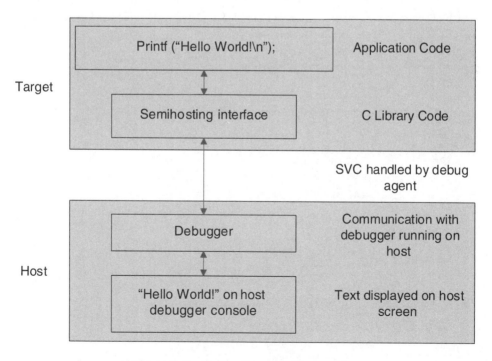

Figure 6.4 Semihosting operations workflow

Semihosting Example Code

Compared to the first code example in this chapter, the example code for semihosting (c06e2) is much simpler:

- `c06e2.c`: The C code implementation `main()` function
- `Makefile`: The makefile to build this project
- `c06e2.ld`: The linker script of the project

Since we use the semihosting facility provided by QEMU and semihosting is supported by Newlib in Sourcery CodeBench, we do not have to write our own startup code or provide system call stubs. The standard input/output goes through the host, which is QEMU, instead of through the serial port of the goldfish platform.

The link script used here is derived from the Sourcery CodeBench Lite general profile (`arm-none-eabi/lib/generic-hosted.ld`). Only one change is made to it:

```
MEMORY
{
    ram (rwx) : ORIGIN = 0x10000, LENGTH = 512M
}
```

We changed the memory location to the goldfish platform–specific location and left the rest of the configuration the same as the default.

Now let's look at the unit test code in Example 6.5, which we have changed from the previous version to accommodate semihosting.

Example 6.5 Semihosting Test Code Example (code/c06/c06e2/c06e2.c)

```c
#include <stdio.h>
#include <stdlib.h>
#include <sys/unistd.h>
int main(int argc, char *argv[])
{
    FILE *fp;
    int c = '\n', i = 0;
    char *buffer = 0;

    /* Unit test 1: write() */
    write(STDERR_FILENO, "Hello, World!\n1", 15);
```

```c
    /* Unit test 2: fopen() */
    fp = fopen("log.txt", "w");
    if(fp == NULL) return 0;

    while (1) {
        /* Unit test 3: malloc() */
        buffer = malloc(128 + i*16);

        /* Unit test 4: printf() */
        printf(". buffer=%x\n", (unsigned int)buffer);
        fprintf(fp, "%c. buffer=%x\n", c, (unsigned int)buffer);

        /* Unit test 5: getchar(), this is a blocking read */
        do {
            c = getchar();
        } while (c == '\n');

        /* Unit test 6: putchar() */
        putchar(c);

        /* Unit test 7: free() */
        if(c != 's') {
            free(buffer);
        }
        if(c == 'q') {
            printf("\nExit from main()...\n");
            break;
        }
        i++;
    }

    /* Unit test 8: fclose() */
    fclose(fp);
    return 1;
}
```

As you can see, the test code looks very similar to Example 6.4. We added some C library functions to verify that the file IO can be provided by the host environment. In

Chapter 6 Using the C Library

test case 2, we opened a file `log.txt` using `fopen`. This `log.txt` file does not exist in the target, which is the Android emulator hardware, but rather is stored in the host environment.

To build the project, we invoke `make` from the project folder:

```
$ make DEBUG=1
   CC    c06e2.c
   LD    gcc/c06e2.axf
```

Now we can debug it:

```
$ make debug
./setup_sdk.sh
Cannot find emulator. Downloading ...
--2015-03-27 12:26:59--  http://downloads.sourceforge.net/project/epwa/emulator_arm.tar.gz?r=&ts=1427204475&use_mirror=master
Resolving downloads.sourceforge.net (downloads.sourceforge.net)... 216.34.181.59
Connecting to downloads.sourceforge.net (downloads.sourceforge.net)|216.34.181.59|:80... connected.
HTTP request sent, awaiting response... 302 Found
Location: http://superb-dca2.dl.sourceforge.net/project/epwa/emulator_arm.tar.gz [following]
--2015-03-27 12:27:00--  http://superb-dca2.dl.sourceforge.net/project/epwa/emulator_arm.tar.gz
Resolving superb-dca2.dl.sourceforge.net (superb-dca2.dl.sourceforge.net)... 209.61.193.20
Connecting to superb-dca2.dl.sourceforge.net (superb-dca2.dl.sourceforge.net)|209.61.193.20|:80... connected.
HTTP request sent, awaiting response... 200 OK
Length: 8118701 (7.7M) [application/x-gzip]
Saving to: './emulator_arm.tar.gz'

100%[======================================>] 8,118,701    714K/s   in 29s

2015-03-27 12:27:30 (274 KB/s) - `./emulator_arm.tar.gz' saved [8118701/8118701]

bin/./
bin/./emulator-ui
bin/./emulator
bin/./emulator-arm
bin/./qemu-android-arm
Find API level 15.
ddd --debugger arm-none-eabi-gdb gcc/c06e2.axf &
```

```
emulator -avd hd2 -qemu -monitor telnet::6666,server -s -S -semihosting -kernel
gcc/c06e2.axf
```
...

If you start the debug the first time using Makefile, you can see that it starts to download an emulator automatically for the semihosting test to avoid the Android emulator bug in your version.

Once we start the program, as shown in Figure 6.5, we actually interact with the ddd command console instead of the emulator serial console. This is exactly what we expect, as semihosting uses the host environment for input/output instead of the target

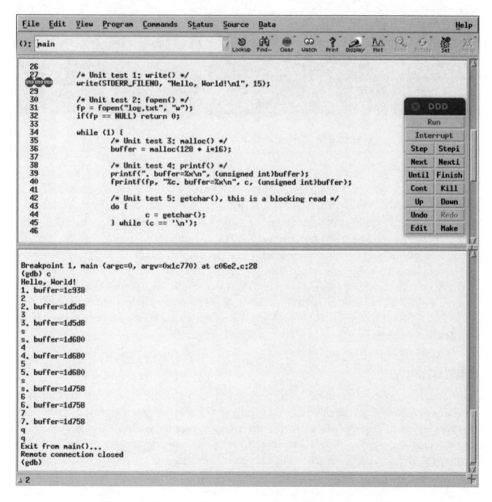

Figure 6.5 The ddd session of the semihosting test code

```
sye1@ubuntu:~/src/epgq/code/c06/c06e2$ emulator -avd hd2 -qemu -monitor telnet::
6666,server -s -S -semihosting -kernel gcc/c06e2.axf
emulator: ERROR: Could not load OpenGLES emulation library: libOpenglRender.so:
cannot open shared object file: No such file or directory
emulator: WARNING: Could not initialize OpenglES emulation, using software rende
rer.
QEMU waiting for connection on: telnet::6666,server
goldfish_tty_add id=0 base=ff002000 80 0
goldfish_tty_add id=1 base=ff011000 80 0
goldfish_tty_add id=2 base=ff012000 80 0
sye1@ubuntu:~/src/epgq/code/c06/c06e2$ ls
c06e2.c  c06e2.ld  gcc  log.txt  Makefile
sye1@ubuntu:~/src/epgq/code/c06/c06e2$ cat log.txt
1. buffer=1c938
2. buffer=1d5d8
3. buffer=1d5d8
s. buffer=1d680
4. buffer=1d680
5. buffer=1d680
s. buffer=1d758
6. buffer=1d758
7. buffer=1d758
sye1@ubuntu:~/src/epgq/code/c06/c06e2$
```

Figure 6.6 Debug output of semihosting example

environment. Consequently, the semihosting build can only be used together with debugger.

In this example, we also allocate and release memory a few times. Notice that the results are similar to those shown in Figure 6.2. The key difference here is that the input and output on screen do not appear on the serial console of the target hardware, but instead on the gdb debugger console. We can also see that log.txt is stored in the same folder from which the debugger is launched. As is evident in the command-line console of Figure 6.6, the debug message on the gdb console (Figure 6.5) can be seen in the log.txt file as well. This is because all the file IO services are provided by the host environment through the debugger.

Summary

After moving from programming in the assembly language to the C language, one immediate need is for C runtime library support. The C runtime library is an important tool that we can use to improve our work efficiency. In this chapter we learned that the C runtime library appears in different formats in different embedded systems. Even though we may call the standard C functions like printf, scanf, and malloc, they will be different in each system. For example, Android uses a C library called Bionic, whereas Linux uses glibc. In this book, we use the C library together with the Sourcery CodeBench Lite variant, which is known as Newlib.

Different flavors of the C library also exist depending on how the system call layer is implemented. Namely, these variants can be hosting or semihosting versions. We provided two examples in this chapter to show the differences between hosting and semihosting.

To use Newlib, we implemented the system call layer required by the Newlib C library. We implemented the necessary system calls such as `_init`, `_read`, `_write`, and `_sbrk`. In the implementation of these system calls, we reused the serial driver from Chapter 5. In this way, we can hide serial port–specific details under the standard C functions. We can use `printf` to send output to a serial port and get input from a serial port using `scanf`.

7
Exception Handling and Timer

We now have a standard programming environment with a C runtime library. This is a good start on our way to build a complete system. Now let's explore bare metal programming in more detail and move toward embedded system programming. Before we try to build a system, including the bootloader, Linux kernel, and file system, however, we should examine the goldfish hardware more closely. We will explore exception handling in this chapter and NAND flash memory in next chapter. This information will help us build a solid foundation before we tackle the task of U-Boot porting.

The goldfish platform provides a unique way to handle interrupts and exceptions. This chapter first provides an overview of the goldfish interrupt controller. Next, we take a close look at goldfish platform exception handling through three examples. The first example is a simple interrupt handler that we use to explore the goldfish interrupt controller and interrupt support of serial ports and timers in the goldfish platform. The second example, which is a little more complicated, introduces nested interrupts handling. In this example, we investigate processor mode switches, nested interrupts, and system calls.

In the third example, we explore a special interrupt in the goldfish platform—the timer. Based on the timer interrupt, we implement a real-time clock (RTC) for the goldfish platform. Both the timer and the RTC are very important modules that we have to support when we work on U-Boot. The code in the third example, then, is used to demonstrate the functionalities of the timer and RTC.

Many other books and resources discuss exception handling on the ARM platform, so we won't spend too much time on the general exception handling concepts such as ARM processor mode, exception priorities, and interrupt handling schemes. If you want more information on general exception handling on the ARM platform, *ARM System Developer's Guide* by Morgan Kaufmann is a good starting point.

Goldfish Interrupt Controller

Before we look at example code, let's look at the goldfish interrupt controller. There is no documentation available for the goldfish interrupt controller, but we can refer to the goldfish kernel source code in Examples 7.1 and 7.2.

Chapter 7 Exception Handling and Timer

Example 7.1 Hardware Interfaces in Goldfish Kernel (arch/arm/mach-goldfish/include/mach/hardware.h)

```
#ifndef __ASM_ARCH_HARDWARE_H
#define __ASM_ARCH_HARDWARE_H

#include <asm/sizes.h>

/*
 * The base address of goldfish devices. This file is copied from the goldfish kernel.
 * It defines only part of goldfish devices.
 */
#define IO_BASE           0xfe000000        /* Base address when MMU is on. */
#define IO_SIZE           0x00800000        /* Size of IO space. */
#define IO_START          0xff000000        /* Base address when MMU is off,
                                               which is the same as physical address. */

#define GOLDFISH_INTERRUPT_BASE            (0x0)
#define GOLDFISH_INTERRUPT_STATUS          (0x00) /* Number of pending interrupts. */
#define GOLDFISH_INTERRUPT_NUMBER          (0x04)
#define GOLDFISH_INTERRUPT_DISABLE_ALL     (0x08)
#define GOLDFISH_INTERRUPT_DISABLE         (0x0c)
#define GOLDFISH_INTERRUPT_ENABLE          (0x10)

#define GOLDFISH_PDEV_BUS_BASE             (0x1000)
#define GOLDFISH_PDEV_BUS_END              (0x100)

#define GOLDFISH_TTY_BASE                  (0x2000)
#define GOLDFISH_TIMER_BASE                (0x3000)

#define IO_ADDRESS(x)                      ((x) + IO_BASE)
#endif
```

Example 7.2 Interrupts in Goldfish Kernel (arch/arm/mach-goldfish/include/mach/irqs.h)

```
#ifndef __ASM_ARCH_IRQS_H
#define __ASM_ARCH_IRQS_H

#define IRQ_PDEV_BUS      (1)
#define IRQ_TIMER         (3)

#define NR_IRQS           (256)

#endif
```

From these two files, we can see that the registers of the goldfish interrupt controller start at address 0xff000000 (IO_START + GOLDFISH_INTERRUPT_BASE). They consist of five 32-bit registers:

- GOLDFISH_INTERRUPT_STATUS at offset 0x0 contains the number of pending interrupts. It is a read-only register.
- GOLDFISH_INTERRUPT_NUMBER at offset 0x4 contains the lowest pending, enabled interrupt number. It is a read-only register.
- GOLDFISH_INTERRUPT_DISABLE_ALL at offset 0x8 is a write-only register. It can be used to disable all interrupts.
- GOLDFISH_INTERRUPT_DISABLE at offset 0xC is a write-only register. Writing an interrupt number to it will disable the specified interrupt.
- GOLDFISH_INTERRUPT_ENABLE at offset 0x10 is a write-only register. Writing an interrupt number to it will enable the specified interrupt.

In irqs.h, only two interrupts (IRQ_PDEV_BUS and IRQ_TIMER) are defined. There are, however, actually a number of interrupts used by the Android emulator. We can find the rest of them by reviewing the kernel debug log:

```
goldfish_new_pdev goldfish_interrupt_controller at ff000000 irq -1
goldfish_new_pdev goldfish_device_bus at ff001000 irq 1
goldfish_new_pdev goldfish_timer at ff003000 irq 3
goldfish_new_pdev goldfish_rtc at ff010000 irq 10
goldfish_new_pdev goldfish_tty at ff002000 irq 4
goldfish_new_pdev goldfish_tty at ff011000 irq 11
goldfish_new_pdev goldfish_tty at ff012000 irq 12
goldfish_new_pdev smc91x at ff013000 irq 13
goldfish_new_pdev goldfish_fb at ff014000 irq 14
goldfish_new_pdev goldfish_audio at ff004000 irq 15
goldfish_new_pdev goldfish_mmc at ff005000 irq 16
goldfish_new_pdev goldfish_memlog at ff006000 irq -1
goldfish_new_pdev goldfish-battery at ff015000 irq 17
goldfish_new_pdev goldfish_events at ff016000 irq 18
goldfish_new_pdev goldfish_nand at ff017000 irq -1
goldfish_new_pdev qemu_pipe at ff018000 irq 19
goldfish_new_pdev goldfish-switch at ff01a000 irq 20
goldfish_new_pdev goldfish-switch at ff01b000 irq 21
goldfish_pdev_worker registered goldfish_interrupt_controller
goldfish_pdev_worker registered goldfish_device_bus
goldfish_pdev_worker registered goldfish_timer
```

```
goldfish_pdev_worker registered goldfish_rtc
goldfish_pdev_worker registered goldfish_tty
goldfish_pdev_worker registered goldfish_tty
goldfish_pdev_worker registered goldfish_tty
goldfish_pdev_worker registered smc91x
goldfish_pdev_worker registered goldfish_fb
goldfish_pdev_worker registered goldfish_audio
goldfish_pdev_worker registered goldfish_mmc
goldfish_pdev_worker registered goldfish_memlog
goldfish_pdev_worker registered goldfish-battery
goldfish_pdev_worker registered goldfish_events
goldfish_pdev_worker registered goldfish_nand
goldfish_pdev_worker registered qemu_pipe
goldfish_pdev_worker registered goldfish-switch
goldfish_pdev_worker registered goldfish-switch
```

The Simplest Interrupt Handler

We create a simple test driver and reusable code in this section to demonstrate the usage of the goldfish interrupt controller. The simplest interrupt handler, the goldfish interrupt controller is used to handle serial port and timer interrupts.

As in other chapters, the files in this chapter are divided into common and project-specific files. Here is a list of the files for the first code example:

Common files:

- `bsp.c`: Includes the API functions for the goldfish interrupt controller.
- `timer.c`: Includes the API functions for the goldfish timer.
- `syscalls_cs3.c`: The implementation of the system service stubs. It is the same as the file in Chapter 6.
- `serial_goldfish.c`: The C code to implement serial port functions. It is the same as the file in Chapter 5.
- `goldfish_uart.S`: The assembly language code to implement serial port–specific functions. It is the same as the file in Chapter 5.

Project-specific files:

- `c07e1.c`: The test code that implements the `main()` function
- `Makefile`: The makefile to build this project
- `c07e1.ld`: The linker script of the project
- `startup_c07e1.S`: The startup code that performs the necessary setup before control is transferred to the C code

For the common files, we implemented serial port–related functions (`serial_goldfish.c` and `goldfish_uart.S`) in Chapter 5. We implemented system service stubs (`syscalls_cs3.c`) in Chapter 6. In this chapter, we implement interrupt controller support functions in `bsp.c` and timer support functions in `timer.c`.

Interrupt Support Functions

The implementation of the interrupt controller support functions is very straightforward, as shown in Example 7.3. We basically provide a wrapper (set/get) function to each of the interrupt controller registers identified in Example 7.1.

Example 7.3 Interrupt Handler (drivers/bsp.c)

```c
#include <hardware.h>           /* Defined all hardware registers used */
#include <timer.h>
#include <bsp.h>                             /* Board Support Package */
#include <isr.h>                 /* Interface to the ISRs (foreground) */

/*
 * Refer to goldfish kernel source at
 * arch/arm/mach-goldfish/board-goldfish.c
 */

/*
 * GOLDFISH_INTERRUPT_DISABLE at offset 0xC is a write-only register.
 * Writing an interrupt number to it will disable the specified interrupt.
 * */
void goldfish_mask_irq(unsigned int irq)
{
    writel(irq, (void *)IO_ADDRESS(GOLDFISH_INTERRUPT_BASE) + GOLDFISH_INTERRUPT_DISABLE);
}

/*
 * GOLDFISH_INTERRUPT_ENABLE at offset 0x10 is a write-only register.
 * Writing an interrupt number to it will enable the specified interrupt.
 * */
void goldfish_unmask_irq(unsigned int irq)
{
    writel(irq, (void *)IO_ADDRESS(GOLDFISH_INTERRUPT_BASE) + GOLDFISH_INTERRUPT_ENABLE);
}
```

Chapter 7 Exception Handling and Timer

```c
/*
 * GOLDFISH_INTERRUPT_DISABLE_ALL at offset 0x8 is a write-only register.
 * Writing any value other than 0 to it will disable all interrupts.
 * */
void goldfish_disable_all_irq(void)
{
    writel(1, (void *)IO_ADDRESS(GOLDFISH_INTERRUPT_BASE) + GOLDFISH_INTERRUPT_DISABLE_ALL);
}

/*
 * GOLDFISH_INTERRUPT_NUMBER at offset 0x4 contains the lowest pending,
 * enabled interrupt number. It is a read-only register.
 * */
int goldfish_get_irq_num(void)
{
    return readl((void *)IO_ADDRESS(GOLDFISH_INTERRUPT_BASE) + GOLDFISH_INTERRUPT_NUMBER);
}

/*
 * GOLDFISH_INTERRUPT_STATUS at offset 0x0 contains the number of pending interrupts.
 * It is a read-only register.
 * */
int goldfish_irq_status(void)
{
    return readl((void *)IO_ADDRESS(GOLDFISH_INTERRUPT_BASE) + GOLDFISH_INTERRUPT_STATUS);
}

void BSP_init(void) {
    uint32_t int_base = IO_START + GOLDFISH_INTERRUPT_BASE;

    /* Hook the exception handlers */
    *(uint32_t volatile *)0x24 = (uint32_t)&ARM_undef;
    *(uint32_t volatile *)0x28 = (uint32_t)&ARM_swi;
    *(uint32_t volatile *)0x2C = (uint32_t)&ARM_pAbort;
```

```
    *(uint32_t volatile *)0x30 = (uint32_t)&ARM_dAbort;
    *(uint32_t volatile *)0x34 = (uint32_t)&ARM_reserved;
    *(uint32_t volatile *)0x38 = (uint32_t)&ARM_irq;
    *(uint32_t volatile *)0x3C = (uint32_t)&ARM_fiq;

    /* Configure goldfish interrupt controller */
    writel(1, (void *)int_base + GOLDFISH_INTERRUPT_DISABLE_ALL);

    /* ARM_INT_UNLOCK(0x1F);            Unlock IRQ/FIQ at the ARM core level */
}

void BSP_abort(char const *msg) {
    /* This function is called when an exception occurs.
     * For production code you need to log the message and go to fail-safe
     * state. You might also want to reset the CPU.
     */
    printf("=>BSP_about.\n");
    for (;;) {
    }
}
```

These functions can be used to enable and disable interrupts, or to get the interrupt status.

The function goldfish_mask_irq() is used to disable interrupts. It writes the interrupt number to the register GOLDFISH_INTERRUPT_DISABLE:

void goldfish_mask_irq(unsigned int irq)

The function goldfish_unmask_irq() is used to enable interrupts. It writes the interrupt number to the register GOLDFISH_INTERRUPT_ENABLE:

void goldfish_unmask_irq(unsigned int irq)

The function goldfish_disable_all_irq() is used to disable all interrupts. It sets the register GOLDFISH_INTERRUPT_DISABLE_ALL:

void goldfish_disable_all_irq(void)

The function goldfish_get_irq_num() returns the current pending interrupt number. This interrupt needs to be handled by the interrupt service routine (ISR). It gets the number from register GOLDFISH_INTERRUPT_NUMBER:

int goldfish_get_irq_num(void)

The function `goldfish_irq_status()` returns the number of current pending interrupts. This is the number of interrupts in the queue to be served. It gets the number from register GOLDFISH_INTERRUPT_STATUS:

int goldfish_irq_status(void)

The timer-related functions are implemented later in the chapter, in Example 7.10.

Implementation of the Simplest Interrupt Handler

Once we have these interrupt and timer support functions, we can work on example code to test the interrupt controller, serial port, and timer. As in all previous examples, we need startup code to initialize the hardware and switch to the C language environment. Example 7.4 is the startup code for this project.

Example 7.4 Startup Code for the Simplest Interrupt Handler (c07/c07e1/startup_c07e1.S)

```
    .text
    .code 32

    .global __cs3_reset
    .global vectors_start
    .global vectors_end

/* Vector table */
vectors_start:
    LDR PC, reset_handler_addr
    LDR PC, undef_handler_addr
    LDR PC, swi_handler_addr
    LDR PC, prefetch_abort_handler_addr
    LDR PC, data_abort_handler_addr
    B .
    LDR PC, irq_handler_addr
    LDR PC, fiq_handler_addr

reset_handler_addr: .word __cs3_reset
undef_handler_addr: .word ARM_undef
swi_handler_addr: .word ARM_swi
prefetch_abort_handler_addr: .word ARM_pAbort
data_abort_handler_addr: .word ARM_dAbort
irq_handler_addr: .word ARM_irq
```

The Simplest Interrupt Handler

```
fiq_handler_addr: .word ARM_fiq

vectors_end:

__cs3_reset:
    /* set Supervisor stack */
    LDR     r0,=__cs3_reset         /* Pass the reset address as the 1st argument */
    LDR     r1,=__cs3_start_asm     /* Pass the return address as the 2nd argument */
    MOV     lr,r1                   /* Set the return address after the remap */
    LDR sp, =__cs3_stack
    /* Copy vector table */
    LDR     r0,=0
    LDR     r1,=vectors_start
    LDR     r2,=vectors_end
1:
    CMP     r1,r2
    LDMLTIA r1!,{r3}
    STMLTIA r0!,{r3}
    BLT     1b

    /* Get program status register */
    MRS r0, cpsr
    /* Go in IRQ mode */
    BIC r1, r0, #0x1F
    ORR r1, r1, #0x12
    MSR cpsr, r1
    /* Set IRQ stack */
    LDR sp, =__irq_stack_top__
    /* Enable IRQs */
    BIC r0, r0, #0x80
    /* Go back in Supervisor mode */
    MSR cpsr, r0

    /* You can add peripherals and memory initialization here on a physical board */
    LDR r0, =__cs3_start_asm
    BX  r0
```

```
__cs3_start_asm:
    /* Call CS3 C startup function __cs3_start_c and transfer to C code */
    LDR  r0, =__cs3_start_c
    BX   r0
    .end
```

As in Chapter 6, we use CS3 startup code. However, for this example we added a stack setup for both Supervisor mode and interrupt request mode. The symbols __cs3_stack and __irq_stack_top__ are the stack bases for Supervisor mode and interrupt request mode, respectively. Since we will handle interrupts on our own, we also need to copy the vector table (vectors_start/vectors_end) to the memory address zero to initialize all exception vectors. Once we have done the initialization in the startup code, we call the CS3 function __cs3_start_c to transfer control to the function main().

Now, let's take a look at our test code for this interrupt handler, shown in Example 7.5.

Example 7.5 Test Code for the Simplest Interrupt Handler (c07/c07e1/c07e1.c)

```c
#include <stdio.h>
#include <stdlib.h>
#include <sys/unistd.h>
#include <hardware.h>
#include <bsp.h>

static int ch = 0;

void __attribute__((interrupt)) ARM_irq(void) {
    int irq = 0, num = 0;
    unsigned long tm = 0;

    irq = goldfish_get_irq_num();
    num = goldfish_irq_status();
    printf("=>Enter ARM_irq(%d), pending num=%d\n", irq, num);

    switch (irq) {
    case IRQ_TTY0:
        printf("=>IRQ_TTY0.\n");
        break;
    case IRQ_TTY1:
        printf("=>IRQ_TTY1.\n");
```

```c
            break;
        case IRQ_TTY2:
            ch = getchar();
            printf("=>IRQ_TTY2. ch=%c\n", ch);

            if(ch == 't') {
                /* Unit test 4: set timer to trigger timer interrupt. */
                goldfish_set_timer(0);
            }
            break;
        case IRQ_TIMER:
            /* We can clear either interrupt or alarm here.
               goldfish_clear_timer_int();
               printf("IRQ_TIMER - clear interrupt.\n");
            */
            goldfish_clear_alarm();
            printf("=>IRQ_TIMER - clear alarm.\n");
            break;
        default:
            printf("=>Unknown IRQ %x.\n", irq);
            break;
    }
    tm = goldfish_timer_read();
    printf("=>Exit ARM_irq(%d). tm=%lu\n", irq, tm);
}

/* All other handlers are infinite loops. */
void __attribute__((interrupt)) ARM_undef(void) {
    printf("Enter ARM_undef() ...\n");
    for(;;);
}

void __attribute__((interrupt)) ARM_swi(void) {
    printf("Enter ARM_swi() ...\n");
}
```

```c
void __attribute__((interrupt)) ARM_pAbort(void) {
    printf("Enter ARM_pAbort() ...\n");
    for(;;);
}

void __attribute__((interrupt)) ARM_dAbort(void) {
    printf("Enter ARM_dAbort() ...\n");
    for(;;);
}

void __attribute__((interrupt)) ARM_reserved(void) {
    printf("Enter ARM_reserved() ...\n");
    for(;;);
}

void __attribute__((interrupt)) ARM_fiq(void) {
    printf("Enter ARM_fiq() ...\n");
    for(;;);
}

/* We will run the unit test of the serial driver in main(). */
int main(int argc, char *argv[])
{
    unsigned long int tm = 0;

    printf("Enter main() ...\n");

    goldfish_unmask_irq(IRQ_TIMER);
    goldfish_unmask_irq(IRQ_TTY2);

    /* We do nothing in main(). */
    for(;;) {
        if(ch != 0) {
            /* Unit test 1: print out serial input and timestamp. */
            printf("1. Command is %c. time=(%lu).\n", ch, tm);

            if(ch == 'd') {
                /* Unit test 2: disable timer interrupt. */
                goldfish_mask_irq(IRQ_TIMER);
```

```
                printf("  - Disabled timer.\n");
            }

            if(ch == 'e') {
                /* Unit test 3: enable timer interrupt. */
                goldfish_unmask_irq(IRQ_TIMER);
                printf("  - Enabled timer.\n");
            }

            ch = 0;
            tm = goldfish_timer_read();
            printf("2. ----- End loop (%lu) -----\n", tm);
        }
        else {
            tm = goldfish_timer_read();
        }
    }
    return 1;
}
```

As we can see in Example 7.5, the functions `ARM_irq`, `ARM_undef`, `ARM_swi`, `ARM_pAbort`, `ARM_dAbort`, `ARM_reserved`, and `ARM_fiq` are registered exception handlers. Other than `ARM_irq`, all of them run in an infinite loop. You might notice that all of the exception handlers are defined using the GCC attribute `__attribute__((interrupt))`. This attribute is used to indicate that the specified function is an interrupt handler. The compiler will generate function entry and exit sequences suitable for use in an interrupt handler when this attribute is present.

There are four unit test cases in this example. In the first test case, the input from the serial console is captured by the interrupt handler and printed on the console, allowing us to confirm that serial input and output work properly. We handled serial input/output in earlier chapters, but, in this example, we capture the serial input in the interrupt handler `ARM_irq`. In the second and third test cases, we try to disable and enable the timer interrupt through the interrupt controller. In the fourth test case, we set an alarm using the timer interrupt. This alarm is set in the interrupt service routine `ARM_irq()` instead of in `main()` because we want to test the nested interrupts. Specifically, we want to show that nested interrupts cannot work in a simple interrupt handler. We will learn how to handle nested interrupts later in this chapter (example c07e2).

Let's build the project:

```
$ make DEBUG=1
   CC    c07e1.c
```

```
AS    startup_c07e1.S
CC    ../../drivers/serial_goldfish.c
AS    ../../drivers/goldfish_uart.S
CC    ../../drivers/syscalls_cs3.c
CC    ../../drivers/bsp.c
CC    ../../drivers/timer.c
LD    gcc/c07e1.axf
```

As usual, we can run the example binary in the Android emulator using the following command:

```
$ make debug
```

Next, we connect to the target, which is a gdbserver in QEMU, from ddd. When the program starts, it generates the message "Enter main() ..." and waits on the serial console for input. Three special input characters are used for different test cases. Table 7.1 describes the usage of these commands: t, d, and e.

Before we test the t, d, and e commands, let's test a random input first, as shown in Figure 7.1. After a serial input (the character a) is captured, we display the debug message on the console. The debug message printed from the interrupt handler starts with =>. In Figure 7.1, we can see that ARM_irq() is called after we key in the character a on the console.

Next, we set and trigger an alarm using the command t. As shown in Figure 7.2, if the input is t, a timer is set within the interrupt handler before it exits from the serial port interrupt handler. Because the alarm is set within the serial port interrupt handler, the timer interrupt is actually triggered inside the serial port interrupt handler. However, because ARM_irq() is a non-nested interrupt handler, the timer interrupt can be served only until the serial interrupt exits. We can also confirm this behavior by examining the timestamp in the debug message. After the timer interrupt is handled, we need to clear the timer interrupt by calling either goldfish_clear_timer_int() or goldfish_clear_alarm().

Table 7.1 Commands Used in the Interrupt Handler Example (c07e1)

Command	Description
t	Set the alarm. This will trigger a timer interrupt.
d	Disable timer interrupt.
e	Enable timer interrupt.

```
emulator: Trace file name is not set

goldfish_add_device: qemu_pipe, base ff017000 2000, irq 18 1
goldfish_add_device: goldfish-switch, base ff019000 1000, irq 19 1
goldfish_add_device: goldfish-switch, base ff01a000 1000, irq 20 1
emulator: autoconfig: -scale 1
emulator: Could not open file: (null)/system/build.prop: No such file or directo
ry
emulator: control console listening on port 5554, ADB on port 5555
emulator: can't connect to ADB server: Connection refused
emulator: ping program: /media/u32/home/sgye/src/Android/android-emulator-201309
28/qemu/objs/ddms
Warning: XmStringGetNextComponent: unknown type 170558216

Warning: XmStringGetNextComponent: unknown type 171109784

goldfish_init(), gtty.base=ff012000
Enter main()
=>Enter ARM_irq(12), pending num=1
=>IRQ_TTY2. ch=a
=>Exit ARM_irq(12). tm=610147903
1. Command is a. time=(609296102).
2. ----- End loop (610687652) -----
```

Figure 7.1 Testing serial input/output

```
emulator: control console listening on port 5554, ADB on port 5555
emulator: can't connect to ADB server: Connection refused
emulator: ping program: /media/u32/home/sgye/src/Android/android-emulator-201309
28/qemu/objs/ddms
Warning: XmStringGetNextComponent: unknown type 170558216

Warning: XmStringGetNextComponent: unknown type 171109784

goldfish_init(), gtty.base=ff012000
Enter main()
=>Enter ARM_irq(12), pending num=1
=>IRQ_TTY2. ch=a
=>Exit ARM_irq(12). tm=610147903
1. Command is a. time=(609296102).
2. ----- End loop (610687652) -----
=>Enter ARM_irq(12), pending num=1
=>IRQ_TTY2. ch=t
=>Exit ARM_irq(12). tm=478030470
=>Enter ARM_irq(3), pending num=1
=>IRQ_TIMER - clear alarm.
=>Exit ARM_irq(3). tm=478548818
1. Command is t. time=(477593759).
2. ----- End loop (478923441) -----
```

Figure 7.2 Testing the alarm

```
=>IRQ_TTY2. ch=a
=>Exit ARM_irq(12). tm=610147903
1. Command is a. time=(609296102).
2. ----- End loop (610687652) -----
=>Enter ARM_irq(12), pending num=1
=>IRQ_TTY2. ch=t
=>Exit ARM_irq(12). tm=478030470
=>Enter ARM_irq(3), pending num=1
=>IRQ_TIMER - clear alarm.
=>Exit ARM_irq(3). tm=478548818
1. Command is t. time=(477593759).
2. ----- End loop (478923441) -----
=>Enter ARM_irq(12), pending num=1
=>IRQ_TTY2. ch=d
=>Exit ARM_irq(12). tm=1645742659
1. Command is d. time=(1645243906).
  - Disabled timer.
2. ----- End loop (1646899167) -----
=>Enter ARM_irq(12), pending num=1
=>IRQ_TTY2. ch=t
=>Exit ARM_irq(12). tm=45935467
1. Command is t. time=(45546911).
2. ----- End loop (46391444) -----
```

Figure 7.3 Disabling the timer interrupt

Finally, let's test the disabling and enabling of the timer interrupt. As shown in Figure 7.3, we can disable the timer interrupt by first giving the command d. Then, we set an alarm using the command t. Now only the serial interrupt is served; the timer interrupt is disabled.

Next, let's re-enable the timer interrupt using the command e. As shown in Figure 7.4, the timer interrupt is triggered immediately after it is enabled. This occurs because an alarm was set when we disabled the timer interrupt in Figure 7.3.

Nested Interrupt Handler

In our simple interrupt handler example, interrupts could be handled only in a sequential fashion. In a real system, however, interrupt handling is much more complicated. To explore this topic a little further and learn more about goldfish's interrupt handling, let's look at another, more complicated interrupt handler example (c07e2). In this example, we create a nested interrupt handler. The example consists of the following files:

Common files:

- bsp.c: Includes the API functions for the goldfish interrupt controller. It is the same as the code for the previous example.
- timer.c: Includes the API functions for the goldfish timer. It is the same as the code for the previous example.

```
=>Exit ARM_irq(3). tm=478548818
1. Command is t. time=(477593759).
2. ----- End loop (478923441) -----
=>Enter ARM_irq(12), pending num=1
=>IRQ_TTY2. ch=d
=>Exit ARM_irq(12). tm=1645742659
1. Command is d. time=(1645243906).
  - Disabled timer.
2. ----- End loop (1646899167) -----
=>Enter ARM_irq(12), pending num=1
=>IRQ_TTY2. ch=t
=>Exit ARM_irq(12). tm=45935467
1. Command is t. time=(45546911).
2. ----- End loop (46391444) -----
=>Enter ARM_irq(12), pending num=1
=>IRQ_TTY2. ch=e
=>Exit ARM_irq(12). tm=1588835732
1. Command is e. time=(1588373998).
=>Enter ARM_irq(3), pending num=1
=>IRQ_TIMER - clear alarm.
=>Exit ARM_irq(3). tm=1590040892
  - Enabled timer.
2. ----- End loop (1590425819) -----
```

Figure 7.4 Enabling the timer interrupt

- `syscalls_cs3.c`: The implementation of system service stubs. It is the same as the code in Chapter 6.
- `serial_goldfish.c`: The C code to implement serial functions. It is the same as the code in Chapter 5.
- `goldfish_uart.S`: The assembly language code to implement serial port–specific functions. It is the same as the code in Chapter 5.
- `arm_exc.S`: In this file, exception vectors are implemented in assembly language code.
- `isr.c`: In this file, a C-level interrupt service routine (ISR) is implemented.
- `low_level_init.c`: Implements a function `low_level_init()`, which performs early initialization of the hardware. Exception vectors are initialized in `low_level_init()`.

Project-specific files:

- `c07e2.c`: The test code to implement the `main()` function
- `Makefile`: The makefile to build this project
- `c07e2.ld`: The linker script of the project
- `startup_c07e2.S`: The startup code that performs the necessary setup before control is transferred to the C code

Implementation of the Nested Interrupt Handler

To enable interrupt nesting, the handler must at some point unlock the interrupts, which are automatically locked at the ARM core level upon the IRQ/FIQ entry. Generally, all documented strategies for handling nested interrupts in the ARM architecture involve switching the mode away from IRQ (or FIQ) and to the mode used by the task-level code before enabling interrupts. The standard techniques also use multiple stacks during interrupt handling. The IRQ/FIQ mode stack is used for saving a part of the interrupt context, and the System/User stack (or sometimes the SVC stack) is used for saving the rest of the context. ARM recommends using System mode while programming reentrant interrupt handlers.

The interrupt handling strategy for the ARM system in this example also switches away from IRQ/FIQ mode and to System mode before enabling interrupt nesting, but differs from the other schemes in that all of the CPU context is saved to the System/User stack—that is, the IRQ/FIQ stacks are not used at all. Saving the context to the separate interrupt stack has value only in multitasking kernels that employ a separate stack for each task. Using multiple stacks in a simple foreground/background architecture with only one background task (the main() loop) does not provide any advantages, but rather simply adds complexity. This approach was proposed by Miro Samek in his article "Building Bare-Metal ARM Systems with GNU" (*http://www.state-machine.com/arm/Building_bare-metal_ARM_with_GNU.pdf*).

Three common files are added in this example: low_level_init.c, arm_exc.S, and isr.c. In the assembly file shown in Example 7.6, all ARM exception handlers are implemented. Pay special attention to ARM_irq(): It is a wrapper of the interrupt service routine (ISR) in assembly language. In this function, the context is saved before the processor mode is switched to System mode. The interrupt is served in the C-level function BSP_irq(). After that, the context is restored and the control returns to the point where the interrupt was triggered.

Example 7.6 Implementation of Exception Handlers (c07/c07e2/arm_exc.S)

```
    .equ    NO_IRQ,     0x80                    /* mask to disable IRQ */
    .equ    NO_FIQ,     0x40                    /* mask to disable FIQ */
    .equ    NO_INT,     (NO_IRQ | NO_FIQ)  /* mask to disable IRQ and FIQ */
    .equ    FIQ_MODE,   0x11
    .equ    IRQ_MODE,   0x12
    .equ    SYS_MODE,   0x1F

    .text
    .code 32

/*
 * Use the special section (.text.fastcode) to fine-tune
 * the placement of this section inside the linker script
```

```
    */
        .section .text.fastcode

/*****************************************************************************
* uint32_t ARM_int_lock_SYS(void);
*/
        .global ARM_int_lock_SYS
        .func   ARM_int_lock_SYS
ARM_int_lock_SYS:
    MRS     r0, cpsr                        /* get the original CPSR in r0 to return */
    MSR     cpsr_c,#(SYS_MODE | NO_INT)     /* disable both IRQ and FIQ */
    BX      lr                              /* return the original CPSR in r0 */

        .size   ARM_int_lock_SYS, . - ARM_int_lock_SYS
        .endfunc


/*****************************************************************************
* void ARM_int_unlock_SYS(uint32_t key);
*/
        .global ARM_int_unlock_SYS
        .func   ARM_int_unlock_SYS
ARM_int_unlock_SYS:
    MSR     cpsr_c, r0                      /* restore the original CPSR from r0 */
    BX      lr                              /* return to ARM or THUMB */

        .size   ARM_int_unlock_SYS, . - ARM_int_unlock_SYS
        .endfunc


/*****************************************************************************
* void ARM_irq(void);
*/
        .global ARM_irq
        .func   ARM_irq
ARM_irq:
/* IRQ entry {{{ */
    MOV     r13,r0                          /* save r0 in r13_IRQ */
    SUB     r0,lr,#4                        /* put return address in r0_SYS */
```

Chapter 7 Exception Handling and Timer

```
        MOV     lr,r1                               /* save r1 in r14_IRQ (lr) */
        MRS     r1,spsr                             /* put the SPSR in r1_SYS */

        MSR     cpsr_c, #(SYS_MODE | NO_IRQ) /* System mode, no IRQ, but FIQ enabled! */
        STMFD   sp!,{r0,r1}                         /* save SPSR and PC on SYS stack */
        STMFD   sp!,{r2-r3,r12,lr}       /* save APCS-clobbered regs on SYS stack */
        MOV     r0, sp                     /* make sp_SYS visible to IRQ mode */
        SUB     sp, sp, #(2*4)             /* make room for stacking (r0_SYS, r1_SYS) */

        MSR     cpsr_c,#(IRQ_MODE | NO_IRQ)         /* IRQ mode, IRQ/FIQ disabled */
        STMFD   r0!,{r13,r14}         /* finish saving the context (r0_SYS,r1_SYS) */

        MSR     cpsr_c,#(SYS_MODE | NO_IRQ)         /* System mode, IRQ disabled */
/* IRQ entry }}} */

/* NOTE: BSP_irq might re-enable IRQ interrupts (FIQ is enabled
 * already), if IRQs are prioritized by an interrupt controller. In our case,
 * we use the goldfish interrupt controller.
 */
        LDR     r12, =BSP_irq
        MOV     lr, pc               /* copy the return address to link register */
        BX      r12                          /* call the C IRQ-handler BSP_irq() */


/* IRQ exit {{{ */
        MSR     cpsr_c,#(SYS_MODE | NO_INT)      /* System mode, IRQ/FIQ disabled */
        MOV     r0,sp                      /* make sp_SYS visible to IRQ mode */
        ADD     sp,sp,#(8*4)         /* fake unstacking 8 registers from sp_SYS */

        MSR     cpsr_c,#(IRQ_MODE | NO_INT)      /* IRQ mode, both IRQ/FIQ disabled */
        MOV     sp,r0                            /* copy sp_SYS to sp_IRQ */
        LDR     r0,[sp,#(7*4)]          /* load the saved SPSR from the stack */
        MSR     spsr_cxsf,r0                     /* copy it into spsr_IRQ */

        LDMFD   sp,{r0-r3,r12,lr}^    /* unstack all saved USER/SYSTEM registers */
        NOP                           /* can't access banked reg immediately */
        LDR     lr,[sp,#(6*4)]     /* load return address from the SYS stack */
        MOVS    pc,lr                   /* return restoring CPSR from SPSR */
/* IRQ exit }}} */
```

```
        .size   ARM_irq, . - ARM_irq
        .endfunc


/***************************************************************************
* void ARM_fiq(void);
*/
        .global ARM_fiq
        .func   ARM_fiq
ARM_fiq:
/* FIQ entry {{{ */
        MOV     r13, r0                         /* save r0 in r13_FIQ */
        SUB     r0, lr, #4                      /* put return address in r0_SYS */
        MOV     lr, r1                          /* save r1 in r14_FIQ (lr) */
        MRS     r1, spsr                        /* put SPSR in r1_SYS */

        MSR     cpsr_c, #(SYS_MODE | NO_INT)    /* System mode, IRQ/FIQ disabled */
        STMFD   sp!, {r0, r1}                   /* save SPSR and PC on SYS stack */
        STMFD   sp!, {r2-r3,r12,lr}             /* save APCS-clobbered regs on SYS stack */
        MOV     r0, sp                          /* make sp_SYS visible to FIQ mode */
        SUB     sp, sp, #(2*4)                  /* make room for stacking (r0_SYS, SPSR) */

        MSR     cpsr_c, #(FIQ_MODE | NO_INT)    /* FIQ mode, IRQ/FIQ disabled */
        STMFD   r0!, {r13, r14}                 /* finish saving the context (r0_SYS,r1_SYS) */

        MSR     cpsr_c, #(SYS_MODE | NO_INT)    /* System mode, IRQ/FIQ disabled */
/* FIQ entry }}} */

        /* NOTE: BSP_fiq must NEVER enable IRQ/FIQ interrrupts!
        */
        LDR     r12, =BSP_fiq
        MOV     lr, pc                          /* store the return address */
        BX      r12                             /* call the C FIQ-handler BSP_fiq() */


/* FIQ exit {{{ */                              /* both IRQ/FIQ disabled (see NOTE above) */
        MOV     r0, sp                          /* make sp_SYS visible to FIQ mode */
        ADD     sp, sp, #(8*4)                  /* fake unstacking 8 registers from sp_SYS */
```

```
        MSR     cpsr_c, #(FIQ_MODE | NO_INT)        /* FIQ mode, IRQ/FIQ disabled */
        MOV     sp, r0                              /* copy sp_SYS to sp_FIQ */
        LDR     r0, [sp, #(7*4)]            /* load the saved SPSR from the stack */
        MSR     spsr_cxsf, r0                       /* copy it into spsr_FIQ */

        LDMFD   sp, {r0-r3, r12, lr}^   /* unstack all saved USER/SYSTEM registers */
        NOP                                 /* can't access banked reg immediately */
        LDR     lr, [sp, #(6*4)]        /* load return address from the SYS stack */
        MOVS    pc, lr                       /* return restoring CPSR from SPSR */
/* FIQ exit }}} */

        .size   ARM_fiq, . - ARM_fiq
        .endfunc


/***************************************************************************
* void ARM_reset(void);
*/
        .global ARM_reset
        .func   ARM_reset
ARM_reset:
        LDR     r0,Csting_reset
        B       ARM_except
        .size   ARM_reset, . - ARM_reset
        .endfunc


/***************************************************************************
* void ARM_undef(void);
*/
        .global ARM_undef
        .func   ARM_undef
ARM_undef:
        LDR     r0,Csting_undef
        B       ARM_except
        .size   ARM_undef, . - ARM_undef
        .endfunc


/***************************************************************************
```

```
 * void ARM_swi(void);
 */
    .global ARM_swi
    .func   ARM_swi
ARM_swi:
    STMFD sp!, {r0-r12,lr}    /* Store registers. */
    LDR r0, [lr, #-4]         /* Calculate address of SWI instruction and load it into r0. */
    BIC r0, r0, #0xff000000   /* Mask off top 8 bits of instruction to give SWI number. */
    BL sw_handler             /* Call C SWI handler sw_handler() */
    LDMFD sp!, {r0-r12,pc}^   /* Restore registers and return */
    .size   ARM_swi, . - ARM_swi
    .endfunc

/****************************************************************************
 * void ARM_pAbort(void);
 */
    .global ARM_pAbort
    .func   ARM_pAbort
ARM_pAbort:
    LDR     r0,Csting_pAbort
    B       ARM_except
    .size   ARM_pAbort, . - ARM_pAbort
    .endfunc

/****************************************************************************
 * void ARM_dAbort(void);
 */
    .global ARM_dAbort
    .func   ARM_dAbort
ARM_dAbort:
    LDR     r0,Csting_dAbort
    B       ARM_except
    .size   ARM_dAbort, . - ARM_dAbort
    .endfunc

/****************************************************************************
```

148   Chapter 7   Exception Handling and Timer

```
 * void ARM_reserved(void);
 */
    .global ARM_reserved
    .func   ARM_reserved
ARM_reserved:
    LDR     r0,Csting_rsrvd
    B       ARM_except
    .size   ARM_reserved, . - ARM_reserved
    .endfunc

/***************************************************************************
 * void ARM_except(void);
 */
    .global ARM_except
    .func   ARM_except
ARM_except:
    SUB     r1, lr, #4              /* set line number to the exception address */
    MSR     cpsr_c, #(SYS_MODE | NO_INT)        /* System mode, IRQ/FIQ disabled */
    LDR     r12, =BSP_abort
    MOV     lr, pc                              /* store the return address */
    BX      r12                     /* call the assertion handler (ARM/THUMB) */
    /* The assertion handler should not return, but in case it does,
     * hang up the machine in the following endless loop
     */
    B       .

Csting_reset:   .string "Reset"
Csting_undef:   .string "Undefined"
Csting_swi:     .string "Software Int"
Csting_pAbort:  .string "Prefetch Abort"
Csting_dAbort:  .string "Data Abort"
Csting_rsrvd:   .string "Reserved Exception"

    .size   ARM_except, . - ARM_except
    .endfunc

    .end
```

Nested Interrupt Handler

BSP_irq() is implemented in Example 7.7. BSP_irq() is the entry point for the interrupt service routine. It blocks the interrupt source for the same interrupt in the goldfish interrupt controller by calling goldfish_mask_irq(). The same interrupt source won't be triggered again before the current interrupt is served. After that, it enables the interrupt to allow nested interrupts. The interrupts from other interrupt sources can be triggered now. The actual interrupt handling is carried out by irq_handler(), which is a project-specific implementation. After it does so, the interrupt source is enabled again but nested interrupts are disabled before the code returns to ARM_irq(). The nested interrupts can be present only inside irq_handler(). Another exception handler that we should notice is ARM_swi(); it is a simple software interrupt handler that we will test later.

Example 7.7 C-Level ISR (c07/c07e2/isr.c)

```
#include "hardware.h"
#include "timer.h"
#include "bsp.h"
#include "isr.h"
#include "serial_goldfish.h"

/*..................................................................*/
__attribute__ ((section (".text.fastcode")))
void BSP_irq(void) {
    int irq = 0;

    irq = goldfish_get_irq_num();

    goldfish_mask_irq(irq);     /* block the same IRQ before IRQ handler return */
    asm("MSR cpsr_c,#(0x1F)");                    /* allow nested interrupts */
    irq_handler(irq);          /* call the IRQ handler via the pointer to function */
    asm("MSR cpsr_c,#(0x1F | 0x80)");             /* lock IRQ before return */
    goldfish_unmask_irq(irq);   /* enable IRQ when IRQ handling is complete */
}

/*..................................................................*/
__attribute__ ((section (".text.fastcode")))
void BSP_fiq(void) {                                /* FIQ ISR */
    /* Handle the FIQ directly. No AIC vectoring overhead necessary. */
}
```

Now that we have the basic framework for nested interrupt handling in place, let's look at the example code that we use to demonstrate nested interrupt handling in the goldfish platform. The startup code shown in Example 7.8 is similar to the code in Example 7.4, albeit with the following differences:

- Even though a separate interrupt stack is not used for this example interrupt handler, there are still three stacks initialized for Supervisor mode, IRQ mode, and System/User mode.
- Two functions, `EnterUserMode()` and `SystemCall()`, are implemented in assembly language. `EnterUserMode()` changes the processor mode from System to User mode, and `SystemCall()` triggers a software interrupt.

Example 7.8 Startup Code for Nested Interrupt Handler (c07/c07e2/startup_c07e2.S)

```
    .text
    .code 32

/* Standard definitions of mode bits and interrupt (I & F) flags in PSRs */
    .equ    I_BIT,      0x80    /* when I bit is set, IRQ is disabled */
    .equ    F_BIT,      0x40    /* when F bit is set, FIQ is disabled */

    .equ    USR_MODE,   0x10
    .equ    FIQ_MODE,   0x11
    .equ    IRQ_MODE,   0x12
    .equ    SVC_MODE,   0x13
    .equ    ABT_MODE,   0x17
    .equ    UND_MODE,   0x1B
    .equ    SYS_MODE,   0x1F

    .global __cs3_reset

__cs3_reset:
    /* Set up stack so that we can call a simple C function. */
    LDR     r0, =__cs3_reset      /* pass the reset address as the 1st argument */
    LDR     r1, =__cs3_start_asm  /* pass the return address as the 2nd argument */
    MOV     lr, r1                /* set the return address after the remap */
    LDR sp, =__cs3_stack
/*
 * Copy vector table to address 0. We moved this to a C function low_level_init().
 */
    BL low_level_init
```

Nested Interrupt Handler   151

```
    MSR     CPSR_c, #(SVC_MODE | I_BIT | F_BIT)
    LDR     sp,=__svc_stack_top__           /* set the SVC stack pointer */

    /* Get program status register */
    MRS r0, cpsr
    /* Go in IRQ mode */
    BIC r1, r0, #0x1F
    ORR r1, r1, #0x12
    MSR cpsr, r1
    /* Set IRQ stack */
    LDR sp, =__irq_stack_top__
    /* Enable IRQs */
    BIC r0, r0, #0x80
    /* Go back in Supervisor mode */
    MSR cpsr, r0
    /* You can add peripherals and memory initialization here */
    MSR CPSR_c, #(SYS_MODE | I_BIT | F_BIT) /* change to SYS_MODE */
    LDR sp, =__cs3_stack            /* set the C stack pointer */
    LDR r0, =__cs3_start_asm        /* call CS3 assembly initialization */
    BX  r0

__cs3_start_asm:
    LDR r0, =__cs3_start_c          /* call CS3 C initialization */
    BX  r0


/*****************************************************************************
* void EnterUserMode(void);
* Switch to user mode using this function.
*/
    .global EnterUserMode
    .func   EnterUserMode
EnterUserMode:
    /* Get program status register */
    MRS r0, cpsr
    /* Change to User mode */
    BIC r1, r0, #0x1F
```

```
        ORR r1, r1, #0x10
        MSR cpsr, r1
        MOV pc, lr
        .endfunc

/**************************************************************************
* void SystemCall(void);
* Make a system call using this function.
*/
        .global SystemCall
        .func   SystemCall
SystemCall:
        SWI 0x8;
        MOV     pc, lr
        .endfunc

        .end
```

The test code in Example 7.9 is similar to the one in Example 7.5. Both serial and timer interrupts are handled in `irq_handler()`. The difference is that `ARM_irq()` in Example 7.5 runs in IRQ mode, whereas `irq_handler()` in Example 7.9 runs in System mode. The function `sw_handler()` is used to handle software interrupts.

Example 7.9 Test Code for Nested Interrupt Handler (c07/c07e2/c07e2.c)

```c
#include <stdio.h>
#include <stdlib.h>
#include <sys/unistd.h>
#include <hardware.h>
#include <arm_exc.h>
#include <bsp.h>

static int ch = 0;

void sw_handler(int num)
{
    printf("=>Inside sw_handler, num=%d.\n", num);
}
```

```c
void irq_handler(int irq)
{
    int num = 0;
    unsigned long tm = 0;

    num = goldfish_irq_status();
    printf("=>Enter ARM_irq(%d), pending num=%d\n", irq, num);

    switch (irq) {
    case IRQ_TTY0:
        printf("=>IRQ_TTY0.\n");
        break;
    case IRQ_TTY1:
        printf("=>IRQ_TTY1.\n");
        break;
    case IRQ_TTY2:
        ch = getchar();
        printf("=>IRQ_TTY2. ch=%c\n", ch);
        if(ch == 't') {
        /* Unit test 1: set timer to trigger timer interrupt. */
            goldfish_set_timer(0);
        }
        break;
    case IRQ_TIMER:
        /* goldfish_mask_irq(IRQ_TIMER); */
        goldfish_clear_timer_int();
        printf("=>IRQ_TIMER - clear interrupt.\n");
        break;
    default:
        printf("=>Unknown IRQ %x.\n", irq);
        break;
    }
    tm = goldfish_timer_read();
    printf("=>Exit ARM_irq(%d). tm=%lu\n", irq, tm);
}
```

Chapter 7 Exception Handling and Timer

```c
/* We will run the unit test of the serial driver in main() */
int main(int argc, char *argv[])
{
    unsigned long tm;
    int i = 0;

    printf("Enter main() ...\n");

    ARM_INT_UNLOCK(0x1F);           /* unlock IRQ/FIQ at the ARM core level */
    goldfish_unmask_irq(IRQ_TIMER);
    goldfish_unmask_irq(IRQ_TTY2);

    EnterUserMode();

    for(;;) {
        if(ch != 0) {
        printf("1. Command is %c. time=(%lu).\n", ch, tm);

            if(ch == 'd') {
                /* disable timer interrupt. */
                goldfish_mask_irq(IRQ_TIMER);
                printf("   - Disabled timer.\n");
            }

            if(ch == 'e') {
                /* disable timer interrupt. */
                goldfish_unmask_irq(IRQ_TIMER);
                printf("   - Enabled timer.\n");
            }

            if(ch == 's') {
                /* Unit test 2: Fire a system call. */
                SystemCall();
                printf("   - Make system call.\n");
            }

            ch = 0;
            tm = goldfish_timer_read();
            printf("2. ----- End loop (%lu) -----\n", tm);
        }
```

```
        else {
            tm = goldfish_timer_read();
        }
    }
    return 1;
}
```

Let's build the project first:

```
$ make DEBUG=1
    CC    c07e2.c
    AS    startup_c07e2.S
    CC    ../../drivers/serial_goldfish.c
    AS    ../../drivers/goldfish_uart.S
    CC    ../../drivers/syscalls_cs3.c
    CC    ../../drivers/low_level_init.c
    AS    ../../drivers/arm_exc.S
    CC    ../../drivers/bsp.c
    CC    ../../drivers/isr.c
    CC    ../../drivers/timer.c
    LD    gcc/c07e2.axf
```

Testing Nested Interrupts and Discovering the Processor Mode Switch

To check the stacks used in different processor modes, we can obtain the stack information using arm-none-eabi-nm as follows:

```
$ arm-none-eabi-nm -n gcc/c07e2.axf
...
000104c8 T __cs3_reset
...
00231950 B __irq_stack_top__
...
00232950 B __svc_stack_top__
...
00233950 B __cs3_stack
...
```

156   Chapter 7 Exception Handling and Timer

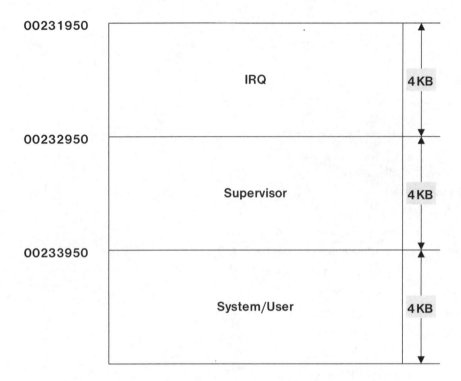

Figure 7.5 Stack structure in the nested interrupt handler

With this output from nm, we can check the three stack pointers shown in the stack structure in Figure 7.5. The stack pointer __cs3_stack located at 0x233950 is used in System mode. The stack pointer __svc_stack_top__ is used in Supervisor mode; its address is 0x232950. The stack pointer __irq_stack_top__, found at 0x231950, is set for IRQ mode, but is not actually used.

> **Note**
> The stack pointer addresses in your environment may not be the same as those mentioned in the text and shown in Figure 7.5. The actual address assignments will depend on your environment's setup.

The program status register and processor modes are used frequently in this example. The processor modes are listed in Table 7.2, and the program status register is shown in Figure 7.6.

Table 7.2 Processor Modes

M[4:0]	Mode
b10000	User
b10001	FIQ
b10010	IRQ
b10011	Supervisor
b10111	Abort
b11011	Undefined
b11111	System

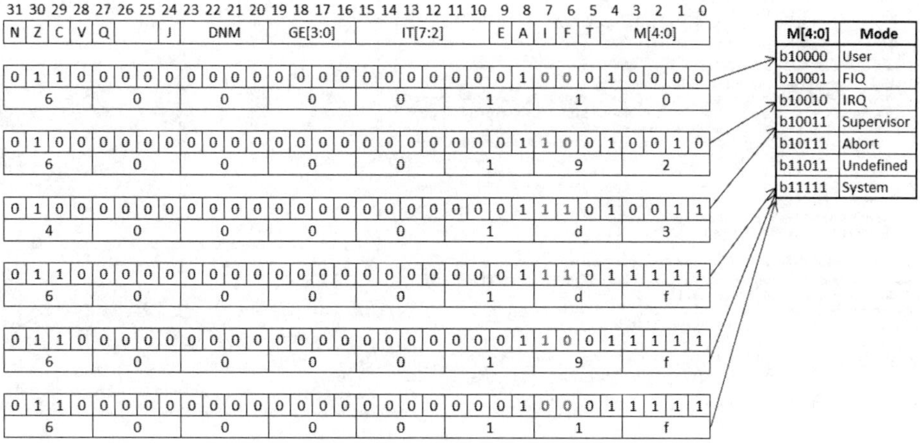

Figure 7.6 Program status register

Let's run this example using the following command:

```
$ make debug
```

As usual, we start the example in the Android emulator and connect to ddd to debug and check the virtual machine status. When powered up, the processor is in Supervisor mode and all registers are set to zero. Both fast interrupt and interrupts are disabled. Figure 7.7 shows the virtual machine status after startup. Refer to Table 7.2 and Figure 7.6 for the meaning of the program status register's value, 0x400001d3.

Chapter 7 Exception Handling and Timer

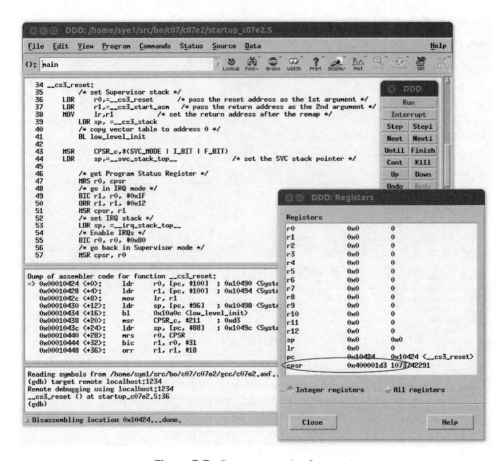

Figure 7.7 Processor mode after reset

Before we return the virtual machine to running status, let's set breakpoints at main(), ARM_irq(), BSP_irq(), irq_handler(), ARM_swi(), and sw_handler(). After we resume running the program, it will hit the first breakpoint at main(), as shown in Figure 7.8. If we look at the program status register value (cpsr) of 0x600001df, we'll see that the virtual machine is running in System mode and that both FIQ and IRQ are disabled.

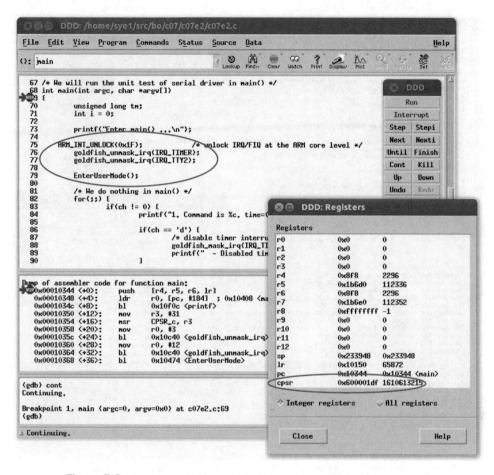

Figure 7.8 In main() before enabling interrupts and entering User mode

Continue running to line 83 as shown in Figure 7.9. Now both FIQ and IRQ are enabled. The virtual machine runs in User mode due to the function call EnterUserMode(). We can check the program status register value of 0x60000110 in Figure 7.9.

Now the console is ready to take input. As we did for the simple interrupt handler example, we type a character t on the console to set an alarm. Once there is input on

160 Chapter 7 Exception Handling and Timer

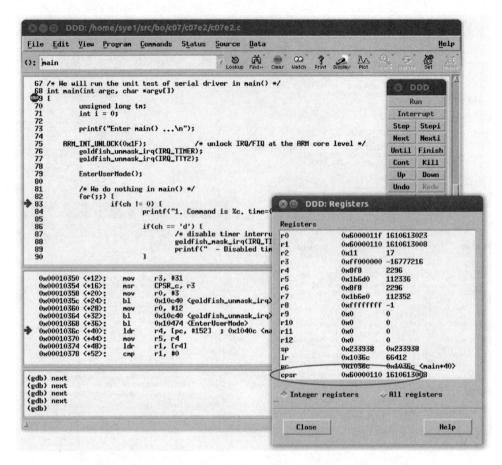

Figure 7.9 In main() with interrupt enabled and in User mode

the console, the serial port interrupt is triggered and we hit the breakpoint ARM_irq(), as shown in Figure 7.10. When we check the program status register value again, we see that we are in IRQ mode now. From the program status register value 0x60000192, we can see that FIQ is enabled and IRQ is disabled.

Let's continue to run the program and go to the next breakpoint, BSP_irq(). As shown in Figure 7.11, from the program status register value of 0x6000019f, we can see that the FIQ and IRQ status is not changed, but we are now running in

Figure 7.10 Breakpoint at ARM_irq()

System mode. Since IRQ is still disabled, the other interrupts cannot be handled at this point.

Let's continue to run the program and go to the next breakpoint, irq_handler(), as shown in Figure 7.12. From the program status register value of 0x6000011f, we can see that we are still in System mode and that IRQ is now enabled. At this stage, interrupts other than serial interrupts can be served, even though we are in the ISR; the ISR handles serial interrupts. Serial interrupts are still disabled in the goldfish interrupt controller, since we called goldfish_mask_irq(irq) in BSP_irq().

Chapter 7 Exception Handling and Timer

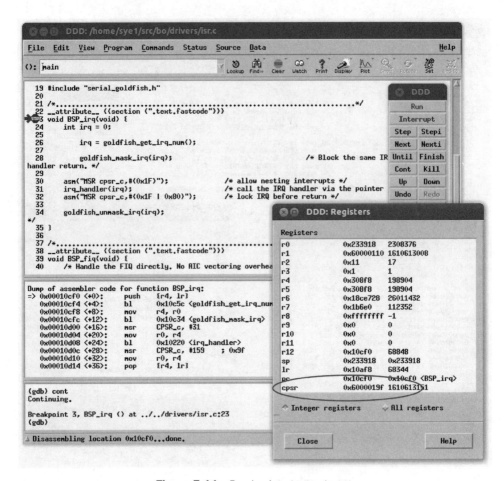

Figure 7.11 Breakpoint at `BSP_irq()`

To test the nested interrupt, we set an alarm inside `irq_handler()`, at the point that it is serving serial interrupts. If we let the program continue to run, we can see that the timer interrupt is served inside the serial interrupt as shown in Figure 7.13. From the timestamp, we can see that timer interrupt exits at time 699542179 while the serial interrupt exits at time 700226749.

Figure 7.12 Breakpoint at `irq_handler()`

Testing System Calls/Software Interrupts

Up to now, we have explored IRQ handling in the goldfish platform. We have tested both simple interrupt handling and nested interrupt handling. Let's take a look at the software interrupt that we added in this example.

Chapter 7 Exception Handling and Timer

```
goldfish_add_device: qemu_pipe, base ff017000 2000, irq 18 1
goldfish_add_device: goldfish-switch, base ff019000 1000, irq 19 1
goldfish_add_device: goldfish-switch, base ff01a000 1000, irq 20 1
emulator: autoconfig: -scale 1
emulator: Could not open file: (null)/system/build.prop: No such file or dire
ctory
emulator: control console listening on port 5554, ADB on port 5555
emulator: can't connect to ADB server: Connection refused
emulator: ping program: /media/u32/home/sgye/src/Android/android-emulator-201
30928/qemu/objs/ddms
goldfish_init(), gtty.base=ff012000
Enter main() ...
=>Enter ARM_irq(12), pending num=0
=>IRQ_TTY2. ch=t
=>Enter ARM_irq(3), pending num=0
=>IRQ_TIMER - clear interrupt.
=>Exit ARM_irq(3). tm=699542179
=>Exit ARM_irq(12). tm=700226749
1. Command is t. time=(696057721).
2. ----- End loop (702934744) -----
```

Figure 7.13 Nested serial and timer interrupts

When we have an operating system, the operating system services are usually implemented in a different processor mode. When an application requests an operating system service, we usually prefer to make a system call. Making a system call involves a processor mode switch—and the software interrupt is used to accomplish this switch. To identify the different system calls, we usually provide a number as the parameter for the software interrupt. This number is usually referred to system call number.

For our example, we'll test the system call using the function SystemCall(). This assembly language implementation uses the instruction SWI 0x8. Although the system call number is 8 in this case, it can actually be any number depending on the system call implementation. Because we didn't implement anything inside the system call, the 8 here is just a dummy number to demonstrate the usage of the software interrupt. After we type the character s in the console, the system call is fired, as shown in Figure 7.14. The SystemCall() function was implemented in Example 7.8. When it hits the instruction SWI 0x8, the software interrupt is triggered and control goes to ARM_swi(). In ARM_swi(), from the program status register's value of 0x60000193, we can see that the software interrupt is running in Supervisor mode. ARM_swi() calls a C-level routine, sw_handler(), to print out the message on the console.

Timer

We used a few timer-related functions in this chapter's first two examples, but we didn't take a close look at them. The hardware specification of the goldfish timer can be found in Chapter 2, where we introduced the various goldfish hardware specifications. There are

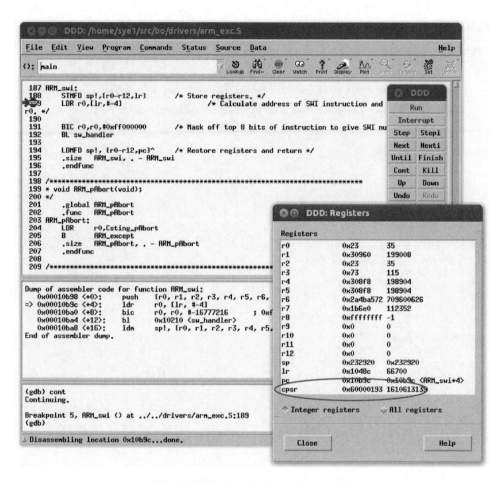

Figure 7.14 Breakpoint at ARM_swi()

a total of six 32-bit registers in the goldfish timer hardware. The combination of two 32-bit read-only registers, TIMER_TIME_LOW and TIMER_TIME_HIGH, provides a 64-bit counter. The value of this 64-bit counter is used as a system tick. The combination of another two 32-bit write-only registers, TIMER_ALARM_LOW and TIMER_ALARM_HIGH, is used to set the timestamp of the timer interrupt. When the system tick reaches this preset timestamp, a timer interrupt is triggered. In the timer interrupt handler, the write-only register TIMER_CLEAR_INTERRUPT or TIMER_CLEAR_ALARM can be used to clear the timer interrupt.

All timer support functions are implemented in Example 7.10. Notice the two kinds of functions in this example. The first group comprises the U-Boot timer application programming interfaces (APIs); these are the timer functions required by U-Boot. The second group consists of the goldfish platform–specific timer functions; these functions are needed to support the timer functionalities in the goldfish platform.

Chapter 7 Exception Handling and Timer

Example 7.10 Timer Interface Functions (code/drivers/timer.c)

```c
#ifndef __BARE_METAL__
/*
 * The macro __BARE_METAL__ is used to define the code for a bare metal environment.
 * The code without this macro defined is used to support U-Boot build.
 */
#include <common.h>
#include <asm/io.h>
#include <configs/goldfish.h>

/*
 * Refer to the goldfish kernel header file for the timer hardware interface:
 * arch/arm/mach-goldfish/include/mach/timer.h
 */
enum {
    TIMER_TIME_LOW          = 0x00,
    TIMER_TIME_HIGH         = 0x04,
    TIMER_ALARM_LOW         = 0x08,
    TIMER_ALARM_HIGH        = 0x0c,
    TIMER_CLEAR_INTERRUPT   = 0x10,
    TIMER_CLEAR_ALARM       = 0x14,
};
#else
#include <hardware.h>
#include <bsp.h>
#include <timer.h>
#endif /* __BARE_METAL__ */

#define TIMER_LOAD_VAL 0xffffffff

#ifndef __BARE_METAL__
/* This data structure is defined in U-Boot. */
DECLARE_GLOBAL_DATA_PTR;

/*
 * timestamp and lastdec are macros in U-Boot, but are global variables in the
 * bare metal environment.
 */
```

```
#define timestamp gd->tbl
#define lastdec gd->lastinc
#else
ulong timestamp;
ulong lastdec;
#endif /* __BARE_METAL__ */

unsigned long get_millisecond(void);

int timer_init (void)
{
    /* Initialize the timestamp and lastdec value */
    reset_timer_masked();

    return 0;
}

/*
 * Timer without interrupts
 */
ulong get_timer (ulong base)
{
    return get_timer_masked () - base;
}

/* Delay x useconds AND preserve advancing timestamp value */
void __udelay (unsigned long usec)
{
    ulong tmo, tmp;

    tmo = usec / CONFIG_SYS_HZ;        /* We support millisecond accuracy */
    tmp = get_timer (0);               /* get current timestamp */
    if( (tmo + tmp + 1) < tmp ) {      /* if setting this forward will roll time
                                          stamp */
reset_timer_masked ();              /* reset "advancing" timestamp to 0, set
                                          lastdec value */
    }
    else
```

Chapter 7 Exception Handling and Timer

```
            tmo += tmp;                     /* else, set advancing stamp wake up
time */

    while (get_timer_masked () < tmo)    /* loop until event */
        /*NOP*/;
}

void reset_timer_masked (void)
{
    ulong rv;

    rv = get_millisecond();

    /* reset time */
    lastdec = rv;        /* capture current decrementer value time */
    timestamp = 0;       /* start "advancing" timestamp from 0 */
}

ulong get_timer_masked (void)
{
    ulong now = 0;                   /* current tick value */

    now = get_millisecond();

    if (now >= lastdec) {            /* normal mode (non-roll) */
        /* normal mode */
        timestamp += now - lastdec;  /* move stamp forward with absolute diff
ticks */
    } else {
/*
 * We have overflow of the countdown timer.
    */
        timestamp += now + TIMER_LOAD_VAL - lastdec;
    }
    lastdec = now;

    return timestamp;
}

/* Waits for specified delay value and resets timestamp */
void udelay_masked (unsigned long usec)
```

```
{
    ulong tmo;
    ulong endtime;
    signed long diff;

    tmo = usec / CONFIG_SYS_HZ;

    endtime = get_timer_masked () + tmo;

    do {
        ulong now = get_timer_masked ();
        diff = endtime - now;
    } while (diff >= 0);
}

/*
 * This function is derived from PowerPC code (read timebase as long long).
 * On ARM, it returns the timer value.
 */
unsigned long long get_ticks(void)
{
    return get_timer(0);
}

/*
 * This function is derived from PowerPC code (timebase clock frequency).
 * On ARM, it returns the number of timer ticks per second.
 */
ulong get_tbclk (void)
{
    ulong tbclk;

    tbclk = CONFIG_SYS_HZ;
    return tbclk;
}

/*
 * Get number of seconds from STARTOFTIME.
 */
```

Chapter 7 Exception Handling and Timer

```
unsigned long get_second(void)
{
    uint32_t timer_base = IO_ADDRESS(GOLDFISH_TIMER_BASE);
    ulong lo, hi, rv;

    lo = readl(timer_base + TIMER_TIME_LOW);
    hi = (int64_t)readl(timer_base + TIMER_TIME_HIGH);

    hi = hi * 4;
    lo = lo >> 30;
    rv = hi + lo;

    return rv;
}

/*
 * Get number of milliseconds from STARTOFTIME.
 */
unsigned long get_millisecond(void)
{
    uint32_t timer_base = IO_ADDRESS(GOLDFISH_TIMER_BASE);
    ulong lo, hi, rv;

    lo = readl(timer_base + TIMER_TIME_LOW);
    hi = (int64_t)readl(timer_base + TIMER_TIME_HIGH);

    hi = hi << 12;
    lo = lo >> 20;
    rv = hi + lo;

    return rv;
}

/*
 * Goldfish-specific timer functions
 */
void goldfish_set_timer(unsigned long cycles)
{
    uint32_t timer_base = IO_ADDRESS(GOLDFISH_TIMER_BASE);
    unsigned long lo, hi, tmp;
```

```c
        lo = readl((void *)timer_base + TIMER_TIME_LOW);
        hi = (int64_t)readl((void *)timer_base + TIMER_TIME_HIGH);

        hi = hi + cycles / 4096;              /* move 12 bits left */
        tmp = lo + ((cycles % 4096) << 20);
        if(lo > tmp) {
            lo = tmp;
            hi = hi + 1;
        }
        else {
            lo = tmp;
        }

        writel(hi, (void *)timer_base + TIMER_ALARM_HIGH);
        writel(lo, (void *)timer_base + TIMER_ALARM_LOW);
}

void goldfish_clear_timer_int(void)
{
    uint32_t timer_base = IO_ADDRESS(GOLDFISH_TIMER_BASE);

    writel(1, (void *)timer_base + TIMER_CLEAR_INTERRUPT);
}

unsigned long goldfish_timer_read(void)
{
    uint32_t timer_base = IO_ADDRESS(GOLDFISH_TIMER_BASE);
    unsigned long  rv;

    rv = readl((void *)timer_base + TIMER_TIME_LOW);
    rv |= (int64_t)readl((void *)timer_base + TIMER_TIME_HIGH) << 32;

    return rv;
}

void goldfish_clear_alarm(void)
{
    uint32_t timer_base = IO_ADDRESS(GOLDFISH_TIMER_BASE);

    writel(1, (void *)timer_base + TIMER_CLEAR_ALARM);
}
```

Goldfish-Specific Timer Functions

In Example 7.10, the names of goldfish platform–specific functions start with the prefix `goldfish_`. These functions provide the timer interrupt support:

- `void goldfish_set_timer(unsigned long cycles)`: This function sets the timer interrupt to a number of milliseconds. The parameter `cycles` is in milliseconds. The function reads the current timestamp and adds a timeout value. After that, it sets an alarm register.

- `void goldfish_clear_timer_int(void)` and `void goldfish_clear_alarm(void)`: Both `goldfish_clear_timer_int` and `goldfish_clear_alarm` can be used to clear the timer interrupt.

U-Boot API

To support U-Boot (covered in Chapter 9), we implemented a few U-Boot timer APIs in Example 7.10. U-Boot uses a global data structure to maintain the system status. Two fields are related to the timer: the timestamp (`gd->tbl`) and the last system tick (`gd->lastinc`). Both are part of the U-Boot global data structure `gd`. Since we haven't encountered this data structure yet, we'll define the timestamp and the last system tick as the global variables `timestamp` and `lastdec`, respectively, in the chapter's last example.

The function `timer_init` initializes the global variables `timestamp` and `lastdec`. The variable `timestamp` is initialized to 0, while `lastdec` is initialized to the current system tick value. Both `get_timer` and `get_timer_masked` return the value of the global variable `timestamp`. In our implementation, the timestamp is implemented as a tick in units of milliseconds. To implement this, we create two functions, `get_millisecond` and `get_second`, to support the system tick and the real-time clock (RTC; discussed in the next section). The function `get_millisecond` returns the number of milliseconds that have passed since the emulator booted up, and the function `get_second` returns the number of seconds that have passed since the emulator booted up. U-Boot API also provides two delay functions: `__udelay` and `udelay_masked`. Both of these functions provide a delay in units of microseconds, although we actually support only a precision measured in milliseconds.

The function `get_tbclk` returns the number of ticks per second. Because we support a precision of milliseconds, the function `get_tbclk` returns 1000 in our implementation. This hardware-dependent function actually reflects the frequency of the system's oscillator.

Real-Time Clock

U-Boot supports the real-time clock through three functions: `rtc_reset`, `rtc_get`, and `rtc_set`. We implement these three functions in Example 7.11. The RTC provides an interface so that we can convert the system tick or timestamp to a corresponding calendar date. The actual functions that perform the conversion work are found in a U-Boot file, `date.c`. The function `to_tm` converts a timestamp to the RTC data structure `rtc_time`. The function `mktime` converts the RTC data structure `rtc_time` to a timestamp.

When the system starts up, the RTC is initialized to a fixed calendar date and time. In the case of U-Boot, the date is set to 1970-01-01 00:00:00. Once the system is up and running, we can use a U-Boot command to set the date to the current date. This command actually calls the function rtc-set, which sets the system date back to the initial value.

Example 7.11 RTC Implementation (code/c07/c07e3/rtc-goldfish.c)

```
#ifndef __BARE_METAL__
#include <common.h>
#include <command.h>
#include <rtc.h>
#include <asm/io.h>
#include <asm/arch/hardware.h>
#else
#include <hardware.h>
#include <bsp.h>
#include "rtc.h"
#endif

#if defined(CONFIG_CMD_DATE)

/* This is the offset for the rtc_set(). */
static unsigned long rtc_offset = 0;

int rtc_get(struct rtc_time *tmp)
{
    ulong rv;

    rv = get_second() + rtc_offset;

    to_tm(rv, tmp);

    return 0;
}

int rtc_set(struct rtc_time *tmp)
{
    unsigned long rv;

    rv = mktime (tmp->tm_year, tmp->tm_mon,
            tmp->tm_mday, tmp->tm_hour,
            tmp->tm_min, tmp->tm_sec);
```

```
    rtc_offset = rv - get_second();

    return 0;
}

void rtc_reset(void)
{
    rtc_offset = 0;
}
#endif
```

Unit Test of Timer and RTC

In this chapter we have discussed timers and the RTC. Let's use an example test program (c07e3) to test our implementation. This example consists of the following files:
Common files:

- `bsp.c`: Includes the API functions for the goldfish interrupt controller. It is the same as the code in the previous example.
- `timer.c`: Includes the API functions for the goldfish timer.
- `syscalls_cs3.c`: Includes the implementation of the system service stubs. It is the same as the code in Chapter 6.
- `serial_goldfish.c`: The C code to implement serial functions. It is the same as the code in Chapter 5.
- `goldfish_uart.S`: The assembly language code for implementing serial port–specific functions. It is the same as the code in Chapter 5.
- `arm_exc.S`: In this file, exception vectors are implemented in assembly language code.
- `isr.c`: In this file, a C-level interrupt service routine (ISR) is implemented.
- `low_level_init.c` i: Implements a function `low_level_init()` that performs early initialization of the hardware. Exception vectors are initialized in `low_level_init()`.

Project-specific files:

- `c07e3.c`: The test code for implementing the `main()` function. This is the unit test code.
- `rtc-goldfish.c`: The implementation of the RTC.
- `date.c`: U-Boot code that provides date and timestamp conversion functions.
- `Makefile`: The makefile to build this project.
- `c07e3.ld`: The linker script of the project.
- `startup_c07e3.S`: The startup code that performs the necessary setup before control is transferred to the C code.

Let's take a look at the test program, shown in Example 7.12. It consists of test cases for the timer and RTC. This test program is similar to our earlier nested interrupt handler example, which included a `main()` function and an interrupt handler, `irq_handler()`.

Example 7.12 Test Code for Timer and RTC (code/c07/c07e3/c07e3.c)

```
#include <stdio.h>
#include <stdlib.h>
#include <sys/unistd.h>
#include <hardware.h>
#include <arm_exc.h>
#include <bsp.h>

#include "rtc.h"

static int ch = 0;
static int timeout = 0;
static int timer_irq = 0;

void sw_handler(int num)
{
    printf("=>Inside sw_handler, num=%d.\n", num);
}

void irq_handler(int irq)
{
    int num = 0;
    unsigned long tm = 0;

    num = goldfish_irq_status();
    printf("\n<=Enter IRQ(%d), %d pending, ", irq, num);
    switch (irq) {
    case IRQ_TTY0:
        printf("=>IRQ_TTY0.\n");
        break;
    case IRQ_TTY1:
        printf("=>IRQ_TTY1.\n");
        break;
```

```
        case IRQ_TTY2:
            ch = getchar();
            printf("IRQ_TTY2, ch=%c, ", ch);
            if(ch == 't') {
                /* Timer unit test 1: set timeout to trigger timer interrupt. */
                printf("timeout = %d ", timeout);
                goldfish_set_timer(timeout);
                timeout = timeout + 1;
                timer_irq = 1;
            }

            /* Timer unit test 2: change the timeout value of timer interrupt. */
            if(ch == 'x') {
                if(timeout > 0) {
                    timeout = timeout * 10;
                }
            }

            /* RTC unit test 3: reset date and time. */
            if(ch == 'r') {
                timeout = 0;
                rtc_reset();
            }
            break;
        case IRQ_TIMER:
            /* goldfish_mask_irq(IRQ_TIMER); */
            goldfish_clear_timer_int();
            printf("IRQ_TIMER ");
            timer_irq = 0;
            break;
        default:
            printf("=>Unknown IRQ %x.\n", irq);
            break;
    }
    tm = get_ticks();
```

```c
        printf("Exit IRQ(%d) tm=%lu =>\n", irq, tm);
}

int main(int argc, char *argv[])
{
    struct rtc_time rtc;

    printf("Starting c07e3 ...\n");

    ARM_INT_UNLOCK(0x1F);           /* Unlock IRQ/FIQ at the ARM core level. */
    goldfish_unmask_irq(IRQ_TIMER);
    goldfish_unmask_irq(IRQ_TTY2);

    EnterUserMode();

    /* Initialize timer. */
    timer_init();

    for(;;) {
        if(ch != 0) {

            if(ch == 'd') {
                /* Disable timer interrupt. */
                goldfish_mask_irq(IRQ_TIMER);
                printf("  - Disabled timer.\n");
            }

            if(ch == 'e') {
                /* Enable timer interrupt. */
                goldfish_unmask_irq(IRQ_TIMER);
                printf("  - Enabled timer.\n");
            }

            if(ch == 'g') {
                /* RTC unit test 1: get date and time. */
                rtc_get(&rtc);

                printf("Get DATE: %4d-%02d-%02d (wday=%d)   TIME: %2d:%02d:%02d (%lu)\n", rtc.tm_year, rtc.tm_mon, rtc.tm_mday, rtc.tm_wday, rtc.tm_hour, rtc.tm_min, rtc.tm_sec, get_millisecond());
            }
```

```c
            if(ch == 's') {
                /* RTC unit test 2: set date to 2014-04-11 12:30:55. */
                rtc.tm_year = 2014;
                rtc.tm_mon = 4;
                rtc.tm_mday = 11;
                rtc.tm_hour = 12;
                rtc.tm_min = 30;
                rtc.tm_sec = 55;

                rtc_set(&rtc);
                printf("  - set RTC. ");
                printf("Get DATE: %4d-%02d-%02d (wday=%d)   TIME: %2d:%02d:%02d (%lu)\n", rtc.tm_year, rtc.tm_mon, rtc.tm_mday, rtc.tm_wday, rtc.tm_hour, rtc.tm_min, rtc.tm_sec, get_millisecond());
            }
            ch = 0;
        }
        else {
            if(timeout > 1000 && timer_irq > 0) {
                /* Timer unit test 3: print out debug message every 1 second for large timeout value. */
                rtc_get(&rtc);
                printf("Get DATE: %4d-%02d-%02d (wday=%d)   TIME: %2d:%02d:%02d (%lu)\n", rtc.tm_year, rtc.tm_mon, rtc.tm_mday, rtc.tm_wday, rtc.tm_hour, rtc.tm_min, rtc.tm_sec, get_millisecond());
                __udelay(1000000);
            }
            else {
                __udelay(1000);
            }
        }
    }
    return 1;
}
```

This test program supports seven commands to test timer and RTC functions. We will actually use eight test cases, as listed in Table 7.3.

Real-Time Clock

Table 7.3 Commands for Testing Timer and RTC Functions

Test Case	Command	Description
1. Get the date and time	g	Call `rtc_get()` to get the current date and time.
2. Set the date and time	s	Call `rtc_set()` to set the date to a particular date.
3. Set timeout	t	Set the timeout of the timer interrupt.
4. Increase timeout	x	Increase the timeout value by 10 times.
5. Reset timeout and RTC	r	Reset the timeout and RTC to the default values.
6. Test delay function		When the timeout value is larger than 1 second, print out the current time per second.
7. Disable timer interrupt	d	Disable the timer interrupt. This was tested in the examples given earlier in this chapter.
8. Enable timer interrupt	e	Enable the timer interrupt. This was tested in the examples given earlier in this chapter.

Let's build the example now:

```
$ make DEBUG=1
   CC    c07e3.c
   AS    startup_c07e3.S
   CC    ../../drivers/serial_goldfish.c
   AS    ../../drivers/goldfish_uart.S
   CC    ../../drivers/syscalls_cs3.c
   CC    ../../drivers/low_level_init.c
   AS    ../../drivers/arm_exc.S
   CC    ../../drivers/bsp.c
   CC    ../../drivers/isr.c
   CC    date.c
   CC    rtc-goldfish.c
   CC    ../../drivers/timer.c
   LD    gcc/c07e3.axf
```

We can start the test program using the predefined make target:

```
$ make run
```

Alternatively, we can run the emulator directly:

```
$ emulator -avd hd2 -shell -kernel gcc/c07e3.axf
```

Chapter 7 Exception Handling and Timer

```
ools/ddms ping emulator 22.2.1.0 "VMware, Inc." "Gallium 0.4 on SVGA3D; build: R
ELEASE;  " "2.1 Mesa 9.0"
goldfish_init(), gtty.base=ff012000
Starting c07e3 ...
1. <=Enter IRQ(12), 0 pending, IRQ_TTY2, ch=g, Exit IRQ(12) tm=5290 =>
   Get DATE: 1970-01-01 (wday=4)    TIME: 0:00:05 (5294)
2. <=Enter IRQ(12), 0 pending, IRQ_TTY2, ch=s, Exit IRQ(12) tm=20686 =>
   set RTC. Get DATE: 2014-04-11 (wday=4)  TIME: 12:30:55 (20690)
   <=Enter IRQ(12), 0 pending, IRQ_TTY2, ch=t, timeout = 0
3. <=Enter IRQ(3), 0 pending, IRQ_TIMER Exit IRQ(3) tm=85808 =>
   Exit IRQ(12) tm=85808 =>
4. <=Enter IRQ(12), 0 pending, IRQ_TTY2, ch=x, Exit IRQ(12) tm=88652 =>
   <=Enter IRQ(12), 0 pending, IRQ_TTY2, ch=x, Exit IRQ(12) tm=89201 =>
   <=Enter IRQ(12), 0 pending, IRQ_TTY2, ch=x, Exit IRQ(12) tm=89985 =>
   <=Enter IRQ(12), 0 pending, IRQ_TTY2, ch=t, timeout = 1000 Exit IRQ(12) tm=95301
   =>
   Get DATE: 2014-04-11 (wday=5)    TIME: 12:32:08 (95306)
```

Figure 7.15 Timer and RTC unit test 1

In Figure 7.15, we can see the following test scenarios (refer to the corresponding numbers in Figure 7.15):

- First, when the system starts up, the default date and time is 1970-01-01 00:00:00.
- After we set the date to a particular date, the system clock can be changed. In this test, we set the system date to 2014-04-11 12:30:55.
- We then trigger a timer interrupt using the command t. The default timeout value is 0, so the timer interrupt is triggered immediately. Since we use a nested interrupt handler, we can see that the timer interrupt is triggered inside the serial interrupt. The timestamp indicates that timer interrupt exits at `tm=85808`; likewise, the serial interrupt exits at `tm=85808`.
- Next, we give the command x to increase the timeout value to 1000 milliseconds—that is, 10 times the current value. The implementation of `irq_handler()` appears in Example 7.12.

Two test cases are in Figure 7.16. When we trigger the timer interrupt again, we can see that the timer interrupt is triggered after 1 second, because we previously increased timeout to 1000 milliseconds.

In the `main()` function of Example 7.12, we added code to print out the current time, if the timer is set and the timeout value is larger than 1 second. We can see the debug message before the timer interrupt is triggered. In the following debug message, the serial interrupt exits at timestamp 109638. After about 1000 milliseconds, the debug message of the timer interrupt exits at timestamp 110640.

```
<=Enter IRQ(12), 0 pending, IRQ_TTY2, ch=x, Exit IRQ(12) tm=88652 =>
<=Enter IRQ(12), 0 pending, IRQ_TTY2, ch=x, Exit IRQ(12) tm=89201 =>
<=Enter IRQ(12), 0 pending, IRQ_TTY2, ch=x, Exit IRQ(12) tm=89985 =>
<=Enter IRQ(12), 0 pending, IRQ_TTY2, ch=t, timeout = 1000 Exit IRQ(12) tm=95301
=>
Get DATE: 2014-04-11 (wday=5)   TIME: 12:32:08 (95306)

<=Enter IRQ(3), 0 pending, IRQ_TIMER Exit IRQ(3) tm=96300 =>

<=Enter IRQ(12), 0 pending, IRQ_TTY2, ch=t, timeout = 1001 Exit IRQ(12) tm=10963
8 =>
Get DATE: 2014-04-11 (wday=5)   TIME: 12:32:22 (109644)
Get DATE: 2014-04-11 (wday=5)   TIME: 12:32:23 (110644)

<=Enter IRQ(3), 0 pending, IRQ_TIMER Exit IRQ(3) tm=110640 =>

<=Enter IRQ(12), 0 pending, IRQ_TTY2, ch=r, Exit IRQ(12) tm=131730 =>
<=Enter IRQ(12), 0 pending, IRQ_TTY2, ch=g, Exit IRQ(12) tm=177833 =>
Get DATE: 1970-01-01 (wday=4)   TIME:  0:02:53 (177836)
```

Figure 7.16 Timer and RTC unit test 2

```
<=Enter IRQ(12), 0 pending, IRQ_TTY2, ch=t, timeout = 1001 Exit IRQ(12) tm=109638 =>
Get DATE: 2014-04-11 (wday=5)    TIME: 12:32:22 (109644)
Get DATE: 2014-04-11 (wday=5)    TIME: 12:32:23 (110644)

<=Enter IRQ(3), 0 pending, IRQ_TIMER Exit IRQ(3) tm=110640 =>
```

In the second test case in Figure 7.16, we can use command r to reset the system date to the default value:

```
<=Enter IRQ(12), 0 pending, IRQ_TTY2, ch=r, Exit IRQ(12) tm=131730 =>
<=Enter IRQ(12), 0 pending, IRQ_TTY2, ch=g, Exit IRQ(12) tm=177830 =>
Get DATE: 1970-01-01 (wday=4)    TIME:  0:02:53 (177836)
```

Summary

In this chapter, we explored the goldfish interrupt controller and timer. We used three examples to demonstrate interrupt handling and use of the timer/RTC in the goldfish platform. To test our code, we first created a simple interrupt handler to test the serial and timer interrupts. Next, we used a more complicated example to demonstrate a nested interrupt handler. Finally, we explained how the timer and RTC can be implemented on the goldfish platform. In the third example, we then tested both the timer and the RTC. The code to handle the goldfish interrupt controller and the timer will be used in U-Boot porting later in this book.

8
NAND Flash Support in Goldfish

To boot an embedded system, we don't really need to initialize all hardware interfaces. Instead, we can leave it to the operating system to initialize the entire platform. Nevertheless, we have to initialize at least a minimum set of hardware so that the system can boot up. In this book, the goal is to demonstrate how to boot up the Android system using U-Boot. Through this process, we learn about the various hardware interfaces and the basics about U-Boot.

In Chapter 7, we discussed serial ports, interrupt controllers, and the real-time clock (RTC)—all hardware interfaces included in the minimum list that we have to initialize. In this chapter, we explore the NAND flash support in the goldfish platform. We will store the kernel image and RAM disk image in NAND flash memory when we boot the Android system in Chapter 10. In this chapter, we investigate the use of the NAND flash programming interface in the Android emulator. We use an example program to demonstrate how to access this NAND flash programming interface. This example code will be reused in Chapter 9, when we work on U-Boot porting.

Android File System

In the Android SDK, file system and user storage images are provided as part of the Android emulator. Each Android version has dedicated system and user data images. Four image files are provided for each Android release:

- `kernel-qemu`: Android Linux kernel image
- `ramdisk.img`: Android RAM disk image
- `system.img`: Android system file image
- `userdata.img`: Android user data file image

These files can be found with the following path name: {SDK root folder}/system-images/{Android version}/{hardware architecture}.

Let's use Android 4.3 as an example to look at these image files.

For ARM architecture, the image files can be found in folders similar to the following:

- `system-images/android-18/armeabi-v7a/`: Android 4.3 version ARM images

  ```
  $ ls system-images/android-18/armeabi-v7a/
  build.prop    NOTICE.txt    source.properties    userdata.img
  kernel-qemu   ramdisk.img   system.img
  ```

For x86 architecture, the image files can be found in folders similar to the following:

- `system-images/android-18/x86/`: Android 4.3 version x86 images

  ```
  $ ls system-images/android-18/x86
  build.prop    NOTICE.txt    source.properties    userdata.img
  kernel-qemu   ramdisk.img   system.img
  ```

Notice that, for each Android emulator instance, the image file list is the same.

The file `kernel-qemu` is a standard Linux kernel (zImage), and the file `ramdisk.img` is in Linux RAM disk image format. We will discuss how to generate these files later in the book.

In Android versions 2.2 and prior, the storage would usually be mounted as YAFFS2 partitions on NAND flash memory. Handset manufacturers have slowly been moving toward eMMC instead of NAND flash memory, however, so the file system type is now changing from YAFFS2 on NAND flash to ext4 on eMMC. The file system type in the Android SDK did not change until Android 4.4 SDK was released. Both `system.img` and `userdata.img` are NAND flash images in YAFFS2; they were used in Android 4.3 and earlier versions. In Android 4.4 SDK and later, these images were changed to the ext4 format.

> **NAND Flash, eMMC, SD/MMC, and SSD**
>
> You can search on the Internet if you want to explore the differences between NAND flash, SD/MMC, eMMC, and SSD in greater detail. For our purposes here, a brief explanation of these differences from a hardware point of view will suffice. NAND flash is a kind of raw flash memory that can be used to build different kinds of storage devices such as SD/MMC, USB storage, or SSD. SD/MMC is a memory card format that includes a microcontroller and NAND flash. The microcontroller implements a Flash Translation Layer (FTL) that translates block access to NAND flash operations. eMMC is a SD/MMC memory card built into a device, such as a handset. Solid State Drive (SSD) combines a controller and NAND flash; the controller uses the SATA protocol and a connector connected to the host, which can achieve better performance than SD/MMC.

If we issue the `mount` command in the `adb` shell of the Android emulator, we will see the following message:

```
shell@android:/ $ mount
rootfs / rootfs ro 0 0
tmpfs /dev tmpfs rw,nosuid,mode=755 0 0
devpts /dev/pts devpts rw,mode=600 0 0
proc /proc proc rw 0 0
```

```
sysfs /sys sysfs rw 0 0
none /acct cgroup rw,cpuacct 0 0
tmpfs /mnt/secure tmpfs rw,mode=700 0 0
tmpfs /mnt/asec tmpfs rw,mode=755,gid=1000 0 0
tmpfs /mnt/obb tmpfs rw,mode=755,gid=1000 0 0
none /dev/cpuctl cgroup rw,cpu 0 0
/dev/block/mtdblock0 /system yaffs2 ro 0 0
/dev/block/mtdblock1 /data yaffs2 rw,nosuid,nodev 0 0
/dev/block/mtdblock2 /cache yaffs2 rw,nosuid,nodev 0 0
```

The system folder, data folder, and cache are mounted to different partitions in NAND flash. As the output of the `mount` command shows, in this case `system.img` and `userdata.img` are simulated as MTD block device partitions. The `system.img` image is mounted to a read-only folder at `/system`. The `userdata.img` image is mounted to a read and write folder at `/data`. The file system format is yaffs2.

NAND Flash Properties

NAND flash is very common in embedded systems and is the major storage hardware in most embedded devices. NAND flash is very similar to a hard disk drive in that it is block based. It is programmed (written to) and read on a page basis and is erased on a block basis. That is, to erase a page, you must also erase the rest of the block containing the page. Erasing a block sets all bits to 1 (and all bytes to 0xff). When you program a NAND flash device, you change erased bits from 1 to 0. The smallest entity that can be programmed is 1 byte.

An 8-bit 2GB NAND flash device, as an example, is organized as 2048 blocks, with 64 pages per block (see Figure 8.1). Each page is 2112 bytes, consisting of a 2048-byte data area and a 64-byte spare area for out-of-band data. The spare area is typically used for ECC, wear leveling, and other software overhead functions, although it is physically the same as the rest of the page. In the NAND flash programming interface, the spare area is called out-of-band (OOB) data; in the Linux kernel source code, it is called either the spare area or out-of-band data.

Many NAND flash devices are offered with either an 8-bit interface or a 16-bit interface. Host data is sent to and received from the NAND flash memory via an 8-bit- or 16-bit-wide bidirectional data bus. For 16-bit devices, commands and addresses use the lower 8 bits (7:0). The upper 8 bits of the 16-bit data bus are used only during data-transfer cycles.

To calculate the amount of NAND storage available, we can use the following formulas:

$\quad$ 1 page = (2048 data + 64 OOB data) bytes = 2112 bytes

$\quad$ 1 block = (2048 + 64) × 64 pages = (128K + 4K) bytes

$\quad$ A 8-bit 2GB NAND device = (128K + 4K) × 2048 blocks = (256M + 8M) bytes

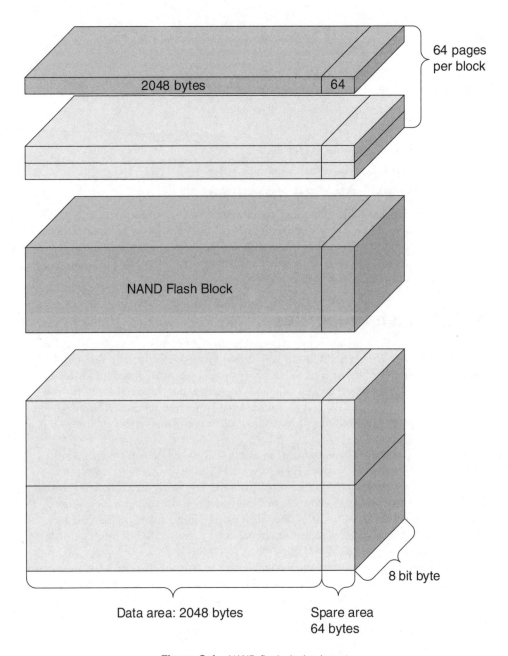

Figure 8.1 NAND flash device layout

NAND Flash Programming Interface in the Goldfish Platform

In the goldfish platform, the NAND flash controller register base address starts from either 0xff016000 or 0xff017000, depending on the version of the Android emulator being used. It consists of sixteen 32-bit registers:

- Register NAND_VERSION at offset 0x000 contains the version of the NAND flash controller. It is a read-only register. During the initialization, it should be compared with the defined macro NAND_VERSION_CURRENT in the Linux kernel. If these two values do not match, the kernel cannot support the right version of NAND flash hardware. This case could arise, for example, when you run the latest Android image on an old Android emulator.

- Register NAND_NUM_DEV at offset 0x004 contains the number of NAND flash chips in the system. A NAND flash chip is simulated using an image file, such as system.img or userdata.img.

- Register NAND_DEV at offset 0x008 is a write-only register. Before a NAND command can be executed, the NAND flash device number must be written to this register.

- Register NAND_DEV_FLAGS at offset 0x010 is a read-only register. It contains the capabilities of the NAND flash device. It can be a combination of properties (e.g., MTD_WRITEABLE, MTD_BIT_WRITEABLE, MTD_NO_ERASE, and MTD_STUPID_LOCK).

- Register NAND_DEV_NAME_LEN at offset 0x014 is a read-only register that contains the length of the device name.

- Register NAND_DEV_PAGE_SIZE at offset 0x018 is a read-only register that contains the page size of the device.

- Register NAND_DEV_EXTRA_SIZE at offset 0x01c is a read-only register that contains the out-of-band data size of the device.

- Register NAND_DEV_ERASE_SIZE at offset 0x020 is a read-only register that contains the erase block size of device.

- Register NAND_DEV_SIZE_LOW at offset 0x028 is a read-only register that contains the lowest 32 bits of the size of the device's capacity.

- Register NAND_DEV_SIZE_HIGH at offset 0x02c is a read-only register that contains the top 32 bits of the size of the device's capacity.

- Register NAND_RESULT at offset 0x040 is a read-only register that is used to store the return status of a NAND flash controller command.

- Register NAND_COMMAND at offset 0x044 is a write-only register for NAND flash commands. The goldfish NAND flash controller supports six commands: NAND_CMD_GET_DEV_NAME, NAND_CMD_READ, NAND_CMD_WRITE, NAND_CMD_ERASE, NAND_CMD_BLOCK_BAD_GET, and NAND_CMD_BLOCK_BAD_SET.

- Register NAND_DATA at offset 0x048 is a write-only register that is used to store the data output pointer in the memory.

- Register `NAND_TRANSFER_SIZE` at offset 0x04c is a write-only register that is used to store the size of data to be transferred.

- Register `NAND_ADDR_LOW` at offset 0x050 is a write-only register that contains the lowest 32 bits of the data address in NAND flash.

- Register `NAND_ADDR_HIGH` at offset 0x054 is a write-only register that contains the top 32 bits of the data address in NAND flash.

There registers can be divided into three groups. The first group, which includes `NAND_VERSION` and `NAND_NUM_DEV`, comprises registers at the NAND flash controller level. They are used to verify the version of NAND flash controller and to detect the number of devices connected to the NAND flash controller.

The second group of registers is device specific. The names of these registers start with the prefix "`NAND_DEV_`". These registers are used to get the properties of the specific NAND flash device.

The third group of registers is used to execute commands supported by the NAND flash controller. The system can communicate with NAND flash devices through these commands, such as those to read, write, or erase a page or block.

Now that we have an understanding of the NAND flash programming interface, we are ready to implement a software programming interface on top of it. We don't have to do all of the work from scratch, because we can refer to the Linux kernel device driver code from Google.

Memory Technology Device Support

An embedded system includes many storage solutions that can be used to support file system. A NAND flash device is one of them. In Linux, the Memory Technology Device (MTD) subsystem provides an abstraction layer (kernel structure) for raw flash devices. MTD makes it possible to use the same API when working with different flash types and technologies (e.g., NAND, OneNAND, NOR, AG-AND, ECC'd NOR). When we use the MTD subsystem, the work to support different flash types is simplified dramatically.

The MTD subsystem, however, is not compatible with block devices like MMC, eMMC, SD, and CompactFlash. These devices are not raw flashes, but rather have a Flash Translation Layer (FTL) inside, which makes them look like block devices. These devices are the subject of the Linux block subsystem, not MTD.

The MTD interface has also been ported to U-Boot to support different flash types as boot devices. In this chapter, we will port the MTD subsystem to a bare metal environment to support NAND flash in the goldfish platform.

Reading from flash memory is fast, easy, and not much different than reading from other memory devices. However, writing data to a flash memory device is more difficult. To overcome these challenges, it often makes sense to create a flash driver for the purpose of hiding chip-specific details from the rest of the software.

Many types of memory devices are available. Writing software for each type of memory device requires a deep knowledge of its architecture, capabilities, and limitations, as well as

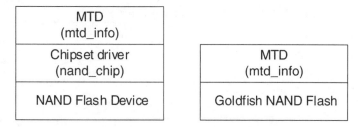

Figure 8.2 NAND flash device driver

how to effectively use each type of memory. Sometimes there may be significant physical differences in the underlying hardware, requiring a bundle of different tools for different devices. To help avoid this inefficient approach to handling memory devices, the MTD subsystem was created; it enables the driver developer to concentrate on dealing with the hardware differences at the device driver layer.

In Linux and U-Boot, the NAND flash device driver in the MTD layer is implemented through the interfaces defined in the file include/linux/mtd/nand.h. The NAND device driver at the chip level doesn't need to perform the read(), write(), read_oob(), and write_oob() operations defined in the data structure mtd_info. Instead, its main task focuses on the nand_chip data structure. MTD uses the nand_chip data structure to represent a NAND flash chip. This structure includes low-level control mechanisms such as address information, read/write method, ECC mode, and hardware control of the NAND flash. The implementation of these NAND chip functions can be found in the file drivers/mtd/nand/nand_base.c.

In the goldfish platform, the Android emulator uses software to simulate NAND flash. As a consequence, the programming interface is much simpler compared to the real hardware and can provide the MTD support directly. As shown in Figure 8.2, for our purposes, we eliminated the chipset driver implementation in the goldfish platform. The goldfish NAND controller provides a layer that can support MTD interfaces directly. To support the MTD subsystem, we can use goldfish's NAND flash programming interface to implement the MTD API. You should take note of these changes when you work on your own projects.

MTD API

The mtd_info structure is the most important structure in the MTD subsystem. In the goldfish kernel code, the NAND flash support can be found in the following files:

- drivers/mtd/devices/goldfish_nand.c
- drivers/mtd/devices/goldfish_nand_reg.h

The file goldfish_nand.c implements the mtd_info structure. We can reuse most of the code for the bare metal environment both here and in our later U-Boot code.

In the header file shown in Example 8.1, all goldfish NAND controller registers and commands are defined. This file can be used directly in our program.

Example 8.1 Goldfish NAND Flash Registers (goldfish_nand_reg.h)

```c
#ifndef GOLDFISH_NAND_REG_H
#define GOLDFISH_NAND_REG_H

enum nand_cmd {
    NAND_CMD_GET_DEV_NAME,  // Write device name for NAND_DEV to NAND_DATA (vaddr)
    NAND_CMD_READ,
    NAND_CMD_WRITE,
    NAND_CMD_ERASE,
    NAND_CMD_BLOCK_BAD_GET, // NAND_RESULT is 1 if block is bad, 0 if it is not
    NAND_CMD_BLOCK_BAD_SET
};

enum nand_dev_flags {
    NAND_DEV_FLAG_READ_ONLY = 0x00000001
};

#define NAND_VERSION_CURRENT (1)

enum nand_reg {
    // Global
    NAND_VERSION        = 0x000,
    NAND_NUM_DEV        = 0x004,
    NAND_DEV            = 0x008,

    // Dev info
    NAND_DEV_FLAGS      = 0x010,
    NAND_DEV_NAME_LEN   = 0x014,
    NAND_DEV_PAGE_SIZE  = 0x018,
    NAND_DEV_EXTRA_SIZE = 0x01c,
    NAND_DEV_ERASE_SIZE = 0x020,
    NAND_DEV_SIZE_LOW   = 0x028,
    NAND_DEV_SIZE_HIGH  = 0x02c,

    // Command
    NAND_RESULT         = 0x040,
    NAND_COMMAND        = 0x044,
    NAND_DATA           = 0x048,
```

```
        NAND_TRANSFER_SIZE   = 0x04c,
        NAND_ADDR_LOW        = 0x050,
        NAND_ADDR_HIGH       = 0x054,
};

#endif
```

The data structure `mtd_info` is defined in the file `include/linux/mtd/mtd.h`. Both the Linux kernel and U-Boot have their own versions of `mtd.h`. U-Boot has ported the entire MTD source code from the Linux kernel and uses a modified version of `mtd.h`. Example 8.2 shows our modified U-Boot version of `mtd.h` for the bare metal environment. We use a macro `__BARE_METAL__` to deal with the bare metal environment–specific code. In this way, the source code can be compiled in this chapter and then recompiled in U-Boot. Notice that we made a minor modification to the original file, replacing some header files with the versions that we copied from the U-Boot source code. The changed part is included in the macro `__BARE_METAL__`.

Because this `mtd.h` is a U-Boot version, we also removed some interfaces and data fields as identified with the following comment: `/* XXX U-BOOT XXX */`. These interfaces are not supported in U-Boot.

Example 8.2 Modified MTD Header File (mtd.h)

```
#ifndef __MTD_MTD_H__
#define __MTD_MTD_H__

#ifndef __BARE_METAL__
#include <linux/types.h>
#include <div64.h>
#include <linux/mtd/mtd-abi.h>
#else
/* This is the only change that we made on top of the U-Boot version. */
#include "div64.h"
#include "mtd-abi.h"
#endif

...

struct mtd_info {
    u_char type;
    u_int32_t flags;
    uint64_t size;       /* Total size of the MTD */
```

```c
/* "Major" erase size for the device. Naïve users may take this
 * to be the only erase size available, or may use the more detailed
 * information below if they desire.
 */
u_int32_t erasesize;
/* Minimal writable flash unit size. In case of NOR flash, it is 1 (even
 * though individual bits can be cleared); in case of NAND flash, it is
 * one NAND page (or half, or one-fourth of it); in case of ECC-ed NOR,
 * it is of ECC block size; etc. It is illegal to have writesize = 0.
 * Any driver registering a struct mtd_info must ensure a writesize of
 * 1 or larger.
 */
u_int32_t writesize;

u_int32_t oobsize;   /* Amount of OOB data per block (e.g., 16) */
u_int32_t oobavail;  /* Available OOB bytes per block */

/* Kernel-only stuff starts here. */
const char *name;
int index;

/* ECC layout structure pointer: read-only! */
struct nand_ecclayout *ecclayout;

/* Data for variable erase regions. If numeraseregions is zero,
 * it means that the whole device has erasesize as given above.
 */
int numeraseregions;
struct mtd_erase_region_info *eraseregions;

/*
 * Erase is an asynchronous operation. Device drivers are supposed
 * to call instr->callback() whenever the operation completes, even
 * if it completes with a failure.
 * Callers are supposed to pass a callback function and wait for it
 * to be called before writing to the block.
 */
int (*erase) (struct mtd_info *mtd, struct erase_info *instr);
```

```c
/* This stuff for eXecute-In-Place */
/* phys is optional and may be set to NULL. */
int (*point) (struct mtd_info *mtd, loff_t from, size_t len,
        size_t *retlen, void **virt, phys_addr_t *phys);

/* We probably shouldn't allow XIP if unpoint isn't a NULL. */
void (*unpoint) (struct mtd_info *mtd, loff_t from, size_t len);

int (*read) (struct mtd_info *mtd, loff_t from, size_t len, size_t *retlen,
u_char *buf);
int (*write) (struct mtd_info *mtd, loff_t to, size_t len, size_t *retlen,
const u_char *buf);

/* In black box (flight recorder)-like scenarios, we want to make successful
    writes in an interrupt context. panic_write() is intended to be
    called only when it's known the kernel is about to panic and we need the
    write to succeed. Since the kernel will not be running for much
    longer, this function can break locks and delay to ensure the write
    succeeds (but not sleep). */

int (*panic_write) (struct mtd_info *mtd, loff_t to, size_t len, size_t
*retlen, const u_char *buf);

int (*read_oob) (struct mtd_info *mtd, loff_t from,
        struct mtd_oob_ops *ops);
int (*write_oob) (struct mtd_info *mtd, loff_t to,
        struct mtd_oob_ops *ops);

/*
 * Methods to access the protection register area, present in some
 * flash devices. The user data is one-time programmable; the
 * factory data is read-only.
 */
int (*get_fact_prot_info) (struct mtd_info *mtd, struct otp_info *buf, size_t
len);
int (*read_fact_prot_reg) (struct mtd_info *mtd, loff_t from, size_t len,
size_t *retlen, u_char *buf);
int (*get_user_prot_info) (struct mtd_info *mtd, struct otp_info *buf, size_t
len);
int (*read_user_prot_reg) (struct mtd_info *mtd, loff_t from, size_t len,
size_t *retlen, u_char *buf);
```

```c
    int (*write_user_prot_reg) (struct mtd_info *mtd, loff_t from, size_t len,
size_t *retlen, u_char *buf);

    int (*lock_user_prot_reg) (struct mtd_info *mtd, loff_t from, size_t len);

/* XXX U-BOOT XXX */
#if 0
    /* kvec-based read/write methods.
       NB: The 'count' parameter is the number of _vectors_, each of
       which contains an (ofs, len) tuple.
    */
    int (*writev) (struct mtd_info *mtd, const struct kvec *vecs, unsigned long count, loff_t to, size_t *retlen);
#endif

    /* Sync */
    void (*sync) (struct mtd_info *mtd);

    /* Chip-supported device locking */
    int (*lock) (struct mtd_info *mtd, loff_t ofs, uint64_t len);
    int (*unlock) (struct mtd_info *mtd, loff_t ofs, uint64_t len);

    /* Bad block management functions */
    int (*block_isbad) (struct mtd_info *mtd, loff_t ofs);
    int (*block_markbad) (struct mtd_info *mtd, loff_t ofs);

/* XXX U-BOOT XXX */
#if 0
    struct notifier_block reboot_notifier;  /* Default mode before reboot */

    /* ECC status information */
    struct mtd_ecc_stats ecc_stats;
#endif
    /* Subpage shift (NAND) */
    int subpage_sft;

    void *priv;

    struct module *owner;
    int usecount;
```

```
    /* If the driver is something smart, like UBI, it may need to maintain
     * its own reference counting. The following functions are only for drivers.
     * A driver may register its callbacks. These callbacks are not
     * supposed to be called by MTD users. */
    int (*get_device) (struct mtd_info *mtd);
    void (*put_device) (struct mtd_info *mtd);
};

...

#endif /* __MTD_MTD_H__ */
```

In Example 8.3 (goldfish_nand.c), we removed most of the Linux-specific stuff and kept the necessary functions to support NAND flash in our environment. In the modified version of goldfish_nand.c shown in this example, there are two kinds of functions. The first group relates to the U-Boot API, which we must support so that our code can be integrated with the U-Boot source code. The second group consists of goldfish-specific support functions; their names start with the prefix goldfish_.

Example 8.3 Modified Version of Goldfish NAND Flash Driver (goldfish_nand.c)

```
#ifndef __BARE_METAL__
#include <div64.h>
#include <asm/io.h>
#include <linux/mtd/mtd.h>
#include <asm/errno.h>
#include <configs/goldfish.h>
#include <ubi_uboot.h>
#include <nand.h>
#else
/* We use a different set of header files in a bare metal environment. */
#include <hardware.h>
#include <bsp.h>
#include "mtd.h"
#include "div64.h"
#endif /* __BARE_METAL__ */

#include "goldfish_nand_reg.h"
```

```c
#define GOLDFISH_DEV_NAME_MAX_LEN 64

struct goldfish_nand {
    unsigned char __iomem   *base;
    size_t                  mtd_count;
    struct mtd_info         *mtd;
};

struct goldfish_nand goldfish_nand_info;

#ifdef __BARE_METAL__
/* This data structure is a global data structure using by U-Boot. It is defined
 * outside this file in U-Boot. We define it as a global variable here.
 */
typedef struct mtd_info nand_info_t;

nand_info_t nand_info[CONFIG_SYS_MAX_NAND_DEVICE];
#else
extern nand_info_t nand_info[CONFIG_SYS_MAX_NAND_DEVICE];
#endif

static char goldfish_dev_name[CONFIG_SYS_MAX_NAND_DEVICE][GOLDFISH_DEV_NAME_MAX_LEN];

/*
 * This is the major NAND flash operation sequence. All other goldfish NAND
 * flash functions use this function to talk to the NAND flash controller.
 */
static uint32_t goldfish_nand_cmd(struct mtd_info *mtd, enum nand_cmd cmd,
                    uint64_t addr, uint32_t len, void *ptr)
{
    struct goldfish_nand *nand = mtd->priv;
    uint32_t rv;
    unsigned char __iomem *base = nand->base;

    writel(mtd - nand->mtd, base + NAND_DEV);
    writel((uint32_t)(addr >> 32), base + NAND_ADDR_HIGH);
    writel((uint32_t)addr, base + NAND_ADDR_LOW);
    writel(len, base + NAND_TRANSFER_SIZE);
    writel((unsigned long)ptr, base + NAND_DATA);
```

```c
    writel(cmd, base + NAND_COMMAND);
    rv = readl(base + NAND_RESULT);

    return rv;
}

/* Erase NAND flash block. */
static int goldfish_nand_erase(struct mtd_info *mtd, struct erase_info *instr)
{
    loff_t ofs = instr->addr;
    uint32_t len = instr->len;
    uint32_t rem;

    if (ofs + len > mtd->size)
        goto invalid_arg;
    rem = do_div(ofs, mtd->writesize);
    if(rem)
        goto invalid_arg;
    ofs *= (mtd->writesize + mtd->oobsize);

    if(len % mtd->writesize)
        goto invalid_arg;
    len = len / mtd->writesize * (mtd->writesize + mtd->oobsize);

    if(goldfish_nand_cmd(mtd, NAND_CMD_ERASE, ofs, len, NULL) != len) {
        debug("goldfish_nand_erase: erase failed, start %llx, len %x, dev_size "
            "%llx, erase_size %x\n", ofs, len, mtd->size, mtd->erasesize);
        return -EIO;
    }

    instr->state = MTD_ERASE_DONE;
    mtd_erase_callback(instr);

    return 0;
invalid_arg:
    debug("goldfish_nand_erase: invalid erase, start %llx, len %x, dev_size "
        "%llx, erase_size %x\n", ofs, len, mtd->size, mtd->erasesize);
    return -EINVAL;
}
```

```c
/* Read a block with out-of-band data. */
static int goldfish_nand_read_oob(struct mtd_info *mtd, loff_t ofs,
                                  struct mtd_oob_ops *ops)
{
    uint32_t rem;

    if(ofs + ops->len > mtd->size)
        goto invalid_arg;
    if(ops->datbuf && ops->len && ops->len != mtd->writesize)
        goto invalid_arg;
    if(ops->ooblen + ops->ooboffs > mtd->oobsize)
        goto invalid_arg;

    rem = do_div(ofs, mtd->writesize);
    if(rem)
        goto invalid_arg;
    ofs *= (mtd->writesize + mtd->oobsize);

    if(ops->datbuf)
        ops->retlen = goldfish_nand_cmd(mtd, NAND_CMD_READ, ofs,
                                        ops->len, ops->datbuf);
    ofs += mtd->writesize + ops->ooboffs;
    if(ops->oobbuf)
        ops->oobretlen = goldfish_nand_cmd(mtd, NAND_CMD_READ, ofs,
                                           ops->ooblen, ops->oobbuf);
    return 0;

invalid_arg:
    debug("goldfish_nand_read_oob: invalid read, start %llx, len %x, "
          "ooblen %x, dev_size %llx, write_size %x\n",
          ofs, ops->len, ops->ooblen, mtd->size, mtd->writesize);
    return -EINVAL;
}

/* Write a block with out-of-band data. */
static int goldfish_nand_write_oob(struct mtd_info *mtd, loff_t ofs,
                                   struct mtd_oob_ops *ops)
```

```
{
    uint32_t rem;

    if(ofs + ops->len > mtd->size)
        goto invalid_arg;
    if(ops->len && ops->len != mtd->writesize)
        goto invalid_arg;
    if(ops->ooblen + ops->ooboffs > mtd->oobsize)
        goto invalid_arg;

    rem = do_div(ofs, mtd->writesize);
    if(rem)
        goto invalid_arg;
    ofs *= (mtd->writesize + mtd->oobsize);

    if(ops->datbuf)
        ops->retlen = goldfish_nand_cmd(mtd, NAND_CMD_WRITE, ofs,
                                ops->len, ops->datbuf);
    ofs += mtd->writesize + ops->ooboffs;
    if(ops->oobbuf)
        ops->oobretlen = goldfish_nand_cmd(mtd, NAND_CMD_WRITE, ofs,
                                ops->ooblen, ops->oobbuf);
    return 0;
invalid_arg:
    debug("goldfish_nand_write_oob: invalid write, start %llx, len %x, "
        "ooblen %x, dev_size %llx, write_size %x\n",
        ofs, ops->len, ops->ooblen, mtd->size, mtd->writesize);
    return -EINVAL;
}

/* Read a NAND flash block. */
static int goldfish_nand_read(struct mtd_info *mtd, loff_t from, size_t len,
                    size_t *retlen, u_char *buf)
{
    uint32_t rem;

    if(from + len > mtd->size)
        goto invalid_arg;
```

```c
    if(len != mtd->writesize)
        goto invalid_arg;

    rem = do_div(from, mtd->writesize);
    if(rem)
        goto invalid_arg;
    from *= (mtd->writesize + mtd->oobsize);

    *retlen = goldfish_nand_cmd(mtd, NAND_CMD_READ, from, len, buf);
    return 0;

invalid_arg:
    debug("goldfish_nand_read: invalid read, start %llx, len %x, dev_size %llx"
           ", write_size %x\n", from, len, mtd->size, mtd->writesize);
    return -EINVAL;
}

/* Write a NAND flash block. */
static int goldfish_nand_write(struct mtd_info *mtd, loff_t to, size_t len,
                                size_t *retlen, const u_char *buf)
{
    uint32_t rem;

    if(to + len > mtd->size)
        goto invalid_arg;
    if(len != mtd->writesize)
        goto invalid_arg;

    rem = do_div(to, mtd->writesize);
    if(rem)
        goto invalid_arg;
    to *= (mtd->writesize + mtd->oobsize);

    *retlen = goldfish_nand_cmd(mtd, NAND_CMD_WRITE, to, len, (void *)buf);
    return 0;

invalid_arg:
    debug("goldfish_nand_write: invalid write, start %llx, len %x, dev_size %llx"
           ", write_size %x\n", to, len, mtd->size, mtd->writesize);
    return -EINVAL;
}
```

```c
/* Check if it is a bad block. */
static int goldfish_nand_block_isbad(struct mtd_info *mtd, loff_t ofs)
{
    uint32_t rem;

    if(ofs >= mtd->size)
        goto invalid_arg;

    rem = do_div(ofs, mtd->erasesize);
    if(rem)
        goto invalid_arg;

    ofs *= mtd->erasesize / mtd->writesize;
    ofs *= (mtd->writesize + mtd->oobsize);

    return goldfish_nand_cmd(mtd, NAND_CMD_BLOCK_BAD_GET, ofs, 0, NULL);

invalid_arg:
    debug("goldfish_nand_block_isbad: invalid arg, ofs %llx, dev_size %llx, "
            "write_size %x\n", ofs, mtd->size, mtd->writesize);
    return -EINVAL;
}

/* Mark a bad block. */
static int goldfish_nand_block_markbad(struct mtd_info *mtd, loff_t ofs)
{
    uint32_t rem;

    if(ofs >= mtd->size)
        goto invalid_arg;

    rem = do_div(ofs, mtd->erasesize);
    if(rem)
        goto invalid_arg;

    ofs *= mtd->erasesize / mtd->writesize;
    ofs *= (mtd->writesize + mtd->oobsize);

    if(goldfish_nand_cmd(mtd, NAND_CMD_BLOCK_BAD_SET, ofs, 0, NULL) != 1)
        return -EIO;
    return 0;
```

```c
invalid_arg:
    debug("goldfish_nand_block_markbad: invalid arg, ofs %llx, dev_size %llx, "
            "write_size %x\n", ofs, mtd->size, mtd->writesize);
    return -EINVAL;
}

/* Initialize a NAND flash device. */
static int goldfish_nand_init_device(struct goldfish_nand *nand, int id)
{
    uint32_t name_len;
    uint32_t result;
    uint32_t flags;
    unsigned char __iomem *base = nand->base;
    struct mtd_info *mtd = &nand->mtd[id];
    char *name;

    writel(id, base + NAND_DEV);
    flags = readl(base + NAND_DEV_FLAGS);
    name_len = readl(base + NAND_DEV_NAME_LEN);
    mtd->writesize = readl(base + NAND_DEV_PAGE_SIZE);
    mtd->size = readl(base + NAND_DEV_SIZE_LOW);
    mtd->size |= (uint64_t)readl(base + NAND_DEV_SIZE_HIGH) << 32;
    mtd->oobsize = readl(base + NAND_DEV_EXTRA_SIZE);
    mtd->oobavail = mtd->oobsize;
    mtd->erasesize = readl(base + NAND_DEV_ERASE_SIZE) /
                    (mtd->writesize + mtd->oobsize) * mtd->writesize;
    do_div(mtd->size, mtd->writesize + mtd->oobsize);
    mtd->size *= mtd->writesize;
    mtd->priv = nand;

    if(name_len > GOLDFISH_DEV_NAME_MAX_LEN) {
        debug("goldfish_nand_init_device: name_len=%d, larger than maximum length.", name_len);
        return -ENOMEM;
    }
    mtd->name = name = &goldfish_dev_name[id];
```

```c
        result = goldfish_nand_cmd(mtd, NAND_CMD_GET_DEV_NAME, 0, name_len, name);
        if(result != name_len) {
            mtd->name = NULL;
            debug("goldfish_nand_init_device failed to get dev name %d != %d\n",
                    result, name_len);
            return -ENODEV;
        }
        ((char *) mtd->name)[name_len] = '\0';

        /* Set up the MTD structure. */
        mtd->type = MTD_NANDFLASH;
        mtd->flags = MTD_CAP_NANDFLASH;
        if(flags & NAND_DEV_FLAG_READ_ONLY)
            mtd->flags &= ~MTD_WRITEABLE;

        mtd->owner = THIS_MODULE;
        mtd->erase = goldfish_nand_erase;
        mtd->read = goldfish_nand_read;
        mtd->write = goldfish_nand_write;
        mtd->read_oob = goldfish_nand_read_oob;
        mtd->write_oob = goldfish_nand_write_oob;
        mtd->block_isbad = goldfish_nand_block_isbad;
        mtd->block_markbad = goldfish_nand_block_markbad;

        return 0;
}
/*
 * This U-Boot function is the entry point to initialize the NAND flash
 * controller. It is called by U-Boot to initialize NAND flash.
 */
void board_nand_init(void)
{
    uint32_t num_dev;
    int i;
    int err;
```

```c
        uint32_t num_dev_working;
        uint32_t version;
        struct goldfish_nand *nand;
        unsigned char __iomem *base = (void *)IO_ADDRESS(GOLDFISH_NAND_BASE);

        debug("base=%x\n", (unsigned int)base);
        version = readl(base + NAND_VERSION);
        if(version != NAND_VERSION_CURRENT) {
            debug("goldfish_nand_init: version mismatch, got %d, expected %d\n",
                    version, NAND_VERSION_CURRENT);
            err = -ENODEV;
            goto err_no_dev;
        }
        num_dev = readl(base + NAND_NUM_DEV);
        if(num_dev == 0 || num_dev > CONFIG_SYS_MAX_NAND_DEVICE) {
            err = -ENODEV;
            debug("goldfish_nand_init: NAND_NUM_DEV=%d, fatal error!", num_dev);
            goto err_no_dev;
        }

        nand = &goldfish_nand_info;

        nand->base = base;
        nand->mtd_count = num_dev;
        nand->mtd = &nand_info[0];

        num_dev_working = 0;
        for(i = 0; i < num_dev; i++) {
            /* There are three NAND flash devices in goldfish (system, user data,
               and cache). We need to initialize them one by one. */
            err = goldfish_nand_init_device(nand, i);
            if(err == 0) {
                num_dev_working++;
#ifndef __BARE_METAL__
                /* After the device is initialized, it is registered in U-Boot. */
                nand_register(i);
#endif
                debug("goldfish_nand_init: id=%d: name=%s, nand_name=%s\n",
```

```
            i, nand->mtd[i].name, goldfish_dev_name[i]);

      }
  }
  if(num_dev_working == 0) {
      err = -ENODEV;
      goto err_no_working_dev;
  }
  return;

err_no_working_dev:
err_no_dev:
  return;
}
```

U-Boot API to Support NAND Flash

The function `board_nand_init()` is created for both the bare metal environment and U-Boot. This function will be called by the U-Boot initialization code so that NAND flash can be initialized during U-Boot initialization. First, it checks the revision of the NAND controller and gets the number of devices (e.g., system or user data) connected to it. Then, it calls the function `goldfish_nand_init_device()` to initialize each device that is found. Notice the global variable `goldfish_nand_info` included in this function—it is the data structure used to store an array of `mtd_info`. Each NAND device maps to one element in the `mtd_info` array.

The function `goldfish_nand_init_device()` associates each device with an instance of the data structure `mtd_info`. It populates `mtd_info` with NAND devices' properties, such as the page size, block size, OOB data size, device name, device capability flag, and so on. It also populates `mtd_info` with the methods that can operate on the NAND device, such as read, write, and erase methods. The next section provides details on these methods.

Goldfish NAND Flash Driver Functions

The function `goldfish_nand_cmd()` is common to all NAND flash commands. This function implements a general NAND flash command sequence for the goldfish NAND flash controller. The goldfish NAND flash controller command sequence is as follows:

1. Write the NAND DEV ID.
2. Write the NAND device address.
3. Write the size of the data being transferred.
4. Write the data address in memory.
5. Write the NAND flash command.
6. Read the execution result.

Seven other functions also support NAND flash commands. These functions are the methods that are initialized in the `mtd_info` data structure to support the MTD subsystem in both U-Boot and the Linux kernel:

- `goldfish_nand_erase()`: Erases a NAND block.
- `goldfish_nand_read_oob()`: Reads both page and OOB data.
- `goldfish_nand_read()`: Reads page data.
- `goldfish_nand_write_oob()`: Writes both page and OOB data.
- `goldfish_nand_write()`: Writes page data.
- `goldfish_nand_isbad()`: Gets the bad block data.
- `goldfish_nand_markbad()`: Sets the bad block data.

NAND Flash Programming Interface Test Program

After we have implemented the NAND flash programming interface, we must create a test program to test it. To verify the test result, we can compare it with the corresponding result from the Android SDK.

NAND Flash Information from the Linux Kernel

Earlier in this chapter, we discussed the file system for the Android emulator. The Android system runs on top of a Linux kernel, and this Linux kernel provides the NAND flash programming interface support. We can use the debug information from this Linux kernel as a reference to check the result of our test program. To do so, we can run the Android Virtual Device hd2 that we created in Chapter 2 (see Figure 2.3) with the following command-line options:

```
$ emulator -verbose -show-kernel -avd hd2
```

After the emulator boots up, the following information is printed to the console. It includes the NAND flash capacity, page size, OOB data size, and erase block size.

```
goldfish nand dev0: size c9c0000, page 2048, extra 64, erase 131072
goldfish nand dev1: size c200000, page 2048, extra 64, erase 131072
goldfish nand dev2: size 4000000, page 2048, extra 64, erase 131072
```

After the Android system is ready in the emulator, we can connect to the emulator instance through the `adb` command to get more detailed information about the NAND flash. In particular, we can use the `adb` command console to print the contents of the file /proc/yaffs:

```
$ adb shell
* daemon not running. starting it now on port 5037 *
* daemon started successfully *
```

```
root@android:/ # cat /proc/yaffs
YAFFS built:Mar  7 2014 15:57:44
$Id$
$Id$

Device 0 "system"
startBlock......... 0
endBlock........... 1613
totalBytesPerChunk. 2048
nDataBytesPerChunk. 2048
chunkGroupBits..... 0
chunkGroupSize..... 1
nErasedBlocks...... 4
nReservedBlocks.... 5
blocksInCheckpoint. 3
nTnodesCreated..... 8000
nFreeTnodes........ 71
nObjectsCreated.... 1000
nFreeObjects....... 99
nFreeChunks........ 286
nPageWrites........ 159
nPageReads......... 46248
nBlockErasures..... 0
nGCCopies.......... 0
garbageCollections. 0
passiveGCs......... 0
nRetriedWrites..... 0
nShortOpCaches..... 10
nRetireBlocks...... 0
eccFixed........... 0
eccUnfixed......... 0
tagsEccFixed....... 0
tagsEccUnfixed..... 0
cacheHits.......... 0
nDeletedFiles...... 0
nUnlinkedFiles..... 0
```

```
nBackgroudDeletions 0
useNANDECC......... 1
isYaffs2........... 1
inbandTags......... 0

Device 1 "userdata"
startBlock......... 0
endBlock........... 1551
totalBytesPerChunk. 2048
nDataBytesPerChunk. 2048
chunkGroupBits..... 0
chunkGroupSize..... 1
nErasedBlocks...... 1395
nReservedBlocks.... 5
blocksInCheckpoint. 0
nTnodesCreated..... 500
nFreeTnodes........ 101
nObjectsCreated.... 500
nFreeObjects....... 36
nFreeChunks........ 95199
nPageWrites........ 909
nPageReads......... 2089
nBlockErasures..... 0
nGCCopies.......... 0
garbageCollections. 0
passiveGCs......... 0
nRetriedWrites..... 0
nShortOpCaches..... 10
nRetireBlocks...... 0
eccFixed........... 0
eccUnfixed......... 0
tagsEccFixed....... 0
tagsEccUnfixed..... 0
cacheHits.......... 92
nDeletedFiles...... 1
```

```
nUnlinkedFiles..... 90
nBackgroudDeletions 0
useNANDECC......... 1
isYaffs2........... 1
inbandTags......... 0
Device 2 "cache"
startBlock......... 0
endBlock........... 511
totalBytesPerChunk. 2048
nDataBytesPerChunk. 2048
chunkGroupBits..... 0
chunkGroupSize..... 1
nErasedBlocks...... 511
nReservedBlocks.... 5
blocksInCheckpoint. 0
nTnodesCreated..... 0
nFreeTnodes........ 0
nObjectsCreated.... 200
nFreeObjects....... 96
nFreeChunks........ 32766
nPageWrites........ 4
nPageReads......... 5
nBlockErasures..... 0
nGCCopies.......... 0
garbageCollections. 0
passiveGCs......... 0
nRetriedWrites..... 0
nShortOpCaches..... 10
nRetireBlocks...... 0
eccFixed........... 0
eccUnfixed......... 0
tagsEccFixed....... 0
tagsEccUnfixed..... 0
cacheHits.......... 0
```

```
nDeletedFiles...... 0
nUnlinkedFiles..... 0
nBackgroudDeletions 0
useNANDECC......... 1
isYaffs2........... 1
inbandTags......... 0
```

From this information, we can identify the items listed in Table 8.1 that are related to NAND flash. In this case, we use the device "system" as an example.

NAND Flash Test Program

The test program shown in Example 8.4 is created on top of the example code we created earlier in Chapter 7. We have the following common and project-specific files:
Common files:

- `bsp.c`: Includes the API functions for the goldfish interrupt controller. It is the same as the code in Chapter 7.
- `timer.c`: Includes the API functions for the goldfish timer. It is the same as the code in Chapter 7.
- `syscalls_cs3.c`: Implementation of system service stubs. It is the same as the code in Chapter 6.
- `serial_goldfish.c`: The C code to implement serial functions. It is the same as the code in Chapter 5.
- `goldfish_uart.S`: The assembly language code to implement serial port–specific functions. It is the same as the code in Chapter 5.
- `arm_exc.S`: Exception vectors are implemented in assembly language code.

Table 8.1 NAND Flash Device System

Item	Value
Size	The size of flash device system is 0xc9c0000 (211550208).
Number of pages in a block	Each block has 64 pages (131072/2048).
Block size	The block size is 131072 (0x20000 or 128KB).
Number of blocks	From the file `/proc/yaffs`, we can see that the start block is 0 and the end block is 1613, so the total number of blocks is 1614.
Page size	The page size is 2048 (0x800 or 2KB).
Number of pages	The number of pages is 103296 (1614*64).
Extra data size	The size allocated for extra data is 64 bytes.

- `isr.c` : In this file, a C-level interrupt service routine (ISR) is implemented.
- `low_level_init.c`: Implements a function `low_level_init()` that performs early initialization of the hardware. Exception vectors are initialized in `low_level_init()`.

Project-specific files:

- `c08e1.c`: The test code that implements the `main()` function
- `goldfish_nand.c`: The file that includes all the NAND flash support functions
- `Makefile`: The makefile to build this project
- `c08e1.ld`: The linker script of the project
- `startup_c08e1.S`: The startup code

Example 8.4 NAND Flash Programming Interface Test Program (c08e1.c)

```
#include <stdio.h>
#include <stdlib.h>
#include <string.h>
#include <sys/unistd.h>
#include <hardware.h>
#include <arm_exc.h>
#include <bsp.h>
#include "div64.h"
#include "mtd.h"

void EnterUserMode(void);
void SystemCall(void);

struct goldfish_nand {
    unsigned char __iomem   *base;
    size_t                  mtd_count;
    struct mtd_info         *mtd;
};

extern struct goldfish_nand goldfish_nand_info;

uint32_t __div64_32(uint64_t *n, uint32_t base)
{
    uint64_t rem = *n;
    uint64_t b = base;
```

```c
    uint64_t res, d = 1;
    uint32_t high = rem >> 32;

    /* Reduce the thing a bit first */
    res = 0;
    if (high >= base) {
        high /= base;
        res = (uint64_t) high << 32;
        rem -= (uint64_t) (high*base) << 32;
    }

    while ((int64_t)b > 0 && b < rem) {
        b = b+b;
        d = d+d;
    }

    do {
        if (rem >= b) {
            rem -= b;
            res += d;
        }
        b >>= 1;
        d >>= 1;
    } while (d);

    *n = res;
    return rem;
}

void sw_handler(int num)
{
    printf("=>Inside sw_handler, num=%d.\n", num);
}

void irq_handler(int irq)
{
    int num = 0;
    unsigned long tm = 0;
```

```c
        num = goldfish_irq_status();
        printf("=>Enter ARM_irq(%d), pending num=%d\n", irq, num);
    switch (irq) {
    case IRQ_TTY0:
        printf("=>IRQ_TTY0.\n");
        break;
    case IRQ_TTY1:
        printf("=>IRQ_TTY1.\n");
        break;
    case IRQ_TTY2:
        printf("=>IRQ_TTY2.\n");
        break;
    case IRQ_TIMER:
        /* goldfish_mask_irq(IRQ_TIMER); */
        goldfish_clear_timer_int();
        printf("=>IRQ_TIMER - clear interrupt.\n");
        break;
    default:
        printf("=>Unknown IRQ %x.\n", irq);
        break;
    }
    tm = get_ticks();
    printf("=>Exit ARM_irq(%d). tm=%lu\n", irq, tm);
}

/* We will run the unit test of the serial driver in main() */
int main(int argc, char *argv[])
{
    struct mtd_info *mtd;
    int i;
    int num_dev = 0;

    printf("Enter main(), test goldfish NAND flash ...\n");

    EnterUserMode();
```

```
    /* Initialize NAND devices */
    board_nand_init();

    num_dev = goldfish_nand_info.mtd_count;
    if(num_dev > 0) {
        for(i = 0; i < num_dev; i++) {
            mtd = &goldfish_nand_info.mtd[i];
            printf("Device %d %s\n", i, mtd->name);
            printf("Flags............ 0x%x %s\n", i, mtd->flags);
            printf("Size............. %d\n", mtd->size);
            printf("Block/Page....... %d\n", mtd->erasesize/mtd->writesize);
            printf("Block Size....... %d\n", mtd->erasesize);
            printf("No. of Blocks.... %d\n", mtd->size/mtd->erasesize);
            printf("Page Size........ %d\n", mtd->writesize);
            printf("No. of Pages..... %d\n", mtd->size/mtd->writesize);
            printf("Extra Data Size... %d\n\n", mtd->oobsize);
        }
    }

    while(1) {};

    return 1;
}
```

This is a very simple test program. We call U-Boot API `board_nand_init()` to initialize NAND devices. After NAND devices are initialized, the `mtd_info` data structure for each device is available. We can print out the information for each device from its `mtd_info` data structure.

Let's build the project first:

```
$ make DEBUG=1
    CC     c08e1.c
    CC     goldfish_nand.c
    AS     startup_c08e1.S
    CC     ../../drivers/serial_goldfish.c
    AS     ../../drivers/goldfish_uart.S
    CC     ../../drivers/syscalls_cs3.c
    CC     ../../drivers/low_level_init.c
    AS     ../../drivers/arm_exc.S
```

```
CC      ../../drivers/bsp.c
CC      ../../drivers/isr.c
CC      ../../drivers/timer.c
LD      gcc/c08e1.axf
```

To run our test program, we can start the emulator with the -show-kernel option:

$ **emulator -show-kernel -netfast -avd hd2 -shell -qemu -kernel gcc/c08e1.axf**

...

```
goldfish_init(), gtty.base=ff012000
Enter main(), test goldfish NAND flash ...
base=ff017000
goldfish_nand_init: id=0: name=system, nand_name=system
goldfish_nand_init: id=1: name=userdata, nand_name=userdata
goldfish_nand_init: id=2: name=cache, nand_name=cache
Device 0 system
Flags............ 0x0
Size............. 211550208
Block/Page....... 64
Block Size....... 131072
No. of Blocks.... 1614
Page Size........ 2048
No. of Pages..... 103296
Extra Data Size.. 64

Device 1 userdata
Flags............ 0x1
Size............. 203423744
Block/Page....... 64
Block Size....... 131072
No. of Blocks.... 1552
Page Size........ 2048
No. of Pages..... 99328
Extra Data Size.. 64

Device 2 cache
Flags............ 0x2
Size............. 67108864
```

```
Block/Page........ 64
Block Size........ 131072
No. of Blocks..... 512
Page Size......... 2048
No. of Pages...... 32768

Extra Data Size... 64
```

...

From the console output, we discover the same set of NAND flash devices (system, user data, and cache), which we can see in the Linux kernel log. When we compare the information from the preceding debug output with the information in Table 8.1, we see that we got a consistent result.

Summary

In this chapter, we continued exploring the goldfish hardware through examples. To test the NAND flash interface, we created a NAND flash driver by analyzing the goldfish Linux kernel source code. Similar to the work done in previous chapters, the driver code can be used in U-Boot porting later. We also created a NAND flash driver around the data structure `mtd_info`. This data structure is used by both U-Boot and the Linux kernel.

To test a NAND flash interface, we read the NAND flash information from the emulated hardware using our driver. We can then compare these results with those from the Linux kernel. In this chapter, we did only minimal testing of the NAND flash driver. We will do more extensive testing of this driver when we discuss how to boot Android from NAND flash in Chapter 10.

II

U-Boot

9 U-Boot Porting

10 Using U-Boot to Boot the Goldfish Kernel

9

U-Boot Porting

In Part I of this book, we discussed how to create applications directly on top of hardware—that is, bare metal applications. In Part II, we talk about a special bare metal application: U-Boot. In this chapter, we discuss porting U-Boot to the goldfish platform. Since QEMU includes a mini-bootloader, it can boot a Linux kernel directly. Consequently, no one has ported U-Boot to the goldfish platform. This workaround is not really a complete boot process, like the processes we would see in a real hardware environment.

In this chapter, we begin by building the U-Boot source code. We then discuss how to port U-Boot to the goldfish platform, working through this process step by step. By the end of this chapter, you should be able to boot the entire Android platform using our own U-Boot and goldfish kernel. Along the way, you will learn how to build a new platform from scratch. This process is very similar to the hardware board build phase, except that we cannot use the same debugging tool in the real hardware environment. In that environment, we would probably use a JTAG-based hardware debugging tool.

Introducing U-Boot

U-Boot is an open source bootloader available for a wide range of embedded processor architectures. It could be compared to BIOS on a desktop PC or laptop. In the embedded system, U-Boot initializes the hardware and finds the available boot image. When a bootable image is found, it loads it into memory and passes control to this process.

At a minimum, a bootloader for an embedded system should provide the following functionalities:

- Initialize the hardware, such as memory, flash device, timer, serial port, and so on
- Provide boot parameters for the Linux kernel
- Transfer control to the Linux kernel

Additionally, most bootloaders provide a command-line interface or menu interface that provides the following functionalities:

- Change the configuration of hardware devices
- Upload binary images to the memory via a serial, USB, or Ethernet port
- Copy binary images from RAM to flash memory

U-Boot can be considered to be a bare metal application even though it is quite complicated. In reality, it lies somewhere between an operating system and an application. From a functionality perspective, it is an application, because the only thing U-Boot does is boot an operating system. However, from a programming architecture perspective, it has a lot of the same elements that an operating system usually has. For example, it supports almost all hardware interfaces on a hardware board. To support these hardware interfaces, U-Boot has its own driver architecture. A lot of its drivers are borrowed directly from the Linux kernel.

Downloading and Compiling U-Boot

The official release of U-Boot is maintained by Wolfgang Denx and hosted at *http://www.denx.de/wiki/U-Boot*. Many U-Boot projects besides the official release exist. One of them is specifically maintained for ARM SoC by the Linaro project. This release, which is the one we will use, is available at *http://www.linaro.org/downloads/1304*.

> **Note**
> Linaro was established in June 2010 by founding members ARM, Freescale, IBM, Samsung, ST-Ericsson, and Texas instruments (TI). It is a nonprofit organization focused on improving Linux on ARM. Linaro follows a monthly release cycle. At the time of this book's writing, the current release number was 13.04.

The U-Boot source code can be cloned from the Linaro git repository using the following command:

```
$ git clone git://git.linaro.org/boot/u-boot-linaro-stable.git
```

Multiple branches and tags can be found in the Linaro git repository. We will create a goldfish port on top of the latest stable version. Once we decide what the baseline should be, we will use it to create a branch for the goldfish port:

```
$ git branch goldfish
```

To make it easier for readers to repeat the porting process, I created a source code repository on GitHub for the U-Boot on goldfish platform. I recommend that you use this GitHub version so that you can follow along with the instructions in this chapter instead of working on the source code taken directly from Linaro. To check out the source code from GitHub, you can use the following command:

```
$ git clone https://github.com/shugaoye/u-boot.git
```

To follow the steps in this chapter and create your own U-Boot, you can check out the original branch:

```
$ git checkout -b versatileqemu remotes/origin/versatileqemu
```

```
Branch versatileqemu set up to track remote branch versatileqemu from origin.
Switched to a new branch 'versatileqemu'
```

If you want to find all of the changes made for the goldfish platform, you can check out the branch for Linux kernel 2.6.29:

```
$ git checkout -b android-armemu-2.6.29 remotes/origin/android-armemu-2.6.29
Branch versatileqemu set up to track remote branch versatileqemu from origin.
Switched to branch 'android-armemu-2.6.29'
```

Once you have these two branches available locally, you can easily discover the changes that we will make in this chapter by giving the `git-diff` command:

```
$ git diff --name-only versatileqemu android-armemu-2.6.29
.gitignore
AndroidU-Boot.mk
arch/arm/cpu/arm926ejs/goldfish/Makefile
arch/arm/cpu/arm926ejs/goldfish/reset.S
arch/arm/cpu/arm926ejs/goldfish/timer.c
arch/arm/include/asm/mach-types.h
board/google/goldfish/Makefile
board/google/goldfish/goldfish.c
board/google/goldfish/lowlevel_init.S
boards.cfg
common/image.c
common/main.c
config.mk
drivers/mmc/Makefile
drivers/mmc/goldfish_mmc.c
drivers/mtd/nand/Makefile
drivers/mtd/nand/goldfish_nand.c
drivers/mtd/nand/goldfish_nand_reg.h
drivers/net/smc91111.c
drivers/rtc/Makefile
drivers/rtc/rtc-goldfish.c
drivers/serial/Makefile
drivers/serial/goldfish_uart.S
drivers/serial/serial_goldfish.c
drivers/serial/serial_goldfish.h
fs/yaffs2/yaffs_uboot_glue.c
include/configs/goldfish.h
```

Chapter 9 U-Boot Porting

Before we have our own U-Boot for goldfish platform, we might want to test a known U-Boot configuration on the Android platform. The most similar hardware board configuration is ARM Versatile Platform Baseboard, a hardware reference board from ARM. It is supported by QEMU. One special configuration is present in the Linaro U-Boot source for Versatile PB QEMU (versatileqemu). We will use this configuration as the foundation for our work in this chapter.

Before we go further, it is important to understand the difference between the Android emulator and QEMU. The Android emulator is a special build of QEMU that has been created to support only the goldfish platform, whereas QEMU is an emulator that can support multiple platforms. Versatile PB QEMU is only one of the supported configurations of QEMU.

Note also that we use the branch versatileqemu, which we checked out previously, as the starting point in this chapter.

To build our Versatile PB QEMU configuration, we go to the U-Boot source tree and run the following commands in a Linux console:

```
$ make versatileqemu_config arch=ARM CROSS_COMPILE=arm-none-eabi-
```

Configuring for versatileqemu - Board: versatile, Options: ARCH_VERSATILE_QEMU, ARCH_VERSATILE_PB

```
$ make all arch=ARM CROSS_COMPILE=arm-none-eabi-
```

After the build completes, we can boot it in QEMU and get the U-Boot command-line prompt:

```
$ qemu-system-arm -M versatilepb -nographic -kernel u-boot.bin
oss: Could not initialize DAC

oss: Failed to open '/dev/dsp'

oss: Reason: No such file or directory

oss: Could not initialize DAC

oss: Failed to open '/dev/dsp'

oss: Reason: No such file or directory

audio: Failed to create voice 'lm4549.out'


U-Boot 2013.01.-rc1-00002-ga93e8a7 (May 26 2013 - 16:12:46)

U-Boot code: 00010000 -> 00029A2C  BSS: -> 0002D1DC
monitor len: 0001D1DC
ramsize: 08000000
TLB table at: 07ff0000
Top of RAM usable for U-Boot at: 07ff0000
Reserving 116k for U-Boot at: 07fd2000
Reserving 136k for malloc() at: 07fb0000
Reserving 32 Bytes for Board Info at: 07faffe0
```

```
Reserving 120 Bytes for Global Data at: 07faff68
New Stack Pointer is: 07faff58
RAM Configuration:
Bank #0: 00000000 128 MiB
relocation Offset is: 07fc2000
WARNING: Caches not enabled
monitor flash len: 0001CF2C
Now running in RAM - U-Boot at: 07fd2000
Using default environment

Destroy Hash Table: 07feb640 table = 00000000
Create Hash Table: N=80
INSERT: table 07feb640, filled 1/83 rv 07fb02d0 ==> name="bootargs" value="root=/
dev/nfs mem=128M ip=dhcp netdev=25,0,0xf1010000,0xf1010010,eth0"
INSERT: table 07feb640, filled 2/83 rv 07fb045c ==> name="bootdelay" value="2"
INSERT: table 07feb640, filled 3/83 rv 07fb0168 ==> name="baudrate" value="38400"
INSERT: table 07feb640, filled 4/83 rv 07fb0234 ==> name="bootfile" value="/
tftpboot/uImage"
INSERT: free(data = 07fb0008)
INSERT: done
In:    serial
Out:   serial
Err:   serial
Net:   SMC91111-0
Warning: SMC91111-0 using MAC address from net device

### main_loop entered: bootdelay=2

### main_loop: bootcmd="<UNDEFINED>"
VersatilePB #
```

> **Note**
>
> If you cannot find the command `qemu-system-arm` in your environment, you can install it using the following command:
>
> `$ sudo apt-get install qemu-system`

In this command line, we use the option `-M versatilepb` to specify the hardware board that we want to simulate.

Now let's run the same U-Boot binary in the Android emulator and see what happens. We can see from the console log that it displays nothing on the console—it seems to have gotten stuck somewhere:

```
$ emulator -show-kernel -netfast -avd hd2 -shell -qemu -kernel u-boot.bin
```

Even though we don't know why this build does not work on the goldfish platform, we can use gdb to trace this U-Boot build and see exactly what happened. This is a wonderful advantage of using the Android emulator or QEMU to debug programs—it is not possible to perform such a trace in a hardware development board.

Debugging U-Boot with GDB

Debugging U-Boot is very similar to our process of debugging applications in the previous chapters. The only special information that we need to know is that U-Boot will relocate itself during the boot-up. We have to reload the debug symbol after that step.

We start the emulator first and let it wait for a gdb connection:

```
$ emulator -verbose -show-kernel -netfast -avd hd2 -qemu -serial stdio -s -S
-kernel u-boot
```

emulator: found SDK root at /home/sgye/adt-bundle-linux-x86-20130219/sdk

emulator: Android virtual device file at: /home/sgye/.android/avd/hd2.ini

emulator: virtual device content at /home/sgye/.android/avd/hd2.avd

emulator: virtual device config file: /home/sgye/.android/avd/hd2.avd/config.ini

...

emulator: mapping 'system' NAND image to /tmp/android-sgye/emulator-Brbv03

emulator: rounding devsize up to a full eraseunit, now cc0f000

emulator: nand_add_dev:
userdata,size=0xc800000,file=/home/sgye/.android/avd/hd2.avd/userdata-qemu.img

emulator: rounding devsize up to a full eraseunit, now c810000

emulator: registered 'boot-properties' qemud service

emulator: Adding boot property: 'dalvik.vm.heapsize' = '32m'

emulator: Adding boot property: 'qemu.sf.lcd_density' = '240'

emulator: Adding boot property: 'qemu.hw.mainkeys' = '1'

emulator: Adding boot property: 'qemu.sf.fake_camera' = 'none'

emulator: nand_add_dev:
cache,size=0x4200000,file=/home/sgye/.android/avd/hd2.avd/cache.img

emulator: Initializing hardware OpenGLES emulation support

Let's launch gdb through ddd and connect to the emulator:

```
$ ddd --debugger arm-none-eabi-gdb u-boot
```

GNU DDD 3.3.12 (i686-pc-linux-gnu), by Dorothea Lütkehaus and Andreas Zeller.

Copyright © 1995-1999 Technische Universität Braunschweig, Germany.

Copyright © 1999-2001 Universität Passau, Germany.

Copyright © 2001 Universität des Saarlandes, Germany.

Copyright © 2001-2004 Free Software Foundation, Inc.

Reading symbols from /media/u64/home/sgye/src/u-boot/u-boot...done.

(gdb) **target remote localhost:1234**

_start () at start.S:64

(gdb)

We have to use the `target remote` command to connect to the Android emulator from gdb first, as shown in Figure 9.1. U-Boot is loaded at address 0x10000 and is started from the reset vector.

The `versatileqemu` configuration builds the same CPU model (`arm926ejs`) as the Android emulator does, so this build can run until it reaches a point somewhere in the

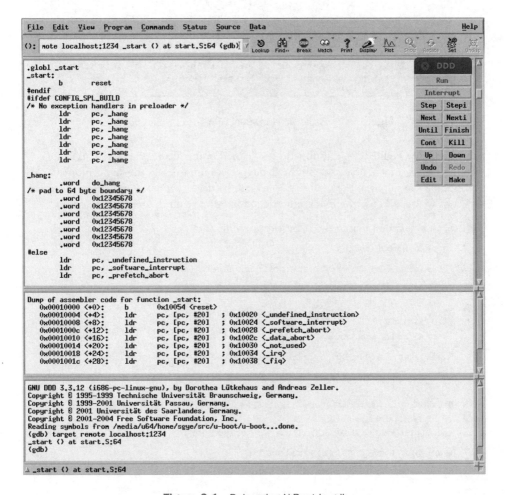

Figure 9.1 Debugging U-Boot in gdb

Chapter 9 U-Boot Porting

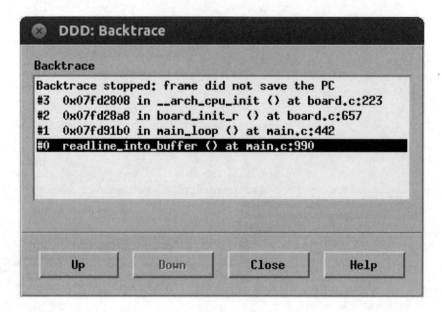

Figure 9.2 Backtrace of U-Boot (versatileqemu build)

main_loop (see Figure 9.2). This function is defined in the file common/main.c. To step through the U-Boot source code in the debugger, we must debug the application after U-Boot relocates itself in the memory. To reload the debug symbol again after the relocation step, we need to use the following method in gdb to find the relocation address:

1. Set a breakpoint before the relocation starting point:

    (gdb) **b board_init_f**

    Breakpoint 1 at 0x108e0: file board.c, line 276.

    (gdb) **c**

    Breakpoint 1, board_init_f (bootflag=0) at board.c:276

    (gdb) **b relocate_code**

    Breakpoint 2 at 0x1007c: file start.S, line 229.

    (gdb) **c**

    Breakpoint 2, relocate_code () at start.S:229

2. Calculate the relocation address. As we can see here, it is at 0x7fd2000:

    (gdb) **p/x ((gd_t *)$r1)->relocaddr**

    $1 = 0x7fd2000

3. Reload the symbol to the address 0x7fd2000:

    (gdb) **add-symbol-file u-boot 0x7fd2000**

```
add symbol table from file "u-boot" at
    .text_addr = 0x7fd2000
```

4. Set a breakpoint in the function that is invoked after the relocation is complete:

   (gdb) **b board_init_r**

   ```
   Breakpoint 3 at 0x10808: file board.c, line 489. (2 locations)
   ```

   (gdb) **c**

   ```
   Breakpoint 3, board_init_r (id=0x7faff68, dest_addr=134029312) at board.c:489
   ```

   (gdb)

To make this process easier for the readers, I created a gdb script that is available at GitHub: *https://github.com/shugaoye/build/blob/master/bin/u-boot.gdb*.

After the relocation, we can continue debugging until the program enters into an infinite loop. We can see this point in the backtrace as shown in Figure 9.2.

As shown in Figure 9.2, U-Boot hangs at the function `readline_into_buffer()`. From this information, we can guess that it may be blocked at the point where input of the serial device should be received, when we expect a U-Boot command from the console. Goldfish has a special serial interface, while the `versatileqemu` build uses a normal UART based on PrimeCell PL010/PL011. Without a goldfish serial driver, we won't be able to see any output or type any U-Boot commands at the command prompt. Next we'll port U-Boot to the goldfish platform.

U-Boot Relocation

U-Boot relocates itself to RAM during the boot-up process. There are two primary reasons for this relocation. First, U-Boot usually starts from ROM—and the performance of read-only memory is much slower than the performance of random access memory (RAM). Second, when U-Boot runs from ROM, it starts from the processor's internal RAM or uses the processor cache as RAM. However, there is no memory available yet. Thus U-Boot has to perform at least a minimum initialization of MMU before it can copy itself into RAM.

Porting U-Boot to the Goldfish Platform

The basic steps to port U-Boot to a new hardware platform are as follows:

1. *Create a new board.* We need to add a new board configuration.
2. *Make processor-level changes.* We need to make processor-level changes if we will support a new processor architecture.
3. *Make board-level changes.* Board-level changes make the U-Boot driver framework available on the new hardware board.
4. *Make device driver changes.* This is the major work required with U-Boot porting. We have to add new hardware drivers or modify existing hardware drivers to support the hardware.

Creating a New Board

To port U-Boot to the goldfish platform, we need to create a new target board to make U-Boot work. We must complete a few basic steps to do this. Depending on the specific version of U-Boot, the steps to create a new target board may differ slightly.

First, we need to add a new board configuration in the `boards.cfg` file located under the root of the U-Boot source tree. The following line is added in file `boards.cfg`:

```
# Target        ARCH CPU           Board name Vendor SoC       Options
#########################################################################
goldfish arm   arm926ejs goldfish    google goldfish    goldfish:ARCH_GOLDFISH,ARCH_VERSATILE_QEMU,ARCH_VERSATILE_PB
```

This is a single, very long line that wraps to multiple lines. Table 9.1 breaks its components down to make the line easier to read.

As this line indicates, we will create a platform with goldfish on top of Versatile PB. The configuration ARCH_GOLDFISH is dependent on two configurations, ARCH_VERSATILE_PB and ARCH_VERSATILE_QEMU. To create the goldfish on Versatile PB platform, we can duplicate two folders and a header file from Versatile PB to create the base of the goldfish source code tree:

arch/arm/cpu/arm926ejs/versatile/ -> arch/arm/cpu/arm926ejs/goldfish/

board/armltd/versatile/ -> board/google/goldfish/

include/configs/versatile.h -> include/configs/goldfish.h

With this change, we can now build the new configuration:

```
$ make goldfish_config arch=ARM CROSS_COMPILE=arm-none-eabi-
```

Configuring for goldfish - Board: goldfish, Options: ARCH_GOLDFISH, ARCH_VERSATILE_QEMU, ARCH_VERSATILE_PB

```
$ make all arch=ARM CROSS_COMPILE=arm-none-eabi-
```

Table 9.1 Goldfish Board Configuration

Field	Value
Target	goldfish
ARCH	arm
CPU	arm926ejs
Board name	goldfish
Vendor	google
SoC	goldfish
Options	goldfish:ARCH_GOLDFISH, ARCH_VERSATILE_QEMU, ARCH_VERSATILE_PB

At this point, we have the code base for the new configuration. To make this new configuration work on Android emulator, however, we must also make a few changes to account for the hardware difference between Versatile PB and goldfish. We will continue working on processor level, board level, and device drivers in the next three sections.

Processor-Specific Changes

Since Versatile PB and goldfish use the same processor model, most of the processor-level code can be reused. The processor-level files are located at arch/arm/cpu/arm926ejs/ goldfish. There are two files within this folder: reset.S and timer.c.

The file reset.S includes a few lines of assembly code for the startup. They are the same as for Versatile PB, which is copied from TI's OMAP1610/OMAP730 code. The major changes for the goldfish platform are timer specific. The file timer.c is created to handle timer initialization and provide timer functions. Since we have developed all timer functions in Chapter 7, we can copy our timer.c file from Chapter 7 and use it here.

Board-Specific Changes

Board-level files are found in the folder board/google/goldfish. There are two files within this folder: goldfish.c and lowlevel_init.S.

The assembly file lowlevel_init.S includes only a stub for the function lowlevel_ init(), which is required by U-Boot. The most important files are goldfish.c and the header file include/configs/goldfish.h provided in Example 9.1. The board-specific implementation is found in goldfish.c and board-specific definitions are defined in goldfish.h. Recall from the header file hardware.h in Example 5.6 that goldfish.h is extended on top of hardware.h with U-Boot–specific configuration information. At the bottom of goldfish.h, all base addresses for goldfish registers and interrupt numbers are copied from hardware.h.

In the U-Boot–specific definitions, CONFIG_SMC91111 is defined to include the Ethernet driver from U-Boot, because an existing implementation is already available. CONFIG_GOLDFISH_SERIAL is defined to include our own serial driver. The creation of a serial driver will be discussed later in this chapter. CONFIG_USE_IRQ is defined to support interrupt handling—interrupt handling is an optional implementation in U-Boot architecture. Goldfish-specific interrupt support is implemented in goldfish.c. Another important definition is PHYS_SDRAM_1_SIZE: We defined the RAM size as 0x20000000 (512MB) in PHYS_SDRAM_1_SIZE, and this size should be the same in our U-Boot code because we configured it in the Android emulator as shown in Figure 2.3.

Example 9.1 Goldfish Hardware Configuration (include/configs/goldfish.h)

```
#ifndef __GOLDFISH_CONFIG_H
#define __GOLDFISH_CONFIG_H

/*
 * High-level configuration options
 */
#define CONFIG_ARM926EJS          1           /* This is an arm926ejs CPU core */
#define CONFIG_VERSATILE          1              /* in Versatile Platform Board */
#define CONFIG_ARCH_VERSATILE     1                /* Specifically, a Versatile */
#define CONFIG_USE_IRQ
#define CONFIG_STACKSIZE_IRQ (4*1024)
#define CONFIG_STACKSIZE_FIQ (4*1024)

#define CONFIG_SYS_MEMTEST_START  0x100000
#define CONFIG_SYS_MEMTEST_END    0x10000000
#define CONFIG_SYS_HZ             (1000000 / 256)
#define CONFIG_SYS_TIMERBASE      IO_ADDRESS(GOLDFISH_TIMER_BASE) /* Timer base */

#define CONFIG_SYS_TIMER_INTERVAL 10000
#define CONFIG_SYS_TIMER_RELOAD   (CONFIG_SYS_TIMER_INTERVAL >> 4)
#define CONFIG_SYS_TIMER_CTRL     0x84                  /* Enable, Clock / 16 */

#define CONFIG_CMDLINE_TAG        1                  /* Enable passing of ATAGs */
#define CONFIG_SETUP_MEMORY_TAGS  1
#define CONFIG_MISC_INIT_R        1
/*
 * Size of malloc() pool
 */
#define CONFIG_ENV_SIZE           8192
#define CONFIG_SYS_MALLOC_LEN     (CONFIG_ENV_SIZE + 128 * 1024)

/*
 * Hardware drivers
 */

#define CONFIG_SMC91111
#define CONFIG_SMC_USE_32_BIT
#define CONFIG_SMC91111_BASE      IO_ADDRESS(GOLDFISH_smc91x_BASE)
#undef CONFIG_SMC91111_EXT_PHY
```

```
/*
 *  GOLDFISH serial
 */

#define CONFIG_GOLDFISH_SERIAL

#define CONFIG_CONS_INDEX        0

#define CONFIG_BAUDRATE          38400
#define CONFIG_SYS_SERIAL0       IO_ADDRESS(GOLDFISH_TTY1_BASE)
#define CONFIG_SYS_SERIAL1       IO_ADDRESS(GOLDFISH_TTY2_BASE)

/*
 *  Command-line configuration
 */
#define CONFIG_CMD_BDI
#define CONFIG_CMD_DHCP
#define CONFIG_CMD_FLASH
#define CONFIG_CMD_IMI
#define CONFIG_CMD_MEMORY
#define CONFIG_CMD_NET
#define CONFIG_CMD_PING
#define CONFIG_CMD_SAVEENV

/*
 *  BOOTP options
 */
#define CONFIG_BOOTP_BOOTPATH
#define CONFIG_BOOTP_GATEWAY
#define CONFIG_BOOTP_HOSTNAME
#define CONFIG_BOOTP_SUBNETMASK

/*
 *  Boot delay and Linux kernel parameters
 */
#define CONFIG_BOOTDELAY    2
#define CONFIG_BOOTARGS "qemu.gles=1 qemu=1 console=ttyS0 android.qemud=ttyS1 androidboot.console=ttyS2 android.checkjni=1 ndns=1"
#define CONFIG_BOOTCOMMAND "bootm 0x210000 0x410000"
#define CONFIG_INITRD_TAG 1
```

```c
/*
 * Static configuration when assigning fixed address
 */
#define CONFIG_BOOTFILE         "/tftpboot/uImage" /* file to load */

/*
 * Miscellaneous configurable options
 */
#define CONFIG_SYS_LONGHELP                         /* undef to save memory */
#define CONFIG_SYS_CBSIZE      256                  /* Console I/O buffer size */
/* Monitor command prompt     */
# define CONFIG_SYS_PROMPT     "Goldfish # "
/* Print buffer size */
#define CONFIG_SYS_PBSIZE      \
         (CONFIG_SYS_CBSIZE + sizeof(CONFIG_SYS_PROMPT) + 16)
#define CONFIG_SYS_MAXARGS     16                   /* Max number of command args */
#define CONFIG_SYS_BARGSIZE    CONFIG_SYS_CBSIZE    /* Boot argument buffer size */

#define CONFIG_SYS_LOAD_ADDR   0x7fc0               /* Default load address */

/*-----------------------------------------------------------------------
 * Physical memory map
 */
#define CONFIG_NR_DRAM_BANKS   1                    /* We have 1 bank of DRAM */
#define PHYS_SDRAM_1           0x00000000           /* SDRAM Bank #1 */
#define PHYS_SDRAM_1_SIZE      0x20000000           /* 512 MB */
#define PHYS_FLASH_SIZE        0x04000000           /* 64MB */

#define CONFIG_SYS_SDRAM_BASE      PHYS_SDRAM_1
#define CONFIG_SYS_INIT_RAM_ADDR   0x00800000
#define CONFIG_SYS_INIT_RAM_SIZE   0x000FFFFF
#define CONFIG_SYS_GBL_DATA_OFFSET     (CONFIG_SYS_INIT_RAM_SIZE - \
                GENERATED_GBL_DATA_SIZE)
#define CONFIG_SYS_INIT_SP_ADDR    (CONFIG_SYS_INIT_RAM_ADDR + \
                CONFIG_SYS_GBL_DATA_OFFSET)

#define CONFIG_BOARD_EARLY_INIT_F
```

```
/*-----------------------------------------------------------------
 * FLASH and environment organization
 */
#define CONFIG_SYS_TEXT_BASE        0x10000
#define CONFIG_SYS_NO_FLASH
#define CONFIG_ENV_IS_NOWHERE
#define CONFIG_SYS_MONITOR_LEN      0x80000

/*
 * Goldfish IO address definition; refer to <mach/hardware.h> in goldfish
 * Linux kernel: where in virtual memory the IO devices (timers, system
 controllers, and so on) are found
 */
#define IRQ_PDEV_BUS       (1)
#define IRQ_TIMER          (3)
#define IRQ_TTY0           (4)
#define IRQ_RTC            (10)
#define IRQ_TTY1           (11)
#define IRQ_TTY2           (12)
#define IRQ_smc91x         (13)
#define IRQ_FB             (14)
#define IRQ_AUDIO          (15)
#define IRQ_EVENTS         (16)
#define IRQ_PIPE           (17)
#define IRQ_SWITCH0        (18)
#define IRQ_SWITCH1        (19)
#define IRQ_RANDOM         (20)

#define LAST_IRQ RANDOM_IRQ
#define N_IRQS 21

/*
 * Base address of memory mapped the IO devices (timers, system controllers,
 * and so on)
 */
#define IO_BASE         0xfe000000              /* MMU on */
#define IO_SIZE         0x00800000
#define IO_START        0xff000000              /* MMU off */
```

```c
/* Goldfish interrupt controller */
#define GOLDFISH_INTERRUPT_BASE         (0x0)
#define GOLDFISH_INTERRUPT_STATUS       (0x00)
#define GOLDFISH_INTERRUPT_NUMBER       (0x04)
#define GOLDFISH_INTERRUPT_DISABLE_ALL  (0x08)
#define GOLDFISH_INTERRUPT_DISABLE      (0x0c)
#define GOLDFISH_INTERRUPT_ENABLE       (0x10)

/* Offset of I/O devices */
#define GOLDFISH_PDEV_BUS_BASE   (0x1000)
#define GOLDFISH_PDEV_BUS_END    (0x100)
#define GOLDFISH_TTY_BASE        (0x2000)
#define GOLDFISH_TIMER_BASE      (0x3000)
#define GOLDFISH_AUDIO_BASE      (0x4000)
#define GOLDFISH_MEMLOG_BASE     (0x6000)
#define GOLDFISH_RTC_BASE        (0x10000)
#define GOLDFISH_TTY1_BASE       (0x11000)
#define GOLDFISH_TTY2_BASE       (0x12000)
#define GOLDFISH_smc91x_BASE     (0x13000)
#define GOLDFISH_FB_BASE         (0x14000)
#define GOLDFISH_EVENTS_BASE     (0x15000)
#define GOLDFISH_NAND_BASE       (0x16000)
#define GOLDFISH_PIPE_BASE       (0x17000)
#define GOLDFISH_SWITCH0_BASE    (0x19000)
#define GOLDFISH_SWITCH1_BASE    (0x1a000)

/* Macro to get at I/O base address */
#if 1
    #define IO_ADDRESS(x) ((x) + IO_START)
#else
    #define IO_ADDRESS(x) ((x) + IO_BASE)
#endif

#endif   /* __GOLDFISH_CONFIG_H */
```

In the board-level implementation of goldfish shown in Example 9.2, we can see that a set of board-level initialization functions is implemented, such as board_early_init_f(), board_init(), misc_init_r(), dram_init(), and board_eth_init(). These functions can be called during the U-Boot boot-up process to support a board-specific implementation. The implementation is very simple and straightforward for goldfish.

Porting U-Boot to the Goldfish Platform

Example 9.2 Board-Level Support (board/google/goldfish/goldfish.c)

```
#include <common.h>
#include <netdev.h>
#include <asm/io.h>
#include <configs/goldfish.h>


DECLARE_GLOBAL_DATA_PTR;

#ifdef CONFIG_USE_IRQ
struct _irq_handler {
    void *m_data;
    void (*m_func)( void *data);
};

static struct _irq_handler IRQ_HANDLERS[N_IRQS];
#endif /* CONFIG_USE_IRQ */

#if defined(CONFIG_SHOW_BOOT_PROGRESS)
void show_boot_progress(int progress)
{
    printf("Boot reached stage %d\n", progress);
}
#endif

#define COMP_MODE_ENABLE ((unsigned int)0x0000EAEF)

/*
 * Miscellaneous platform-dependent initializations
 */

int board_early_init_f (void)
{
    return 0;
}

int board_init (void)
{
    /* Arch number of GOLDFISH board */
    gd->bd->bi_arch_number = MACH_TYPE_GOLDFISH;
```

Chapter 9 U-Boot Porting

```c
    /* Address of boot parameters */
    gd->bd->bi_boot_params = 0x00000100;

    gd->flags = 0;

    icache_enable ();

    return 0;
}

int misc_init_r (void)
{
    setenv("verify", "n");
    return (0);
}

/*****************************
 Routine:
 Description:
 *****************************/
int dram_init (void)
{
    /* dram_init must store the complete ramsize in gd->ram_size */
    gd->ram_size = get_ram_size((void *)CONFIG_SYS_SDRAM_BASE,
                PHYS_SDRAM_1_SIZE);
    return 0;
}

#ifdef CONFIG_CMD_NET
int board_eth_init(bd_t *bis)
{
    int rc = 0;
#ifdef CONFIG_SMC91111
    rc = smc91111_initialize(0, CONFIG_SMC91111_BASE);
#endif
    return rc;
}
#endif
```

```c
#ifdef CONFIG_USE_IRQ
/*
 * GOLDFISH_INTERRUPT_DISABLE at offset 0xC is a write-only register.
 * Writing an interrupt number to it will disable the specified interrupt.
 */
void goldfish_mask_irq(unsigned int irq)
{
    writel(irq, (void *)IO_ADDRESS(GOLDFISH_INTERRUPT_BASE) + GOLDFISH_INTERRUPT_DISABLE);
}

/*
 * GOLDFISH_INTERRUPT_ENABLE at offset 0x10 is a write-only register.
 * Writing an interrupt number to it will enable the specified interrupt.
 */
void goldfish_unmask_irq(unsigned int irq)
{
    writel(irq, (void *)IO_ADDRESS(GOLDFISH_INTERRUPT_BASE) + GOLDFISH_INTERRUPT_ENABLE);
}

/*
 * GOLDFISH_INTERRUPT_DISABLE_ALL at offset 0x8 is a write-only register.
 * Writing any value other than 0 to it will disable all interrupts.
 */
void goldfish_disable_all_irq(void)
{
    writel(1, (void *)IO_ADDRESS(GOLDFISH_INTERRUPT_BASE) + GOLDFISH_INTERRUPT_DISABLE_ALL);
}

/*
 * GOLDFISH_INTERRUPT_NUMBER at offset 0x4 contains the lowest pending,
 * enabled interrupt number. It is a read-only register.
 */
int goldfish_get_irq_num(void)
{
```

```c
    return readl((void *)IO_ADDRESS(GOLDFISH_INTERRUPT_BASE) + GOLDFISH_
INTERRUPT_NUMBER);
}

/*
 * GOLDFISH_INTERRUPT_STATUS at offset 0x0 contains the number of pending
interrupts.
 * It is a read-only register.
 * */
int goldfish_irq_status(void)
{
    return readl((void *)IO_ADDRESS(GOLDFISH_INTERRUPT_BASE) + GOLDFISH_
INTERRUPT_STATUS);
}

static void default_isr(void *data)
{
    printf("default_isr(): called for IRQ %d\n", (int)data);
}

static int next_irq(void)
{
    return goldfish_irq_status();
}

void do_irq (struct pt_regs *pt_regs)
{
    int irq = next_irq();

    IRQ_HANDLERS[irq].m_func(IRQ_HANDLERS[irq].m_data);
}

void irq_install_handler (int irq, interrupt_handler_t handle_irq, void *data)
{
    if (irq >= N_IRQS || !handle_irq)
        return;

    IRQ_HANDLERS[irq].m_data = data;
    IRQ_HANDLERS[irq].m_func = handle_irq;
}
```

```
int arch_interrupt_init (void)
{
    int i;

    /* install default interrupt handlers */
    for (i = 0; i < N_IRQS; i++)
        irq_install_handler(i, default_isr, (void *)i);

    return (0);
}
#endif /* CONFIG_USE_IRQ */
```

Another portion of the implementation is enabled by the macro `CONFIG_USE_IRQ`. It is used to support interrupt handling. The goldfish interrupt controller must be used for this purpose. Goldfish interrupt-related functions (whose names start with the prefix `goldfish_`), such as `goldfish_mask_irq()` and `goldfish_unmask_irq()`, are copied from Example 7.3 (part of the discussion of goldfish's interrupt controllers in Chapter 7). In addition, other functions are called to support the U-Boot interrupt interface—for example, `do_irq()` and `arch_interrupt_init()`. During the initialization of U-Boot, `arch_interrupt_init()` is called to initialize all interrupt handlers. When an interrupt is fired, `do_irq()` is called to serve the interrupt.

Device Driver Changes

In the goldfish platform, we want to support Ethernet, NAND flash, serial ports, and RTC, among other peripherals. The Android emulator emulates a standard SCM91111-based Ethernet hardware, and we can reuse the existing U-Boot code for it. Support for serial ports, NAND flash, and RTC in goldfish requires goldfish-specific implementations; however, we also have to create new drivers.

In U-Boot, to add a driver for a particular class of peripherals, you need to do the following:

- Implement the APIs specified in the driver class header file.
- Add configuration option(s) for the peripheral to the board configuration file in the folder `include/configs`. In this case, it is `goldfish.h`.
- Add or modify the source code for the driver in the device driver tree, such as `drivers/serial`.

Serial Driver

Let's create the new serial driver first. We can reuse the code in `serial_goldfish.c` and `goldfish_uart.S` from Chapter 5 to create this new driver.

In Chapter 5, we implemented the APIs specified in `include/serial.h`. The required APIs are defined in the data structure `serial_device`, as shown in Example 9.3.

Example 9.3 Serial APIs (include/serial.h)

...
```
struct serial_device {
    char    name[16];

    int     (*start)(void);
    int     (*stop)(void);
    void    (*setbrg)(void);
    int     (*getc)(void);
    int     (*tstc)(void);
    void    (*putc)(const char c);
    void    (*puts)(const char *s);
#if CONFIG_POST & CONFIG_SYS_POST_UART
    void    (*loop)(int);
#endif
    struct serial_device    *next;
};

void default_serial_puts(const char *s);
```
...

Once we have the implementation of serial APIs in `serial_goldfish.c` and `goldfish_uart.S`, we can add the related definitions in the configuration file `goldfish.h` as shown in Example 9.4. In addition, we can update the serial driver Makefile to include `serial_goldfish.c` and `goldfish_uart.S`.

Example 9.4 Adding Serial Driver Configuration in goldfish.h

...
```
/*
 * GOLDFISH serial
 */
#define CONFIG_GOLDFISH_SERIAL

#define CONFIG_CONS_INDEX       0

#define CONFIG_BAUDRATE                 38400
#define CONFIG_SYS_SERIAL0              IO_ADDRESS(GOLDFISH_TTY1_BASE)
#define CONFIG_SYS_SERIAL1              IO_ADDRESS(GOLDFISH_TTY2_BASE)
```
...

Let's copy `serial_goldfish.c` and `goldfish_uart.S` from Chapter 5 to the folder `drivers/serial` and update `Makefile`, as shown in Example 9.5.

Example 9.5 Updating Serial Driver Makefile

...

```
COBJS-$(CONFIG_GOLDFISH_SERIAL) += serial_goldfish.o
COBJS-$(CONFIG_GOLDFISH_SERIAL) += goldfish_uart.o
```
...

By using the bare-metal program example for serial hardware in Chapter 5 and integrating it into the U-Boot driver in this section, we can separately debug the hardware interface and implement the actual driver. The same technique can also be used in Linux driver development. In this way, we can separate hardware driver debugging from the complexity of the operating system driver architecture.

NAND Flash Driver

We did most of the work for adding the NAND flash driver in Chapter 8. Here, we must simply integrate that work into the U-Boot framework.

To do so, we copy the files `goldfish_nand.c` and `goldfish_nand_reg.h` from Chapter 8 to the U-Boot folder `drivers/mtd/nand`. In U-Boot, we have to implement the interface defined in the header file `include/nand.h`. In this header file, the NAND driver implements the interface defined by the data structure `nand_info_t`, which is a redefinition of the data structure `mtd_info`. We have implemented the necessary functions required by `mtd_info` in `goldfish_nand.c`.

In Example 9.6 (`include/nand.h`), two versions of `board_nand_init()` are defined. The one with a parameter of `nand_chip` (data structure) is required for a chip-level implementation of the NAND driver. In the goldfish platform, we don't need a chip-level implementation for this driver, so we defined the macro `CONFIG_SYS_NAND_SELF_INIT` and implemented the version of `board_nand_init()` without parameters.

Example 9.6 NAND Flash Initialization Function Header File (include/nand.h)

...

```
extern void nand_init(void);

#include <linux/compat.h>
#include <linux/mtd/mtd.h>
#include <linux/mtd/nand.h>

#ifdef CONFIG_SYS_NAND_SELF_INIT
void board_nand_init(void);
int nand_register(int devnum);
#else
extern int board_nand_init(struct nand_chip *nand);
```

Chapter 9 U-Boot Porting

```
#endif

typedef struct mtd_info nand_info_t;

extern int nand_curr_device;
extern nand_info_t nand_info[];
```
...

After we put goldfish_nand.c in drivers/mtd/nand, we need to add related macro definitions in goldfish.h, as shown in Example 9.7.

Example 9.7 Adding NAND Support in goldfish.h

```
...
/*
 * NAND configuration
 */
#ifdef CONFIG_CMD_NAND
#define CONFIG_NAND_GOLDFISH
#define CONFIG_SYS_NAND_SELF_INIT
#define CONFIG_SYS_MAX_NAND_DEVICE      3       /* Max number of NAND devices */
#endif

#define MTDIDS_DEFAULT       "nand0=system_nand,nand1=data_nand,nand2=cache_nand"
#define MTDPARTS_DEFAULT
"mtdparts=system_nand:197m(system);data_nand:194m(data);cache_nand:64m(cache)"

/*
 * File system
 */
#define CONFIG_CMD_FAT
#define CONFIG_CMD_EXT2
#define CONFIG_CMD_UBI
#define CONFIG_CMD_UBIFS
#define CONFIG_CMD_MTDPARTS
#define CONFIG_MTD_DEVICE
#define CONFIG_MTD_PARTITIONS
#define CONFIG_YAFFS2
#define CONFIG_RBTREE
#define CONFIG_LZO

...
```

We also need to change the `Makefile` in `drivers/mtd/nand` to include `goldfish_nand.c`:

COBJS-$(CONFIG_NAND_GOLDFISH) += goldfish_nand.o

At this point, we have done almost everything necessary to support goldfish NAND flash in U-Boot. One little problem remains, however: As mentioned earlier, we don't want to touch the data structure `nand_chip`. This data structure is used to encapsulate a chip-level specific implementation. It is necessary to make chip-level changes for most of the real-world NAND drivers. We have to change one part of `fs/yaffs2/yaffs_uboot_glue.c` as a workaround for this issue, as shown in Example 9.8. Specifically, we skip the code that changes the field `inband_tags`. This field is part of the `nand_chip` data structure, which is not initialized in goldfish U-Boot code. For this reason, we check the address `IO_ADDR_R`; if it is the same as the goldfish NAND flash base address (0xff016000 or 0xff017000), we skip the initialization of `inband_tags`.

Example 9.8 Changes in yaffs_uboot_glue.c

```
...
        if(chip->IO_ADDR_R != (void __iomem *)0xff017000 && chip->IO_ADDR_R != (void __iomem *)0xff016000) {
                if (chip->ecc.layout->oobavail < sizeof(struct yaffs_packed_tags2)) {
                        dev->param.inband_tags = 1;
                }
        }
...
```

The file `fs/yaffs2/yaffs_uboot_glue.c` is not part of the NAND flash driver, but rather part of the YAFFS2 source code. This change is needed because YAFFS2 support is already included in the U-Boot code base. We added the macro `CONFIG_YAFFS2` to turn it on in Example 9.7.

RTC Driver

To support RTC, we must implement the functions defined in Example 9.9. As we have done for other drivers, we can reuse the code developed in earlier chapters. In this case, we can reuse `rtc-goldfish.c` from Chapter 7.

Example 9.9 U-Boot RTC Interface (include/rtc.h)

```
/*
 * Generic RTC interface
 */
#ifndef _RTC_H_
#define _RTC_H_
```

```c
/* bcd<->bin functions are needed by almost all RTC drivers; let's include
 * them there instead of in every single driver */

#include <bcd.h>

/*
 * The struct used to pass data from the generic interface code to
 * the hardware depends on low-level code, and vice versa. Identical
 * to the struct rtc_time used by the Linux kernel.
 *
 * Note that there are small but significant differences in the
 * common "struct time":
 *
 *         struct time:      struct rtc_time:
 * tm_mon    0 ... 11         1 ... 12
 * tm_year   years since 1900 years since 0
 */
struct rtc_time {
    int tm_sec;
    int tm_min;
    int tm_hour;
    int tm_mday;
    int tm_mon;
    int tm_year;
    int tm_wday;
    int tm_yday;
    int tm_isdst;
};

int rtc_get (struct rtc_time *);
int rtc_set (struct rtc_time *);
void rtc_reset (void);

void GregorianDay (struct rtc_time *);
void to_tm (int, struct rtc_time *);
unsigned long mktime (unsigned int, unsigned int, unsigned int,
            unsigned int, unsigned int, unsigned int);

#endif   /* _RTC_H_ */
```

Porting U-Boot to the Goldfish Platform

Since we have implemented `rtc_get`, `rtc_set`, and `rtc_reset` in `rtc-goldfish.c`, we can copy this file to `drivers/rtc/rtc-goldfish.c`. We need to change the `Makefile` in the folder `drivers/rtc` to include `rtc-goldfish.c`:

```
COBJS-$(CONFIG_RTC_GOLDFISH) += rtc-goldfish.o
```

The next step is to add the macro `CONFIG_RTC_GOLDFISH` in the platform configuration file `include/configs/goldfish.h`:

```
#define CONFIG_CMD_DATE
/*
 * RTC driver configuration
 */
#ifdef CONFIG_CMD_DATE
#define CONFIG_RTC_GOLDFISH
#endif /* CONFIG_CMD_DATE */
```

With RTC support, when we boot to the U-Boot command prompt, we can set the date using a U-Boot command:

```
Goldfish # date
Date: 1970-01-01 (Thursday)    Time:  0:02:42
Goldfish # date 041417482014
Date: 2014-04-14 (Monday)    Time: 17:48:00
```

Ethernet Driver

Since the Android emulator simulates standard SMC91111 Ethernet hardware, we can turn on the existing implementation in U-Boot by changing the board configuration file `goldfish.h`, as shown in Example 9.10.

Example 9.10 Turning on SMC91111 Ethernet Support in goldfish.h

---

```
...
#define CONFIG_SMC91111
#define CONFIG_SMC_USE_32_BIT
#define CONFIG_SMC91111_BASE         IO_ADDRESS(GOLDFISH_smc91x_BASE)
#define CONFIG_SMC91111_EXT_PHY
...
```

With this definition `CONFIG_SMC91111`, the existing driver file `smc91111.c` in the folder `drivers/net` will be built into the goldfish configuration, as shown here, as part of the Ethernet driver `Makefile`:

```
...
COBJS-$(CONFIG_SMC91111) += smc91111.o
...
```

Summary

In this chapter, we ported U-Boot to the goldfish platform. We now have a basic understanding of how to port U-Boot based on an existing platform to a new platform. You can apply the same process to your own real-world projects as necessary.

During the porting process, we learned that we can reuse code that we created previously for another purpose. This technique can be used in real projects as well. In fact, we can create most pure hardware-related code in a bare metal environment. This approach allows us to concentrate on hardware enabling and to avoid the complexity of dealing with U-Boot and the Linux kernel. Once we have enabled the hardware as needed, we can merge that work with either a bootloader framework or an operating system driver. This is a good practice to reduce the complexity of embedded system programming.

This chapter covered the general steps for porting U-Boot. In this case, we first chose the hardware platform "Versatile" as the base of our U-Boot porting. We changed processor-specific and board-specific code as necessary. We reused the code from Chapter 7 for the timer and interrupt controller. We then added three drivers (serial, NAND flash, and Ethernet) to the goldfish U-Boot. In doing so, we learned how to add both new and existing drivers to U-Boot. For the serial driver and the NAND flash driver, we reused code from Chapter 5 and Chapter 8, respectively. For the Ethernet driver, we used the existing U-Boot code directly.

Table 9.2 summarizes the configuration changes that we have made in this chapter. They include processor- and board-level changes, device driver changes, and a few build-related changes. Table 9.2 also indicates how discussions and examples from other chapters relate to this chapter.

Table 9.2 Goldfish Board Configuration

File	Remarks	Related Changes

`arch/arm/cpu/arm926ejs/goldfish/Makefile`
`arch/arm/cpu/arm926ejs/goldfish/reset.S`
`arch/arm/cpu/arm926ejs/goldfish/timer.c`
`arch/arm/include/asm/mach-types.h`
`board/google/goldfish/Makefile`
`board/google/goldfish/goldfish.c`
`board/google/goldfish/lowlevel_init.S`
`include/configs/goldfish.h`
`common/image.c`
`boards.cfg`
	Reuse interrupt controller and timer support from Chapter 7 and `hardware.h`	Processor- and board-level changes

File	Remarks	Related Changes

`drivers/mtd/nand/Makefile`
`drivers/mtd/nand/goldfish_nand.c`
`drivers/mtd/nand/goldfish_nand_reg.h`
`fs/yaffs2/yaffs_uboot_glue.c`
	Reuse NAND flash support from Chapter 8	NAND flash driver

`drivers/rtc/Makefile` `drivers/rtc/rtc-goldfish.c`	Reuse RTC support from Chapter 7	RTC driver

`drivers/serial/Makefile`
`drivers/serial/goldfish_uart.S`
`drivers/serial/serial_goldfish.c`
`drivers/serial/serial_goldfish.h`
	Reuse serial port support from Chapter 5	Serial port driver

`common/main.c` `config.mk`	Change the boot delay timing and turn on debug build	Miscellaneous changes

10

Using U-Boot to Boot the Goldfish Kernel

Once we have U-Boot ready for the goldfish platform, we can use it to boot the Linux kernel in the Android emulator. Ideally, the boot process starts from nonvolatile memory (such as flash memory). Many kind of storage devices can be used in an embedded system, though NOR and NAND flash devices are the most popular options. In this chapter, we will build a goldfish Linux kernel first. We then explore how to boot Android from NOR flash and NAND flash using U-Boot and this kernel.

Building the Goldfish Kernel

Ideally, we might like to build everything on our own—from the bootloader, to the kernel, to the file system. Except for Google-specific applications, everything in Android is hosted in a project called Android Open Source Project (AOSP). However, we will lose our focus if we go into too much detail about every aspect of the build process right now. We will discuss AOSP builds in Part III of this book. If you want to learn how to build AOSP from scratch, the book *Embedded Android* by Karim Yaghmour is a good reference. In addition, the Internet provides plenty of articles that explain how to work on AOSP.

To build the kernel, we need two things: a prebuilt toolchain and goldfish kernel source code. The recommended option is to use the prebuilt toolchain from AOSP, which can be downloaded from the Google source git repository. Other prebuilt toolchains can be used as well. For example, we could use a prebuilt toolchain from a vendor such as Mentor Graphics (i.e., Sourcery CodeBench).

If you already have an AOSP source tree, you can use the prebuilt toolchain from AOSP directly. If you don't have an AOSP source tree, the instructions in this chapter explain how to download this toolchain. If you installed your toolchain using the script `install.sh` introduced in Appendix A, you should have the toolchain from CodeBench Lite. In this case, you can skip the steps for downloading AOSP toolchain given in this chapter.

We will use the file system included with the Android SDK to boot up our kernel. When an Android virtual device is created, a corresponding file system is created as well. We will use the virtual device `hd2` that we created in Chapter 2 in this chapter. The file system image for `hd2` can be found at `~/.android/avd/hd2.avd`.

You might wonder why we want to build the kernel ourselves instead of using the original kernel in the Android SDK to demonstrate the boot-up process. The reason is that we may not be able to boot up the Linux kernel as smoothly as we think. Actually, this process will most likely fail when we first attempt it. Thus we need a debug build to debug the boot process.

The porting of U-Boot actually includes two steps. First, we must add the necessary hardware support so that we can run U-Boot until the command-line prompt becomes available. Second, we must change U-Boot to prepare the proper environment for the Linux kernel so that control can be transferred to the kernel and the kernel can be started normally. In the second step, if we don't have a debug version of kernel, it will be very difficult for us to debug U-Boot itself. We will demonstrate how to debug both U-Boot and the Linux kernel at the source code level in this chapter.

Prebuilt Toolchain and Kernel Source Code

The latest information about how to build an Android kernel using a prebuilt toolchain can be found at *https://source.android.com/*. Given that AOSP changes from time to time, be aware that the procedure in this chapter is what was available at the time of this book's writing—and that a newer version may have been released since then.

You can download the prebuilt toolchain from the AOSP git repository using the following command:

```
$ git clone https://android.googlesource.com/platform/prebuilts/gcc/linux-x86/arm/arm-eabi-4.7
```

It may take a while for this command to complete its work. After the prebuilt toolchain is downloaded, we can set up the path environment variable to include it:

```
$ export PATH=$(pwd)/arm-eabi-4.7/bin:$PATH
```

The next step is to get the goldfish kernel source code. We can use the following command to get a copy of kernel from AOSP repository:

```
$ git clone https://android.googlesource.com/kernel/goldfish.git
$ cd goldfish
$ git branch -a
* master
  remotes/origin/HEAD -> origin/master
  remotes/origin/android-goldfish-2.6.29
  remotes/origin/android-goldfish-3.4
  remotes/origin/linux-goldfish-3.0-wip
  remotes/origin/master
$ git checkout -t origin/android-goldfish-2.6.29 -b goldfish
```

To build the kernel, use the following commands:

```
$ export ARCH=arm
$ export SUBARCH=arm
$ export CROSS_COMPILE=arm-eabi-
$ make goldfish_armv7_defconfig
$ make
```

After the build is completed, we have a release build of the goldfish kernel by default.

To debug the kernel, we need to turn on debugging options in the kernel configuration file. To do so, we can either edit the .config file directly or run menuconfig. To run menuconfig, you have to install the package libncurses5-dev first, if you haven't already installed it:

```
$ sudo apt-get install libncurses5-dev
$ make menuconfig CROSS_COMPILE=arm-eabi-
```

After menuconfig starts, we can select Kernel hacking, Compile the kernel with debug info, as shown in Figure 10.1.

An alternative approach, as mentioned earlier, is to edit the .config file directly. In the .config file, we can set CONFIG_DEBUG_INFO=y.

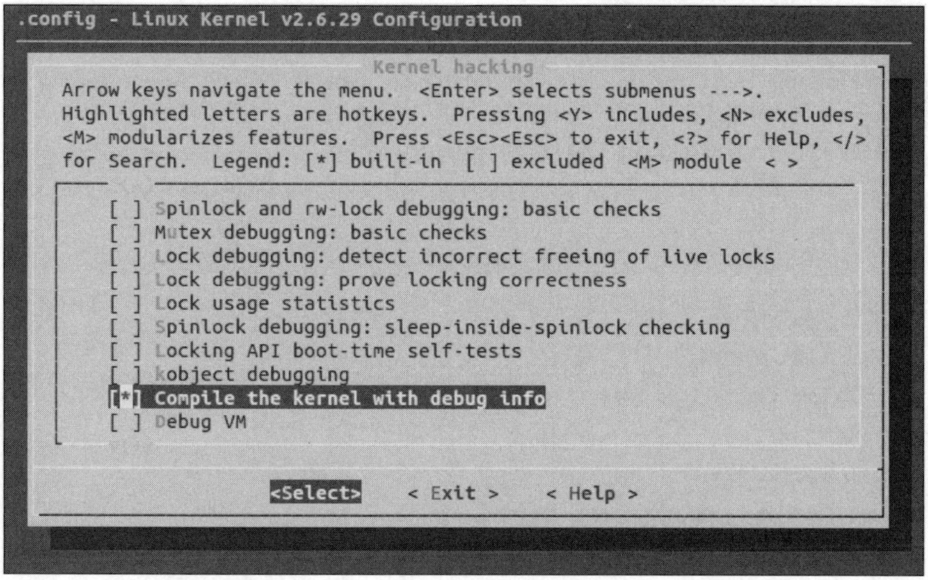

Figure 10.1 Enabling debugging in menuconfig

Even though these steps look quite simple, problems may occasionally occur. Yet another alternative is to follow the instructions in Appendix B to set up the development environment and build everything in this book using the `Makefile` and scripts in the repository `build` in GitHub.

Running and Debugging the Kernel in the Emulator

After the build process is finished, we can run and debug the kernel in the Android emulator. The compressed kernel image can be found at `arch/arm/boot/zImage`. This image can be used to run the kernel in the emulator. The image file `vmlinux` is in ELF format; it can be used by gdb to get the debug symbol. We give the following command to start the Android emulator using our own kernel image:

```
$ emulator -verbose -show-kernel -netfast -avd hd2 -qemu -serial stdio -s -S
-kernel arch/arm/boot/zImage
```

After the emulator is running, we can start the gdb debugger to debug the kernel. We will use the graphical interface ddd to start the gdb debugger; it produces a more user-friendly environment. In the following command line, we tell ddd to use `arm-eabi-gdb` as the debugger and `vmlinux` as the binary image:

$ ddd --debugger arm-eabi-gdb vmlinux

After gdb starts, it needs to connect to the gdbserver in the emulator using the command `target remote localhost:1234`. To track the boot-up progress, we can set a breakpoint at the function `start_kernel`:

```
GNU DDD 3.3.12 (i686-pc-linux-gnu), by Dorothea Lütkehaus and Andreas Zeller.
Copyright © 1995-1999 Technische Universität Braunschweig, Germany.
Copyright © 1999-2001 Universität Passau, Germany.
Copyright © 2001 Universität des Saarlandes, Germany.
Copyright © 2001-2004 Free Software Foundation, Inc.
Reading symbols from /home/sgye/src/Android/goldfish/vmlinux...done.
```
(gdb) **target remote localhost:1234**

0x00000000 in ?? ()

(gdb) **b start_kernel**

Breakpoint 1 at 0xc0008858: file init/main.c, line 531.

(gdb) **c**

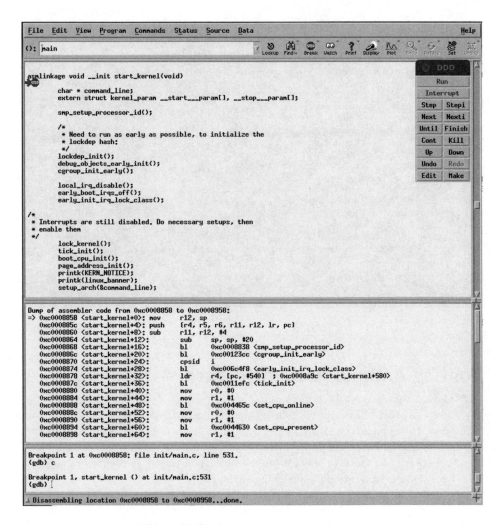

Figure 10.2 Boot-up stop at start_kernel

After starting the process, gdb will stop at start_kernel, as shown in Figure 10.2.

After the system boots up, a console like that shown in Figure 10.3 appears. The entire Android system should be ready to use at this point. From here, we boot the kernel in the Android emulator directly. In the next few sections, we will boot this kernel using U-Boot.

```
<6>yaffs: dev is 32505858 name is "mtdblock2"
yaffs: dev is 32505858 name is "mtdblock2"
<6>yaffs: passed flags ""
yaffs: passed flags ""
yaffs: Attempting MTD mount on 31.2, "mtdblock2"
yaffs: Attempting MTD mount on 31.2, "mtdblock2"
yaffs_read_super: isCheckpointed 0
yaffs_read_super: isCheckpointed 0
<3>init: cannot find '/system/etc/install-recovery.sh', disabling 'flash_recover
y'
init: cannot find '/system/etc/install-recovery.sh', disabling 'flash_recovery'
<3>init: untracked pid 47 exited
init: untracked pid 47 exited
<6>warning: `rild' uses 32-bit capabilities (legacy support in use)
warning: `rild' uses 32-bit capabilities (legacy support in use)
<6>eth0: link up
eth0: link up
shell@android:/ $ <7>eth0: no IPv6 routers present
<6>request_suspend_state: wakeup (3->0) at 35350000414 (2013-05-25 13:53:51.1612
96804 UTC)
request_suspend_state: wakeup (3->0) at 35350000414 (2013-05-25 13:53:51.1612968
04 UTC)

shell@android:/ $
```

Figure 10.3 Linux console after boot-up

Booting Android from NOR Flash

QEMU doesn't provide NOR flash emulation on the goldfish platform. To make things simple, we will use RAM to create a boot-up process that is similar to the boot process from NOR flash. This approach builds a binary image that includes U-Boot, the Linux kernel, and the RAMDISK image and passes this image to QEMU through the -kernel option.

Before we start, let's look at how QEMU boots a Linux kernel. To boot up a Linux kernel, the bootloader prepares the following environment:

- The processor is in SVC (Supervisor) mode and IRQ and FIQ are disabled.
- MMU is disabled.
- Register r0 is set to 0.
- Register r1 contains the ARM Linux machine type.
- Register r2 contains the address of the kernel parameter list.

After power-up, QEMU starts to run from address 0x00000000. Before it loads a kernel image, QEMU prepares the environment described previously; it then jumps to address 0x00010000. Figure 10.4 shows a memory dump before the point at which QEMU launches a kernel image. Notice the five lines of assembly code before control is transferred to the kernel image—these lines are hard-coded by QEMU when the system starts. The first line (0x00000000) sets register r0 to 0. The second line (0x00000004) and third line (0x00000008) set register r1 to 0x5a1, which is the machine type of the goldfish

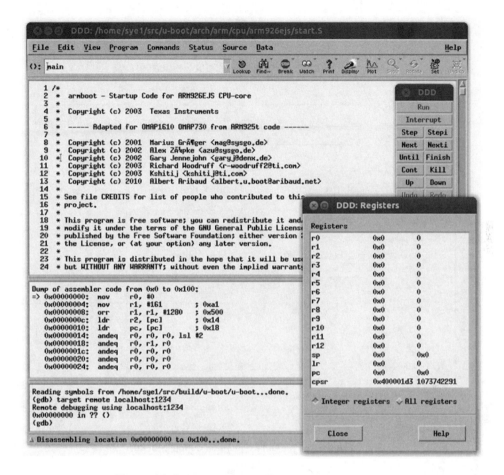

Figure 10.4 Memory dump of mini-bootloader at reset

platform. The fourth line (0x0000000c) sets the value of register r2 to 0x100, which is the start address of the kernel parameter list. The fifth line (0x00000010) sets the register pc to 0x10000, so the execution jumps to address 0x10000. QEMU assumes the kernel image is loaded at address 0x10000.

As outlined in Figure 10.5, we will create an image including U-Boot, the Linux kernel, and RAMDISK for testing. U-Boot is located at address 0x00010000, which is the address that QEMU will invoke. The Linux kernel is located at address 0x00210000, and the RAMDISK image is located at address 0x00410000. Both the kernel and RAMDISK images are placed at a distance of 2MB starting from address 0x00010000. After U-Boot is relocated, it will move itself to address 0x1ff59000 (this address may change for each build) and free about 2MB from the starting address 0x00010000. We can inform U-Boot about the kernel and RAMDISK image locations through the bootm command, given

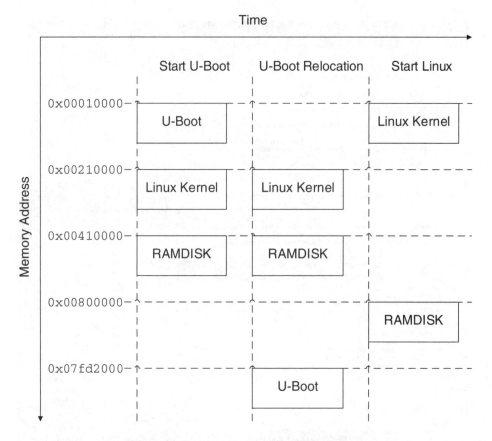

Figure 10.5 Memory relocation during boot-up

from the U-Boot command line. Alternatively, you can set the default `bootm` parameter in `include/configs/goldfish.h`. We can add the default `bootm` and kernel parameters in `goldfish.h` as follows:

```
#define CONFIG_BOOTARGS "qemu.gles=1 qemu=1 console=ttyS0 android.qemud=ttyS1
androidboot.console=ttyS2 android.checkjni=1 ndns=1"
```

```
#define CONFIG_BOOTCOMMAND "bootm 0x210000 0x410000"
```

The U-Boot command `bootm` then copies the kernel image into 0x00010000 and the RAMDISK image into 0x00800000. At that point, U-Boot jumps to address 0x00010000 to start the Linux kernel.

Creating the RAMDISK Image

Besides U-Boot and the kernel image, we need a RAMDISK image to support the boot process. In Android, RAMDISK is used as the root file system. We can customize the boot process by changing the RAMDISK content. Let's create a RAMDISK image so that we can build the flash image for testing. Given that we are using the Android emulator, we can take advantage of the RAMDISK image from the Android SDK as the base for our image. The RAMDISK image can be found in the system image folder in the Android SDK. For an example, the RAMDISK image for Android 4.0.3 (API 15) can be found at {Android SDK installation path}/system-images/android-15/armeabi-v7a/ramdisk.img.

If we want to modify this image, we can create a folder and extract the image to that folder using the following command:

$ **mkdir initrd**

$ **cd initrd**

$ **gzip -dc < ../ramdisk.img | cpio --extract**

Once we extract the RAMDISK image, we can see its content:

$ **ls -F**

```
data/         dev/      init.goldfish.rc*  proc/   sys/      ueventd.goldfish.rc
default.prop  init*     init.rc*                   sbin/   system/   ueventd.rc
```

The RAMDISK includes the folders and startup scripts for the root file system. The actual system files are stored in system.img, and the user data files are stored in userdata.img. Both system.img and userdata.img are emulated as NAND flash. They are mounted as /system and /data folders, respectively, under the root file system.

We can inspect file systems after boot-up as follows:

```
shell@android:/ $ mount
rootfs / rootfs ro 0 0
tmpfs /dev tmpfs rw,nosuid,mode=755 0 0
devpts /dev/pts devpts rw,mode=600 0 0
proc /proc proc rw 0 0
sysfs /sys sysfs rw 0 0
none /acct cgroup rw,cpuacct 0 0
tmpfs /mnt/secure tmpfs rw,mode=700 0 0
tmpfs /mnt/asec tmpfs rw,mode=755,gid=1000 0 0
tmpfs /mnt/obb tmpfs rw,mode=755,gid=1000 0 0
none /dev/cpuctl cgroup rw,cpu 0 0
/dev/block/mtdblock0 /system yaffs2 ro 0 0
/dev/block/mtdblock1 /data yaffs2 rw,nosuid,nodev 0 0
/dev/block/mtdblock2 /cache yaffs2 rw,nosuid,nodev 0 0
shell@android:/ $
```

Now we can change the files in this folder as desired. After we've made those changes, we can generate the new RAMDISK image using the following commands:

```
$ find . > ../initrd.list
$ cpio -o -H newc -O ../ramdisk.img < ../initrd.list
$ cd ..
$ gzip ramdisk.img
$ mv ramdisk.img.gz rootfs.img
```

Creating the Flash Image

Now that all of the image files (U-Boot, Linux kernel, and RAMDISK) are ready, we can start to create the flash image to boot the system.

U-Boot can boot a variety of file types (e.g., ELF, BIN), but these file types have to first be repackaged in the U-Boot image format (i.e., uImage). This format stores information about the operating system type, the load address, the entry point, basic integrity verification (via CRC), compression types, free description text, and so on.

To create a U-Boot image format, we need a utility called mkimage. If this tool is not installed in the host system, it can be installed in Ubuntu using the following command:

```
$ sudo apt-get install uboot-mkimage
```

With this utility, we can repackage the kernel image and RAMDISK image in the U-Boot format using the following commands:

```
$ mkimage -A arm -C none -O linux -T kernel -d zImage -a 0x00010000 -e 0x00010000 zImage.uimg

$ gzip -c rootfs.img > rootfs.img.gz

$ mkimage -A arm -C none -O linux -T ramdisk -d rootfs.img.gz -a 0x00800000 -e 0x00800000 rootfs.uimg
```

Once we have uImage files in hand, we can generate a flash image using the `dd` command as follows:

```
$ dd if=/dev/zero of= flash.bin bs=1 count=6M
$ dd if=u-boot.bin of= flash.bin conv=notrunc bs=1
$ dd if= zImage.uimg of= flash.bin conv=notrunc bs=1 seek=2M
$ dd if= rootfs.uimg of= flash.bin conv=notrunc bs=1 seek=4M
```

The file `flash.bin` includes all three images that we will use to boot up the system.

There are multiple steps to build the Linux kernel and generate all images. Please refer to Appendix A for the detailed procedures. All related `Makefiles` and scripts can be found in repository `build` in GitHub.

Booting Up the Flash Image

Finally, we are ready to boot the flash image that we built. Let's run it in the Android emulator and stop in the U-Boot command-line interface first. In U-Boot, we set a

2-second delay before U-Boot starts autoboot. Before autoboot starts, any keystroke will take us to the U-Boot command prompt. We can use a U-Boot command to verify the kernel and RAMDISK image, thereby making sure they are correct:

```
$ emulator -verbose -show-kernel -netfast -avd hd2 -qemu -serial stdio -kernel flash.bin
...
U-Boot 2013.01.-rc1-00003-g54217a1 (Feb 09 2014 - 23:28:59)

U-Boot code: 00010000 -> 00029B0C  BSS: -> 0002D36C

IRQ Stack: 0badc0de

FIQ Stack: 0badc0de

monitor len: 0001D36C

ramsize: 20000000

TLB table at: 1fff0000

Top of RAM usable for U-Boot at: 1fff0000

Reserving 116k for U-Boot at: 1ffd2000

Reserving 136k for malloc() at: 1ffb0000

Reserving 32 Bytes for Board Info at: 1ffaffe0

Reserving 120 Bytes for Global Data at: 1ffaff68

Reserving 8192 Bytes for IRQ stack at: 1ffadf68

New Stack Pointer is: 1ffadf58

RAM Configuration:

Bank #0: 00000000 512 MiB

relocation Offset is: 1ffc2000

goldfish_init(), gtty.base=ff012000

WARNING: Caches not enabled

monitor flash len: 0001D0D4

Now running in RAM - U-Boot at: 1ffd2000

Using default environment

Destroy Hash Table: 1ffeb724 table = 00000000

Create Hash Table: N=89

INSERT: table 1ffeb724, filled 1/89 rv 1ffb02a4 ==> name="bootargs" value="qemu.gles=1 qemu=1 console=ttyS0 android.qemud=ttyS1 androidboot.console=ttyS2 android.checkjni=1 ndns=1"

INSERT: table 1ffeb724, filled 2/89 rv 1ffb0160 ==> name="bootcmd" value="bootm 0x210000 0x410000"

INSERT: table 1ffeb724, filled 3/89 rv 1ffb02f8 ==> name="bootdelay" value="2"

INSERT: table 1ffeb724, filled 4/89 rv 1ffb0178 ==> name="baudrate" value="38400"
```

```
INSERT: table 1ffeb724, filled 5/89 rv 1ffb0154 ==> name="bootfile" value="/
tftpboot/uImage"
INSERT: free(data = 1ffb0008)
INSERT: done
In:    serial
Out:   serial
Err:   serial
Net:   SMC91111-0
Warning: SMC91111-0 using MAC address from net device

### main_loop entered: bootdelay=2

### main_loop: bootcmd="bootm 0x210000 0x410000"
Hit any key to stop autoboot:  0
Goldfish # iminfo 0x210000

## Checking Image at 00210000 ...
   Legacy image found
   Image Name:
   Image Type:   ARM Linux Kernel Image (uncompressed)
   Data Size:    1722596 Bytes = 1.6 MiB
   Load Address: 00010000
   Entry Point:  00010000
   Verifying Checksum ... OK
Goldfish # iminfo 0x410000

## Checking Image at 00410000 ...
   Legacy image found
   Image Name:
   Image Type:   ARM Linux RAMDisk Image (uncompressed)
   Data Size:    187687 Bytes = 183.3 KiB
   Load Address: 00800000
   Entry Point:  00800000
   Verifying Checksum ... OK
Goldfish #
```

In the preceding code, notice that we use the `iminfo` command to check the image at 0x00210000 and 0x00410000. U-Boot recognizes the data at these addresses as the Linux kernel image and Linux RAMDISK image, respectively. Also notice the load address: U-Boot loads the kernel image to address 0x00010000 and the RAMDISK image to address 0x00800000.

We can boot the system using the `bootm` command as follows:

```
Goldfish # bootm 0x210000 0x410000
## Current stack ends at 0x1ffadb10 *  kernel: cmdline image address = 0x00210000
## Booting kernel from Legacy Image at 00210000 ...
   Image Name:
   Image Type:   ARM Linux Kernel Image (uncompressed)
   Data Size:    1722596 Bytes = 1.6 MiB
   Load Address: 00010000
   Entry Point:  00010000
   kernel data at 0x00210040, len = 0x001a48e4 (1722596)
*  ramdisk: cmdline image address = 0x00410000
## Loading init Ramdisk from Legacy Image at 00410000 ...
   Image Name:
   Image Type:   ARM Linux RAMDisk Image (uncompressed)
   Data Size:    187687 Bytes = 183.3 KiB
   Load Address: 00800000
   Entry Point:  00800000
   ramdisk start = 0x00800000, ramdisk end = 0x0082dd27
   Loading Kernel Image ... OK
CACHE: Misaligned operation at range [00010000, 006a2390]
OK
   kernel loaded at 0x00010000, end = 0x001b48e4
using: ATAGS
## Transferring control to Linux (at address 00010000)...

Starting kernel ...

Uncompressing Linux.......................................................
......................................... done, booting the kernel.
goldfish_fb_get_pixel_format:167: display surface,pixel format:
   bits/pixel:  16
   bytes/pixel: 2
   depth:       16
   red:         bits=5 mask=0xf800 shift=11 max=0x1f
   green:       bits=6 mask=0x7e0 shift=5 max=0x3f
```

```
    blue:       bits=5 mask=0x1f shift=0 max=0x1f
    alpha:      bits=0 mask=0x0 shift=0 max=0x0
Initializing cgroup subsys cpu
Linux version 2.6.29-ge3d684d (sgye@sgye-Latitude-E6510) (gcc version 4.6.3
(Sourcery CodeBench Lite 2012.03-57) ) #1 Sun Feb 9 23:32:29 CST 2014
CPU: ARMv7 Processor [410fc080] revision 0 (ARMv7), cr=10c5387f
CPU: VIPT nonaliasing data cache, VIPT nonaliasing instruction cache
Machine: Goldfish
Memory policy: ECC disabled, Data cache writeback
Built 1 zonelists in Zone order, mobility grouping on.  Total pages: 130048
Kernel command line: qemu.gles=1 qemu=1 console=ttyS0 android.qemud=ttyS1
androidboot.console=ttyS2 android.checkjni=1 ndns=1
Unknown boot option 'qemu.gles=1': ignoring
Unknown boot option 'android.qemud=ttyS1': ignoring
Unknown boot option 'androidboot.console=ttyS2': ignoring
Unknown boot option 'android.checkjni=1': ignoring
PID hash table entries: 2048 (order: 11, 8192 bytes)
Console: colour dummy device 80x30
Dentry cache hash table entries: 65536 (order: 6, 262144 bytes)
Inode-cache hash table entries: 32768 (order: 5, 131072 bytes)
Memory: 512MB = 512MB total
Memory: 515456KB available (2944K code, 707K data, 124K init)
Calibrating delay loop... 370.27 BogoMIPS (lpj=1851392)
Mount-cache hash table entries: 512
Initializing cgroup subsys debug
Initializing cgroup subsys cpuacct
Initializing cgroup subsys freezer
CPU: Testing write buffer coherency: ok
net_namespace: 936 bytes
NET: Registered protocol family 16
bio: create slab <bio-0> at 0
NET: Registered protocol family 2
IP route cache hash table entries: 16384 (order: 4, 65536 bytes)
TCP established hash table entries: 65536 (order: 7, 524288 bytes)
TCP bind hash table entries: 65536 (order: 6, 262144 bytes)
TCP: Hash tables configured (established 65536 bind 65536)
```

```
TCP reno registered
NET: Registered protocol family 1
checking if image is initramfs... it is
Freeing initrd memory: 180K
goldfish_new_pdev goldfish_interrupt_controller at ff000000 irq -1
goldfish_new_pdev goldfish_device_bus at ff001000 irq 1
goldfish_new_pdev goldfish_timer at ff003000 irq 3
goldfish_new_pdev goldfish_rtc at ff010000 irq 10
goldfish_new_pdev goldfish_tty at ff002000 irq 4
goldfish_new_pdev goldfish_tty at ff011000 irq 11
goldfish_new_pdev goldfish_tty at ff012000 irq 12
goldfish_new_pdev smc91x at ff013000 irq 13
goldfish_new_pdev goldfish_fb at ff014000 irq 14
goldfish_new_pdev goldfish_audio at ff004000 irq 15
goldfish_new_pdev goldfish_mmc at ff005000 irq 16
goldfish_new_pdev goldfish_memlog at ff006000 irq -1
goldfish_new_pdev goldfish-battery at ff015000 irq 17
goldfish_new_pdev goldfish_events at ff016000 irq 18
goldfish_new_pdev goldfish_nand at ff017000 irq -1
goldfish_new_pdev qemu_pipe at ff018000 irq 19
goldfish_new_pdev goldfish-switch at ff01a000 irq 20
goldfish_new_pdev goldfish-switch at ff01b000 irq 21
goldfish_pdev_worker registered goldfish_interrupt_controller
goldfish_pdev_worker registered goldfish_device_bus
goldfish_pdev_worker registered goldfish_timer
goldfish_pdev_worker registered goldfish_rtc
goldfish_pdev_worker registered goldfish_tty
goldfish_pdev_worker registered goldfish_tty
goldfish_pdev_worker registered goldfish_tty
goldfish_pdev_worker registered smc91x
goldfish_pdev_worker registered goldfish_fb
goldfish_pdev_worker registered goldfish_audio
goldfish_pdev_worker registered goldfish_mmc
goldfish_pdev_worker registered goldfish_memlog
goldfish_pdev_worker registered goldfish-battery
```

```
goldfish_pdev_worker registered goldfish_events
goldfish_pdev_worker registered goldfish_nand
goldfish_pdev_worker registered qemu_pipe
goldfish_pdev_worker registered goldfish-switch
goldfish_pdev_worker registered goldfish-switch
ashmem: initialized
Installing knfsd (copyright (C) 1996 okir@monad.swb.de).
fuse init (API version 7.11)
yaffs Feb  9 2014 23:30:30 Installing.
msgmni has been set to 1007
alg: No test for stdrng (krng)
io scheduler noop registered
io scheduler anticipatory registered (default)
io scheduler deadline registered
io scheduler cfq registered
allocating frame buffer 480 * 800, got ffa00000
console [ttyS0] enabled
brd: module loaded
loop: module loaded
nbd: registered device at major 43
goldfish_audio_probe
tun: Universal TUN/TAP device driver, 1.6
tun: (C) 1999-2004 Max Krasnyansky <maxk@qualcomm.com>
smc91x.c: v1.1, sep 22 2004 by Nicolas Pitre <nico@cam.org>
eth0 (smc91x): not using net_device_ops yet
eth0: SMC91C11xFD (rev 1) at e080c000 IRQ 13 [nowait]
eth0: Ethernet addr: 52:54:00:12:34:56
goldfish nand dev0: size c5e0000, page 2048, extra 64, erase 131072
goldfish nand dev1: size c200000, page 2048, extra 64, erase 131072
goldfish nand dev2: size 4000000, page 2048, extra 64, erase 131072
mice: PS/2 mouse device common for all mice
*** events probe ***
events_probe() addr=0xe0814000 irq=18
events_probe() keymap=qwerty2
input: qwerty2 as /devices/virtual/input/input0
```

```
goldfish_rtc goldfish_rtc: rtc core: registered goldfish_rtc as rtc0
device-mapper: uevent: version 1.0.3
device-mapper: ioctl: 4.14.0-ioctl (2008-04-23) initialised: dm-devel@redhat.com
logger: created 64K log 'log_main'
logger: created 256K log 'log_events'
logger: created 64K log 'log_radio'
Netfilter messages via NETLINK v0.30.
nf_conntrack version 0.5.0 (8192 buckets, 32768 max)
CONFIG_NF_CT_ACCT is deprecated and will be removed soon. Please use
nf_conntrack.acct=1 kernel parameter, acct=1 nf_conntrack module option or
sysctl net.netfilter.nf_conntrack_acct=1 to enable it.
ctnetlink v0.93: registering with nfnetlink.
NF_TPROXY: Transparent proxy support initialized, version 4.1.0
NF_TPROXY: Copyright (c) 2006-2007 BalaBit IT Ltd.
xt_time: kernel timezone is -0000
ip_tables: (C) 2000-2006 Netfilter Core Team
arp_tables: (C) 2002 David S. Miller
TCP cubic registered
NET: Registered protocol family 10
ip6_tables: (C) 2000-2006 Netfilter Core Team
IPv6 over IPv4 tunneling driver
NET: Registered protocol family 17
NET: Registered protocol family 15
RPC: Registered udp transport module.
RPC: Registered tcp transport module.
802.1Q VLAN Support v1.8 Ben Greear <greearb@candelatech.com>
All bugs added by David S. Miller <davem@redhat.com>
VFP support v0.3: implementor 41 architecture 3 part 30 variant c rev 0
goldfish_rtc goldfish_rtc: setting system clock to 2014-02-20 08:54:53 UTC (1392886493)
Freeing init memory: 124K
mmc0: new SD card at address e118
mmcblk0: mmc0:e118 SU02G 100 MiB
 mmcblk0:
init: cannot open '/initlogo.rle'
yaffs: dev is 32505856 name is "mtdblock0"
```

Chapter 10 Using U-Boot to Boot the Goldfish Kernel

```
yaffs: passed flags ""
yaffs: Attempting MTD mount on 31.0, "mtdblock0"
yaffs_read_super: isCheckpointed 0
save exit: isCheckpointed 1
yaffs: dev is 32505857 name is "mtdblock1"
yaffs: passed flags ""
yaffs: Attempting MTD mount on 31.1, "mtdblock1"
yaffs_read_super: isCheckpointed 0
yaffs: dev is 32505858 name is "mtdblock2"
yaffs: passed flags ""
yaffs: Attempting MTD mount on 31.2, "mtdblock2"
yaffs_read_super: isCheckpointed 0
init: untracked pid 39 exited
eth0: link up
shell@android:/ $ warning: 'zygote' uses 32-bit capabilities (legacy support in use)
```

Source-Level Debugging of the Flash Image

At this point, we can use a flash image that includes both U-Boot and the goldfish kernel to boot up the system. But can we do source-level debugging as well? If we are working on a real hardware board with JTAG debugger, it is quite difficult to do source-level debugging for both U-Boot and the kernel. However, no such problem arises in a virtual environment. With this approach, we can closely observe the transition from bootloader to Linux kernel using source-level debugging. This is a convenient way to debug the U-Boot boot-up process. We can track the interaction between U-Boot and Linux kernel by tracing the execution of the source code.

Let's start the Android emulator with gdb support:

$ emulator -verbose -show-kernel -netfast -avd hd2 -shell -qemu -s -S -kernel flash.bin

We connect to the Android emulator using gdb:

$ ddd --debugger arm-none-eabi-gdb u-boot/u-boot

As shown in Figure 10.6, we load U-Boot in gdb with source-level debugging information.

Now we can perform source-level debugging for U-Boot. Since U-Boot will reload itself, we must use the same technique that we applied in Chapter 9 to continue the source-level debugging after memory relocation occurs.

Each time we start U-Boot in gdb, we have to go through a series of steps. It is much easier (and faster) to put these steps into a gdb script, as shown in Example 10.1. This script can be found in the folder bin of the repository build.

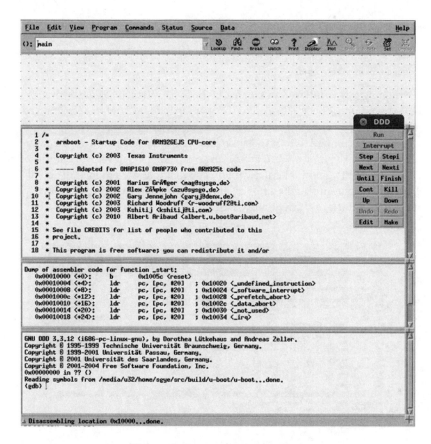

Figure 10.6 Loading U-Boot to gdb

Example 10.1 GDB Startup Script for U-Boot (u-boot.gdb)

```
# Debug u-boot
b board_init_f
c
b relocate_code
c
p/x ((gd_t *)$r1)->relocaddr
d
symbol-file ./u-boot/u-boot
add-symbol-file ./u-boot/u-boot 0x1ff59000
b board_init_r
```

268 Chapter 10 Using U-Boot to Boot the Goldfish Kernel

We can load this script in the gdb console using the following command:

(gdb) **target remote localhost:1234**

(gdb) **source bin/u-boot.gdb**

After running this script, we can see that U-Boot has stopped at board_init_f() and the U-Boot symbol has been reloaded to the memory address after its relocation, as shown in Figure 10.7.

Let's continue running U-Boot to a point after memory relocation. In the script u-boot.gdb, the breakpoint is set to board_init_r(). After U-Boot stops at this breakpoint, we can load the goldfish kernel symbol. The multiple steps to load the goldfish kernel can also be put into a gdb script, as shown in Example 10.2. This script can also be found in the folder bin of the repository build.

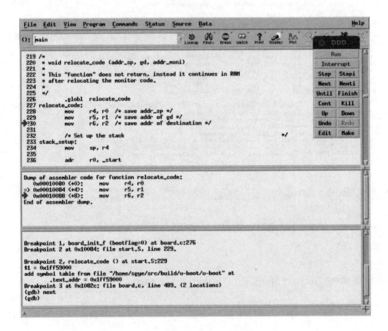

Figure 10.7 Reload the U-Boot symbol after relocation

Example 10.2 GDB Script for Debugging Goldfish Kernel (goldfish.gdb)

```
# Debug goldfish kernel
d
symbol-file ./goldfish/vmlinux
add-symbol-file ./goldfish/vmlinux 0x00010000
b start_kernel
```

We can load the script `goldfish.gdb` to the gdb console as follows:

(gdb) source bin/goldfish.gdb
```
add symbol table from file "/home/sgye/src/build/goldfish/vmlinux" at
    .text_addr = 0x10000
Breakpoint 4 at 0xc00086b4: file /home/sgye/src/goldfish/init/main.c, line 535.
(2 locations)
...
warning: (Internal error: pc 0x10088 in read in psymtab, but not in symtab.)

(gdb) c
warning: (Internal error: pc 0x10088 in read in psymtab, but not in symtab.)

Breakpoint 4, start_kernel () at /home/sgye/src/goldfish/init/main.c:535
(gdb)
```

In the script `goldfish.gdb`, the kernel symbol is loaded from `vmlinux` at memory address 0x10000 and a breakpoint is set at `start_kernel()`. After loading the kernel symbol, we can continue running U-Boot. Now the system stops at the Linux kernel code, as shown in Figure 10.8.

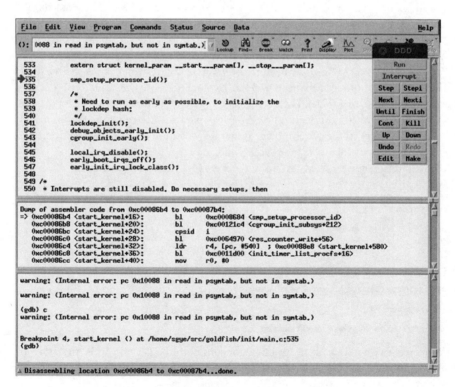

Figure 10.8 The goldfish kernel at `start_kernel()`

As we can see in this session, we have much more control over the system in the virtual environment compared to what is possible in the real hardware. In turn, we can perform a deeper analysis of the code by tracing the execution path at the source level. We can work at the source level, starting from the first line of code and working all the way to the point at which the operating system fully boots up.

Booting Android from NAND Flash

With U-Boot, we can also boot Android from NAND flash. This approach is very similar to that used in real-world cases. When using this approach, we keep everything (kernel, RAMDISK image, and file system) in NAND flash and boot from there. As discussed in Chapter 8, three flash devices—`system`, `userdata`, and `cache`—are connected to the Android emulator. Even though Android mounts the RAMDISK as root, all system files are included in `system.img`. We can put both the kernel and RAMDISK images in `system.img` as well, allowing us to then boot the entire system from `system.img`.

Preparing system.img

To put the kernel and RAMDISK images into `system.img`, we have to recreate them. As mentioned previously, in Android 4.3 and earlier, `system.img` is in the YAFFS2 format. In Android 4.4 or later, it is in the ext4 format. In the ext4 format, we can mount the `system.img` file directly and copy both the kernel and RAMDISK in it. In this chapter, we will continue to use the Android Virtual Device `hd2` that we created in Chapter 2; it is in YAFFS2 format and relies on Android version 4.0.3.

To regenerate `system.img`, we need to use YAFFS2 utilities. You can get them after you check out the `build` repository from GitHub. Two utilities—`mkyaffs2image` and `unyaffs`—can be found in the `bin` folder. Their source code can be found at *http://code.google.com*.

We have to extract `system.img` first. After we extract it, we can copy the kernel and RAMDISK images to the system image folder. As we did in the previous section, we need them in the U-Boot format (`zImage.uimg` and `rootfs.uimg`).

We can regenerate `system.img` using the `mkyaffs2image` command:

```
$ mkdir system

$ cd system

$ unyaffs ../system.img

$ cd ..

$ cp ./rootfs.uimg system/ramdisk.uimg

$ cp ./zImage.uimg system/zImage.uimg

$ rm ./system.img

$ mkyaffs2image system ./system.img
```

Now we have a new `system.img` that contains both the kernel and RAMDISK images. We can use it to boot Android with U-Boot. For the exact procedures, refer to the build target `rootfs` of `Makefile` in the `build` repository.

Booting from NAND Flash

To boot Android from NAND flash, we need to use the -system option to tell the emulator to use our version of system.img instead of the one that comes with the Android SDK:

```
$ emulator -show-kernel -netfast -avd hd2 -shell -system ./system.img -ramdisk ./ramdisk.img  -qemu -kernel ./u-boot.bin
...
U-Boot 2013.01.-rc1-00005-g4627a3e-dirty (Mar 07 2014 - 15:55:45)

U-Boot code: 00010000 -> 0006E2BC  BSS: -> 000A6450
IRQ Stack: 0badc0de
FIQ Stack: 0badc0de
monitor len: 00096450
ramsize: 20000000
TLB table at: 1fff0000
Top of RAM usable for U-Boot at: 1fff0000
Reserving 601k for U-Boot at: 1ff59000
Reserving 4104k for malloc() at: 1fb57000
Reserving 32 Bytes for Board Info at: 1fb56fe0
Reserving 120 Bytes for Global Data at: 1fb56f68
Reserving 8192 Bytes for IRQ stack at: 1fb54f68
New Stack Pointer is: 1fb54f58
RAM Configuration:
Bank #0: 00000000 512 MiB
relocation Offset is: 1ff49000
goldfish_init(), gtty.base=ff012000
WARNING: Caches not enabled
monitor flash len: 00065AD4
Now running in RAM - U-Boot at: 1ff59000
NAND:   base=ff017000
goldfish_nand_init: id=0: name=nand0, nand_name=system
goldfish_nand_init: id=1: name=nand1, nand_name=userdata
goldfish_nand_init: id=2: name=nand2, nand_name=cache
459 MiB
Using default environment
```

Chapter 10 Using U-Boot to Boot the Goldfish Kernel

```
Destroy Hash Table: 1ffb5fe4 table = 00000000
Create Hash Table: N=89
INSERT: table 1ffb5fe4, filled 1/89 rv 1fb572a4 ==> name="bootargs" value="qemu.
gles=1 qemu=1 console=ttyS0 android.qemud=ttyS1 androidboot.console=ttyS2
android.checkjni=1 ndns=1"
INSERT: table 1ffb5fe4, filled 2/89 rv 1fb57160 ==> name="bootcmd" value="bootm
0x210000 0x410000"
INSERT: table 1ffb5fe4, filled 3/89 rv 1fb572f8 ==> name="bootdelay" value="2"
INSERT: table 1ffb5fe4, filled 4/89 rv 1fb57178 ==> name="baudrate" value="38400"
INSERT: table 1ffb5fe4, filled 5/89 rv 1fb57154 ==> name="bootfile" value="/
tftpboot/uImage"
INSERT: free(data = 1fb57008)
INSERT: done
In:    serial
Out:   serial
Err:   serial
Net:   SMC91111-0
Warning: SMC91111-0 using MAC address from net device

### main_loop entered: bootdelay=2

### main_loop: bootcmd="bootm 0x210000 0x410000"
Hit any key to stop autoboot:  0
## Current stack ends at 0x1fb54b00 *  kernel: cmdline image address = 0x00210000
Wrong Image Format for bootm command
ERROR: can't get kernel image!
Command failed, result=1
Goldfish #
```

After the emulator is running, we are sent to the U-Boot command prompt because we have interrupted the autoboot process. We can then mount system.img from the U-Boot command line. First, we use the U-Boot command ydevconfig to configure the NAND device. We configure the device name as sys starting from block 0 to 0x64d (1613). The device number is 0:

Goldfish # **ydevconfig sys 0 0x0 0x64d**

Configures yaffs mount sys: dev 0 start block 0, end block 1613

We can check the configuration using the command ydevls:

Goldfish # **ydevls**

sys   0 0x00000 0x0064d not mounted

Booting Android from NAND Flash

Next, we use the `ymount` command to mount the device `sys`. After mounting the device, we can list its contents using the command `yls`:

```
Goldfish # ymount sys
Mounting yaffs2 mount point sys
Goldfish # yls sys
build.prop
media
fonts
lib
ramdisk.uimg
usr
zImage.uimg
xbin
etc
framework
tts
bin
app
lost+found
```

Once we find both the kernel and RAMDISK image (`zImage.uimg` and `ramdisk.uimg`), we need to load them into memory using the command `yrdm` before we can boot the system. After we load them into memory, we can use the command `iminfo` to verify them:

```
Goldfish # yrdm sys/ramdisk.uimg 0x410000
Copy sys/ramdisk.uimg to 0x00410000...      [DONE]
Goldfish # iminfo 0x410000

## Checking Image at 00410000 ...
   Legacy image found
   Image Name:
   Image Type:   ARM Linux RAMDisk Image (uncompressed)
   Data Size:    187703 Bytes = 183.3 KiB
   Load Address: 00800000
   Entry Point:  00800000
   Verifying Checksum ... OK
Goldfish # yrdm sys/zImage.uimg 0x210000
```

```
Copy sys/zImage.uimg to 0x00210000...      [DONE]
Goldfish # iminfo 0x210000

## Checking Image at 00210000 ...
   Legacy image found
   Image Name:
   Image Type:   ARM Linux Kernel Image (uncompressed)
   Data Size:    1722852 Bytes = 1.6 MiB
   Load Address: 00010000
   Entry Point:  00010000
   Verifying Checksum ... OK
```

Now we are ready to boot the system. This stage is the same as what we did when booting with NOR flash in the previous section. We use the umount command to dismount the YAFFS2 file system first and use the bootm command to boot the system:

```
Goldfish # yumount sys
Unmounting yaffs2 mount point sys
Goldfish # bootm 0x210000 0x410000
## Current stack ends at 0x1fb54b10 *  kernel: cmdline image address = 0x00210000
## Booting kernel from Legacy Image at 00210000 ...
   Image Name:
   Image Type:   ARM Linux Kernel Image (uncompressed)
   Data Size:    1722852 Bytes = 1.6 MiB
   Load Address: 00010000
   Entry Point:  00010000
   kernel data at 0x00210040, len = 0x001a49e4 (1722852)
*  ramdisk: cmdline image address = 0x00410000
## Loading init Ramdisk from Legacy Image at 00410000 ...
   Image Name:
   Image Type:   ARM Linux RAMDisk Image (uncompressed)
   Data Size:    187703 Bytes = 183.3 KiB
   Load Address: 00800000
   Entry Point:  00800000
   ramdisk start = 0x00800000, ramdisk end = 0x0082dd37
   Loading Kernel Image ... OK
CACHE: Misaligned operation at range [00010000, 006a2790]
```

```
OK
   kernel loaded at 0x00010000, end = 0x001b49e4
using: ATAGS
## Transferring control to Linux (at address 00010000)...

Starting kernel ...

Uncompressing Linux.......................................................
...................................... done, booting the kernel.
goldfish_fb_get_pixel_format:167: display surface,pixel format:
   bits/pixel:   16
   bytes/pixel:  2
   depth:        16
   red:          bits=5 mask=0xf800 shift=11 max=0x1f
   green:        bits=6 mask=0x7e0 shift=5 max=0x3f
   blue:         bits=5 mask=0x1f shift=0 max=0x1f
   alpha:        bits=0 mask=0x0 shift=0 max=0x0
Initializing cgroup subsys cpu
Linux version 2.6.29-ge3d684d (sye1@ubuntu) (gcc version 4.6.3 (Sourcery
CodeBench Lite 2012.03-57) ) #4 Fri Mar 7 15:59:39 CST 2014
CPU: ARMv7 Processor [410fc080] revision 0 (ARMv7), cr=10c5387f
CPU: VIPT nonaliasing data cache, VIPT nonaliasing instruction cache
Machine: Goldfish
Memory policy: ECC disabled, Data cache writeback
Built 1 zonelists in Zone order, mobility grouping on.  Total pages: 130048
Kernel command line: qemu.gles=1 qemu=1 console=ttyS0 android.qemud=ttyS1
androidboot.console=ttyS2 android.checkjni=1 ndns=1
Unknown boot option 'qemu.gles=1': ignoring
Unknown boot option 'android.qemud=ttyS1': ignoring
Unknown boot option 'androidboot.console=ttyS2': ignoring
Unknown boot option 'android.checkjni=1': ignoring
PID hash table entries: 2048 (order: 11, 8192 bytes)
Console: colour dummy device 80x30
Dentry cache hash table entries: 65536 (order: 6, 262144 bytes)
Inode-cache hash table entries: 32768 (order: 5, 131072 bytes)
Memory: 512MB = 512MB total
Memory: 515456KB available (2956K code, 707K data, 124K init)
```

```
Calibrating delay loop... 452.19 BogoMIPS (lpj=2260992)
Mount-cache hash table entries: 512
Initializing cgroup subsys debug
Initializing cgroup subsys cpuacct
Initializing cgroup subsys freezer
CPU: Testing write buffer coherency: ok
net_namespace: 936 bytes
NET: Registered protocol family 16
bio: create slab <bio-0> at 0
NET: Registered protocol family 2
IP route cache hash table entries: 16384 (order: 4, 65536 bytes)
TCP established hash table entries: 65536 (order: 7, 524288 bytes)
TCP bind hash table entries: 65536 (order: 6, 262144 bytes)
TCP: Hash tables configured (established 65536 bind 65536)
TCP reno registered
NET: Registered protocol family 1
checking if image is initramfs... it is
Freeing initrd memory: 180K
goldfish_new_pdev goldfish_interrupt_controller at ff000000 irq -1
goldfish_new_pdev goldfish_device_bus at ff001000 irq 1
goldfish_new_pdev goldfish_timer at ff003000 irq 3
goldfish_new_pdev goldfish_rtc at ff010000 irq 10
goldfish_new_pdev goldfish_tty at ff002000 irq 4
goldfish_new_pdev goldfish_tty at ff011000 irq 11
goldfish_new_pdev goldfish_tty at ff012000 irq 12
goldfish_new_pdev smc91x at ff013000 irq 13
goldfish_new_pdev goldfish_fb at ff014000 irq 14
goldfish_new_pdev goldfish_audio at ff004000 irq 15
goldfish_new_pdev goldfish_mmc at ff005000 irq 16
goldfish_new_pdev goldfish_memlog at ff006000 irq -1
goldfish_new_pdev goldfish-battery at ff015000 irq 17
goldfish_new_pdev goldfish_events at ff016000 irq 18
goldfish_new_pdev goldfish_nand at ff017000 irq -1
goldfish_new_pdev qemu_pipe at ff018000 irq 19
```

```
goldfish_new_pdev goldfish-switch at ff01a000 irq 20
goldfish_new_pdev goldfish-switch at ff01b000 irq 21
goldfish_pdev_worker registered goldfish_interrupt_controller
goldfish_pdev_worker registered goldfish_device_bus
goldfish_pdev_worker registered goldfish_timer
goldfish_pdev_worker registered goldfish_rtc
goldfish_pdev_worker registered goldfish_tty
goldfish_pdev_worker registered goldfish_tty
goldfish_pdev_worker registered goldfish_tty
goldfish_pdev_worker registered smc91x
goldfish_pdev_worker registered goldfish_fb
goldfish_pdev_worker registered goldfish_audio
goldfish_pdev_worker registered goldfish_mmc
goldfish_pdev_worker registered goldfish_memlog
goldfish_pdev_worker registered goldfish-battery
goldfish_pdev_worker registered goldfish_events
goldfish_pdev_worker registered goldfish_nand
goldfish_pdev_worker registered qemu_pipe
goldfish_pdev_worker registered goldfish-switch
goldfish_pdev_worker registered goldfish-switch
ashmem: initialized
Installing knfsd (copyright (C) 1996 okir@monad.swb.de).
fuse init (API version 7.11)
yaffs Mar  7 2014 15:57:44 Installing.
msgmni has been set to 1007
alg: No test for stdrng (krng)
io scheduler noop registered
io scheduler anticipatory registered (default)
io scheduler deadline registered
io scheduler cfq registered
allocating frame buffer 480 * 800, got ffa00000
console [ttyS0] enabled
brd: module loaded
loop: module loaded
```

```
nbd: registered device at major 43
goldfish_audio_probe
tun: Universal TUN/TAP device driver, 1.6
tun: (C) 1999-2004 Max Krasnyansky <maxk@qualcomm.com>
smc91x.c: v1.1, sep 22 2004 by Nicolas Pitre <nico@cam.org>
eth0 (smc91x): not using net_device_ops yet
eth0: SMC91C11xFD (rev 1) at e080c000 IRQ 13 [nowait]
eth0: Ethernet addr: 52:54:00:12:34:56
goldfish nand dev0: size c9c0000, page 2048, extra 64, erase 131072
goldfish nand dev1: size c200000, page 2048, extra 64, erase 131072
goldfish nand dev2: size 4000000, page 2048, extra 64, erase 131072
mice: PS/2 mouse device common for all mice
*** events probe ***
events_probe() addr=0xe0814000 irq=18
events_probe() keymap=qwerty2
input: qwerty2 as /devices/virtual/input/input0
goldfish_rtc goldfish_rtc: rtc core: registered goldfish_rtc as rtc0
device-mapper: uevent: version 1.0.3
device-mapper: ioctl: 4.14.0-ioctl (2008-04-23) initialised: dm-devel@redhat.com
logger: created 64K log 'log_main'
logger: created 256K log 'log_events'
logger: created 64K log 'log_radio'
Netfilter messages via NETLINK v0.30.
nf_conntrack version 0.5.0 (8192 buckets, 32768 max)
CONFIG_NF_CT_ACCT is deprecated and will be removed soon. Please use
nf_conntrack.acct=1 kernel parameter, acct=1 nf_conntrack module option or
sysctl net.netfilter.nf_conntrack_acct=1 to enable it.
ctnetlink v0.93: registering with nfnetlink.
NF_TPROXY: Transparent proxy support initialized, version 4.1.0
NF_TPROXY: Copyright (c) 2006-2007 BalaBit IT Ltd.
xt_time: kernel timezone is -0000
ip_tables: (C) 2000-2006 Netfilter Core Team
arp_tables: (C) 2002 David S. Miller
TCP cubic registered
```

```
NET: Registered protocol family 10
ip6_tables: (C) 2000-2006 Netfilter Core Team
IPv6 over IPv4 tunneling driver
NET: Registered protocol family 17
NET: Registered protocol family 15
RPC: Registered udp transport module.
RPC: Registered tcp transport module.
802.1Q VLAN Support v1.8 Ben Greear <greearb@candelatech.com>
All bugs added by David S. Miller <davem@redhat.com>
VFP support v0.3: implementor 41 architecture 3 part 30 variant c rev 0
goldfish_rtc goldfish_rtc: setting system clock to 2014-03-10 10:04:08 UTC (1394445848)
Freeing init memory: 124K
mmc0: new SD card at address e118
mmcblk0: mmc0:e118 SU02G 100 MiB
 mmcblk0:
init: cannot open '/initlogo.rle'
yaffs: dev is 32505856 name is "mtdblock0"
yaffs: passed flags ""
yaffs: Attempting MTD mount on 31.0, "mtdblock0"
yaffs_read_super: isCheckpointed 0
save exit: isCheckpointed 1
yaffs: dev is 32505857 name is "mtdblock1"
yaffs: passed flags ""
yaffs: Attempting MTD mount on 31.1, "mtdblock1"
yaffs_read_super: isCheckpointed 0
yaffs: dev is 32505858 name is "mtdblock2"
yaffs: passed flags ""
yaffs: Attempting MTD mount on 31.2, "mtdblock2"
yaffs_read_super: isCheckpointed 0
init: cannot find '/system/etc/install-recovery.sh', disabling 'flash_recovery'
eth0: link up
shell@android:/ $ warning: 'rild' uses 32-bit capabilities (legacy support in use)
```

Summary

In this chapter, we used U-Boot to demonstrate two scenarios for operating system boot-up. First, we booted Android from NOR flash using U-Boot. Even though the Android emulator doesn't have NOR flash, we created an image to simulate it. Second, we booted Android from NAND flash. In this case, we put the kernel and RAMDISK images inside system.img and used U-Boot to boot the system.

We can build almost everything on our own to boot the Android system, except RAMDISK and the file system. To make our own RAMDISK and file system, we hacked them from the Android SDK. In next two chapters, we will go even further; that is, we will explore how to build everything, including the Android file system, from source code.

III

Android System Integration

11 Building Your Own AOSP and CyanogenMod

12 Customizing Android and Creating Your Own Android ROM

11
Building Your Own AOSP and CyanogenMod

In Chapter 10, we booted Android using our own U-Boot. We've now learned how to create almost everything from scratch except the file system. The file system includes the actual Android system. To have a complete picture, this chapter explores how to build Android from source code using AOSP and CyanogenMod.

Introducing AOSP and CyanogenMod

Android Open Source Project (AOSP) is an open source project managed by Google. A typical Android system usually includes two parts: the foundation of the Android system built from AOSP, and a variety of applications and services collectively known as Google Mobile Services (GMS). Many popular applications from Google are part of GMS, such as Gmail, Google Search, and Google Maps. GMS is independent of Android and under a separate license from Google. It runs as an add-on above AOSP.

Some Android products are built using AOSP with GMS. Many other products are built using AOSP only, especially those products targeted at emerging markets. According to a report from the marketing research company ABI Research,[1] sales of AOSP-based smartphones grew 20% from first quarter 2014 to second quarter 2014 (by comparison, the total market for smartphones grew 3% over the same period) and accounted for 20% of the smartphone market. Certified or OHA Android products still lead the market, representing 65% of the total, but are growing at a much slower pace (13% from first to second quarter 2014). Collectively, Android AOSP and OHA accounted for 278 million shipped smartphones—a staggering 86% share—in the second quarter of 2014.

Since AOSP is an open source project, not only can mobile device companies build Android products using it, but the developer communities can also create child projects on top of it. Many so-called third-party ROM development communities exist, such as CyanogenMod, AOKP, and MIUI.

---

[1] The report from ABI Research can be found at https://www.abiresearch.com/press/2q-2014-smartphone-results-forked-android-aosp-gro/.

Table 11.1 ASOP and CyanogenMod Releases

Nickname	AOSP	CyanogenMod
Donut	Android 1.6	CM4
Eclair	Android 2.0/2.1	CM5
Froyo	Android 2.2	CM6
Gingerbread	Android 2.3	CM7
Honeycomb	Android 3.x	CM8
Ice Cream Sandwich	Android 4.0	CM9
Jelly Bean	Android 4.1	CM10
Jelly Bean	Android 4.2	CM10.1
Jelly Bean	Android 4.3	CM10.2
KitKat	Android 4.4	CM11
Lollipop	Android 5.0	CM12

Among the denizens of the ROM development communities, CyanogenMod and MIUI are the most famous. Their products are used by many Android users as well as in commercial products. For example, when the mobile device company OnePlus released its OnePlus One series of products, the devices used CyanogenMod ROM. Xiaomi has successfully developed Android products using MIUI ROM. The initial development of MIUI is also built on top of CyanogenMod.

Multiple versions of CyanogenMod releases exist, all built on top of AOSP releases. Table 11.1 lists the various AOSP and CyanogenMod releases.

Setting Up an Android Virtual Device

Before we start to build our own Android ROM, let's investigate the use of the Google Android SDK in more depth. We will create an Android 4.4-based virtual device and then explore how to create our own ROM using the same version of AOSP and CyanogenMod.

We installed the Android SDK in Chapter 3. We can now launch Android Virtual Device Manager (Figure 11.1) using the following command:

```
$ android avd
```

Click the *Create…* button in Android Virtual Device Manager and create a new virtual device named `armemu`, as shown in Figure 11.2, with the following configuration:

- Android 4.4.2: API Level 19
- 512MB RAM
- 200MB SD Card
- 200MB Internal Storage
- 5.1″ WVGA (480 × 800: mdpi)

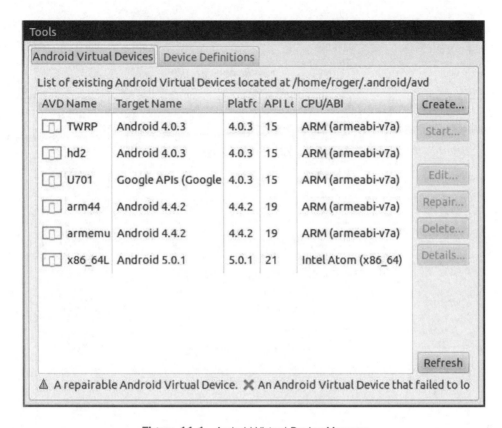

Figure 11.1 Android Virtual Device Manager

Once we have created the virtual device, we can launch it in the Android emulator using the following command:

```
$ emulator -avd armemu -verbose -show-kernel -shell
emulator:Found AVD name 'armemu'
emulator:Found AVD target architecture: arm
emulator:Looking for emulator-arm to emulate 'arm' CPU
emulator:Probing program: ./emulator64-arm
...
```

To monitor the status of our virtual device, we decide to use the following Android emulator options:

- **-verbose**: Shows the emulator debug information
- **-show-kernel**: Shows kernel debug information
- **-shell**: Uses stdio as the command-line prompt

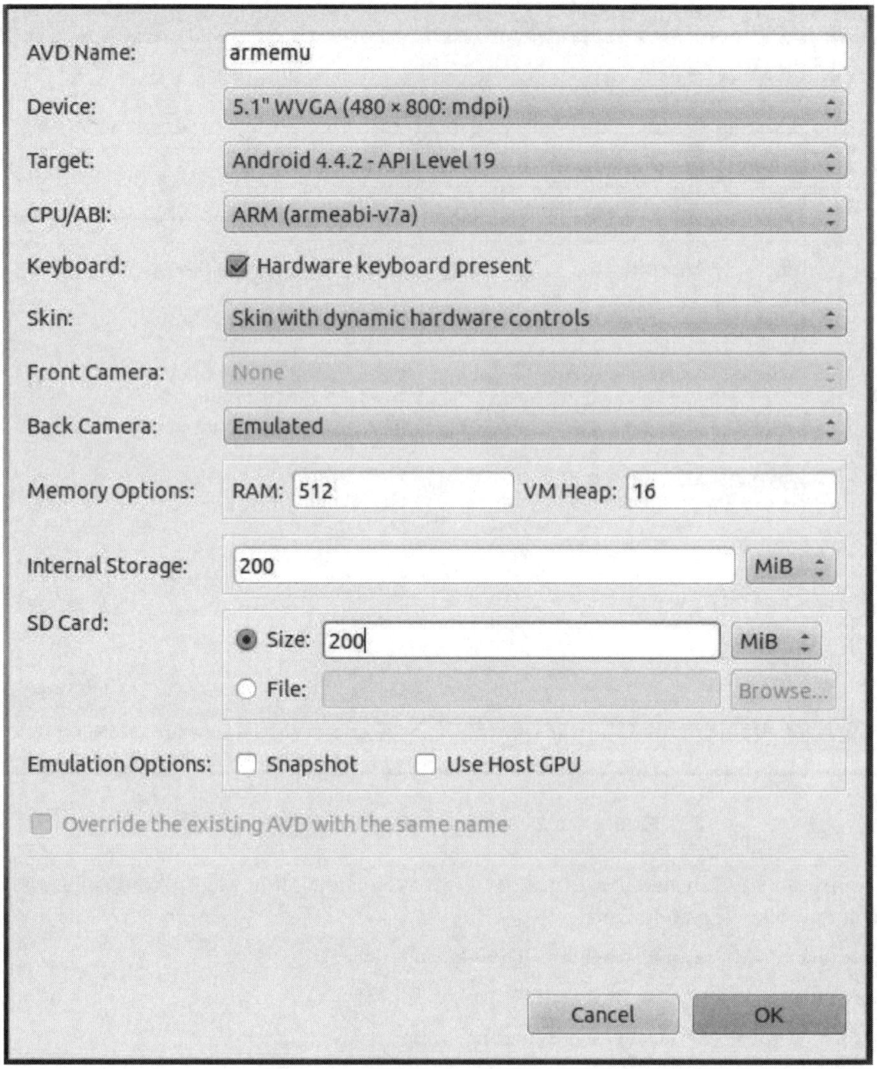

286 Chapter 11 Building Your Own AOSP and CyanogenMod

Figure 11.2 Virtual Device `armemu`

After the Android device starts successfully, from the Android UI, we can go to *Settings > About Phone* and see the screen shown in Figure 11.3.

Pay attention to the following information on the *About Phone* screen:

- Model number: sdk
- Android version: 4.4.2
- Kernel version: 3.4.0-gd853d22
- Build number: sdk-eng 4.4.2 KK 938007 test-keys

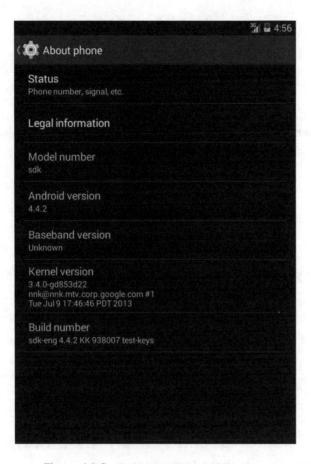

Figure 11.3 Android version of SDK images

The device model number is provided by the device's manufacturer. For example, LG-D802 is the model number for LG G2 device. Here we can see that the model number is *sdk*, which is a build configuration of the emulator.

The AOSP-based Android system includes two parts: the AOSP release and an Android-compatible Linux kernel. They are built separately and are covered under different licenses. The preferred license for the AOSP is the Apache Software License, while the Linux kernel is under the GPLv2 license.

Pay attention to these differences, because they also mean the AOSP build doesn't include the kernel build. That is, we have to build the kernel separately. In the next chapter, we'll talk about how to integrate the Linux kernel and U-Boot build in the AOSP build.

The Android version in Figure 11.3 indicates the AOSP release version, while kernel version gives the compatible Linux kernel version. The build number is the specific AOSP build number.

AOSP Android Emulator Build

To create our own Android system, we have to set up the AOSP build environment and build our own AOSP target for the Android emulator. We will talk about how to create our own Android system in Chapter 12. In this section, we explore the process of setting up the AOSP build environment and creating a standard Android emulator image.

Many good references are available on the Internet and as printed books that explain how to build AOSP. If you want to explore more about this topic, Chapters 3 and 4 of the book *Embedded Android* by Karim Yaghmour are a great starting point. Because Android remains under rapid development, however, the build process and environment setup may change from time to time. You can always refer to Google's website to obtain the latest information: https://source.android.com/source/building.html.

While the resources mentioned previously give general guidelines and procedures for AOSP builds, in this section we look specifically at how to build AOSP for the Android emulator.

AOSP Build Environment

The first thing we have to do before building an AOSP target is to set up a build environment. Always refer to Google's website for the latest build environment information.

Installing the Required Packages

As noted in Chapter 3 of this book, we are using Ubuntu 12.04 64-bit version as our host operating system. We have to install all necessary software packages as follows for Ubuntu 12.04. If you use a different Linux distribution, you can refer to Google's website or search on the Internet for the appropriate setup procedures. To install all necessary packages for Ubuntu 12.04, we execute the following commands:

```
$ sudo apt-get install git gnupg flex bison gperf build-essential \
  zip curl libc6-dev libncurses5-dev:i386 x11proto-core-dev \
  libx11-dev:i386 libreadline6-dev:i386 libgl1-mesa-glx:i386 \
  libgl1-mesa-dev g++-multilib mingw32 tofrodos \
  python-markdown libxml2-utils xsltproc zlib1g-dev:i386
$ sudo ln -s /usr/lib/i386-linux-gnu/mesa/libGL.so.1 /usr/lib/i386-linux-gnu/libGL.so
```

Installing the JDK

To build a different version of AOSP, we need a different version of JDK. To build Android 4.4, we need Sun JDK 1.6. To build the latest version, Android 5.0, we need to install OpenJDK 7. Since we will build Android 4.4 in this chapter, we execute the following commands from the Linux console to install Sun JDK 1.6:

```
$ sudo add-apt-repository "deb http://archive.canonical.com/ natty partner"
$ sudo apt-get update
$ sudo apt-get install sun-java6-jdk
```

Now we have a build environment ready. You might want to refer to Google's website to set up other features. For example, you might want to use `ccache` to speed up the build or create a separate output directory from the AOSP tree.

Downloading the AOSP Source

Once our build environment is ready, we need to get the AOSP source code. Again, refer to Google's website or Chapter 3 of *Embedded Android* for more information on this process.

For the code presented here, you need to download the Android 4.4.4 source code from source.android.com. Ideally, we would use the latest version of Android to explain the topics in this book, which was Android 5.0 (Lollipop) at the time of writing. However, this chapter and Chapter 12 compare AOSP and CyanogenMod—and when this book was published, Android 5.0's support for CyanogenMod was not stable. Instead, we use the stable version of CyanogenMod, CM-11, which is supported by Android 4.4.4.

Installing Repo

AOSP consists of a large number of git repositories, and we have to use the `repo` tool to manage them. To download and install `repo`, we give the following commands:

```
$ mkdir ~/bin
```

```
$ PATH=~/bin:$PATH
```

```
$ curl https://storage.googleapis.com/git-repo-downloads/repo > ~/bin/repo
```

```
$ chmod a+x ~/bin/repo
```

Initializing a Repo Client and Downloading the AOSP Source Tree

After we have the `repo` tool, we can initialize the repository and download the AOSP source tree by executing the following commands:

```
$ repo init -u https://android.googlesource.com/platform/manifest -b android-4.4.4_r2
```

```
$ repo sync
```

It will take quite a long time to get the AOSP source tree. After we get the source tree, let's take a look at the top-level folders:

```
$ ls
```

```
abi       cts          docs        libcore          packages    tools
art       dalvik       external    libnativehelper  pdk
bionic    developers   filelist    Makefile         prebuilts
bootable  development  frameworks  ndk              sdk
build     device       hardware    out              system
```

We won't go into the details of the content in this list here. Instead, we'll consider the specific problem of how to add a new device in the AOSP source tree in this chapter and the next. We will look at the entire structure from this angle. For the general information about the AOSP source tree, please refer to Table 3.1 in the book *Embedded Android*.

Building AOSP Android Emulator Images

To create an Android emulator build, we can execute the following commands from the AOSP top-level folder:

```
$ . build/envsetup.sh
including device/samsung/manta/vendorsetup.sh
including device/lge/mako/vendorsetup.sh
including device/lge/hammerhead/vendorsetup.sh
including device/asus/flo/vendorsetup.sh
including device/asus/deb/vendorsetup.sh
including device/asus/tilapia/vendorsetup.sh
including device/asus/grouper/vendorsetup.sh
including device/generic/x86/vendorsetup.sh
including device/generic/armv7-a-neon/vendorsetup.sh
including device/generic/mips/vendorsetup.sh
including sdk/bash_completion/adb.bash
$ lunch

You're building on Linux

Lunch menu... pick a combo:
     1. aosp_arm-eng
     2. aosp_x86-eng
     3. aosp_mips-eng
     4. vbox_x86-eng
     5. aosp_manta-userdebug
     6. aosp_mako-userdebug
     7. aosp_hammerhead-userdebug
     8. aosp_flo-userdebug
     9. aosp_deb-userdebug
     10. aosp_tilapia-userdebug
     11. aosp_grouper-userdebug
     12. mini_x86-userdebug
     13. mini_armv7a_neon-userdebug
     14. mini_mips-userdebug

Which would you like? [aosp_arm-eng]

=============================================
```

```
PLATFORM_VERSION_CODENAME=REL
PLATFORM_VERSION=4.4.4
TARGET_PRODUCT=aosp_arm
TARGET_BUILD_VARIANT=eng
TARGET_BUILD_TYPE=release
TARGET_BUILD_APPS=
TARGET_ARCH=arm
TARGET_ARCH_VARIANT=armv7-a
TARGET_CPU_VARIANT=generic
HOST_ARCH=x86
HOST_OS=linux
HOST_OS_EXTRA=Linux-3.8.0-44-generic-x86_64-with-Ubuntu-12.04-precise
HOST_BUILD_TYPE=release
BUILD_ID=KTU84Q
OUT_DIR=out
============================================
```

We set up the environment variables first using the startup script envsetup.sh. After that, we execute the command **lunch** to choose a build target. To build for the Android emulator, we can choose the default target aosp_arm-eng, which will build an Android emulator version for ARM. To learn more about the script file envsetup.sh and the command **lunch**, refer to the Google website at *https://source.android.com*.

The actual build starts when we execute the following **make** command:

```
$ make -j4
============================================
PLATFORM_VERSION_CODENAME=REL
PLATFORM_VERSION=4.4.4
TARGET_PRODUCT=aosp_arm
TARGET_BUILD_VARIANT=eng
TARGET_BUILD_TYPE=release
TARGET_BUILD_APPS=
TARGET_ARCH=arm
TARGET_ARCH_VARIANT=armv7-a
TARGET_CPU_VARIANT=generic
HOST_ARCH=x86
HOST_OS=linux
HOST_OS_EXTRA=Linux-3.8.0-44-generic-x86_64-with-Ubuntu-12.04-precise
HOST_BUILD_TYPE=release
```

```
BUILD_ID=KTU84Q

OUT_DIR=out

============================================

including ./abi/cpp/Android.mk ...

including ./art/Android.mk ...

…

make_ext4fs -S out/target/product/generic/root/file_contexts -l 576716800 -a
system out/target/product/generic/obj/PACKAGING/systemimage_intermediates/system.
img out/target/product/generic/system

+ make_ext4fs -S out/target/product/generic/root/file_contexts -l 576716800 -a
system out/target/product/generic/obj/PACKAGING/systemimage_intermediates/system.
img out/target/product/generic/system

Creating filesystem with parameters:
    Size: 576716800
    Block size: 4096
    Blocks per group: 32768
    Inodes per group: 7040
    Inode size: 256
    Journal blocks: 2200
    Label:
    Blocks: 140800
    Block groups: 5
    Reserved block group size: 39
Created filesystem with 1277/35200 inodes and 82235/140800 blocks
+ '[' 0 -ne 0 ']'
Install system fs image: out/target/product/generic/system.img
out/target/product/generic/system.img+ maxsize=588791808 blocksize=2112
total=576716800 reserve=5947392
```

The total build time required depends on your hardware configuration. Even on a high-end CORE i7 Intel processor, it may take approximately 40 minutes.

Testing AOSP Images

After the build is completed, we can find all images in the following folder:

```
$ ls out/target/product/generic/
android-info.txt    data                obj                         symbols
cache               dex_bootjars        previous_build_config.mk    system
cache.img           fake_packages       ramdisk.img                 system.img
clean_steps.mk      installed-files.txt root                        userdata.img
```

The images `system.img`, `userdata.img`, and `ramdisk.img` are necessary to run the emulator, but—as you can see—there is no kernel image. We will discuss building the kernel in Chapter 12. For now, we use the kernel image from the Android SDK to test our AOSP build.

In addition to all the images for the target device, the AOSP build process produces emulator binaries that can be executed on the Linux host. We can find all the tools for Linux host under the following folder:

```
$ ls out/host/linux-x86/bin
```

aapt	clang++	e2fsck	hprof-conv	mkyaffs2image
acp	clang-tblgen	emulator	insertkeys.py	oatdump
adb	dalvik	emulator64-arm	llvm-as	rs-spec-gen
aidl	dalvikvm	emulator64-mips	llvm-link	simg2img
apicheck	dex2oat	emulator64-x86	llvm-rs-cc	tblgen
aprotoc	dexdeps	emulator-arm	make_ext4fs	validatekeymaps
bcc_strip_attr	dexdump	emulator-mips	make_g2g	zipalign
checkfc	dexlist	emulator-x86	minigzip	
checkpolicy	dexopt	fastboot	mkbootfs	
checkseapp	dmtracedump	grxmlcompile	mksnapshot.arm	
clang	dx	hierarchyviewer1	mkuserimg.sh	

Before we can test our own AOSP emulator and images, we have to do some setup work. Ideally, you will have installed the Android SDK in the same folder as the AOSP tree as follows:

```
$ ls ..
adt-bundle-linux-x86_64-20140702    android-4.4.4_r2
```

We have to create two soft-links so that our emulator can find all the images in the default folders. Let's create a soft-link for the platform folder in SDK first:

```
$ cd out/host/linux-x86

$ ln -s ../../../../adt-bundle-linux-x86_64-20140702/sdk/platforms/ .

$ ls -l platforms
lrwxrwxrwx 1 roger mcafee 59 Feb 12 16:36 platforms -> ../../../../adt-bundle-
linux-x86_64-20140702/sdk/platforms/
```

Then, we need to create a soft-link to replace the `system-images` folder using our build:

```
$ mkdir -p system-images/android-19

$ cd system-images/android-19

$ ln -s ../../../../target/product/generic/ armeabi-v7a

$ ls -al armeabi-v7a
```

```
lrwxrwxrwx 1 roger mcafee 35 Feb 12 16:40 armeabi-v7a -> ../../../../target/
product/generic/
```

Now the environment is ready. Let's go to the host folder and try to test our emulator and images:

$ **cd ../..**

$ **ls**

```
add-ons  bin  framework  lib  obj  platforms  system-images  usr
```

$ **bin/emulator -avd armemu -verbose -show-kernel -shell**

emulator: found SDK root at /home/android/aosp/android-4.4.4_r2/out/host/linux-x86

emulator: Android virtual device file at: /home/roger/.android/avd/armemu.ini

emulator: virtual device content at /home/roger/.android/avd/armemu.avd

emulator: virtual device config file: /home/roger/.android/avd/armemu.avd/config.ini

emulator: using core hw config path: /home/roger/.android/avd/armemu.avd/hardware-qemu.ini

emulator: Found AVD target API level: 19

emulator: 'magic' skin format detected: 480x800

emulator: autoconfig: -skin 480x800

emulator: autoconfig: -skindir (null)

emulator: keyset loaded from: /home/roger/.android/default.keyset

emulator: found SDK root at /home/android/aosp/android-4.4.4_r2/out/host/linux-x86

emulator: found magic skin width=480 height=800 bpp=16

emulator: ERROR: This AVD's configuration is missing a kernel file!!

You can see that our attempt generated an error message. The kernel file is missing, as mentioned earlier. Let's copy the kernel file from the Android SDK and try it again:

$ **cp ../../../../adt-bundle-linux-x86_64-20140702/sdk/system-images/android-19/armeabi-v7a/kernel-qemu system-images/android-19/armeabi-v7a/kernel-qemu**

$ **bin/emulator -avd armemu -verbose -show-kernel -shell**

emulator: found SDK root at /home/android/aosp/android-4.4.4_r2/out/host/linux-x86

emulator: Android virtual device file at: /home/roger/.android/avd/armemu.ini

emulator: virtual device content at /home/roger/.android/avd/armemu.avd

emulator: virtual device config file: /home/roger/.android/avd/armemu.avd/config.ini

emulator: using core hw config path: /home/roger/.android/avd/armemu.avd/hardware-qemu.ini

emulator: Found AVD target API level: 19

emulator: 'magic' skin format detected: 480x800

emulator: autoconfig: -skin 480x800

emulator: autoconfig: -skindir (null)

emulator: keyset loaded from: /home/roger/.android/default.keyset

emulator: found SDK root at /home/android/aosp/android-4.4.4_r2/out/host/linux-x86

emulator: found magic skin width=480 height=800 bpp=16

...

emulator: control console listening on port 5554, ADB on port 5555

emulator: sent '0012host:emulator:5555' to ADB server

emulator: ping program: /home/android/aosp/android-4.4.4_r2/out/host/linux-x86/bin/ddms

Uncompressing Linux... done, booting the kernel.

goldfish_fb_get_pixel_format:167: display surface,pixel format:

    bits/pixel: 16

    bytes/pixel: 2

    depth: 16

    red: bits=5 mask=0xf800 shift=11 max=0x1f

    green: bits=6 mask=0x7e0 shift=5 max=0x3f

    blue: bits=5 mask=0x1f shift=0 max=0x1f

    alpha: bits=0 mask=0x0 shift=0 max=0x0

Booting Linux on physical CPU 0

Initializing cgroup subsys cpu

Linux version 3.4.0-gd853d22 (nnk@nnk.mtv.corp.google.com) (gcc version 4.6.x-google 20120106 (prerelease) (GCC)) #1 PREEMPT Tue Jul 9 17:46:46 PDT 2013

CPU: ARMv7 Processor [410fc080] revision 0 (ARMv7), cr=10c53c7d

CPU: PIPT / VIPT nonaliasing data cache, VIPT nonaliasing instruction cache

Machine: Goldfish

Memory policy: ECC disabled, Data cache writeback

Built 1 zonelists in Zone order, mobility grouping on. Total pages: 130048

Kernel command line: qemu.gles=0 qemu=1 console=ttyS0 android.qemud=ttyS1 androidboot.console=ttyS2 android.checkjni=1 ndns=1

PID hash table entries: 2048 (order: 1, 8192 bytes)

Dentry cache hash table entries: 65536 (order: 6, 262144 bytes)

Inode-cache hash table entries: 32768 (order: 5, 131072 bytes)

Memory: 512MB = 512MB total

...

Chapter 11 Building Your Own AOSP and CyanogenMod

As the preceding message indicates, the emulator treats the host output folder `out/host/linux-x86` as the SDK root and uses the images in this folder. We linked the target output folder `out/target/product/generic` to `system-images/android-19/armeabi-v7a` under the SDK root.

After the emulator starts, we can check the version information as we did earlier. Figure 11.4 shows the version information for the AOSP images. Let's compare this information with that for the SDK images.

From Table 11.2, we can see that the model number is *AOSP on ARM Emulator* instead of *sdk*. The Android version is 4.4.4 instead of 4.4.2, indicating which SDK version we used. The build number is the build target `aosp_arm-eng`; the build information also includes the date and time of the build.

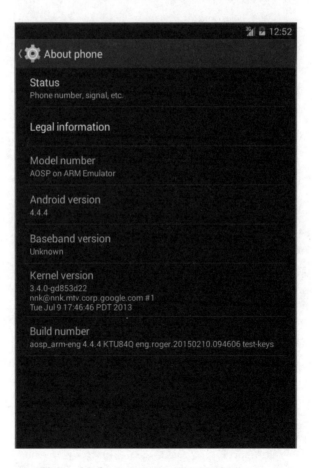

Figure 11.4 Android version of AOSP images

Table 11.2 SDK and AOSP Versions

	SDK	AOSP
Model number	sdk	AOSP on ARM Emulator
Android version	4.4.2	4.4.4
Kernel version	3.4.0-gd853d22	3.4.0-gd853d22
Build number	sdk-eng 4.4.2 KK 938007 test-keys	aosp_arm-eng 4.4.4 KTU84Q eng. roger.20150210.0944606 test-keys

CyanogenMod Android Emulator Build

The process for creating a CyanogenMod-specific Android emulator build is almost the same as the corresponding process for the AOSP build. You will notice, however, a minor difference later: In CyanogenMod, we choose a CyanogenMod-specific build target `cm_goldfish-eng` instead of the default build target `aosp_arm-eng` in AOSP build.

This section provides a good reference for how to create an Android emulator build on CyanogenMod. Many articles cover ways to build CyanogenMod for specific devices, but it is more difficult to find a guide for the Android emulator build.

As we have already set up the AOSP build environment, we don't have to repeat that process here. CyanogenMod uses the same build environment as AOSP.

Downloading the CyanogenMod Source

We will put the CyanogenMod source tree at the same level as the AOSP source tree. We can download the CyanogenMod source tree using the `repo` tool:

```
$ mkdir cm-11
$ cd cm-11
$ repo init -u git://github.com/CyanogenMod/android.git -b cm-11.0
$ repo sync
```

Again, we have to wait a long time for this. After we download the source tree, we see something similar to the AOSP source tree:

```
$ ls
abi       build        device     kernel          out         sdk
android   cts          docs       libcore         packages    system
art       dalvik       external   libnativehelper pdk         tools
bionic    developers   frameworks Makefile        prebuilt    vendor
bootable  development  hardware   ndk             prebuilts
```

Building CyanogenMod Android Emulator Images

The build process for a CyanogenMod-specific Android emulator is similar to that for the AOSP build, except the build options are different. We initialize the environment and select the build target first:

$ **. build/envsetup.sh**

including device/generic/armv7-a-neon/vendorsetup.sh

including device/generic/goldfish/vendorsetup.sh

including device/generic/mips/vendorsetup.sh

including device/generic/x86/vendorsetup.sh

including vendor/cm/vendorsetup.sh

including sdk/bash_completion/adb.bash

including vendor/cm/bash_completion/git.bash

including vendor/cm/bash_completion/repo.bash

$ **lunch**

You're building on Linux

Lunch menu... pick a combo:

1. aosp_arm-eng
2. aosp_x86-eng
3. aosp_mips-eng
4. vbox_x86-eng
5. mini_armv7a_neon-userdebug
6. cm_goldfish-eng
7. cm_goldfish-userdebug
8. cm_goldfish-user
9. mini_mips-userdebug
10. mini_x86-userdebug
11. cm_a700-userdebug
12. cm_apexqtmo-userdebug
13. cm_aries-userdebug
14. cm_captivatemtd-userdebug
15. cm_crespo-userdebug
16. cm_d2lte-userdebug
17. cm_d710-userdebug
18. cm_d800-userdebug
19. cm_d801-userdebug
20. cm_dogo-userdebug
21. cm_e973-userdebug
22. cm_encore-userdebug
23. cm_endeavoru-userdebug
24. cm_enrc2b-userdebug
25. cm_epicmtd-userdebug
26. cm_exhilarate-userdebug
27. cm_expressatt-userdebug
28. cm_fireball-userdebug
29. cm_galaxysbmtd-userdebug
30. cm_galaxysmtd-userdebug
31. cm_hercules-userdebug
32. cm_hlteusc-userdebug
33. cm_hltevzw-userdebug
34. cm_huashan-userdebug

35. cm_hummingbird-userdebug
36. cm_i9100-userdebug
37. cm_i9100g-userdebug
38. cm_i925-userdebug
39. cm_i9300-userdebug
40. cm_i9305-userdebug
41. cm_i9500-userdebug
42. cm_jem-userdebug
43. cm_jflte-userdebug
44. cm_kltespr-userdebug
45. cm_klteusc-userdebug
46. cm_kltevzw-userdebug
47. cm_l01f-userdebug
48. cm_m4-userdebug
49. cm_m7spr-userdebug
50. cm_maguro-userdebug
51. cm_moto_msm8960_jbbl-userdebug
52. cm_n1-userdebug
53. cm_n5100-userdebug
54. cm_n5110-userdebug
55. cm_n5120-userdebug
56. cm_n7000-userdebug
57. cm_n7100-userdebug
58. cm_odin-userdebug
59. cm_otter-userdebug
60. cm_otter2-userdebug
61. cm_otterx-userdebug
62. cm_ovation-userdebug
63. cm_p1-userdebug
64. cm_p3100-userdebug
65. cm_p3110-userdebug
66. cm_p5100-userdebug
67. cm_p5110-userdebug
68. cm_p880-userdebug
69. cm_p930-userdebug
70. cm_pollux-userdebug
71. cm_pollux_windy-userdebug
72. cm_r950-userdebug
73. cm_skyrocket-userdebug
74. cm_sprout-userdebug
75. cm_superior-userdebug
76. cm_t769-userdebug
77. cm_tate-userdebug
78. cm_tf700t-userdebug
79. cm_tf701t-userdebug
80. cm_vs920-userdebug
81. cm_vs980-userdebug
82. cm_w7-userdebug
83. cm_ypg1-userdebug
84. cm_yuga-userdebug

```
Which would you like? [aosp_arm-eng] 6
Looking for dependencies

============================================
PLATFORM_VERSION_CODENAME=REL
PLATFORM_VERSION=4.4.4
CM_VERSION=11-20150212-UNOFFICIAL-goldfish
TARGET_PRODUCT=cm_goldfish
TARGET_BUILD_VARIANT=eng
```

```
TARGET_BUILD_TYPE=release

TARGET_BUILD_APPS=

TARGET_ARCH=arm

TARGET_ARCH_VARIANT=armv7-a

TARGET_CPU_VARIANT=generic

HOST_ARCH=x86

HOST_OS=linux

HOST_OS_EXTRA=Linux-3.8.0-44-generic-x86_64-with-Ubuntu-12.04-precise

HOST_BUILD_TYPE=release

BUILD_ID=KTU84Q

OUT_DIR=/home/android/aosp/cm-11/out

============================================
```

As you can see, CyanogenMod offers many more options compared to the AOSP build. It supports many device families directly, while AOSP is the base that can be used for Android platform development.

Pay attention to the build target that we chose. We did not choose the default target (aosp_arm-eng), as we did for the AOSP build. CyanogenMod supports a few build targets for the Android Emulator build directly. For the emulator engineering build, we selected the target cm_goldfish-eng.

The development guide for CyanogenMod lists several commands besides **lunch** that can be used to configure and build CyanogenMod images. For example, the command called **breakfast** can be used instead of **lunch** for the CyanogenMod build. You can refer to xdadevelopers to obtain more information about device builds in CyanogenMod: *http://forum.xda-developers.com/nexus-4/general/guide-cm11-how-to-build-cyanogenmod-11-t2515305*.

Following are the options for the **breakfast** command:

$ **breakfast**

```
including vendor/cm/vendorsetup.sh

You're building on Linux

Breakfast menu... pick a combo:

    1. full-eng                          7. cm_d21te-userdebug

    2. cm_a700-userdebug                 8. cm_d710-userdebug

    3. cm_apexqtmo-userdebug             9. cm_d800-userdebug

    4. cm_aries-userdebug                10. cm_d801-userdebug

    5. cm_captivatemtd-userdebug         11. cm_dogo-userdebug

    6. cm_crespo-userdebug               12. cm_e973-userdebug
```

13. cm_encore-userdebug
14. cm_endeavoru-userdebug
15. cm_enrc2b-userdebug
16. cm_epicmtd-userdebug
17. cm_exhilarate-userdebug
18. cm_expressatt-userdebug
19. cm_fireball-userdebug
20. cm_galaxysbmtd-userdebug
21. cm_galaxysmtd-userdebug
22. cm_hercules-userdebug
23. cm_hlteusc-userdebug
24. cm_hltevzw-userdebug
25. cm_huashan-userdebug
26. cm_hummingbird-userdebug
29. cm_i925-userdebug
30. cm_i9300-userdebug
31. cm_i9305-userdebug
32. cm_i9500-userdebug
33. cm_jem-userdebug
34. cm_jflte-userdebug
35. cm_kltespr-userdebug
36. cm_klteusc-userdebug
37. cm_kltevzw-userdebug
38. cm_l01f-userdebug
39. cm_m4-userdebug
40. cm_m7spr-userdebug
41. cm_maguro-userdebug
42. cm_moto_msm8960_jbbl-userdebug
43. cm_n1-userdebug
44. cm_n5100-userdebug
45. cm_n5110-userdebug
46. cm_n5120-userdebug
47. cm_n7000-userdebug
48. cm_n7100-userdebug
49. cm_odin-userdebug
50. cm_otter-userdebug
51. cm_otter2-userdebug
52. cm_otterx-userdebug
53. cm_ovation-userdebug
54. cm_p1-userdebug
55. cm_p3100-userdebug
56. cm_p3110-userdebug
57. cm_p5100-userdebug
58. cm_p5110-userdebug
59. cm_p880-userdebug
60. cm_p930-userdebug
61. cm_pollux-userdebug
62. cm_pollux_windy-userdebug
63. cm_r950-userdebug
64. cm_skyrocket-userdebug
67. cm_t769-userdebug
68. cm_tate-userdebug
69. cm_tf700t-userdebug
70. cm_tf701t-userdebug
71. cm_vs920-userdebug
72. cm_vs980-userdebug
73. cm_w7-userdebug
74. cm_ypg1-userdebug
75. cm_yuga-userdebug

... and don't forget the bacon!

Which would you like? [aosp_arm-eng]

We see a similar list of options for the **breakfast** command as for the **lunch** command, but there are some differences. Most importantly, the Android emulator build targets are not available in the **breakfast** command—which is the reason we chose the **lunch** command. The **breakfast** command is also more specific to CyanogenMod; it does something more than the **lunch** command. When we execute the **breakfast** command, it tries to download so-called supported device configurations from github and add them to the lunch combo. After that, it calls the **lunch** command to do the work. That behavior explains why the list generated by the **breakfast** command includes only supported devices: The emulator build is not in the supported list for CyanogenMod.

Another command in CyanogenMod, called **brunch**, is a combination of the **breakfast** and **make** commands.

After we select the build target using the **lunch** command, the actual build command is the same as with AOSP. We execute the **make** command to fire a build:

```
$ make -j4
```

Testing CyanogenMod Images

After the build is complete, we can review the following output folder:

```
$ ls out/target/product/generic/
```

android-info.txt	dex_bootjars	previous_build_config.mk	root
boot.img	external	ramdisk.img	symbols
cache	fake_packages	ramdisk-recovery.cpio	system
cache.img	installed-files.txt	ramdisk-recovery.img	system.img
clean_steps.mk	kernel	recovery	userdata.img
data	obj	recovery.img	utilities

As you can see, the output of the CyanogenMod build is similar to the output of the AOSP build, except there are more images in the CyanogenMod build than in the AOSP build. Also included are images for recovery (`ramdisk-recover.img`) and the kernel.

To test our CyanogenMod build, we can repeat the same procedure as we did for the AOSP images:

```
$ ls ..
adt-bundle-linux-x86_64-20140702   android-4.4.4_r2   cm-11
```

The Android SDK, AOSP, and CyanogenMod source tree appear at the same folder level. We can create the same soft-links as we did for the AOSP test. Let's create the soft-link for the `platforms` folder first:

```
$ cd out/host/linux-x86
```
```
$ ln -s ../../../../adt-bundle-linux-x86_64-20140702/sdk/platforms/ .
```
```
$ ls -l platforms
lrwxrwxrwx 1 roger mcafee 59 Feb 13 14:41 platforms -> ../../../../adt-bundle-linux-x86_64-20140702/sdk/platforms/
```

Then, we need to create a soft-link to use our CyanogenMod images as a `system-images` folder:

```
$ mkdir -p system-images/android-19
$ cd system-images/android-19
$ ln -s ../../../../target/product/generic/ armeabi-v7a
$ ls -l armeabi-v7a
lrwxrwxrwx 1 roger mcafee 35 Feb 13 14:50 armeabi-v7a ->
../../../../target/product/generic/
```

Now the environment is ready. Before we start the emulator, we need to change `kernel` to `kernel-qemu`. Since the CyanogenMod build has a Linux kernel available, we can use our own kernel build for testing purposes:

```
$ cd armeabi-v7a
$ ln -s ./kernel kernel-qemu
```

We can start the emulator now. Let's go to the host folder and test our emulator and images:

```
$ cd ../../..
$ bin/emulator -avd armemu -verbose -show-kernel -shell
```

emulator: found SDK root at /home/android/aosp/cm-11/out/host/linux-x86

emulator: Android virtual device file at: /home/roger/.android/avd/armemu.ini

emulator: virtual device content at /home/roger/.android/avd/armemu.avd

emulator: virtual device config file: /home/roger/.android/avd/armemu.avd/config.ini

emulator: using core hw config path: /home/roger/.android/avd/armemu.avd/hardware-qemu.ini

emulator: Found AVD target API level: 19

emulator: 'magic' skin format detected: 480x800

emulator: autoconfig: -skin 480x800

emulator: autoconfig: -skindir (null)

emulator: keyset loaded from: /home/roger/.android/default.keyset

emulator: found SDK root at /home/android/aosp/cm-11/out/host/linux-x86

...

emulator: control console listening on port 5554, ADB on port 5555

emulator: sent '0012host:emulator:5555' to ADB server

emulator: ping program: /home/android/aosp/cm-11/out/host/linux-x86/bin/ddms

```
Uncompressing Linux.......................................................
....................................... done, booting the kernel.
goldfish_fb_get_pixel_format:167: display surface,pixel format:
  bits/pixel:   16
  bytes/pixel:  2
  depth:        16
  red:          bits=5 mask=0xf800 shift=11 max=0x1f
  green:        bits=6 mask=0x7e0 shift=5 max=0x3f
  blue:         bits=5 mask=0x1f shift=0 max=0x1f
  alpha:        bits=0 mask=0x0 shift=0 max=0x0
Initializing cgroup subsys cpu
Linux version 2.6.29-g1059d20 (roger@sz-lin-003) (gcc version 4.7 (GCC) ) #1 Tue
Feb 10 17:07:45 CST 2015
CPU: ARMv7 Processor [410fc080] revision 0 (ARMv7), cr=10c5387f
CPU: VIPT nonaliasing data cache, VIPT nonaliasing instruction cache
Machine: Goldfish
...
healthd: wakealarm_init: timerfd_create failed
healthd: BatteryVoltagePath not found
healthd: BatteryTemperaturePath not found
binder: 32:32 transaction failed 29189, size0-0
binder: 32:32 transaction failed 29189, size0-0
```

We see that the system couldn't start properly and we keep getting the error message "binder: 32:32 transaction failed 29189, size0-0." This error is generated because the kernel version in the CyanogenMod source tree does work with Android version 4.4.4. The kernel version from the debug output follows:

```
Linux version 2.6.29-g1059d20 (roger@sz-lin-003) (gcc version 4.7 (GCC) ) #1 Tue
Feb 10 17:07:45 CST 2015
```

From the date and name, we see that it is our build, but the kernel version is an old 2.6.29 version kernel. Let's fix this by using the kernel from Android SDK as we did for the AOSP test:

```
$ cd system-images/android-19/armeabi-v7a
```

```
$ ln -s ../../../../../adt-bundle-linux-x86_64-20140702/sdk/system-images/
android-19/armeabi-v7a/kernel-qemu .
```

```
$ ls -al kernel-qemu
```

```
lrwxrwxrwx 1 roger mcafee 100 Feb 13 15:05 kernel-qemu -> ../../../../../adt-
bundle-linux-x86_64-20140702/sdk/system-images/android-19/armeabi-v7a/kernel-qemu
```

We can temporarily fix this issue now. In the next chapter, we'll discuss how to integrate the kernel and U-Boot builds with AOSP and CyanogenMod; at that point, we'll resolve this issue completely. Let's try it again with the new kernel:

```
$ cd ../../..
$ bin/emulator -avd armemu -verbose -show-kernel -shell
emulator: found SDK root at /home/android/aosp/cm-11/out/host/linux-x86
emulator: Android virtual device file at: /home/roger/.android/avd/armemu.ini
emulator: virtual device content at /home/roger/.android/avd/armemu.avd
emulator: virtual device config file: /home/roger/.android/avd/armemu.avd/config.ini
emulator: using core hw config path: /home/roger/.android/avd/armemu.avd/hardware-qemu.ini
emulator: Found AVD target API level: 19
...
emulator: control console listening on port 5554, ADB on port 5555
emulator: sent '0012host:emulator:5555' to ADB server
emulator: ping program: /home/android/aosp/cm-11/out/host/linux-x86/bin/ddms
Uncompressing Linux... done, booting the kernel.
goldfish_fb_get_pixel_format:167: display surface,pixel format:
  bits/pixel:  16
  bytes/pixel: 2
  depth:       16
  red:         bits=5 mask=0xf800 shift=11 max=0x1f
  green:       bits=6 mask=0x7e0 shift=5 max=0x3f
  blue:        bits=5 mask=0x1f shift=0 max=0x1f
  alpha:       bits=0 mask=0x0 shift=0 max=0x0
Booting Linux on physical CPU 0
Initializing cgroup subsys cpu
Linux version 3.4.0-gd853d22 (nnk@nnk.mtv.corp.google.com) (gcc version 4.6.x-google 20120106 (prerelease) (GCC) ) #1 PREEMPT Tue Jul 9 17:46:46 PDT 2013
CPU: ARMv7 Processor [410fc080] revision 0 (ARMv7), cr=10c53c7d
CPU: PIPT / VIPT nonaliasing data cache, VIPT nonaliasing instruction cache
Machine: Goldfish
Memory policy: ECC disabled, Data cache writeback
...
SELinux: Loaded policy from /sepolicy
```

Chapter 11 Building Your Own AOSP and CyanogenMod

```
SELinux: Loaded file_contexts from /file_contexts
init: /dev/hw_random not found
healthd: wakealarm_init: timerfd_create failed
healthd: BatteryVoltagePath not found
healthd: BatteryTemperaturePath not found
eth0: link up
shell@generic:/ $ warning: 'zygote' uses 32-bit capabilities (legacy support in
use)

shell@generic:/ $
```

We can boot to the Linux shell and see the CyanogenMod lock screen now. After we unlock the screen, we see CyanogenMod's setup screen (Figure 11.5), including the version information. Much as we did earlier for the SDK and AOSP images, we can compare the version information in Table 11.3 for the SDK, AOSP, and CyanogenMod builds.

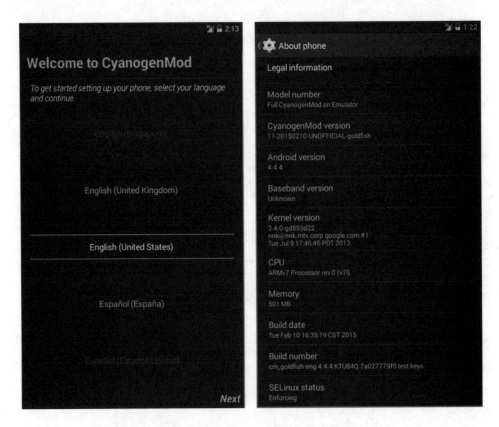

Figure 11.5 Android version of CyanogenMod images

Table 11.3 Comparison of SDK, AOSP, and CyanogenMod

	SDK	AOSP	CyanogenMod
Model number	sdk	AOSP on ARM Emulator	Full CyanogenMod on Emulator
Android version	4.4.2	4.4.4	4.4.4
Kernel version	3.4.0-gd853d22	3.4.0-gd853d22	3.4.0-gd853d22
Build number	sdk-eng 4.4.2 KK 938007 test-keys	aosp_arm-eng 4.4.4 KTU84Q eng. roger.20150210.0944606 test-keys	cm_goldfish-eng 4.4.4 KTU84Q 7a027779f5 test-keys

As you can see, the model number is CyanogenMod specific. The build number indicates that we chose `cm_goldfish-eng` as our build target. In the test of all three build, we use the same kernel version, `3.4.0-gd853d22`, which will work with Android 4.4.x.

Summary

In this chapter, we set up the environment for SDK, AOSP, and CyanogenMod. We built the Android emulator images for both AOSP and CyanogenMod. We tested our Android images in the Android SDK, AOSP, and CyanogenMod. All of these steps are necessary before we can continue exploring how to create our own Android system in the next chapter.

12
Customizing Android and Creating Your Own Android ROM

In the last chapter, we learned how to build Android emulator images from an AOSP or CyanogenMod source tree. In this chapter, we explore how to create our own Android ROM, just like most mobile application developers do. First, we create a new device in the source tree of both AOSP and CyanogenMod. Then, we integrate the kernel and bootloader in the source tree for the new device. Finally, we use U-Boot to boot up this new ROM.

Supporting New Hardware in AOSP

Since you are reading this book, most likely you are interested in low-level development for the Android system. You might be a software engineer who is working for a system on a chip (SoC) company and trying to support a new SoC on the roadmap of your company. You might be just an enthusiast who wants to do something amazing on your own devices. For example, one of the incredible things that enthusiasts have done is port Android to an HTC HD2 Windows Mobile device. This old device can run the latest Android version even though it is a Windows Mobile phone that was released by HTC in 2009. Enthusiasts made this device a legend in the history of smartphones. Whether you're a full-fledged professional or an inventive amateur, however, the first thing you have to do is add new hardware support in the Android build system—and that's the topic of this chapter.

As we have done throughout this book, to allow a more general discussion, we will use a virtual device instead of a specific hardware board to explore the topic at hand. In the Android emulator, each virtual device is actually a new piece of hardware. You can imagine these devices as using the same processor but having different sizes of memory and unique displays. We will use the virtual device created in Figure 11.2 as an example to discuss how to support new hardware in Android. As you will recall, this virtual device's name is `armemu`. Be aware that most of the discussion in this chapter pertains to the build aspect for this device.

Chapter 12 Customizing Android and Creating Your Own Android ROM

To support new hardware, we start by creating an entry in the device folder of the AOSP source tree. The hierarchy in the device folder is in vendor-name/device-name format. For example, the Nexus S from Samsung can be found in the folder samsung/crespo. The device name of Nexus S is crespo. We can create a virtual device that is put under a common folder generic, as follows. The folder name for our device is generic/armemu.

$ **cd device/generic**

$ **mkdir armemu**

Assume we are at the top level of the AOSP source tree. We create a new folder for the device armemu.

> **Note**
> Be aware of the name convention that we use. Our device name is armemu. The folder in which we store our device is also called armemu.
> The process followed to support a new device is similar to AOSP for other third-party source trees such as CyanogenMod. We will use CyanogenMod as an example for the discussion of third-party source trees. Refer to Chapter 4 in the book *Embedded Android* for a detailed explanation of the Android Open Source Project (AOSP) build system.

We next create skeleton files in the folder generic/armemu. The first thing we need to do is create an Android makefile Android.mk in this folder as follows:

```
LOCAL_PATH := $(call my-dir)

include $(CLEAR_VARS)

ifneq ($(filter armemu,$(TARGET_DEVICE)),)
include $(call all-makefiles-under,$(LOCAL_PATH))
endif
```

Next, we create a product make file AndroidProducts.mk as follows:

```
PRODUCT_MAKEFILES := $(LOCAL_DIR)/full_armemu.mk
```

In the AndroidProducts.mk file, a variable PRODUCT_MAKEFILES is defined. This variable points to another makefile, full_armemu.mk, which defines the product attributes. We can actually point to multiple makefiles using the variable PRODUCT_MAKEFILES to define several product configurations. The configurations can be different settings for the same product to match different requirements. Following is the content of the makefile full_armemu.mk:

```
$(call inherit-product, $(SRC_TARGET_DIR)/product/languages_full.mk)

$(call inherit-product, $(SRC_TARGET_DIR)/product/full.mk)
```

```
PRODUCT_NAME := full_armemu
PRODUCT_DEVICE := armemu
PRODUCT_BRAND := AOSP_ARMEMU
PRODUCT_MODEL := Full_Android_ARMEMU

LOCAL_KERNEL := prebuilts/qemu-kernel/arm/kernel-qemu-armv7
PRODUCT_COPY_FILES += \
    $(LOCAL_KERNEL):kernel
```

Let's look at the attributes defined in the makefile `full_armemu.mk`.

First, `PRODUCT_NAME` is the build target. We can select it as a `lunch` combo or pass it as part of the combo parameter to `lunch`, as follows:

$ lunch full_armemu-eng

Second, `PRODUCT_DEVICE` is the name of the actual product that we build. This name has to match an entry in `device/generic/`, since that's where the build looks for the corresponding `BoardConfig.mk` file. We use the same name, `armemu`, as we used for our virtual device created by the Virtual Device Manager. We can find the images for the device `armemu` in the folder `out/target/product/armemu/`, after the build is completed.

Third, `PRODUCT_MODEL` is the name of this product as provided in the model number in the "About the phone" section in the settings. This variable is stored as the `ro.product.model` global property, which is accessible on the device.

Fourth, The value of the `PRODUCT_BRAND` variable is available as the `ro.product.brand` global property, which is accessible on the device.

Finally, we set the variable `LOCAL_KERNEL` to a prebuilt kernel in the `prebuilts` folder and add it to the variable `PRODUCT_COPY_FILES` so that the kernel binary is copied to the output folder.

Now we need to describe which kind of hardware we want to build in the board configuration file `BoardConfig.mk`:

```
TARGET_NO_BOOTLOADER := true
TARGET_NO_KERNEL := true

TARGET_ARCH := arm
TARGET_ARCH_VARIANT := armv7-a
TARGET_CPU_VARIANT := generic
TARGET_CPU_ABI := armeabi-v7a
```

In `BoardConfig.mk`, we specify the processor architecture details about the device. We can add more hardware-specific items if necessary; we provide some examples of such items later in this chapter.

Next, we make the device we just added visible to envsetup.sh and **lunch**. To do so, we need to create a file called vendorsetup.sh in the same folder with the following content:

```
for i in eng userdebug user; do
        add_lunch_combo full_armemu-${i}
done
```

As you can see, we created three different build configurations for our device. We also need to make sure that it's executable if it's to be operational:

$ **chmod 755 vendorsetup.sh**

We can now go back to the AOSP's root and select armemu in the command **lunch**:

$ **. build/envsetup.sh**
including device/samsung/manta/vendorsetup.sh
including device/lge/mako/vendorsetup.sh
including device/lge/hammerhead/vendorsetup.sh
including device/asus/flo/vendorsetup.sh
including device/asus/deb/vendorsetup.sh
including device/asus/tilapia/vendorsetup.sh
including device/asus/grouper/vendorsetup.sh
including device/generic/x86/vendorsetup.sh
including device/generic/armv7-a-neon/vendorsetup.sh
including device/generic/armemu/vendorsetup.sh
including device/generic/mips/vendorsetup.sh
including sdk/bash_completion/adb.bash
$ **lunch**

You're building on Linux

Lunch menu... pick a combo:
     1. aosp_arm-eng
     2. aosp_x86-eng
     3. aosp_mips-eng
     4. vbox_x86-eng
     5. aosp_manta-userdebug
     6. aosp_mako-userdebug
     7. aosp_hammerhead-userdebug
     8. aosp_flo-userdebug

9. aosp_deb-userdebug

10. aosp_tilapia-userdebug

11. aosp_grouper-userdebug

12. mini_x86-userdebug

13. mini_armv7a_neon-userdebug

14. full_armemu-eng

15. full_armemu-userdebug

16. full_armemu-user

17. mini_mips-userdebug

Which would you like? [aosp_arm-eng]14

We select 14, 15, or 16 to build our device `armemu`. After the build is complete, we can take a look at our output:

$ make -j4

...

host Executable: mkyaffs2image (out/host/linux-x86/obj/EXECUTABLES/ mkyaffs2image_intermediates/mkyaffs2image)

Install: out/host/linux-x86/bin/mkyaffs2image

Installed file list: out/target/product/armemu/installed-files.txt

Target userdata fs image: out/target/product/armemu/userdata.img

Target system fs image: out/target/product/armemu/obj/PACKAGING/systemimage_ intermediates/system.img

Running: mkyaffs2image -f out/target/product/armemu/data out/target/product/ armemu/userdata.img out/target/product/armemu/root/file_contexts data

Running: mkyaffs2image -f out/target/product/armemu/system out/target/ product/armemu/obj/PACKAGING/systemimage_intermediates/system.img out/target/ product/armemu/root/file_contexts system

Install system fs image: out/target/product/armemu/system.img

The build results include the output for both the host and the target. The output or images for the device `armemu` can be found in the folder out/target/product/armemu/ as follows:

$ ls out/target/product/armemu/

android-info.txt	data	obj	symbols
cache	fake_packages	previous_build_config.mk	system
cache.img	installed-files.txt	ramdisk.img	system.img
clean_steps.mk	kernel	root	userdata.img

Chapter 12 Customizing Android and Creating Your Own Android ROM

We have all the images for our virtual hardware now. Let's try it out, just as we did in the previous chapter. The build results for the host include the Android emulator, which we can use to test our images. Recall that we have to set up the soft-links so that we can use our own emulator build and images for testing purposes. To make this step much easier, let's create a shell script `setup_emu.sh` to do the job:

```
echo Please run this script from the root of AOSP. Setup armemu ...
cd out/host/linux-x86
pwd
ln -s ../../../../adt-bundle-linux-x86_64-20140702/sdk/platforms/ .
mkdir -p system-images/android-19
cd system-images/android-19
ln -s ../../../../target/product/$1/ armeabi-v7a
cd armeabi-v7a
ln -s ../../../../../adt-bundle-linux-x86_64-20140702/sdk/system-images/android-18/armeabi-v7a/kernel-qemu kernel-qemu
cd ../../../..
```

Notice that we use the kernel from the Android SDK for testing here, because our own kernel build isn't available yet. Now, let's set up the environment and run our images:

```
$ setup_emu.sh armemu
$ bin/emulator -avd armemu -verbose -show-kernel -shell
emulator: found SDK root at /home/android/aosp/android-4.4.4_r2/out/host/linux-x86
...
Uncompressing Linux... done, booting the kernel.
goldfish_fb_get_pixel_format:167: display surface,pixel format:
  bits/pixel:   16
  bytes/pixel:  2
  depth:        16
  red:          bits=5 mask=0xf800 shift=11 max=0x1f
  green:        bits=6 mask=0x7e0  shift=5  max=0x3f
  blue:         bits=5 mask=0x1f   shift=0  max=0x1f
  alpha:        bits=0 mask=0x0    shift=0  max=0x0
Booting Linux on physical CPU 0
Initializing cgroup subsys cpu
Linux version 3.4.0-gd853d22 (nnk@nnk.mtv.corp.google.com) (gcc version 4.6.x-google 20120106 (prerelease) (GCC) ) #1 PREEMPT Tue Jul 9 17:46:46 PDT 2013
```

```
CPU: ARMv7 Processor [410fc080] revision 0 (ARMv7), cr=10c53c7d
...
init: cannot open '/initlogo.rle'
EXT4-fs (mtdblock0): VFS: Can't find ext4 filesystem
fs_mgr: Cannot mount filesystem on /dev/block/mtdblock0 at /system
init: fs_mgr_mount_all returned an error
init: /dev/hw_random not found
init: Unable to open persistent property directory /data/property errno: 2
init: cannot find '/system/bin/servicemanager', disabling 'servicemanager'
init: cannot find '/system/bin/vold', disabling 'vold'
init: cannot find '/system/bin/qemu-props', disabling 'qemu-props'
init: cannot find '/system/bin/netd', disabling 'netd'
init: cannot find '/system/bin/debuggerd', disabling 'debuggerd'
init: cannot find '/system/bin/rild', disabling 'ril-daemon'
init: cannot find '/system/bin/surfaceflinger', disabling 'surfaceflinger'
init: cannot find '/system/bin/app_process', disabling 'zygote'
...
```

From the preceding log, we can see that the system cannot be launched as expected. Instead, we get the following error message:

```
EXT4-fs (mtdblock0): VFS: Can't find ext4 filesystem
```

The kernel log tells us that the file system cannot be mounted in ext4 format. What's going wrong here? If we compare the result to the build log for our device, we can see that the system.img file is in YAFFS2 format instead of ext4 format:

```
...
Running: mkyaffs2image -f out/target/product/armemu/system out/target/product/armemu/obj/PACKAGING/systemimage_intermediates/system.img out/target/product/armemu/root/file_contexts system
Install system fs image: out/target/product/armemu/system.img
```

As mentioned earlier, we can use the BoardConfig.mk file to set the board-level configuration to generate the file system in ext4 format, we can add the following configuration in BoardConfig.mk:

```
TARGET_USERIMAGES_USE_EXT4 := true
BOARD_SYSTEMIMAGE_PARTITION_SIZE := 576716800
BOARD_USERDATAIMAGE_PARTITION_SIZE := 209715200
BOARD_CACHEIMAGE_PARTITION_SIZE := 69206016
```

```
BOARD_CACHEIMAGE_FILE_SYSTEM_TYPE := ext4

BOARD_FLASH_BLOCK_SIZE := 512

TARGET_USERIMAGES_SPARSE_EXT_DISABLED := true
```

With this change, we can build again and review the build log. From the following build log, we can see that the file system is generated in ext4 format now:

```
$ make -j4
...
make_ext4fs -S out/target/product/armemu/root/file_contexts -l 576716800 -a
system out/target/product/armemu/obj/PACKAGING/systemimage_intermediates/
system.img out/target/product/armemu/system

+ make_ext4fs -S out/target/product/armemu/root/file_contexts -l 576716800 -a
system out/target/product/armemu/obj/PACKAGING/systemimage_intermediates/
system.img out/target/product/armemu/system

Creating filesystem with parameters:
    Size: 576716800
    Block size: 4096
    Blocks per group: 32768
    Inodes per group: 7040
    Inode size: 256
    Journal blocks: 2200
    Label:
    Blocks: 140800
    Block groups: 5
    Reserved block group size: 39
Created filesystem with 1166/35200 inodes and 68257/140800 blocks
+ '[' 0 -ne 0 ']'
Install system fs image: out/target/product/armemu/system.img
out/target/product/armemu/system.img+ maxsize=588791808 blocksize=2112
total=576716800 reserve=5947392
```

Let's start the emulator and test our images again. When we do so, we see that everything works correctly now. Let's go to the About page and check the version information.

In Figure 12.1, both the model number and the build number reflect the definitions we set in the makefile `full_armemu.mk`. We used the prebuilt kernel image released with Android 4.4.4, and we can see that this is exactly the same kernel we used in the Android SDK image from Android 4.4.2.

We have now created our own device `armemu` and built the corresponding images. We can also boot our virtual device using the images built from the AOSP source tree. Let's

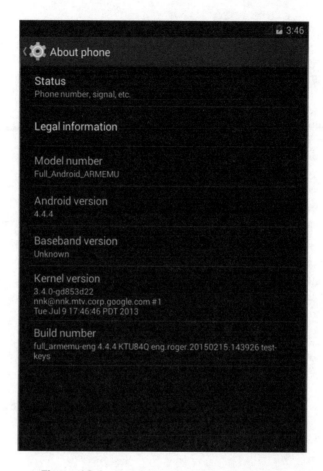

Figure 12.1 Android version of armemu images

go even further, and build U-Boot and the kernel in the AOSP source tree for this virtual device `armemu`.

Building the Kernel with AOSP

As mentioned in Chapter 11, the kernel build is separate from the AOSP build system for various reasons. The official reference for the kernel build from Google can be found at *https://source.android.com/source/building-kernels.html*.

Nevertheless, it is possible to build the kernel within the AOSP source tree. In fact, many vendors include the kernel build in their own AOSP projects. Some third parties, such as CyanogenMod, also provide better integration of the kernel build in their source trees.

This section introduces an approach based on the Nexus 5 Hammerhead kernel build to show how to integrate a kernel build in AOSP. We can use the same approach to integrate the U-Boot build in the AOSP source tree. CyanogenMod uses a different approach, which is much cleaner in integrating various kernel builds. The problem with its approach, however, is that we would have to change the build system itself. It's hard to contribute changes to the AOSP source tree, so we won't use that method for AOSP.

In this section, we'll build a kernel for our virtual device `armemu`. The same approach can be used for other devices as well.

The first step is to download the goldfish kernel for our virtual device. Recall that we built this kernel in Chapter 10, when we discussed booting the goldfish kernel using U-Boot. We follow the same steps to download the goldfish kernel and put it under the AOSP source tree:

```
$ git clone https://android.googlesource.com/kernel/goldfish.git kernel
```

All of the source code in this book is in GitHub, so you can download the kernel source code from there as well:

```
$ git clone https://github.com/shugaoye/goldfish.git kernel
$ git checkout -b android-armemu-3.4 remotes/origin/android-armemu-3.4
```

Next, we copy a makefile `AndroidKernel.mk` from the Nexus 5 kernel source code to our kernel source tree:

```
$ ls kernel/AndroidKernel.mk
kernel/AndroidKernel.mk
```

> **Note**
>
> If you clone the kernel source code from GitHub, the makefile *AndroidKernel.mk* is already in the branch `android-armemu-3.4`. You don't need to copy it from the Nexus 5 kernel source tree.

To utilize `AndroidKernel.mk` to build our kernel, we have to add the following rules in `full_armemu.mk`:

```
TARGET_KERNEL_SOURCE := kernel

TARGET_KERNEL_CONFIG := goldfish_armv7_defconfig

PRODUCT_OUT ?= out/target/product/armemu

include $(TARGET_KERNEL_SOURCE)/AndroidKernel.mk

.PHONY: $(TARGET_PREBUILT_KERNEL) $(TARGET_PREBUILT_U-BOOT)
```

We specify the path of the kernel source code in `TARGET_KERNEL_SOURCE` and the kernel configuration in `TARGET_KERNEL_CONFIG`. The kernel makefile shown in Example 12.1 (`AndroidKernel.mk`) is included in `full_armemu.mk`.

Example 12.1 Kernel Makefile AndroidKernel.mk

```
ifeq ($(TARGET_PREBUILT_KERNEL),)

TARGET_OUT_INTERMEDIATES ?= $(PRODUCT_OUT)/obj
KERNEL_OUT := $(TARGET_OUT_INTERMEDIATES)/KERNEL_OBJ
KERNEL_CONFIG := $(KERNEL_OUT)/.config
TARGET_PREBUILT_INT_KERNEL := $(KERNEL_OUT)/arch/arm/boot/zImage
KERNEL_HEADERS_INSTALL := $(KERNEL_OUT)/usr
KERNEL_MODULES_INSTALL := system
KERNEL_MODULES_OUT := $(TARGET_OUT)/lib/modules
KERNEL_IMG=$(KERNEL_OUT)/arch/arm/boot/Image

ifeq ($(TARGET_USES_UNCOMPRESSED_KERNEL),true)
$(info Using uncompressed kernel)
TARGET_PREBUILT_KERNEL := $(KERNEL_OUT)/piggy
else
TARGET_PREBUILT_KERNEL := $(TARGET_PREBUILT_INT_KERNEL)
endif

define mv-modules
mdpath=`find $(KERNEL_MODULES_OUT) -type f -name modules.dep`;\
if [ "$$mdpath" != "" ];then\
mpath=`dirname $$mdpath`;\
ko=`find $$mpath/kernel -type f -name *.ko`;\
for i in $$ko; do mv $$i $(KERNEL_MODULES_OUT)/; done;\
fi
endef

define clean-module-folder
mdpath=`find $(KERNEL_MODULES_OUT) -type f -name modules.dep`;\
if [ "$$mdpath" != "" ];then\
mpath=`dirname $$mdpath`; rm -rf $$mpath;\
fi
endef
```

```
$(KERNEL_OUT):
    mkdir -p $(KERNEL_OUT)

$(KERNEL_CONFIG): $(KERNEL_OUT)
    $(MAKE) -C kernel O=../$(KERNEL_OUT) ARCH=arm CROSS_COMPILE=arm-eabi-
$(TARGET_KERNEL_CONFIG)

$(KERNEL_OUT)/piggy : $(TARGET_PREBUILT_INT_KERNEL)
    $(hide) gunzip -c $(KERNEL_OUT)/arch/arm/boot/compressed/piggy.gzip >
$(KERNEL_OUT)/piggy

$(TARGET_PREBUILT_INT_KERNEL): $(KERNEL_OUT) $(KERNEL_CONFIG) $(KERNEL_HEADERS_
INSTALL)
    $(MAKE) -C kernel O=../$(KERNEL_OUT) ARCH=arm CROSS_COMPILE=arm-eabi-
#   $(MAKE) -C kernel O=../$(KERNEL_OUT) ARCH=arm CROSS_COMPILE=arm-eabi-
modules
#   $(MAKE) -C kernel O=../$(KERNEL_OUT) INSTALL_MOD_PATH=../../$(KERNEL_
MODULES_INSTALL) INSTALL_MOD_STRIP=1 ARCH=arm CROSS_COMPILE=arm-eabi- modules_
install
#   $(mv-modules)
#   $(clean-module-folder)

$(KERNEL_HEADERS_INSTALL): $(KERNEL_OUT) $(KERNEL_CONFIG)
    $(MAKE) -C kernel O=../$(KERNEL_OUT) ARCH=arm CROSS_COMPILE=arm-eabi-
headers_install

kerneltags: $(KERNEL_OUT) $(KERNEL_CONFIG)
    $(MAKE) -C kernel O=../$(KERNEL_OUT) ARCH=arm CROSS_COMPILE=arm-eabi- tags

kernelconfig: $(KERNEL_OUT) $(KERNEL_CONFIG)
    env KCONFIG_NOTIMESTAMP=true \
        $(MAKE) -C kernel O=../$(KERNEL_OUT) ARCH=arm CROSS_COMPILE=arm-eabi-
menuconfig
    env KCONFIG_NOTIMESTAMP=true \
        $(MAKE) -C kernel O=../$(KERNEL_OUT) ARCH=arm CROSS_COMPILE=arm-eabi-
savedefconfig
    cp $(KERNEL_OUT)/defconfig kernel/arch/arm/configs/$(TARGET_KERNEL_CONFIG)

endif
```

In Example 12.1, the kernel build environment is defined first and the kernel build process is actually the same as that followed in Chapter 10. The kernel module build is also supported in AndroidKernel.mk, but we comment it out in the goldfish kernel build.

Once we have the build environment set up for AOSP kernel build integration, we can build the AOSP source tree and test our own kernel:

```
$ make -j4
...
$ bin/emulator -avd armemu -verbose -show-kernel -shell
```

After the Android system boots up, we can check the version information in the About page as we did before. As you can see in Figure 12.2, except for the kernel version, everything is the same as in Figure 12.1. The kernel version is 3.4.67-gea97df6, which is different from the prebuilt kernel version (3.4.0-gd853d22).

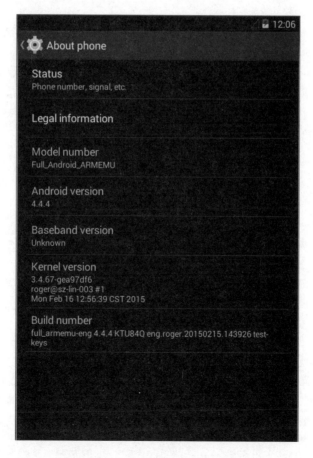

Figure 12.2 Android version of AOSP images with our own kernel build

We have now built the AOSP source tree together with the goldfish kernel for the virtual device `armemu`. Let's take another step and integrate the U-Boot build in the AOSP source tree.

Building U-Boot with AOSP

We use a similar approach to integrate the U-Boot build in the AOSP source tree. As in Chapter 9, we use the U-Boot source code from the Linaro project as the base for porting to the goldfish platform. To make it easier to access the source code in this book, the modified U-Boot code is also provided in GitHub. Let's check out the U-Boot source code from GitHub to the root of AOSP source tree:

```
$ croot
$ git clone https://github.com/shugaoye/u-boot.git u-boot
$ cd u-boot
$ git checkout -b android-armemu-3.4 remotes/origin/android-armemu-3.4
$ ls AndroidU-Boot.mk
```
AndroidU-Boot.mk

We checked out a branch to work with kernel 3.4. The makefile `AndroidU-Boot.mk` (shown in Example 12.2) is similar to the makefile `AndroidKernel.mk` for the kernel build. We can add the following rules in `full_armemu.mk` to invoke `AndroidU-Boot.mk` in the AOSP build:

```
TARGET_U_BOOT_SOURCE := u-boot

TARGET_U_BOOT_CONFIG := goldfish_config

PRODUCT_OUT ?= out/target/product/armemu

.PHONY: $(TARGET_PREBUILT_KERNEL) $(TARGET_PREBUILT_U-BOOT)

include $(TARGET_U_BOOT_SOURCE)/AndroidU-Boot.mk

LOCAL_U_BOOT := $(TARGET_PREBUILT_U-BOOT)

PRODUCT_COPY_FILES += \
    $(LOCAL_U_BOOT):u-boot.bin \
    $(LOCAL_KERNEL):kernel \
    device/generic/armemu/init.recovery.armemu.rc:root/init.recovery.armemu.rc \
    device/generic/armemu/init.recovery.armemu.sh:root/init.recovery.armemu.sh
```

We defined the path of the U-Boot source code in `TARGET_U_BOOT_SOURCE` and defined the U-Boot configuration in `TARGET_U_BOOT_CONFIG`. We now include `AndroidU-Boot.mk` in Example 12.2 in `full_armemu.mk` to invoke the U-Boot build. We also add the build result for both the kernel and U-Boot to the variable `PRODUCT_COPY_FILES`, so that all of these items are copied to output folder.

Example 12.2 U-Boot Makefile AndroidU-Boot.mk

```
TARGET_OUT_INTERMEDIATES ?= $(PRODUCT_OUT)/obj

U-BOOT_OUT := $(TARGET_OUT_INTERMEDIATES)/U-BOOT_OBJ

U-BOOT_CONFIG := $(U-BOOT_OUT)/include/config.mk

TARGET_PREBUILT_INT_U-BOOT := $(U-BOOT_OUT)/u-boot.bin

U-BOOT_IMG=$(U-BOOT_OUT)/u-boot.bin

TARGET_PREBUILT_U-BOOT := $(TARGET_PREBUILT_INT_U-BOOT)

$(U-BOOT_OUT):

    mkdir -p $(U-BOOT_OUT)

$(U-BOOT_CONFIG): $(U-BOOT_OUT)

    export BUILD_DIR=../$(U-BOOT_OUT); cd $(TARGET_U_BOOT_SOURCE); $(MAKE)
$(TARGET_U_BOOT_CONFIG) arch=ARM CROSS_COMPILE=arm-none-eabi-

$(TARGET_PREBUILT_INT_U-BOOT): $(U-BOOT_OUT) $(U-BOOT_CONFIG)

    export BUILD_DIR=../$(U-BOOT_OUT); cd $(TARGET_U_BOOT_SOURCE); $(MAKE) all
arch=ARM CROSS_COMPILE=arm-none-eabi-
```

In Example 12.2, we set up all necessary environment variables first. We then created three build targets—U-BOOT_OUT, U-BOOT_CONFIG, and TARGET_PREBUILT_INT_U-BOOT—to produce the build.

Booting Android with U-Boot from NAND Flash

Chapter 10 demonstrated how to boot Android from NAND flash using U-Boot. In that chapter, we hacked the system image from the Android SDK. That approach in many ways resembled the actions taken by a ROM developer who hacks the original ROM from manufacturers. In this section, however, we play a role like that of an engineer working for a manufacturer—that is, we build our own original ROM instead of hacking one.

We have U-Boot, the Linux kernel, and a file system now. We have to tweak the system a little so that everything can work together. As we did in Chapter 10, we want to store everything in NAND flash. However, the default file system in Android 4.4 (KitKat) is in ext4 format, which is used by the embedded MultiMediaCard (eMMC). To generate a ext4-formatted file system, we added several lines to BoardConfig.mk in the previous section. To use NAND flash, however, we need to build the file system in YAFFS2 format. To generate the file system in this format, we have to make these changes in BoardConfig.mk:

```
# TARGET_USERIMAGES_USE_EXT4 := true

# BOARD_SYSTEMIMAGE_PARTITION_SIZE := 576716800

# BOARD_USERDATAIMAGE_PARTITION_SIZE := 209715200
```

Chapter 12 Customizing Android and Creating Your Own Android ROM

```
# BOARD_CACHEIMAGE_PARTITION_SIZE := 69206016
BOARD_CACHEIMAGE_FILE_SYSTEM_TYPE := yaffs2
# BOARD_FLASH_BLOCK_SIZE := 512
# TARGET_USERIMAGES_SPARSE_EXT_DISABLED := true
```

In this code, we comment out the settings for generating system and data images in the ext4 format and specify the YAFFS2 file system format for the cache image. Now the build system will generate system, data, and cache images in YAFFS2 format. However, we still cannot boot Android properly from NAND flash in the YAFFS2 file system. The kernel and init process will look at the file system configuration `fstab.goldfish` and device-specific startup script `init.goldfish.rc` during the system startup; thus we have to change these two files to reflect our change to the file system format. Both `fstab.goldfish` and `init.goldfish.rc` can be found in the folder `device/generic/goldfish`.

In `fstab.goldfish`, we change the file system type from ext4 to YAFFS2 as follows (be aware of the wrapping of long lines here):

```
/dev/block/mtdblock0      /system    yaffs2   ro,barrier=1    wait
/dev/block/mtdblock1      /data     yaffs2   noatime,nosuid,nodev,barrier=1,
nomblk_io_submit      wait,check
/dev/block/mtdblock2      /cache    yaffs2   noatime,nosuid,nodev,nomblk_io_
submit,errors=panic    wait,check
/devices/platform/goldfish_mmc.0     auto     vfat    defaults
voldmanaged=sdcard:auto
```

In `init.goldfish.rc`, we let the init process mount the YAFFS2 file system from NAND flash instead of mounting the ext4 file system from eMMC:

```
on fs
    # mount mtd partitions
    # Mount /system rw first to give the filesystem a chance to save a checkpoint
    mount yaffs2 mtd@system /system
    mount yaffs2 mtd@system /system ro remount

    mount yaffs2 mtd@userdata /data nosuid nodev

    mount yaffs2 mtd@cache /cache nosuid nodev

    # mount_all /fstab.goldfish
```

As we did in Chapter 10, we need to convert the kernel and RAMDISK to U-Boot image format so that we can load them in U-Boot before system boot-up. We generate all U-Boot images in `full_armemu.mk`, as shown in Example 12.3, which is the final version of `full_armemu.mk`:

Example 12.3 Device Makefile full_armemu.mk

```
$(call inherit-product, $(SRC_TARGET_DIR)/product/languages_full.mk)
$(call inherit-product, $(SRC_TARGET_DIR)/product/full.mk)
PRODUCT_NAME := full_armemu
PRODUCT_DEVICE := armemu
PRODUCT_BRAND := AOSP_ARMEMU
PRODUCT_MODEL := Full_Android_ARMEMU

# define U-Boot and Kernel path and configuration
TARGET_U_BOOT_SOURCE := u-boot
TARGET_U_BOOT_CONFIG := goldfish_config

TARGET_KERNEL_SOURCE := kernel
TARGET_KERNEL_CONFIG := goldfish_armv7_defconfig

PRODUCT_OUT ?= out/target/product/armemu

include $(TARGET_KERNEL_SOURCE)/AndroidKernel.mk
include $(TARGET_U_BOOT_SOURCE)/AndroidU-Boot.mk

# define U-Boot images
TARGET_KERNEL_UIMAGE := $(PRODUCT_OUT)/zImage.uimg
TARGET_RAMDISK_UIMAGE := $(PRODUCT_OUT)/ramdisk.uimg
TARGET_RECOVERY_UIMAGE := $(PRODUCT_OUT)/ramdisk-recovery.uimg

# define build targets for kernel, U-Boot and U-Boot images
.PHONY: $(TARGET_PREBUILT_KERNEL) $(TARGET_PREBUILT_U-BOOT) $(TARGET_KERNEL_
UIMAGE) $(TARGET_RAMDISK_UIMAGE) $(TARGET_RECOVERY_UIMAGE)

$(TARGET_KERNEL_UIMAGE): $(TARGET_PREBUILT_KERNEL)
    mkimage -A arm -C none -O linux -T kernel -d $(TARGET_PREBUILT_INT_KERNEL) -a
0x00010000 -e 0x00010000 $(TARGET_KERNEL_UIMAGE)

$(TARGET_RAMDISK_UIMAGE): $(PRODUCT_OUT)/ramdisk.img
    mkimage -A arm -C none -O linux -T ramdisk -d $(PRODUCT_OUT)/ramdisk.img -a
0x00800000 -e 0x00800000 $(TARGET_RAMDISK_UIMAGE)

$(TARGET_RECOVERY_UIMAGE): $(PRODUCT_OUT)/ramdisk-recovery.img
    mkimage -A arm -C none -O linux -T ramdisk -d $(PRODUCT_OUT)/ramdisk-
recovery.img -a 0x00800000 -e 0x00800000 $(TARGET_RECOVERY_UIMAGE)
```

```
LOCAL_U_BOOT := $(TARGET_PREBUILT_U-BOOT)

ifeq ($(TARGET_PREBUILT_KERNEL),)
LOCAL_KERNEL := prebuilts/qemu-kernel/arm/kernel-qemu-armv7
else
LOCAL_KERNEL := $(TARGET_PREBUILT_KERNEL)
endif

LOCAL_KERNEL_UIMAGE := $(TARGET_KERNEL_UIMAGE)
LOCAL_RAMDISK_UIMAGE := $(TARGET_RAMDISK_UIMAGE)
LOCAL_RECOVERY_UIMAGE := $(TARGET_RECOVERY_UIMAGE)

PRODUCT_COPY_FILES += \
    $(LOCAL_U_BOOT):u-boot.bin \
    $(LOCAL_KERNEL):kernel \
    $(LOCAL_KERNEL_UIMAGE):system/zImage.uimg \
    $(LOCAL_RAMDISK_UIMAGE):system/ramdisk.uimg \
    $(LOCAL_RECOVERY_UIMAGE):system/ramdisk-recovery.uimg \
    device/generic/armemu/init.recovery.armemu.rc:root/init.recovery.armemu.rc \
    device/generic/armemu/init.recovery.armemu.sh:root/init.recovery.armemu.sh
```

In `full_armemu.mk`, we define the U-Boot images path for the kernel, RAMDISK, and recovery RAMDISK in the variables `TARGET_KERNEL_UIMAGE`, `TARGET_RAMDISK_UIMAGE`, and `TARGET_RECOVERY_UIMAGE`. We also define the rules to generate these images. Once we have all the images, we copy them to the `system` folder.

In Chapter 10, we booted Android from the U-Boot console and loaded the kernel and RAMDISK manually using U-Boot commands. We can ask U-Boot to boot Android from NAND flash automatically by changing the definition of `CONFIG_BOOTCOMMAND` in `goldfish.h`:

```
#define CONFIG_BOOTCOMMAND "ydevconfig sys 0 0x0 0x7f0 ; ymount sys ; yrdm sys/
ramdisk.uimg 0x610000 ; yrdm sys/zImage.uimg 0x210000 ; yumount sys ; bootm
0x210000 0x610000"
```

The configuration of `CONFIG_BOOTCOMMAND` is the major difference between kernel 2.6.29 and kernel 3.4. In terms of size, kernel 3.4 is much larger than kernel 2.6.29, so we need more memory space to load this kernel image in U-Boot. We load RAMDISK at the address 0x410000 for kernel 2.6.29, and we load RAMDISK at the address 0x610000 for kernel 3.4.

Now we can fire a build and test our ROM using our own emulator build:

```
$ cd out/host/linux-x86
```

```
$ bin/emulator -avd armemu -verbose -show-kernel -shell
```

...

```
U-Boot 2013.01.-rc1-00002-g259abc1-dirty (Feb 26 2015 - 17:59:35)

U-Boot code: 00010000 -> 00070F2C  BSS: -> 000A9210
IRQ Stack: 0badc0de
FIQ Stack: 0badc0de
monitor len: 00099210
ramsize: 20000000
TLB table at: 1fff0000
```

We can see that the RAM size is 0x20000000 (512MB). This is what we defined in Android Virtual Device Manager.

```
Top of RAM usable for U-Boot at: 1fff0000
Reserving 612k for U-Boot at: 1ff56000
Reserving 4104k for malloc() at: 1fb54000
Reserving 32 Bytes for Board Info at: 1fb53fe0
Reserving 120 Bytes for Global Data at: 1fb53f68
Reserving 8192 Bytes for IRQ stack at: 1fb51f68
New Stack Pointer is: 1fb51f58
RAM Configuration:
Bank #0: 00000000 512 MiB
relocation Offset is: 1ff46000
goldfish_init(), gtty.base=ff012000
WARNING: Caches not enabled
monitor flash len: 00068C54
Now running in RAM - U-Boot at: 1ff56000
NAND:  base=ff017000
goldfish_nand_init: id=0: name=nand0, nand_name=system
goldfish_nand_init: id=1: name=nand1, nand_name=userdata
goldfish_nand_init: id=2: name=nand2, nand_name=cache
```

NAND flash is initialized in U-Boot:

```
511 MiB
MMC:   board_mmc_init called
goldfish_mmc: 0
Using default environment

Destroy Hash Table: 1ffb5bf0 table = 00000000
Create Hash Table: N=104
```

Chapter 12 Customizing Android and Creating Your Own Android ROM

```
INSERT: table 1ffb5bf0, filled 1/107 rv 1fb542b0 ==> name="bootargs" value="qemu.
gles=1 qemu=1 console=ttyS0 android.qemud=ttyS1 androidboot.console=ttyS2
android.checkjni=1 ndns=1"

INSERT: table 1ffb5bf0, filled 2/107 rv 1fb54394 ==> name="bootcmd"
value="ydevconfig sys 0 0x0 0x7e8 ; ymount sys ; yrdm sys/ramdisk.uimg 0x410000 ;
yrdm sys/zImage.uimg 0x210000 ; yumount sys ; bootm 0x210000 0x410000"
```

We have also prepared kernel parameters that will be used by the Linux kernel:

```
INSERT: table 1ffb5bf0, filled 3/107 rv 1fb5440c ==> name="bootdelay" value="2"

INSERT: table 1ffb5bf0, filled 4/107 rv 1fb54478 ==> name="baudrate"
value="38400"

INSERT: table 1ffb5bf0, filled 5/107 rv 1fb54604 ==> name="bootfile" value="/
tftpboot/uImage"

INSERT: free(data = 1fb54008)

INSERT: done

In:     serial

Out:    serial

Err:    serial

Net:    SMC91111-0
Warning: SMC91111-0 using MAC address from net device


### main_loop entered: bootdelay=2


### main_loop: bootcmd="ydevconfig sys 0 0x0 0x7f0 ; ymount sys ; yrdm sys/
ramdisk.uimg 0x610000 ; yrdm sys/zImage.uimg 0x210000 ; yumount sys ; bootm
0x210000 0x610000"

Hit any key to stop autoboot:  0

Configures yaffs mount sys: dev 0 start block 0, end block 2024

Mounting yaffs2 mount point sys

Copy sys/ramdisk.uimg to 0x00610000...      [DONE]

Copy sys/zImage.uimg to 0x00210000...       [DONE]

Unmounting yaffs2 mount point sys
```

After we load RAMDISK and the kernel from NAND flash, we are ready to boot the system:

```
## Current stack ends at 0x1fb51b00 *  kernel: cmdline image address = 0x00210000

## Booting kernel from Legacy Image at 00210000 ...
   Image Name:
   Created:       2015-02-26   9:59:53 UTC
   Image Type:    ARM Linux Kernel Image (uncompressed)
```

```
   Data Size:    1645064 Bytes = 1.6 MiB
   Load Address: 00010000
   Entry Point:  00010000
   kernel data at 0x00210040, len = 0x00191a08 (1645064)
*  ramdisk: cmdline image address = 0x00610000
## Loading init Ramdisk from Legacy Image at 00610000 ...
   Image Name:
   Created:      2015-02-26   9:59:53 UTC
   Image Type:   ARM Linux RAMDisk Image (uncompressed)
   Data Size:    323724 Bytes = 316.1 KiB
   Load Address: 00800000
   Entry Point:  00800000
   ramdisk start = 0x00800000, ramdisk end = 0x0084f08c
   Loading Kernel Image ... OK
OK
   kernel loaded at 0x00010000, end = 0x001a1a08
using: ATAGS
## Transferring control to Linux (at address 00010000)...
```

We are now in the Linux kernel:

```
Starting kernel ...

Uncompressing Linux... done, booting the kernel.
goldfish_fb_get_pixel_format:169: display surface,pixel format:
   bits/pixel:  16
   bytes/pixel: 2
   depth:       16
   red:         bits=5 mask=0xf800 shift=11 max=0x1f
   green:       bits=6 mask=0x7e0 shift=5 max=0x3f
   blue:        bits=5 mask=0x1f shift=0 max=0x1f
   alpha:       bits=0 mask=0x0 shift=0 max=0x0
Booting Linux on physical CPU 0
Initializing cgroup subsys cpu
Linux version 3.4.67-gad65975 (roger@sz-lin-003) (gcc version 4.7 (GCC) ) #1
PREEMPT Tue Mar 24 18:20:18 CST 2015
CPU: ARMv7 Processor [410fc080] revision 0 (ARMv7), cr=10c53c7d
CPU: PIPT / VIPT nonaliasing data cache, VIPT nonaliasing instruction cache
```

```
Machine: Goldfish
Memory policy: ECC disabled, Data cache writeback
Built 1 zonelists in Zone order, mobility grouping on.  Total pages: 130048
Kernel command line: qemu.gles=0 qemu=1 console=ttyS0 android.qemud=ttyS1
androidboot.console=ttyS2 android.checkjni=1 ndns=1
PID hash table entries: 2048 (order: 1, 8192 bytes)
Dentry cache hash table entries: 65536 (order: 6, 262144 bytes)
Inode-cache hash table entries: 32768 (order: 5, 131072 bytes)
Memory: 512MB = 512MB total
Memory: 496864k/496864k available, 27424k reserved, 0K highmem
Virtual kernel memory layout:
    vector  : 0xffff0000 - 0xffff1000   (   4 kB)
    fixmap  : 0xfff00000 - 0xfffe0000   ( 896 kB)
    vmalloc : 0xe0800000 - 0xff000000   ( 488 MB)
    lowmem  : 0xc0000000 - 0xe0000000   ( 512 MB)
      .text : 0xc0008000 - 0xc045fe28   (4448 kB)
      .init : 0xc0460000 - 0xc0485000   ( 148 kB)
      .data : 0xc0486000 - 0xc04bf9c8   ( 231 kB)
       .bss : 0xc04bf9ec - 0xc0609cb8   (1321 kB)
NR_IRQS:256
sched_clock: 32 bits at 100 Hz, resolution 10000000ns, wraps every 4294967286ms
Console: colour dummy device 80x30
Calibrating delay loop... 523.46 BogoMIPS (lpj=2617344)
pid_max: default: 32768 minimum: 301
Security Framework initialized
SELinux:  Initializing.
Mount-cache hash table entries: 512
Initializing cgroup subsys debug
Initializing cgroup subsys cpuacct
Initializing cgroup subsys freezer
CPU: Testing write buffer coherency: ok
Setting up static identity map for 0x36c9e8 - 0x36ca40
NET: Registered protocol family 16
bio: create slab <bio-0> at 0
Switching to clocksource goldfish_timer
NET: Registered protocol family 2
```

```
IP route cache hash table entries: 4096 (order: 2, 16384 bytes)
TCP established hash table entries: 16384 (order: 5, 131072 bytes)
TCP bind hash table entries: 16384 (order: 4, 65536 bytes)
TCP: Hash tables configured (established 16384 bind 16384)
TCP: reno registered
UDP hash table entries: 256 (order: 0, 4096 bytes)
UDP-Lite hash table entries: 256 (order: 0, 4096 bytes)
NET: Registered protocol family 1
RPC: Registered named UNIX socket transport module.
RPC: Registered udp transport module.
RPC: Registered tcp transport module.
RPC: Registered tcp NFSv4.1 backchannel transport module.
Trying to unpack rootfs image as initramfs...
Freeing initrd memory: 316K
goldfish_new_pdev goldfish_interrupt_controller at ff000000 irq -1
goldfish_new_pdev goldfish_device_bus at ff001000 irq 1
goldfish_new_pdev goldfish_timer at ff003000 irq 3
goldfish_new_pdev goldfish_rtc at ff010000 irq 10
goldfish_new_pdev goldfish_tty at ff002000 irq 4
goldfish_new_pdev goldfish_tty at ff011000 irq 11
goldfish_new_pdev goldfish_tty at ff012000 irq 12
goldfish_new_pdev smc91x at ff013000 irq 13
goldfish_new_pdev goldfish_fb at ff014000 irq 14
goldfish_new_pdev goldfish_audio at ff004000 irq 15
goldfish_new_pdev goldfish_mmc at ff005000 irq 16
goldfish_new_pdev goldfish_memlog at ff006000 irq -1
goldfish_new_pdev goldfish-battery at ff015000 irq 17
goldfish_new_pdev goldfish_events at ff016000 irq 18
goldfish_new_pdev goldfish_nand at ff017000 irq -1
goldfish_new_pdev qemu_pipe at ff018000 irq 19
goldfish_new_pdev goldfish-switch at ff01a000 irq 20
goldfish_new_pdev goldfish-switch at ff01b000 irq 21
goldfish_pdev_worker registered goldfish_interrupt_controller
...
shell@armemu:/ $
```

From the log, we see that the system starts from U-Boot. After U-Boot runs the function `main_loop`, it tries to execute boot commands defined in the macro `CONFIG_BOOT-COMMAND`. These U-Boot commands use exactly the same command sequence that we used in Chapter 10. We mount the NAND flash volume first using the `ymount` command. Next, we load the kernel and RAMDISK images from the `system` root into RAM using the `yrdm` command. We then execute the `bootm` command by passing it the memory addresses of the kernel and RAMDISK.

All code that we created under `device/generic/armemu` can be found in GitHub: *https://github.com/shugaoye/armemu.git*. Appendix B outlines a way to download this code as part of the process of downloading the AOSP source using local manifest.

You have now walked through the entire process for creating an Android ROM from source code. Now we'll look at how to do the same for third-party ROM, such as that from CyanogenMod.

Supporting New Hardware in CyanogenMod

Now that we have gone through the process of creating a new device in AOSP, we'll see how to do the same thing in CyanogenMod. CyanogenMod has done a great job in helping developers create the skeleton of a new device automatically. The work that we have done for our device `armemu` in AOSP can be considered a manual process for creating a new device in the AOSP source tree. CyanogenMod actually provides a script to carry out those steps so developers don't have to worry about the environment setup and instead can focus on the real work.

You can visit the CyanogenMod wiki to find more information about this topic: *http://wiki.cyanogenmod.org/w/Doc:_porting_intro*. This article suggests three ways to create the skeleton for the new device:

- **Method 1:** We can use a script `mkvendor.sh` from CyanogenMod to create the skeleton for the new device. This script can be found at the path `build/tools/device/mkvendor.sh` from the root of the CyanogenMod source tree. We use this script to create our device `armemu` in this section.

- **Method 2:** We can make a copy of a similar device source tree and modify it to become our own device source tree. This approach is useful when you start to work on a new device in a similar product family.

- **Method 3:** We can create everything on our own. This is the method we used for our device `armemu` in AOSP.

In this section, we work on our device `armemu` in CyanogenMod using Method 1, then consider the differences between Method 1 and 3. To use the script `mkvendor.sh`, we have to build a package `otatools` first:

```
$ . build/envsetup.sh
$ lunch cm_goldfish-eng
$ make -j4 otatools
```

```
Install: /home/android/aosp/cm-11/out/host/linux-x86/bin/unpackbootimg

Install: /home/android/aosp/cm-11/out/host/linux-x86/bin/mkyaffs2image

Install: /home/android/aosp/cm-11/out/host/linux-x86/bin/fs_config

host StaticLib: libbz (/home/android/aosp/cm-11/out/host/linux-x86/obj/STATIC_
LIBRARIES/libbz_intermediates/libbz.a)

external/bsdiff/bsdiff.c: In function 'main':

external/bsdiff/bsdiff.c:196:5: warning: 'pos' may be used uninitialized in this
function [-Wmaybe-uninitialized]

host Executable: imgdiff (/home/android/aosp/cm-11/out/host/linux-x86/obj/
EXECUTABLES/imgdiff_intermediates/imgdiff)

host Executable: bsdiff (/home/android/aosp/cm-11/out/host/linux-x86/obj/
EXECUTABLES/bsdiff_intermediates/bsdiff)

Install: /home/android/aosp/cm-11/out/host/linux-x86/bin/bsdiff

Install: /home/android/aosp/cm-11/out/host/linux-x86/bin/imgdiff
```

Next, we can use the script mkvendor.sh to generate the skeleton files. If you don't know how to use this script, you can just run it without parameters and the help message will be shown. As you can see, it is quite straightforward to use mkvendor.sh:

$ **build/tools/device/mkvendor.sh**

```
Arguments:

Usage:

  mkvendor.sh manufacturer device [boot.img]

  The boot.img argument is the extracted recovery or boot image.

  The boot.img argument should not be provided for devices

  that have non standard boot images (ie, Samsung).


Example:

  mkvendor.sh motorola sholes ~/Downloads/recovery-sholes.img
```

As you can see, this script requires a boot image to do its work. We can use the boot image we generated for the device armemu in AOSP as the input. In Chapter 11, we saw how to download both the AOSP and CyanogenMod source code. Appendix B also explains how to download both the AOSP and CyanogenMod source code effectively. Ideally, you will put the CyanogenMod source and AOSP source at the same directory level, so that we can then run this script from the root of CyanogenMod:

$ **build/tools/device/mkvendor.sh generic armemu ../android-4.4.4_r2/out/target/product/armemu/boot.img**

```
Arguments: generic armemu ../android-4.4.4_r2/out/target/product/armemu/boot.img

Output will be in /home/android/aosp/cm-11/device/generic/armemu
1151 blocks
```

```
Creating initial git repository.
/home/android/aosp/cm-11/device/generic/armemu /home/android/aosp/cm-11
Initialized empty Git repository in /home/android/aosp/cm-11/device/generic/
armemu/.git/
[master (root-commit) 3b0905f] mkvendor.sh: Initial commit of armemu
 8 files changed, 96 insertions(+)
 create mode 100644 AndroidBoard.mk
 create mode 100644 AndroidProducts.mk
 create mode 100644 BoardConfig.mk
 create mode 100644 cm.mk
 create mode 100644 device_armemu.mk
 create mode 100644 kernel
 create mode 100644 recovery.fstab
 create mode 100644 system.prop
/home/android/aosp/cm-11
Done!
Use the following command to set up your build environment:
  lunch cm_armemu-eng
And use the following command to build a recovery:
  . build/tools/device/makerecoveries.sh cm_armemu-eng
```

As this output indicates, the script generates all of the files that we need to build the new device. Let's take a look at the files generated by the script:

```
$ ls device/generic/armemu
AndroidBoard.mk       BoardConfig.mk    device_armemu.mk   LICENSE     recovery.fstab
AndroidProducts.mk    cm.mk             kernel             README.md   system.prop
```

As you can see, the script generates a similar set of files as we created for the `armemu` AOSP build. We can make changes in `BoardConfig.mk` and `device_armemu.mk` just as we did in the AOSP build. The file `device_armemu.mk` is the equivalent to `full_armemu.mk` in the AOSP build. We'll review the necessary changes in these two files in the next two subsections, where we discuss how to build the kernel and U-Boot in CyanogenMod.

Building the Kernel with CyanogenMod

As mentioned earlier, CyanogenMod uses a much cleaner approach to build the kernel. You can refer to an article in the CyanogenMod wiki, titled "Integrated Kernel Building," for more details: *http://wiki.cyanogenmod.org/w/Doc:_integrated_kernel_building*.

For the CyanogenMod build, we need to check out the kernel source code in a different folder than we used for the AOSP build:

```
$ cd kernel
$ git clone https://github.com/shugaoye/goldfish.git armemu
$ git checkout -b android-armemu-3.4 remotes/origin/android-armemu-3.4
```

In the preceding code, we check out the goldfish kernel code and place it in kernel/armemu instead of in kernel. To build the kernel, we just need to define the kernel path in variable `TARGET_KERNEL_SOURCE` and the kernel configuration in `TARGET_KERNEL_CONFIG` in `device_armemu.mk`. We can even generate a kernel image for U-Boot by defining the variable `BOARD_USES_UBOOT` as true, as shown in Example 12.4 (`device_armemu.mk`). All of the actual build activities are handled by the makefile `build/core/tasks/kernel.mk` in the build system. Because CyanogenMod has the freedom to change anything in the build system, it can actually do a much nicer job than what we did in the previous section for AOSP.

Example 12.4 Device Makefile device_armemu.mk in CyanogenMod

```
$(call inherit-product, $(SRC_TARGET_DIR)/product/languages_full.mk)

# The gps config appropriate for this device
$(call inherit-product, device/common/gps/gps_us_supl.mk)

$(call inherit-product-if-exists, vendor/generic/armemu/armemu-vendor.mk)

DEVICE_PACKAGE_OVERLAYS += device/generic/armemu/overlay

# build kernel
TARGET_KERNEL_SOURCE := kernel/armemu
TARGET_KERNEL_CONFIG := goldfish_armv7_defconfig
BOARD_KERNEL_IMAGE_NAME := uImage
BOARD_USES_UBOOT := true

LOCAL_PATH := out/target/product/armemu/obj/KERNEL_OBJ/arch/arm/boot
ifeq ($(TARGET_PREBUILT_KERNEL),)
    LOCAL_KERNEL := $(LOCAL_PATH)/$(BOARD_KERNEL_IMAGE_NAME)
else
    LOCAL_KERNEL := $(TARGET_PREBUILT_KERNEL)
endif

# convert kernel image to uImage
KERNEL_EXTERNAL_MODULES:
    echo "Build external kernel modules here."
```

```
TARGET_KERNEL_MODULES := KERNEL_EXTERNAL_MODULES

# build U-Boot

PRODUCT_OUT ?= out/target/product/armemu

TARGET_U_BOOT_SOURCE := u-boot

TARGET_U_BOOT_CONFIG := goldfish_config

include $(TARGET_U_BOOT_SOURCE)/AndroidU-Boot.mk

LOCAL_U_BOOT := $(TARGET_PREBUILT_U-BOOT)

# define U-Boot images
# TARGET_KERNEL_UIMAGE := $(PRODUCT_OUT)/zImage.uimg

TARGET_RAMDISK_UIMAGE := $(PRODUCT_OUT)/ramdisk.uimg

TARGET_RECOVERY_UIMAGE := $(PRODUCT_OUT)/ramdisk-recovery.uimg

# define build targets for kernel, U-Boot, and U-Boot images
.PHONY: $(TARGET_PREBUILT_KERNEL) $(TARGET_PREBUILT_U-BOOT) $(TARGET_RAMDISK_UIMAGE) $(TARGET_RECOVERY_UIMAGE)

# $(TARGET_KERNEL_UIMAGE): $(TARGET_PREBUILT_KERNEL)
#     mkimage -A arm -C none -O linux -T kernel -d $(TARGET_PREBUILT_INT_KERNEL) -a 0x00010000 -e 0x00010000 $(TARGET_KERNEL_UIMAGE)

$(TARGET_RAMDISK_UIMAGE): $(INSTALLED_RAMDISK_TARGET)
    mkimage -A arm -C none -O linux -T ramdisk -d $(PRODUCT_OUT)/ramdisk.img -a 0x00800000 -e 0x00800000 $(TARGET_RAMDISK_UIMAGE)

$(TARGET_RECOVERY_UIMAGE): $(PRODUCT_OUT)/ramdisk-recovery.img
    mkimage -A arm -C none -O linux -T ramdisk -d $(PRODUCT_OUT)/ramdisk-recovery.img -a 0x00800000 -e 0x00800000 $(TARGET_RECOVERY_UIMAGE)

# LOCAL_KERNEL_UIMAGE := $(TARGET_KERNEL_UIMAGE)
LOCAL_RAMDISK_UIMAGE := $(TARGET_RAMDISK_UIMAGE)
LOCAL_RECOVERY_UIMAGE := $(TARGET_RECOVERY_UIMAGE)

PRODUCT_COPY_FILES += \
    $(LOCAL_U_BOOT):u-boot.bin \
    $(LOCAL_KERNEL):kernel \
    $(LOCAL_KERNEL):system/zImage.uimg \
    $(LOCAL_RAMDISK_UIMAGE):system/ramdisk.uimg \
    $(LOCAL_RECOVERY_UIMAGE):system/ramdisk-recovery.uimg \
```

```
            device/generic/armemu/init.recovery.armemu.rc:root/init.recovery.armemu.rc \
            device/generic/armemu/init.recovery.armemu.sh:root/init.recovery.armemu.sh

$(call inherit-product, build/target/product/full.mk)

PRODUCT_BUILD_PROP_OVERRIDES += BUILD_UTC_DATE=0
PRODUCT_NAME := full_armemu
PRODUCT_DEVICE := armemu
```

In Example 12.4, we comment out the portion of code that generates the U-Boot image for the kernel—the CyanogenMod makefile will perform that job when `BOARD_USES_UBOOT` is equal to true. However, we still need to generate U-Boot images for RAMDISK ourselves.

Building U-Boot and Booting Up CyanogenMod

Integrating U-Boot and booting up Android using U-Boot in CyanogenMod is the same as what we did in AOSP. We check out U-Boot source code to the CyanogenMod root as follows:

```
$ git clone https://github.com/shugaoye/u-boot.git u-boot
$ cd u-boot
$ git checkout -b android-armemu-3.4 remotes/origin/android-armemu-3.4
```

Refer to Example 12.4 for the U-Boot integration. As mentioned in the discussion on U-Boot AOSP integration, we need to change the default file system in Android 4.4 from ext4 to YAFFS2. We now have to make the same change in `BoardConfig.mk`, as shown in Example 12.5.

Example 12.5 BoardConfig.mk in CyanogenMod

```
USE_CAMERA_STUB := true

# inherit from the proprietary version
-include vendor/generic/armemu/BoardConfigVendor.mk

TARGET_ARCH := arm

TARGET_NO_BOOTLOADER := true

TARGET_BOARD_PLATFORM := unknown

TARGET_CPU_ABI := armeabi-v7a

TARGET_CPU_ABI2 := armeabi

TARGET_ARCH_VARIANT := armv7-a-neon

TARGET_CPU_VARIANT := cortex-a7
```

```
TARGET_CPU_SMP := true

ARCH_ARM_HAVE_TLS_REGISTER := true

TARGET_BOOTLOADER_BOARD_NAME := armemu

BOARD_KERNEL_CMDLINE :=
BOARD_KERNEL_BASE := 0x10000000
BOARD_KERNEL_PAGESIZE := 2048

# fix this up by examining /proc/mtd on a running device
# TARGET_USERIMAGES_USE_EXT4 := true
#BOARD_SYSTEMIMAGE_PARTITION_SIZE := 576716800
#BOARD_USERDATAIMAGE_PARTITION_SIZE := 209715200
# BOARD_CACHEIMAGE_PARTITION_SIZE := 69206016
BOARD_CACHEIMAGE_FILE_SYSTEM_TYPE := yaffs2
# BOARD_FLASH_BLOCK_SIZE := 512
# TARGET_USERIMAGES_SPARSE_EXT_DISABLED := true

BOARD_HAS_NO_SELECT_BUTTON := true
```

We also need to change `fstab.goldfish` and `init.goldfish.rc` in the folder `device/generic/goldfish/` to switch from ext4 to the YAFFS2 file system. We can make exactly the same change as we did in the AOSP build.

Now we can fire a build and test our device following the same process as we did before.

All of the source code that we created under `device/generic/armemu` for Cyanogen-Mod can be found in GitHub at *https://github.com/shugaoye/cm_armemu.git*. Appendix B describes a way to download this code as part of the process of downloading Cyanogen-Mod source code using local manifest.

Summary

In this chapter, we took on the role of an engineer working for a manufacturer. We created a virtual device `armemu` in both the AOSP and CyanogenMod source trees. We learned how to add a new device using different approaches in AOSP and CyanogenMod. We then integrated the kernel and U-Boot build in both environments. The method we used in AOSP kernel integration can be used to integrate other vendor-specific software modules as well. For example, we can integrate the U-Boot build following the same method. Finally, we created our own original Android ROM and we can now boot our own Android images using U-Boot.

IV

Appendixes

A Building the Source Code for This Book
B Using Repo in This Book

A

Building the Source Code for This Book

Since this is a hands-on book, you are encouraged to set up the environment and play with the projects while you read this book. Appendix A explains how to set up the development environment and check out the source code for this book.

If you have a computer with Intel Core i5 or i7 CPU, you will be able to compile all example code in this book. However, the hardware requirements for practicing with the code in Parts I and II in this book are quite different from requirements for Part III. There are not many hardware requirements for implementing the bare metal programming examples in Parts I and II. The major difference between these examples and those in Part III is the amount of disk space required. If you have a few gigabytes of free disk space, it should be sufficient to test all example code in Parts I and II. To compile AOSP or CyanogenMod in Part III, however, the estimated free disk space required is approximately 100GB. To be safe, you may want 150GB of free disk space to try the AOSP or CyanogenMod build.

Setting Up the Build Environment

The 64-bit version of Ubuntu is highly recommended, since the official guidelines at Google for the AOSP build are based on 64-bit Ubuntu. If you choose a different Linux distribution, you may have to spend extra time figuring out the AOSP build environment setup on your own. You can download Ubuntu 12.04 LTS (64-bit) at *http://www.ubuntu.com*.

Once you set up Ubuntu, refer to the guidelines at Google for setting up the AOSP build environment: *https://source.android.com/source/building.html*.

Once you have installed Ubuntu and set up the AOSP build environment, you can check out the `build` folder from GitHub (see Table A.1, which appears later in this appendix). The `build` folder includes utilities and scripts that can help you to set up the build environment used in this book. The build procedures and environment setup are discussed throughout the book. Follow these steps to check out the `build` folder from GitHub:

```
$ mkdir src

$ cd src

$ git clone https://github.com/shugaoye/build.git
```

```
$ ls build/bin
```

clearup.sh	install.sh	setup_emu.sh	u-boot.gdb
goldfish.gdb	mkyaffs2image	setup.sh	unyaffs

After you check out this folder, you will notice several utilities and scripts under the build/bin folder. Run the script install.sh to set up the environment. It takes some time to download the ARM toolchain, Android SDK, and necessary Android SDK images. Be patient and follow these instructions to complete the setup process:

```
$ build/bin/install.sh
```

Initializing x86_64 version ...

This script will download and install CodeBench Lite and Android SDK for you.

Android SDK will be installed at:

  /home/aosp/adt-bundle-linux-x86_64-20140702/sdk

CodeBench Lite will be installed at:

  /home/aosp/arm-2013.11

Do you want to start the installation? [y/n]?y

Starting the installation...

Create download folder.

Downloading CodeBench Lite ...

--2015-03-26 13:20:34-- https://sourcery.mentor.com/public/gnu_toolchain/arm-none-eabi/arm-2013.11-24-arm-none-eabi-i686-pc-linux-gnu.tar.bz2

Resolving sourcery.mentor.com (sourcery.mentor.com)... 54.83.42.164

Connecting to sourcery.mentor.com (sourcery.mentor.com)|54.83.42.164|:443... connected.

HTTP request sent, awaiting response... 200 OK

Length: 46051600 (44M) [application/x-bzip2]

Saving to: '/home/aosp/src/download/arm-2013.11-24-arm-none-eabi-i686-pc-linux-gnu.tar.bz2'

100%[=====================================>] 46,051,600   910K/s   in 47s

2015-03-26 13:21:24 (953 KB/s) - '/home/aosp/src/download/arm-2013.11-24-arm-none-eabi-i686-pc-linux-gnu.tar.bz2' saved [46051600/46051600]

--2015-03-26 13:21:24-- http://sourcery.mentor.com/public/gnu_toolchain/arm-none-linux-gnueabi/arm-2013.11-33-arm-none-linux-gnueabi-i686-pc-linux-gnu.tar.bz2

Resolving sourcery.mentor.com (sourcery.mentor.com)... 54.83.42.164

Connecting to sourcery.mentor.com (sourcery.mentor.com)|54.83.42.164|:80... connected.

HTTP request sent, awaiting response... 200 OK

Length: 101630521 (97M) [application/x-bzip2]

```
Saving to: '/home/aosp/src/download/arm-2013.11-33-arm-none-linux-gnueabi-i686-
pc-linux-gnu.tar.bz2'

100%[======================================>] 101,630,521  1.20M/s   in 91s

2015-03-26 13:22:56 (1.07 MB/s) - '/home/aosp/src/download/arm-2013.11-33-
arm-none-linux-gnueabi-i686-pc-linux-gnu.tar.bz2' saved [101630521/101630521]

Downloading Android SDK ...

--2015-03-26 13:22:56--  https://dl.google.com/android/adt/adt-bundle-
linux-x86_64-20140702.zip

Resolving dl.google.com (dl.google.com)... 173.194.38.137, 173.194.38.128,
173.194.38.135, ...

Connecting to dl.google.com (dl.google.com)|173.194.38.137|:443... connected.

HTTP request sent, awaiting response... 200 OK

Length: 372259418 (355M) [application/zip]

Saving to: '/home/aosp/src/download/adt-bundle-linux-x86_64-20140702.zip'

<!-- output omitted -->

Installing Archives:
  Preparing to install archives
  Downloading SDK Platform Android 4.0.3, API 15, revision 5
  Installing SDK Platform Android 4.0.3, API 15, revision 5
  Downloading ARM EABI v7a System Image, Android API 15, revision 2
  Done. 2 package installed.

Please refer to chapter 2 to create an Android Virtual Device.
Please add /home/aosp/src/build/bin in your path and
add /home/aosp/src/build/bin/setup.sh in your .bashrc.
```

As you can see from the preceding output, Android SDK platform 4.0.3 and system images are installed by the installation script. This is the Android version we use in Chapter 2. Follow the procedure in Chapter 2 and look at Figure 2.3 to create the Android Virtual Device hd2.

Our build environment is now ready for use. To set up the environment variables and execution paths, we can add the following line in the startup script .bashrc:

. ~/src/build/bin/setup.sh

Once you have added this line, you'll see the following output message when you create a new console:

```
Setup development environment for Android SDK and Sourcery CodeBench.
Using CodeBench Lite arm-2013.11-24-arm-none-eabi-i686-pc-linux-gnu.tar.bz2
Android SDK 24.1.2 and API 22
```

```
Initializing x86_64 version ...
Find API level 15.
Find AVD hd2.
TOOLROOT=/home/aosp/arm-2013.11
Android SDK path is /home/aosp/adt-bundle-linux-x86_64-20140702/sdk.
```

You can now use the development environment in the new console.

Setting Up a Virtual Machine

If you don't have a machine to set up Ubuntu, you can always set up the build environment using either VMware or VirtualBox. They can be downloaded from the following URLs:

- VMware Player: *http://www.vmware.com*
- VirtualBox: *http://www.virtualbox.org*

If your operating system is Windows or Linux, you can choose either VMware Player or VirtualBox. If you are using OS X, you may want to use VirtualBox. For this book, virtual machine setup was not tested on OS X. Instead, we used either VMware or VirtualBox on Windows.

Organization of Source Code

All example code in this book has been fully tested and can be found in GitHub: *https://github.com/shugaoye*.

Table A.1 provides a list of git repositories available in GitHub for this book. Since I may fix issues with the code from time to time, you can check out a release tag for the stable version. Read the `README.md` file for each git repository to obtain the release history.

Table A.1 Source Code on GitHub for This Book

Git Repositories	URL	Description
bo	https://github.com/shugaoye/bo.git	Example code (Chapters 3–8)
build	https://github.com/shugaoye/build.git	Build scripts (Chapters 3–12)
u-boot	https://github.com/shugaoye/u-boot.git	U-Boot (Chapters 9–12)
goldfish	https://github.com/shugaoye/goldfish.git	Goldfish kernel (Chapters 9–12)
armemu	https://github.com/shugaoye/armemu.git	Device `armemu` for AOSP (Chapter 12)
cm_armemu	https://github.com/shugaoye/cm_armemu.git	Device `armemu` for CyanogenMod (Chapter 12)

Source Code for Part I

To work with the example code in Part I (including the examples in Chapters 3–8), you can clone the git repository bo as follows:

```
$ cd src
```

```
$ git clone https://github.com/shugaoye/bo.git
```

You can build and test the example code separately. The directory structure of this example code is arranged by chapter; for example, the example code for Chapter 3 is stored in the folder bo/c03. There is more than one example in a chapter, so you will find subfolders under the main folder for each chapter. For example, there are four examples in Chapter 4:

```
$ ls -F bo/c04
```

c04e1/   c04e2/   c04e3/   c04e4/

You can build and test these examples from either the command line or Eclipse.

Building and Testing from the Command Line

To build an example from the command line, you can use the following commands. The command to build c04e1 is used as an example here:

```
$ cd bo/c04/c04e1
```

```
$ make DEBUG=1 VERBOSE=1
```

```
arm-none-eabi-gcc -marm -mno-thumb-interwork -mabi=aapcs-linux -march=armv5te
-fno-common -ffixed-r8 -msoft-float -fno-builtin -ffreestanding -MD -g -D DEBUG
-Dgcc -o gcc/c04e1.o -c c04e1.S

arm-none-eabi-gcc -marm -mno-thumb-interwork -mabi=aapcs-linux -march=armv5te
-fno-common -ffixed-r8 -msoft-float -fno-builtin -ffreestanding -MD -g -D DEBUG
-Dgcc -o gcc/sum-sub.o -c sum-sub.S

arm-none-eabi-ld -T c04e1.ld --entry ResetISR -o gcc/c04e1.axf gcc/c04e1.o gcc/
sum-sub.o /media/u64/home/sgye/CodeSourcery/Sourcery_CodeBench_Lite_for_ARM_EABI/
bin/../lib/gcc/arm-none-eabi/4.6.3/../../../../arm-none-eabi/lib/libm.a /media/
u64/home/sgye/CodeSourcery/Sourcery_CodeBench_Lite_for_ARM_EABI/bin/../lib/
gcc/arm-none-eabi/4.6.3/../../../../arm-none-eabi/lib/libc.a /media/u64/home/
sgye/CodeSourcery/Sourcery_CodeBench_Lite_for_ARM_EABI/bin/../lib/gcc/arm-none-
eabi/4.6.3/libgcc.a

arm-none-eabi-objcopy -O binary gcc/c04e1.axf gcc/c04e1.bin
```

The executable image c04e1.bin can be found in folder gcc. To test this example, you can use the emulator command:

```
$ emulator -verbose -avd hd2 -qemu -kernel gcc/c04e1.bin
```

Alternately, you can make the target be debug:

```
$ make debug
```

Building and Testing in Eclipse

Google released Android Studio 1.0 in December 2014. If you are an application developer, you may want to switch to Android Studio instead of using Eclipse (with an ADT plugin). For Android system developers, Eclipse may still be the best choice, since you have to work on both the C and Java languages, or even assembly language.

If you are still using an ADT bundle with the Android SDK, you can use Eclipse right away. The installation script (`build/bin/install.sh`) installs the ADT bundle for you. If you don't have that, you may download the latest SDK tools from the Android developer website and install Eclipse separately. After that, you can follow the instructions from Google to install the ADT plugin: *http://developer.android.com/sdk/installing/installing-adt.html*.

To build and test examples from Chapters 3 through 8 in Eclipse, follow these steps to set up projects in Eclipse:

1. Start Eclipse and choose the C/C++ perspective, as shown in Figure A.1.

Figure A.1 Choosing a perspective in Eclipse

Source Code for Part I   347

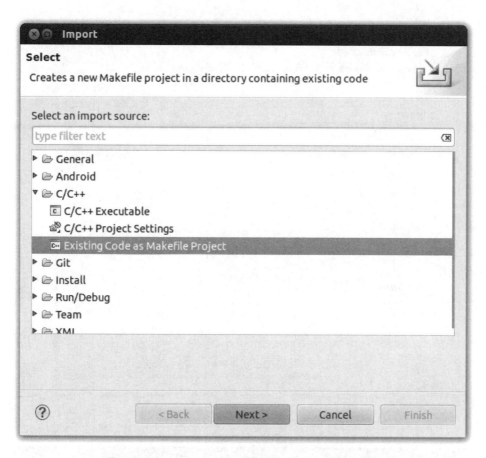

Figure A.2 Selecting Existing Code as Makefile Project

2. From the menu `File->Import...`, choose `Existing Code as the Makefile Project` from C/C++ to import a C/C++ project, as shown in Figure A.2.
3. Click the Next button and choose an example project. Project c03e1 is used as an example here, as shown in Figure A.3.
4. Once you have imported the project into Eclipse, select `Build Project` or `Clean Project` to build or clean the project, respectively. The `Build Project` option will build the release build for you. If you want to build a debug build or debug the project, you can manually add two build targets by selecting `Project->Make Targets` and then `Create...`, as shown in Figure A.4.

348   Appendix A Building the Source Code for This Book

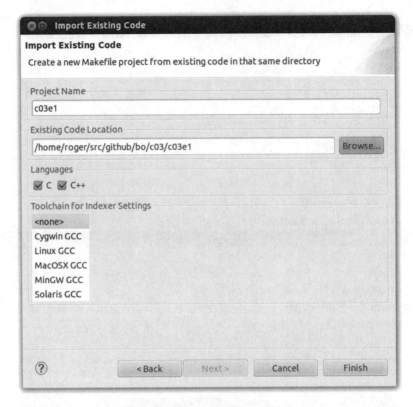

Figure A.3 Choosing a project

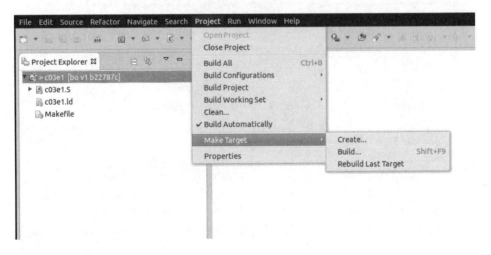

Figure A.4 Selecting make targets

Source Code for Part I 349

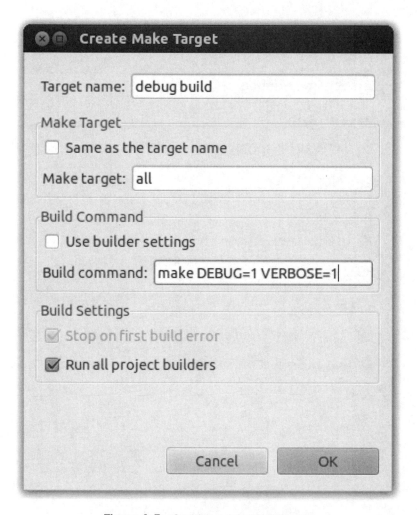

Figure A.5 Creating a debug build target

5. In the Create Make Target dialog box, fill in the Target name with debug build, specify Make target as all, and fill in the Build command with make DEBUG=1 VERBOSE=1, as shown in Figure A.5. You can use this option to create a debug build.
6. Do the same for the debug target as shown in Figure A.6. In this case, just fill in the Target name with debug and leave the rest as the default values.

You can use this option to debug the project. Following the same process, you can import all other projects into Eclipse.

Figure A.6 Creating a debug target

Source Code for Part II

To build and test the source code in Part II (which includes Chapters 9 and 10), you need to clone the git repositories u-boot and goldfish:

```
$ cd ~/src
```
```
$ git clone https://github.com/shugaoye/u-boot.git
```
```
$ cd u-boot
```
```
$ git checkout -b android-armemu-2.6.29 remotes/origin/android-armemu-2.6.29
```

```
Branch android-armemu-2.6.29 set up to track remote branch android-armemu-2.6.29
from origin.

Switched to a new branch 'android-armemu-2.6.29'
```

$ cd ~/src

$ git clone https://github.com/shugaoye/goldfish.git

$ cd goldfish

$ git checkout -b android-armemu-2.6.29 remotes/origin/android-armemu-2.6.29

```
Branch android-armemu-2.6.29 set up to track remote branch android-armemu-2.6.29
from origin.

Switched to a new branch 'android-armemu-2.6.29'
```

We see here the branch android-armemu-2.6.29, which is built for Linux kernel 2.6.29. This version is used because we use Android 4.0.3 in Part I and Part II.

For the examples in Part II, the top-level Makefile is in a separate folder build to make the build process much easier for U-Boot, the Linux kernel, and file system images. This Makefile is a wrapper for the various build steps that we use in Chapters 9 and 10. Also included are various scripts related to the build and debug components in this folder. We checked out the build folder at beginning of this chapter, so now let's take a look at its contents:

$ ls -F build

```
bin/              cm_local_manifest.xml   LICENSE    prep.sh
busybox.config    initrd.list             Makefile   README.md
local_manifest.xml
```

If we list the contents of the build folder, we see that there is a Makefile. We also see two files initrd.list and prep.sh; they are used to generate the RAMDISK image. Appendix B discusses local_manifest.xml and cm_local_manifest.xml in more depth.

The U-Boot and goldfish debug scripts u-boot.gdb and goldfish.gdb for gdb are found in the bin folder:

$ ls -F build/bin

```
clearup.sh*    install.sh*      setup_emu.sh*   u-boot.gdb
goldfish.gdb   mkyaffs2image*   setup.sh*       unyaffs*
```

To build U-Boot, the Linux kernel, or file system images, you can choose the following targets:

$ cd build

$ make {target}

Following is a list of build targets that we can choose in this make command:

- **u-boot_config**: Create a U-Boot configuration.
- **u-boot_build**: Build U-Boot. The result can be found at build/u-boot.

- **goldfish_config**: Create a goldfish configuration.
- **goldfish_build**: Build the goldfish kernel. The result can be found at build/goldfish.
- **flash.bin**: Build the image for the NOR flash boot-up in Chapter 10.
- **rootfs**: Build the image for the NAND flash boot-up in Chapter 10.

You can also create all images using just the following command:

```
$ make
```

Source Code for Part III

To reproduce the builds of AOSP and CyanogenMod in Chapters 11 and 12, you need to clone git repositories in the AOSP and CyanogenMod source trees. Refer to Chapter 11 for information on how to set up the AOSP and CyanogenMod source trees. This section outlines the procedures to build the virtual device armemu.

Building AOSP

To build AOSP for the virtual device armemu, we need to check out the git repositories goldfish, u-boot, and armemu to AOSP. Ideally, you will have already set up the AOSP build for Android 4.4 in the folder android-4.4.4_r2. Let's check out the necessary git repositories:

```
$ cd android-4.4.4_r2
$ . build/envsetup.sh
including device/samsung/manta/vendorsetup.sh
including device/lge/mako/vendorsetup.sh
including device/lge/hammerhead/vendorsetup.sh
including device/asus/flo/vendorsetup.sh
including device/asus/deb/vendorsetup.sh
including device/asus/tilapia/vendorsetup.sh
including device/asus/grouper/vendorsetup.sh
including device/generic/x86/vendorsetup.sh
including device/generic/armv7-a-neon/vendorsetup.sh
including device/generic/mips/vendorsetup.sh
including sdk/bash_completion/adb.bash
$ git clone https://github.com/shugaoye/goldfish.git kernel
$ cd kernel
$ git checkout -b android-armemu-3.4 remotes/origin/android-armemu-3.4
$ croot
```

```
$ git clone https://github.com/shugaoye/u-boot.git
$ cd u-boot
$ git checkout -b android-armemu-3.4 remotes/origin/android-armemu-3.4
$ croot
$ cd device/generic
$ git clone https://github.com/shugaoye/armemu.git
$ croot
$ lunch full_armemu-eng
$ make -j4
```

As you can see, we check out a different branch for U-Boot and the kernel than we did for the code in Part II. We use Android 4.4 in Chapters 11 and 12, so we need the branch `android-armemu-3.4`, which is a Linux kernel version 3.4.x. When the build is completed, all images can be found in the folder `out/target/product/armemu/`.

Building CyanogenMod

We follow a similar process to build CyanogenMod for the virtual device `armemu`. We need to check out the git repositories `goldfish`, `u-boot`, and `cm_armemu` to the CyanogenMod source tree. Ideally, you will have already set up the CyanogenMod 11 build in the folder `cm-11`. Let's check out the necessary git repositories:

```
$ cd cm-11
$ . build/envsetup.sh
including device/generic/armv7-a-neon/vendorsetup.sh
including device/generic/goldfish/vendorsetup.sh
including device/generic/mips/vendorsetup.sh
including device/generic/x86/vendorsetup.sh
including vendor/cm/vendorsetup.sh
including sdk/bash_completion/adb.bash
including vendor/cm/bash_completion/git.bash
including vendor/cm/bash_completion/repo.bash
$ cd kernel
$ git clone https://github.com/shugaoye/goldfish.git armemu
$ cd armemu
$ git checkout -b android-armemu-3.4 remotes/origin/android-armemu-3.4
$ croot
$ git clone https://github.com/shugaoye/u-boot.git
```

```
$ cd u-boot
$ git checkout -b android-armemu-3.4 remotes/origin/android-armemu-3.4
$ croot
$ cd device/generic
$ git clone https://github.com/shugaoye/cm_armemu.git armemu
$ croot
$ lunch cm_armemu-eng
$ make -j4
```

When the build is complete, all images can be found in the folder out/target/product/armemu/.

B
Using Repo in This Book

To help you work on the examples in this book more efficiently, especially building the virtual device armemu in both the AOSP and CyanogenMod source trees, this appendix gives a brief introduction to Repo and discusses key features that should be used in AOSP or CyanogenMod builds. Repo is a repository management tool that can help you manage multiple git repositories for large projects, such as those involving AOSP and CyanogenMod. To build AOSP or CyanogenMod, we have to put hundreds of different git repositories together first before we fire the actual build. It is a time-consuming process to download the entire source tree of AOSP or CyanogenMod. The tips and tricks provided in this appendix may help you save a significant amount of time when downloading source code from various git repositories.

Resources for Repo

In Chapter 11, we use the repo tool to download all of the source code for AOSP and CyanogenMod. The official reference for this tool can be found at the Google website: *https://source.android.com/source/using-repo.html*.

Many resources on the Internet are available that provide helpful tips about how to use repo efficiently. The following two articles from the xdadevelopers forum are referred to in this appendix:

- "Repo: Tips & Tricks": *http://xda-university.com/as-a-developer/repo-tips-tricks*
- "Learn about the Repo Tool, Manifests and Local Manifests and 5 Important Tips!": *http://forum.xda-developers.com/showthread.php?t=2329228*

Syncing a New Source Tree In Minutes

In Chapters 11 and 12, you are asked to build both AOSP and CyanogenMod. The size of each may exceed 10GB. It may take more than a day to download the necessary source code with the usual Internet connection. However, if you already have any AOSP or CyanogenMod builds, you can save a significant amount of time by referring to your current AOSP or CyanogenMod source tree when you download a new source tree. You can also download the AOSP source tree first, and then refer to that while you download the CyanogenMod source tree.

The following example uses CyanogenMod to show how to do this. As mentioned in Appendix A, this example assumes that you have put both AOSP and CyanogenMod in the same folder. It also assumes you have downloaded and built AOSP and you now want to download CyanogenMod. Use the following commands to download CyanogenMod:

```
$ mkdir cm-11
$ cd cm-11
$ ls -F ..
android-4.4.4_r2/   cm-11/
$ repo init --reference=../android-4.4.4_r2 -u git://github.com/CyanogenMod/android.git -b cm-11.0
$ repo sync -j 4
```

Pay attention to the additional option `--reference`. This option can save you a lot of time, because repo quickly copies the identical git repositories from AOSP to CyanogenMod. The repo tool stores the downloaded git repositories in the folder `.repo/projects`. If we look at the local git repositories in both AOSP and CyanogenMod, it is obvious that many of them are the same. Following is a list of the AOSP git repositories downloaded:

```
$ ls -F android-4.4.4_r2/.repo/projects
abi/           cts.git/            docs/           libnativehelper.git/   sdk.git/
art.git/       dalvik.git/         external/       ndk.git/               system/
bionic.git/    developers/         frameworks/     packages/              tools/
bootable/      development.git/    hardware/       pdk.git/
build.git/     device/             libcore.git/    prebuilts/
```

Following is a list of CyanogenMod git repositories downloaded:

```
$ ls -F cm-11/.repo/projects
abi/            cts.git/            external/            ndk.git/          system/
android.git/    dalvik.git/         frameworks/          packages/         tools/
art.git/        developers/         hardware/            pdk.git/          vendor/
bionic.git/     development.git/    kernel/              prebuilt.git/
bootable/       device/             libcore/             prebuilts/
build.git/      docs/               libnativehelper.git/ sdk.git/
```

Downloading Git Repositories Using Local Manifest

When we build either AOSP or CyanogenMod, we downloaded the kernel, U-Boot, and device folder separately. We can actually use a file called *local manifest* to download our own git repositories into the AOSP or CyanogenMod source tree. In this case, you can actually deviate from the git repositories covered here to create your own git repositories and use them to build and test the virtual device. You can create a file `local_manifest.xml` under the folder `.repo/local_manifests` with the following content in the AOSP source tree:

```
<?xml version="1.0" encoding="UTF-8"?>

<manifest>

    <remote  name="shugaoye"
             fetch="https://github.com/shugaoye/" />

        <project path="kernel" name="goldfish" remote="shugaoye" revision="android-armemu-3.4"/>

        <project path="u-boot" name="u-boot" remote="shugaoye" revision="android-armemu-3.4" />

        <project path="device/generic/armemu/" name="armemu" remote="shugaoye" revision="master" />

</manifest>
```

This file can be downloaded from GitHub at *https://github.com/shugaoye/build/blob/master/local_manifest.xml*.

You can create the following similar file for CyanogenMod:

```
<?xml version="1.0" encoding="UTF-8"?>

<manifest>

    <remote  name="shugaoye"
             fetch="https://github.com/shugaoye/" />

        <project path="kernel/armemu" name="goldfish" remote="shugaoye" revision="android-armemu-3.4"/>

        <project path="u-boot" name="u-boot" remote="shugaoye" revision="android-armemu-3.4" />

        <project path="device/generic/armemu/" name="cm_armemu" remote="shugaoye" revision="master" />

</manifest>
```

This file can be downloaded from GitHub at *https://github.com/shugaoye/build/blob/master/cm_local_manifest.xml*.

You have to rename `cm_local_manifest.xml` to `local_manifest.xml` in the CyanogenMod folder `.repo/local_manifests`.

After the `local_manifest.xml` file is ready, you can just run `repo sync` to get all the git repositories from GitHub. Local manifest provides a way to override the default manifest. You can find more information about local manifest on your own by referring to the resources mentioned at the beginning of this appendix.

Index

A

ABI Research, 283
Address alignment, viewing, 31–32
`ALARM_HIGH` register, 19
`ALARM_LOW` register, 19
`align` directive, 44
`all`, build target, 36
Android
    file system, 183–185
    kernel, verifying, 273–274
    virtual devices, setting up, 284–287
`android` command, 16
Android emulator
    configuring virtual devices, 14–16
    description, 11
    illustration, 14
    mobile device hardware features supported, 13–14
Android emulator, building with AOSP
    AOSP build environment, 288–289
    building Android emulator images, 290–292
    downloading AOSP source, 289
    initializing a `repo` client, 289
    installing `repo` tool, 289
    installing required packages, 288
    installing the JDK, 288
    testing AOSP images, 292–297
Android emulator, building with CyanogenMod
    `armemu` virtual device, 332–338, 353–354
    build process, 298–302
    downloading CyanogenMod source, 297
    emulator images, Android version of, 306
    emulator images, building, 298–302
    emulator images, testing, 302–307
    introduction, 297
    releases, 284
Android Open Source Project (AOSP). *See* AOSP (Android Open Source Project).
Android ROM, creating with AOSP
    booting Android with U-Boot from NAND flash, 323–332
    building the kernel, 317–322
    building U-Boot, 322–323
    process description, 309–317
Android ROM, creating with CyanogenMod
    booting CyanogenMod, 337–338
    building the kernel, 334–337

360 Index

Android ROM, creating with
CyanogenMod *(continued)*
building U-Boot, 337–338
introduction, 332–334
Android SDK, setting up, 27, 284–287
Android Virtual Device Manager, 284–287
AOSP (Android Open Source Project). *See also*
CyanogenMod.
`armemu` virtual device, 352–353
introduction, 283–284
releases, 284
AOSP (Android Open Source Project), Android emulator
build
AOSP build environment, 288–289
building Android emulator images, 290–292
downloading AOSP source, 289
initializing a `repo` client, 289
installing `repo` tool, 289
installing required packages, 288
installing the JDK, 288
testing AOSP images, 292–297
AOSP (Android Open Source Project), creating Android
ROM
booting Android with U-Boot from NAND flash,
323–332
building the kernel, 317–322
building U-Boot, 322–323
process description, 309–317
AOSP (Android Open Source Project), supporting new
hardware
booting Android with U-Boot from NAND flash,
323–332
building the kernel, 317–322
building U-Boot, 322–323
process description, 309–317
AOSP-based smartphones, sales growth, 283
APCS registers use convention, 78
Application layer, embedded systems, 7
Architecture of embedded systems, 7–10
ARM Architectural Reference Manual, 5
ARM processors for embedded systems, 8–9. *See also*
specific processors.
ARM register set, 67
ARM System Developer's Guide, 5, 125
ARM926EJ-S processor, 9
`ARM_dAbort()` function, 137
`armemu` virtual device
Android version, illustration, 317, 321
building a kernel for, 318–322
building with AOSP, 352–353
building with CyanogenMod,
353–354
creating, 284–287, 309–317
creating skeleton files for, 310–311
CyanogenMod version, 332–338
`arm_exc.s` file, 141, 142–149
`ARM_fiq()` function, 137
`ARM_irq()` function, 137
`ARM_pAbort()` function, 137
`ARM_reserved()` function, 137
`ARM_swi()` function, 137

`ARM_undef()` function, 137
Assembler directives, 30, 43–44
Assembly initialization phase, 103
Assembly language, 30
AVD Manager, 16. *See also* SDK Manager.
AVDs (Android Virtual Devices), 14–16

B

Banked registers, initializing, 66–68
Banked stack pointers, initializing, 66–68
Bare metal programming. *See also* Embedded system
programming.
common programming languages, 4
definition, 3, 5
resources for, 5
`__BARE_METAL__` macro, 191
Barr, Michael, 5
Ben-Yossef, Gilad, 5
Binary files, 31–32
Bionic, C library variant, 95
`board_early_init_f()` function, 234
`board_init()` function, 234
`board_nand_init()` function, 205
Books and publications. *See also* Online resources.
ARM Architectural Reference Manual, 5
ARM System Developer's Guide, 5, 125
Building Embedded Linux Systems, 5
Embedded Android, 5, 249, 288
Linkers and Loaders, 42
Procedure Call Standard for the ARM Architecture, 78
Programming Embedded System in C and C++, 5
RealView Compilation Tools Developer Guide, 50
RealView Platform Baseboard, 5
Booting
CyanogenMod, 337–338
flash image, 258–266
a Linux kernel, 254
Booting Android from NAND flash
boot process, 271–279
checking the configuration, 272
introduction, 270
preparing `system.img`, 270
with U-Boot, 323–332
verifying the kernel and the RAMDISK image,
273–274
Booting Android from NOR flash
introduction, 254–256
memory relocation, 256
RAMDISK image, creating, 256–258
Booting Android from NOR flash, flash image
booting, 258–266
creating, 258
source-level debugging, 266–270
Booting the goldfish kernel
booting a Linux kernel, 254
building the kernel, 249–250
debugging the kernel, 252–254
kernel source code, 250–252
prebuilt toolchain, 250–252
running the kernel, 252–254

Index

Bootloader. *See* U-Boot.
`bootm` command, 256, 261, 274
`BSP_irq()` function, 149
`.bss` section
    C language in a bare metal environment, 68–78
    zeroing our, 72–78
bss segment, 42
Building Embedded Linux Systems, 5
`byte` directive, 43–44
`BYTES_READY` register, 18

C

C functions, calling from assembly language code, 79–81
C language in a bare metal environment. *See also* C functions.
    `.bss` section, 68–78
    `.data` section, 68–78
    `.global` directive, 81
    `.isr_vector` section, 68–78
    `.rodata` section, 68–78, 80
    `.stack` section, 68–78
    `.text` section, 68–78
    calling assembly language functions from, 81
    calling C functions from assembly language code, 79–81
    calling convention, 78–81
    debugging, 75–76
    global variables, 68
    preparing the stack, 65–68
    prerequisites for, 63–65
    read-only data, 68
    startup code, 68–78
    version information, 80
    viewing symbol placement, 76–78
C language in a bare metal environment, example code
    calling C code from assembly language, 64–65
    linker script, 70–72
C library variants. *See also* Newlib C library; Semihosting support.
    in a bare metal environment, 94–96
    Bionic, 95
    debugging capabilities, 95
    `libcmtd.lib`, 94
    `libcmt.lib`, 94
    Microsoft C runtime libraries, 94
    `msvcmrt.lib`, 94
    `msvcrtd.lib`, 94
    `msvcrt.lib`, 94
    `msvcurt.lib`, 94
    RealView Development Suite, 95
    uclibc, 95
C Run-Time (CRT) libraries, 94
`c04e1.S` file, 42–46
`c04e2.c` file, 53–56
`c04e3.c` file, 56–57
`c04e4.c` file, 58
`c05e1.c` file, 64–65
`c05e1.ld` file, 64, 70–72
`c05e2.c` file, 81, 90–91

`c06e1.c` file, 97, 113–115
`c06e1.ld` file, 97–103
`c06e2.c` file, 118–122
`c07e1.c` file, 128, 134–137
`c07e1.ld` file, 128
`c07e2.c` file, 141, 152–155
`c07e2.ld` file, 141
`c07e3.c` file, 174
`c08e1.c` file, 211–216
`c08e1.ld` file, 211–216
Calling
    assembly language functions from C, 81
    C convention, 78–81
`clean,` build target, 36
`CLEAR_ALARM` register, 19
`CLEAR_INTERRUPT` register, 19
Client development environment, setting up, 25–26
`CMD` register, 18
`CMD_INT_DISABLE` command, 18
`CMD_INT_ENABLE` command, 18
`CMD_READ_BUFFER` command, 18
`CMD_WRITE_BUFFER` command, 18
CodeBench. *See* Sourcery CodeBench.
Coding. *See* Programming.
Commands
    `android`, 16
    `bootm`, 256, 261, 274
    `CMD_INT_DISABLE`, 18
    `CMD_INT_ENABLE`, 18
    `CMD_READ_BUFFER`, 18
    `CMD_WRITE_BUFFER`, 18
    `d`, 138, 179
    `e`, 138, 179
    `g`, 179
    `git-diff`, 221
    `iminfo`, 260, 273
    `ld`, 31–32
    `mount`, 184–185
    `NAND_CMD_BLOCK_BAD_SET`, 187
    `NAND_CMD_ERASE`, 187
    `NAND_CMD_GET_DEV_NAME CO`, 187
    `NAND_CMD_READ`, 187
    `NAND_CMD_WRITE`, 187
    `nm`, 31–32
    `objcopy`, 32
    `q`, 91
    `r`, 179
    `s`, 179
    `t`, 138, 179
    `umount`, 274
    `x`, 179
Comments, assembly language, 30
Common files, folder for, 81
Compiling U-Boot, 220–224
`CONFIG_USE_IRQ` macro, 239
Console
    debugging serial ports, console log example, 91
    interrupts, enabling/disabling, 18

362 Index

Constant names, 69
Copying
   converting file formats, 32
   `.data` to RAM, 57–58,
      68, 72–78
   `objcopy` command, 32
CORTEX-A processors, 8–9
CORTEX-M processors, 8–9
CORTEX-R processors, 8–9
CRT (C Run-Time) libraries, 94
Customizing Android, supporting new hardware with AOSP
   booting Android with U–Boot from NAND flash,
      323–332
   building the kernel, 317–322
   building U–Boot, 322–323
   process description, 309–317
Customizing Android, supporting new hardware with CyanogenMod
   booting CyanogenMod, 337–338
   building the kernel, 334–337
   building U–Boot, 337–338
   introduction, 332–334
CyanogenMod, Android emulator build. *See also* AOSP (Android Open Source Project).
   `armemu` virtual device, 332–338, 353–354
   build process, 298–302
   downloading CyanogenMod source, 297
   emulator images, Android version of, 306
   emulator images, building, 298–302
   emulator images, testing, 302–307
   introduction, 297
   releases, 284
CyanogenMod, creating Android ROM
   booting CyanogenMod, 337–338
   building the kernel, 334–337
   building U–Boot, 337–338
   introduction, 332–334
CyanogenMod, supporting new hardware
   booting CyanogenMod, 337–338
   building the kernel, 334–337
   building U–Boot, 337–338
   introduction, 332–334
CyanogenMod wiki, 332

D

`d` command, 138, 179
Data buffer, checking, 87–88
`.data` section
   copying to RAM, 57–58, 68, 72–78
   placement, 68–78
Data segment, 42
`DATA_LEN` register, 18
`DATA_PTR` register, 18
Date and time
   getting/setting, 179
   resetting, 173
`date.c` file, 174
ddd
   installing, 29
   starting, 33

starting GDB in, 37
stepping through instructions, 35
user interface, 35–36
viewing register contents, 34
`debug`, build target, 37
`DEBUG` option, 37–38
Debugging
   C library variant capabilities, 95
   development environment, 25, 37–38
   the goldfish kernel, 252–254
   `makefile` template, 37–38
   quitting, 91
   serial ports, console log example, 91
   source-level, 75–76
   source-level flash image, 266–270
   U–Boot, with GDB, 224–227
Debugging, GDB (GNU Debugger)
   scripts for, 227, 267–270
   starting in ddd, 37
Denx, Wolfgang, 220
Development environment, debugging, 25, 37–38. *See also* Virtualization environment.
Development environment, setting up
   Android SDK, 27
   building the binary, 30–32
   for client, 25–26
   downloading/installing toolchains, 26–29
   flash memory, emulating, 32–36
   for host, 25–26
   `makefile` template, build targets, 32–36
   output filename, specifying, 31
   running in the Android emulator, 32–36
Device drivers
   adding drivers, 239
   adding to goldfish, 239
   device driver changes, 239–246
   Ethernet drivers, 245
   NAND flash drivers, 241–243
   RTC drivers, 243–245
   serial drivers, 239–241
Disabling. *See* Enabling/disabling.
Dollar sign ($), in assembly language labels, 30
Downloading
   EABI/ELF toolchain, 28–29
   git repositories, 356–357
   GNU/Linux toolchain, 28–29
   Sourcery CodeBench Lite, 28–29
   Sourcery CodeBench trial version, 28–29
   toolchains, 26–29
   U–Boot, 220–224
`dram_init()` function, 234
Drivers. *See* Device drivers.

E

`e` command, 138, 179
EA (empty ascending) stacks, 66
EABI/ELF toolchain, downloading, 28–29
Eclipse editor, 29
ED (empty descending) stacks, 66
Editors, 29

Index

ELF (executable and linkable) format, 32
Embedded Android, 5, 249, 288
Embedded system programming, 5–7. *See also* Bare metal programming.
Embedded systems
   application layer, 7
   architecture of, 7–10
   ARM processors, 8–9
   definition, 3
   software layers, 7–10
eMMC *vs.* NAND flash, 184
Empty ascending (EA) stacks, 66
Empty descending (ED) stacks, 66
Emulators. *See also* Android emulator; Tools.
   QEMU, 11–12
   virtual hardware *vs.* real hardware, 11–12
Enabling/disabling
   `CMD_INT_ENABLE` command, 18
   console interrupts, 18
   `GOLDFISH_INTERRUPT_ENABLE` register, 127
   interrupts, 131
   nested interrupt handler, 142–149
   timer interrupts, 179
`EnterUserMode()` function, 150-152
Environments. *See* Development environment; Virtualization environment.
Erasing, from NAND flash
   block size, 187
   flash blocks, 197, 206
   flash pages, 185
   `goldfish_nand_erase()` function, 206
   `NAND_CMD_ERASE` command, 187
   `NAND_DEV_ERASE_SIZE` register, 187
Ethernet drivers, adding to goldfish, 242, 245
Example code, makefile template for, xx–xxii. *See also specific examples*.
Executable and linkable (ELF) format, 32

F

FA (full ascending) stacks, 66
FD (full descending) stacks, 66
Files
   `arm_exc.S`, 141, 142–149
   `c04e1.S`, 42–46
   `c04e2.c`, 53–56
   `c04e3.c`, 56–57
   `c04e4.c`, 58
   `c05e1.c`, 64–65
   `c05e1.ld`, 64, 70–72
   `c05e2.c`, 81, 90–91
   `c06e1.c`, 97, 113–115
   `c06e1.ld`, 97–103
   `c06e2.c`, 118–122
   `c07e1.c`, 128, 134–137
   `c07e1.ld`, 128
   `c07e2.c`, 141, 152–155
   `c07e2.ld`, 141
   `c07e3.c`, 174

   `c08e1.c`, 211–216
   `c08e1.ld`, 211–216
   common, folder for, 181
   `date.c`, 174
   `goldfish.c`, 229, 235–239
   `goldfish.gdb`, 268–269
   `goldfish.nand.reg.h`, 189, 190–191
   `goldfish_uart.c`, 174
   `kernel-qemu` image, 183–184
   local manifest, 356–357
   `lowlevel_init.S`, 229
   `mtd.h`, 191–195
   `nand.h`, 241–243
   project-specific, folder for, 81
   `ramdisk.img` image, 183–184
   reading/writing to/from, 112
   `rtc-goldfish.c`, 173–174
   `rtc.h`, 243–245
   `serial.h`, 240
   `startup_c07e1.S`, 128, 132–134
   `startup_c07e2.S`, 141, 150–152
   `startup_c07e3.S`, 174
   `startup_c08e1.S`, 211–216
   `startup_cs3.S`, 96, 104
   `syscalls_cs3timer.c`, 210–216
   `system.img` image, 183
   `u-boot.gdb`, 267
   `userdata.img` image, 183
   `yaffs_uboot_glue.c`, 243
Files, `bsp.c`
   NAND flash test program, 210–216
   nested interrupt handler, 140
   simple interrupt handler, 128, 129–131
   unit test of timer and RTC, 174
Files, `goldfish.h`
   adding Ethernet drivers, 242
   description, 229–234
   NAND flash drivers, adding to goldfish, 242
   serial drivers, adding to goldfish, 240
Files, `goldfish_nand.c`
   NAND flash driver, 189, 195–205
   NAND flash test program, 211–216
Files, `goldfish_uart.s`
   goldfish serial port support, 81–83
   NAND flash test program, 210–216
   Newlib C library, 96
   simple interrupt handler, 128, 141
Files, `isr.c`
   NAND flash test program, 211–216
   a simple interrupt handler, 141, 142–149
   unit test of timer and RTC, 174
Files, `low_level_init.c`
   NAND flash test program, 211–216
   a simple interrupt handler, 141
   unit test of timer and RTC, 174
Files, `serial_goldfish.c`
   checking data buffer, 87
   data input/output, 88–89
   goldfish serial port support, 81, 84–85
   implementing nested interrupt handler, 141
   interrupt support functions, 128

Files, `serial_goldfish.c` *(continued)*
  NAND flash test program, 210–216
  Newlib C library, 96
  unit test of timer and RTC, 174
Files, `startup.S`
  calling C code in assembler language, 72–77
  calling **main** from, 80
  goldfish serial support, 81
Files, `syscalls_cs3.c`
  nested interrupt handler, 141
  Newlib C library, 96, 105–112
  a simple interrupt handler, 128
  unit test of timer and RTC, 174
Files, `timer.c`
  description, 128
  NAND flash test program, 210–216
  nested interrupt handler, 140
  timer interface functions, 166–171
  unit test of timer and RTC, 174
Flash devices. *See* NAND flash.
Flash image
  booting, 258–266
  creating, 258
Flash memory. *See also* NAND flash; NOR flash.
  copying `.data` to RAM, 57–58, 68
  definition, 39
  emulating, 32–36
  specifying a file for, 32–36
`4byte` directive, 43–44
FPGA Cores processors, 8–9
FTL (Flash Translation Layer), 188
Full ascending (FA) stacks, 66
Full descending (FD) stacks, 66
Functions
  `ARM_dAbort()` function, 137
  `ARM_fiq()`, 137
  `ARM_irq()`, 137
  `ARM_pAbort()`, 137
  `ARM_reserved()`, 137
  `ARM_swi()`, 137
  `ARM_undef()`, 137
  assembly language, calling from C language, 81
  `board_early_init_f()`, 234
  `board_init()`, 234
  `board_nand_init()`, 205
  `BSP_irq()`, 149
  C language, calling from assembly language, 79–81
  `dram_init()`, 234
  `EnterUserMode()`, 150–152
  `get_millisecond()`, 172
  `get_second()`, 172
  `get_tbclk()`, 172
  `goldfish_disable_all_irq()`, 131
  `goldfish_getc()`, 88–89
  `goldfish_get_irq_num()`, 131
  `goldfish_gets()`, 88–89
  `goldfish_irq_status()`, 132
  `goldfish_mask_irq()`, 131
  `goldfish_nand_cmd()`, 205–206
  `goldfish_nand_erase()`, 206
  `goldfish_nand_init_device()`, 205

  `goldfish_nand_isbad()`, 206
  `goldfish_nand_markbad()`, 206
  `goldfish_nand_read()`, 206
  `goldfish_nand_read_oob()`, 206
  `goldfish_nand_write()`, 206
  `goldfish_nand_write_oob()`, 206
  `goldfish_putc()`, 88–89
  `goldfish_unmask_irq()`, 131
  interrupt support, 128–132
  `misc_init_r()`, 234
  `mktime()`, 174
  `rtc_get()`, 174
  `rtc_reset()`, 174
  `rtc_set()`, 174
  `sw_handler()`, 152–155
  `SystemCall()`, 150–152
  `timer_init()`, 172
  `to_tm()`, 174
  `__udelay()`, 172
  `udelay_masked()`, 172
  `void goldfish_clear_timer()`, 172
  `void goldfish_set_timer()`, 172

G

`g` command, 179
GDB (GNU Debugger)
  scripts for, 227, 267–270
  starting in ddd, 37
gdb command prompt, 81
Gerum, Philippe, 5
`get_millisecond()` function, 172
`get_second()` function, 172
`get_tbclk()` function, 172
Getting started. *See* "Hello World" program.
Git, xvii
git repositories, downloading, 356–357
`git-diff` command, 221
GitHub, xvii
`.global` directive, 81
Global variables, 68
GNU toolchain, 11
GNU/Linux toolchain, 28–29
goldfish interrupt controller. *See* Interrupt controller.
goldfish interrupt handler. *See* Interrupt handler.
goldfish kernel
  source code, URL for, 13
  startup log, example code, 19–24
goldfish kernel, initializing
  hardware interfaces, example code, 21–22
  memory, example code, 20
  NAND flash, example code, 22–24
goldfish platform
  hardware diagram, 15
  serial ports, 18, 81–87
`goldfish.c` file, 229, 235–239
`goldfish_disable_all_irq()` function, 131
`goldfish.gdb` file, 268-269
`goldfish_getc()` function, 88-89
`goldfish_get_irq_num()` function, 131
`goldfish_gets()` function, 88-89

Index

goldfish.h file
  adding Ethernet drivers, 242
  description, 229–234
  NAND flash drivers, adding to goldfish, 242
  serial drivers, adding to goldfish, 240
GOLDFISH_INTERRUPT_DISABLE register, 127
GOLDFISH_INTERRUPT_DISABLE_ALL register, 127
GOLDFISH_INTERRUPT_ENABLE register, 127
GOLDFISH_INTERRUPT_NUMBER register, 127
GOLDFISH_INTERRUPT_STATUS register, 127
goldfish_irq_status() function, 132
goldfish_mask_irq() function, 131
goldfish_nand.c file
  NAND flash driver, 189, 195–205
  NAND flash test program, 211–216
goldfish_nand_cmd() function, 205-206
goldfish_nand_erase() function, 206
goldfish_nand_init_device() function, 205
goldfish_nand_isbad() function, 206
goldfish_nand_markbad() function, 206
goldfish_nand_read() function, 206
goldfish_nand_read_oob() function, 206
goldfish.nand.reg.h file, 189, 190-191
goldfish_nand_write() function, 206
goldfish_nand_write_oob() function, 206
goldfish_putc() function, 88–89
goldfish_uart.c file, 174
goldfish_uart.s file
  goldfish serial port support, 81–83
  NAND flash test program, 210–216
  Newlib C library, 96
  simple interrupt handler, 128, 141
goldfish_unmask_irq() function, 131
Google Android SDK, 284-287

H

Hard reset phase, 103
Hardware
  new, supporting. *See* Supporting new hardware.
  programming directly on. *See* Bare metal programming.
  virtual. *See* Virtual hardware.
Hardware interfaces
  initializing, example code, 21–22
  registers and interrupts, 17
  supported by Android emulator, 17–18
Hardware platform, overview, 11
hardware.h file, 85-87
"Hello World" program, 29–30
Host development environment, setting up, 25–26

I

iminfo command, 260, 273
_init system call, 112
Initializing
  hardware interfaces, example code, 21–22
  memory, example code, 20
  NAND flash, example code, 22–24

Initializing, data in RAM
  accessing memory, 60–61
  copying **.data** to RAM, 57–58, 68
  example code, 56–57, 58–59
  LMA (load memory address), 57–58
  load address, 57–58
  overview, 56–58
  runtime address, 57
  VMA (virtual memory address), 57
Input/output. *See also* Reading/writing.
  serial, testing, 139
  serial ports, 88–89
  serial_goldfish.c file, 88–89
Installing
  ddd, 29
  JDK, 288
  qemu-system-arm command, 223
  repo tool, 289
  required packages for AOSP, 288
  toolchains, 26–29
"Integrated Kernel Building," 334
Interrupt controller, 126–128. *See also* Interrupt handler.
Interrupt handler
  current pending interrupt number, getting, 131
  enabling/disabling interrupts, 131
  example code files, 128. *See also specific files*.
  implementing, 132–134
  interrupt support functions, 129–132
  number of current pending interrupts, getting, 132
  serial input/output, testing, 139
  startup code, 132–134
  testing, 134–140
  timer interrupt, testing, 140
Interrupt handler, nested
  enabling, 142–149
  example code files, 140–141. *See also specific files*.
  implementation, 142–149
  processor mode, changing, 150–152
  processor mode switch, discovering, 155–163
  processor modes, 157
  program status register, 157
  setting breakpoints, 158–163
  software interrupt, triggering, 150–152
  stack pointer addresses, 156
  stack structure, 156
  testing, 155–163
Interrupt handler, simplest form
  alarm, testing, 139
  current pending interrupt number, getting, 131
  enabling/disabling interrupts, 131
  example code files, 128
  implementing, 132–134
  interrupt support functions, 129–132
  number of current pending interrupts, getting, 132
  serial input/output, testing, 139
  startup code, 132–134
  testing, 134–140
  timer interrupt, testing, 140
Interrupts
  console, enabling/disabling, 18
  for hardware interfaces, 17

Index

`isr.c` file
   NAND flash test program, 211–216
   a simple interrupt handler, 141, 142–149
   unit test of timer and RTC, 174
`.isr_vector` section, 68-78

K

Kaufmann, Morgan, 125
Kernel
   Android, verifying, 273–274
   building for `armemu` virtual device, 318–322
   building with AOSP, 317–322
   building with CyanogenMod, 334–337
   "Integrated Kernel Building," 334
   verifying, 273–274
Kernel, Android ROM
   supporting new hardware with AOSP, 317–322
   supporting new hardware with CyanogenMod, 334–337
Kernel, goldfish
   booting a Linux kernel, 254
   building, 249–250
   building the kernel, 249–250
   debugging, 252–254
   Linux, booting, 254
   prebuilt toolchain, 250–252
   running, 252–254
   source code, 250–252
   startup, example code, 19–24
Kernel, Linux
   booting, 254
   testing flash info from, 206–210
`kernel-qemu` image file, 183-184

L

Labels, assembly language, 30
ld command, 31-32
"Learn about the Repo Tool...," 355
Learning embedded system programming, 6
Levine, John R., 42
`libcmtd.lib` runtime library, 94
`libcmt.lib` runtime library, 94
Linaro, history of, 220
Linker. See also Linker script.
   `2byte` directive, 43–44
   `4byte` directive, 43–44
   `align` directive, 44
   assembler directives, 43–44
   bss segment, 42
   `byte` directive, 43–44
   Data segment, 42
   definition, 41
   description, 41–42
   example code, 42–43, 44–46, 46–49
   executable output, 42
   relocatable code, 50
   relocation, 46–49
   section merging, 49–50
   section placement, 50–51
   symbol resolution, 42–43

   Text segment, 42
   `word` directive, 43–44
Linker script. See also Linker.
   . (period), location counter, 52
   * (asterisk), wildcard character, 52
   for C language, example code, 70–72
   description, 51–53
   example code, 53–56
Linkers and Loaders, 42
Linking, 41. See also Linker; Linker script.
Linux
   GNU/Linux toolchain, 28–29
   starting SDK Manager under, 15
Linux kernel
   booting, 254
   testing flash info from, 206–210
LMA (load memory address), 57-58
Load address, 57-58
Local manifest file, 356-357
Location counter, period (.), 52, 69
Logs for goldfish kernel startup, example code, 19–24
`low_level_init.c` file
   NAND flash test program, 211–216
   a simple interrupt handler, 141
   unit test of timer and RTC, 174
`lowlevel_init.s` file, 229

M

`make` command, building a development environment, 30-31
`makedefs.arm` makefile, template for, xx–xxii
`makefile` template
   build targets, 32–36
   debugging, 37–38
   example code, xx–xxi
Masters, Jon, 5
Memory
   initializing, example code, 20
   managing, 112
   relocation, booting Android from NOR flash, 256
Memory map, 39-41
Memory Technology Device (MTD). See MTD (Memory Technology Device).
Mentor Graphics, downloading toolchains, 28–29
Microsoft C runtime libraries, 94
Milliseconds/seconds since boot up, getting, 172
`misc_init_r()` function, 234
MIUI development community, 283–284
`mkimage` utility, 258
`mktime()` function, 174
`mkvendor.sh` script, 332-333
Mobile devices, hardware features supported by Android emulator, 13–14
`mount` command, 184-185
`msvcmrt.lib` runtime library, 94
`msvcrtd.lib` runtime library, 94
`msvcrt.lib` runtime lib, 94
`msvcurt.lib` runtime library, 94
MTD (Memory Technology Device). See also NAND flash.

Index   367

compatibility with block devices, 188
NAND flash support for, 188–189
setting up structure for, example code, 203
support for, 188–189
U-Boot API, 205
MTD (Memory Technology Device), example code
checking for bad blocks, 201
data structure, 196
erasing blocks, 197
getting/setting bad block data, 206
initializing a device, 202–203
initializing NAND flash controller, 203–204
marking bad blocks, 201–202
`mtd_info` structure, implementing, 190–191
operation sequence, 196–197
reading blocks, 199–200
reading/writing blocks with out-of-band, 198
setting up the MTD structure, 203
writing blocks, 200
`mtd.h` file, 191–195
`mtd_info` structure, implementing, 190–191

N

NAND flash. *See also* Booting Android from NAND flash; NOR flash.
available storage, calculating, 185
checking for bad blocks, 201
data structure, 196
vs. eMMC, 184
erasing a page, 185
erasing blocks, 197
FTL (Flash Translation Layer), 188
getting/setting bad block data, 206
initializing, example code, 22–24
initializing a device, 202–203
initializing NAND flash controller, 203–204
marking bad blocks, 201–202
MTD (Memory Technology Device) support, 188–189. *See also* MTD (Memory Technology Device).
`mtd_info` structure, implementing, 190–191
operation sequence, 196–197
vs. SD/MMC, 184
setting up the MTD structure, 203
vs. SSD, 184
NAND flash controller
command execution, 188
commands, 187
initializing, 203–204
number of devices connected, detecting, 188
verifying version of, 188
NAND flash device drivers
example code, 195–205
functions, 205–206
illustration, 189
NAND flash programming interface
erasing block size, 187
erasing blocks, 206
NAND flash programming interface, device information
capabilities, 187
data output pointer, 187

data transfer size, 188
lowest 32 bits of data address, 188
lowest 32 bits of device capacity, 187
name length, 187
number, 187
number of NAND flash chips, 187
out-of-band data size, 187
page size, 187
registers, 187–188
return status of controller commands, 187
top 32 bits of data address, 188
top 32 bits of device capacity, 187
NAND flash programming interface, reading/writing
blocks, 199–200
blocks with out-of-band, 198
out-of-band data, 206
page data, 206
to/from flash memory, 188
NAND flash programming interface, testing
example code, 206–210, 211–216
files, 210. *See also specific files.*
flash info from the Linux kernel, 206–210
NAND flash properties
description, 185
flash device layout, 185
flash info from the Linux kernel, 206–210
getting, 188
`NAND_ADDR_HIGH` register, 188
`NAND_ADDR_LOW` register, 188
`NAND_CMD_BLOCK_BAD_SET` command, 187
`NAND_CMD_ERASE` command, 187
`NAND_CMD_GET_DEV_NAME` CO command, 187
`NAND_CMD_READ` command, 187
`NAND_CMD_WRITE` command, 187
`NAND_COMMAND` register, 187
`NAND_DATA` register, 187
`NAND_DEV` register, 187
`NAND_DEV_ERASE_SIZE` register, 187
`NAND_DEV_EXTRA_SIZE` register, 187
`NAND_DEV_FLAGS` register, 187
`NAND_DEV_NAME_LEN` register, 187
`NAND_DEV_PAGE_SIZE` register, 187
`NAND_DEV_SIZE_HIGH` register, 187
`NAND_DEV_SIZE_LOW` register, 187
`nand.h` file, 241–243
`NAND_NUM_DEV` register, 187
`NAND_RESULT` register, 187
`NAND_TRANSFER_SIZE` register, 188
`NAND_VERSION` register, 187
Nested interrupt handler. *See* Interrupt handler, nested.
Newlib C library
CS3 linker scripts, 97–103
system call implementation, 104–111
Newlib C library, example code. *See also specific files.*
common files, 96
CS3 linker scripts, 97–104
debugging the library, 112–116
project-specific files, 96
running the library, 112–116
semihosting support, 118–122
startup code sequence, 97–103

Index

Newlib C library, startup code sequence
   assembly initialization phase, 103
   C initialization phase, 104
   common, 97
   custom, 103–104
   hard reset phase, 103
`nm` command, 31–32
NOR flash, booting Android from. *See also* NAND flash.
   introduction, 254–256
   memory relocation, 256
   RAMDISK image, creating, 256–258

O

`objcopy` command, 32
Object file formats, converting, 32
Online resources. *See also* Books and publications.
   CyanogenMod wiki, 332
   "Integrated Kernel Building," 334
   "Learn about the Repo Tool…," 355
   "Repo: Tips & Tricks," 355
   source code for this book, 344
OOB (out-of-band) data
   definition, 185
   reading/writing, 206
   reading/writing blocks with, 198
   size, getting, 187

P

Period (.)
   in assembly language directives, 30
   location counter, 52, 69
   in section names, 69
Privileged modes, 66
Procedure Call Standard for the ARM Architecture, 78
Processor mode switch, discovering, 155–163
Processor modes
   changing, 150–152
   list of, 157
Program status register, nested interrupt handler, 157
Programming
   directly on hardware. *See* Bare metal programming.
   your first program, 29–30
Programming Embedded System in C and C++, 5
Project-specific files, folder for, 81
`PUT_CHAR` register, 18

Q

`q` command, 91
QEMU emulator, 11–12
`qemu-system-arm` command, installing, 223
Quitting debugging, 91

R

`r` command, 179
RAMDISK image
   creating, 256–258
   verifying, 273–274

`ramdisk.img` image file, 183–184
Read buffer command. *See* `CMD_READ_BUFFER` command.
`_read` system call, 112
Reading/writing, NAND flash programming interface. *See also* Input/output.
   blocks, 199–200
   blocks with out-of-band, 198
   out-of-band data, 206
   page data, 206
   to/from flash memory, 188
Reading/writing to/from file, 112
Read-only data, 68
Real-time clock (RTC). *See* RTC (real-time clock), and timer.
Real-time operating system (RTOS). *See also* Embedded system programming.
   description, 5
   vs. a full operating system, 9
RealView Compilation Tools Developer Guide, 50
RealView Development Suite, 95
RealView Platform Baseboard, 5
Registers
   `ALARM_HIGH`, 19
   `ALARM_LOW`, 19
   APCS use convention, 78
   ARM register set, 67
   banked, initializing, 66–68
   `BYTES_READY`, 18
   `CLEAR_ALARM`, 19
   `CLEAR_INTERRUPT`, 19
   `CMD`, 18
   `DATA_LEN`, 18
   `DATA_PTR`, 18
   `GOLDFISH_INTERRUPT_DISABLE`, 127
   `GOLDFISH_INTERRUPT_DISABLE_ALL`, 127
   `GOLDFISH_INTERRUPT_ENABLE`, 127
   `GOLDFISH_INTERRUPT_NUMBER`, 127
   `GOLDFISH_INTERRUPT_STATUS`, 127
   for hardware interfaces, 17
   `NAND_ADDR_HIGH`, 188
   `NAND_ADDR_LOW`, 188
   `NAND_COMMAND`, 187
   `NAND_DATA`, 187
   `NAND_DEV`, 187
   `NAND_DEV_ERASE_SIZE`, 187
   `NAND_DEV_EXTRA_SIZE`, 187
   `NAND_DEV_FLAGS`, 187
   `NAND_DEV_NAME_LEN`, 187
   `NAND_DEV_PAGE_SIZE`, 187
   `NAND_DEV_SIZE_HIGH`, 187
   `NAND_DEV_SIZE_LOW`, 187
   `NAND_NUM_DEV`, 187
   `NAND_RESULT`, 187
   `NAND_TRANSFER_SIZE`, 188
   `NAND_VERSION`, 187
   `PUT_CHAR`, 18
   `TIME_HIGH`, 19
   `TIME_LOW`, 19

Index   369

for timer controller, 18–19
`TIMER_TIME_HIGH`, 165
`TIMER_TIME_LOW`, 165
viewing contents of, 34–36
Relocatable code, 50
Relocation, 46-49, 227
"Repo: Tips & Tricks," 355
`repo` tool
downloading git repositories, 356–357
initializing a client, 289
installing, 289
local manifest file, 356–357
online resources for, 355
syncing a new source tree, 355–356
`.rodata` section, 68-78, 80
ROM. *See* **Android ROM.**
RTC (real-time clock), and timer. *See also* **Timer.**
commands, 179. *See also specific commands.*
converting to/from a timestamp, 172
date and time, getting/setting, 179
description, 172–173
example code, 173–174, 175–179
resetting, 179
system date, resetting, 173
test delay function, 179
timeout, setting/increasing/resetting, 179
timer interrupts, enabling/disabling, 179
unit test, example code, 174–179
RTC drivers, adding to goldfish, 243-245
`rtc_get()` function, 174
`rtc-goldfish.c` file, 173-174
`rtc.h` file, 243-245
`rtc_reset()` function, 174
`rtc_set()` function, 174
RTOS (real-time operating system). *See also* **Embedded system programming.**
description, 5
vs. a full operating system, 9
Runtime address, 57
Runtime library support. *See* **C library variants.**

S

`s` command, 179
`_sbrk` system call, 112
SDK. *See* **Android SDK.**
SDK Manager. *See also* **AVD Manager.**
starting under Linux, 15
version used in this book, 26
SD/MMC *vs.* NAND flash, 184
Seconds/milliseconds since boot up, getting, 172
Section merging, 49-50
Section placement, 50-51
SecurCore processors, 8-9
Semihosting support
definition,
example code, 118–122
Newlib C library, 118–122
QEMU ARM semihosting, 116–122
Serial drivers, adding to goldfish, 239-241

Serial ports, goldfish platform
base addresses, 18
checking the data buffer, 87–88
debugging, console log example, 91
getting data from, 87–89
input/output, 88–89
providing support for, 81–87
sending data to, 88–89
test cases, example code, 90–91
unit test, 90–91
Serial ports, initializing, 112
`serial_goldfish.c` file
checking data buffer, 87
data input/output, 88–89
goldfish serial port support, 81, 84–85
implementing nested interrupt handler, 141
interrupt support functions, 128
NAND flash test program, 210–216
Newlib C library, 96
unit test of timer and RTC, 174
`serial.h` file, 240
Setting up a development environment. *See* **Development environment, setting up.**
Sloss, Andrew N., 5
Software interrupt, triggering, 150-152
Software layers of embedded systems, 7-10
Source code for this book
AOSP, building, 352–353
build environment, setting up, 341–344
CyanogenMod, building, 353–354
organization of, 344
virtual machine, setting up, 344
Source code for this book, building
from the command line, 345
from Eclipse, 346–350
Source code for this book, overview
Part I, 345–350
Part II, 350–352
Part III, 352–354
Source code for this book, testing
from the command line, 345
from Eclipse, 346–350
Source tree, syncing, 355-356
Source-level debugging a flash image, 266-270
Sourcery CodeBench Lite, downloading, 28-29
Sourcery CodeBench trial version, downloading, 28-29
Spare area. *See* **OOB (out-of-band) data.**
SSD *vs.* NAND flash, 184
Stack
banked stack pointers, initializing, 66–68
EA (empty ascending), 66
ED (empty descending), 66
FA (full ascending), 66
FD (full descending), 66
preparing for a bare metal environment, 65–68
types of, 66
Stack pointer addresses, nested interrupt handler, 156
Stack pointers, initializing, 66-68, 72

Index

.stack section, 68-78
Stack structure, nested interrupt handler, 156
Startup code for C language, 68-78
Startup code for Newlib C library
    assembly initialization phase, 103
    C initialization phase, 104
    common, 97
    CS3 linker scripts, 97-103
    custom, 103-104
    hard reset phase, 103
startup_c07e1.S file, 128, 132-134
startup_c07e2.S file, 141, 150-152
startup_c07e3.S file, 174
startup_c08e1.S file, 211-216
startup_cs3.S file, 96, 104
startup.S file
    calling C code in assembler language, 72-77
    calling main from, 80
    goldfish serial support, 81
Stepping through instructions with ddd, 35
Supporting new hardware, with AOSP
    booting Android with U-Boot from NAND flash, 323-332
    building the kernel, 317-322
    building U-Boot, 322-323
    process description, 309-317
Supporting new hardware, with CyanogenMod
    booting CyanogenMod, 337-338
    building the kernel, 334-337
    building U-Boot, 337-338
    introduction, 332-334
sw_handler() function, 152-155
Symbol placement, viewing, 76-78
Symbol resolution, 42-43
Symes, Dominic, 5
Syncing a new source tree, 355-356
syscalls_cs3.c file
    nested interrupt handler, 141
    Newlib C library, 96, 105-112
    a simple interrupt handler, 128
    unit test of timer and RTC, 174
syscalls_cs3timer.c file, 210-216
System call implementation, 104-112
System date
    getting/setting, 173
    resetting, 179
SystemCall() function, 150-152
system.img
    booting Android from NAND flash, 270
    description, 257
    preparing for booting Android, 270
system.img image file, 183

T

t command, 138, 179
Test delay function, 179
Testing
    from the command line, 345
    from Eclipse, 346-350
    a known configuration of U-Boot, 222-224
    unit test of timer and RTC, 174
Testing, interrupt handler
    alarms, 139
    example code, 134-140
    serial input/output, 139
Testing, nested interrupt handler
    nested interrupt handler, 155-163
    RTC (real-time clock) unit test, 174-179
    setting breakpoints, 158-163
    software interrupts, 163-164
    system calls, 163-164
    timer, 174-179
    timer interrupt, 140
.text section, 68-78
Text segment, 42
TIME_HIGH register, 19
TIME_LOW register, 19
Timeout, setting/increasing/resetting, 179
Timer
    delay functions, 172
    description, 164-171
    example code, 19-24
    goldfish-specific functions, 172
    interface functions, example code, 166-171
    last system tick, initializing, 172
    number of ticks per second, getting, 172
    registers, 18-19
    seconds/milliseconds since boot up, getting, 172
    setting/clearing timer interrupts, 172
    timestamp, initializing, 172
    U-Boot API, 172
Timer, and RTC
    converting to/from a timestamp, 172
    date and time, getting/setting, 179
    description, 172-173
    example code, 173-174, 175-179
    system date, resetting, 173
    test delay function, 179
    timeout, setting/increasing/resetting, 179
    timer interrupts, enabling/disabling, 179
    unit test, example code, 174-179
Timer interrupts
    alarms, setting/clearing, 19
    enabling/disabling, 179
timer.c file
    description, 128
    NAND flash test program, 210-216
    nested interrupt handler, 140
    timer interface functions, 166-171
    unit test of timer and RTC, 174
timer_init() function, 172
TIMER_TIME_HIGH register, 165
TIMER_TIME_LOW register, 165
Timestamp, 172
Toolchains
    cross-compilaton, identifying, 31
    downloading, 26-29
    installing, 26-29

Tools. *See also* Android emulator; QEMU emulator; *specific tools*.
    downloading, 28–29
    GNU toolchain, 11
    GNU/Linux toolchain, 28–29
    prebuilt toolchain, 250–252
to_tm() function, 174
2byte directive, 43–44

U

U-Boot
    debugging with GDB, 224–227
    downloading and compiling, 220–224
    introduction, 219–220
    NAND flash API, 205
    recommended version, 220
    relocation, 227
    required functionalities, 219–220
    testing a known configuration, 222–224
U-Boot, booting Android from NAND flash
    boot process, 271–279
    checking the configuration, 272
    introduction, 270
    preparing system.img, 270
    verifying the kernel and the RAMDISK image, 273–274
U-Boot, booting Android from NOR flash
    flash image, booting, 258–266
    flash image, creating, 258
    flash image, source-level debugging, 266–270
    introduction, 254–256
    memory relocation, 256
    RAMDISK image, creating, 256–258
U-Boot, booting the goldfish kernel
    booting a Linux kernel, 254
    building the kernel, 249–250
    debugging the kernel, 252–254
    kernel source code, 250–252
    prebuilt toolchain, 250–252
    running the kernel, 252–254
U-Boot, building with
    AOSP, 322–323
    CyanogenMod, 337–338
U-Boot, porting to the goldfish platform
    adding drivers, 239
    basic steps, 227
    board changes, summary of, 246–247
    board-level initialization functions, 234
    board-specific changes, 229–239
    creating a new board, 228–229
    device driver changes, 239–246
    Ethernet drivers, 245
    example code, 230–239
    NAND flash drivers, 241–243
    RTC drivers, 243–245
    serial drivers, 239–241
u-boot.gdb file, 267
Ubuntu, downloading, 341, 344

uclibc, library variant, 95
__udelay() function, 172
udelay_masked() function, 172
umount command, 274
Underscore (_)
    in assembly language labels, 30
    in symbol names, 69
Unit test
    Newlib C library, 112–116
    serial ports, 90–91
Uppercase letters in constant names, 69
userdata.img, 257
userdata.img image file, 183

V

VERBOSE option, 37–38
Verifying
    Android kernel, 273–274
    RAMDISK image, 273–274
Versatile PB vs. goldfish, 229
versatileqemu program, 222–224
Version information, 80
Virtual devices
    configuring, 14–16
    setting up, 284–287
Virtual hardware
    overview, 13–14
    vs. real hardware, 11
VirtualBox, 344
Virtualization environment. *See also* Development environment.
    definition, 6
    learning embedded system programming, 6
VMA (virtual memory address), 57
VMware Player, 344
void goldfish_clear_timer() function, 172
void goldfish_set_timer() function, 172

W

Wildcard character, asterisk (*), 52
word directive, 43–44
Wright, Chris, 5
Write buffer command. *See* CMD_WRITE_BUFFER command.
_write system call, 112

X

x command, 179

Y

yaffs_uboot_glue.c file, 243
Yaghmour, Karim, 5, 249, 288
ydevconfig command, 272
ydevls command, 272
ymount command, 273
yrdm command, 273

Essential Resources for Android Developers
informit.com/android

Developing Android User Interfaces LiveLessons (Video Training)
Adam Porter
ISBN-13: 978-0-134-0-3773-8

Android User Interface Design
Ian G. Clifton
ISBN-13: 978-0-321-88673-6

Bulletproof Android: Practical Advice for Building Secure Apps
Godfrey Nolan
ISBN-13: 978-0-133-99332-5

Android Security Essentials LiveLessons (Video Training)
Godfrey Nolan
ISBN-13: 978-0-133-82904-4

Apache Cordova 4 Programming
John M. Wargo
ISBN-13: 978-0-134-04819-2

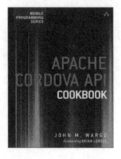

Apache Cordova API Cookbook
John M. Wargo
ISBN-13: 978-0-321-99480-6

Advanced Android Application Development, 4th Edition
Joseph Annuzzi, Lauren Darcey, and Shane Conder
ISBN-13: 978-0-133-89238-3

Titles are available in print and/or eBook formats.

 For more information and to read sample material, please visit informit.com/android.

 Titles are also available at safari.informit.com.

informIT.com

THE TRUSTED TECHNOLOGY LEARNING SOURCE

PEARSON InformIT is a brand of Pearson and the online presence for the world's leading technology publishers. It's your source for reliable and qualified content and knowledge, providing access to the leading brands, authors, and contributors from the tech community.

Addison-Wesley • Cisco Press • IBM Press • Microsoft Press
PEARSON IT CERTIFICATION • PRENTICE HALL • QUE • SAMS • vmware PRESS

LearnIT at InformIT

Looking for a book, eBook, or training video on a new technology? Seeking timely and relevant information and tutorials. Looking for expert opinions, advice, and tips? **InformIT has a solution**.

- Learn about new releases and special promotions by subscribing to a wide variety of monthly newsletters. Visit **informit.com/newsletters**.
- FREE Podcasts from experts at **informit.com/podcasts**.
- Read the latest author articles and sample chapters at **informit.com/articles**.
- Access thousands of books and videos in the Safari Books Online digital library. **safari.informit.com**.
- Get Advice and tips from expert blogs at **informit.com/blogs**.

Visit **informit.com** to find out all the ways you can access the hottest technology content.

Are you part of the IT crowd?

Connect with Pearson authors and editors via RSS feeds, Facebook, Twitter, YouTube and more! Visit **informit.com/socialconnect**.

PEARSON

Register the Addison-Wesley, Exam Cram, Prentice Hall, Que, and Sams products you own to unlock great benefits.

To begin the registration process, simply go to **informit.com/register** to sign in or create an account. You will then be prompted to enter the 10- or 13-digit ISBN that appears on the back cover of your product.

Registering your products can unlock the following benefits:
- Access to supplemental content, including bonus chapters, source code, or project files.
- A coupon to be used on your next purchase.

Registration benefits vary by product. Benefits will be listed on your Account page under Registered Products.

About InformIT — THE TRUSTED TECHNOLOGY LEARNING SOURCE

INFORMIT IS HOME TO THE LEADING TECHNOLOGY PUBLISHING IMPRINTS Addison-Wesley Professional, Cisco Press, Exam Cram, IBM Press, Prentice Hall Professional, Que, and Sams. Here you will gain access to quality and trusted content and resources from the authors, creators, innovators, and leaders of technology. Whether you're looking for a book on a new technology, a helpful article, timely newsletters, or access to the Safari Books Online digital library, InformIT has a solution for you.

THE TRUSTED TECHNOLOGY LEARNING SOURCE

Addison-Wesley | Cisco Press | Exam Cram
IBM Press | Que | Prentice Hall | Sams
SAFARI BOOKS ONLINE